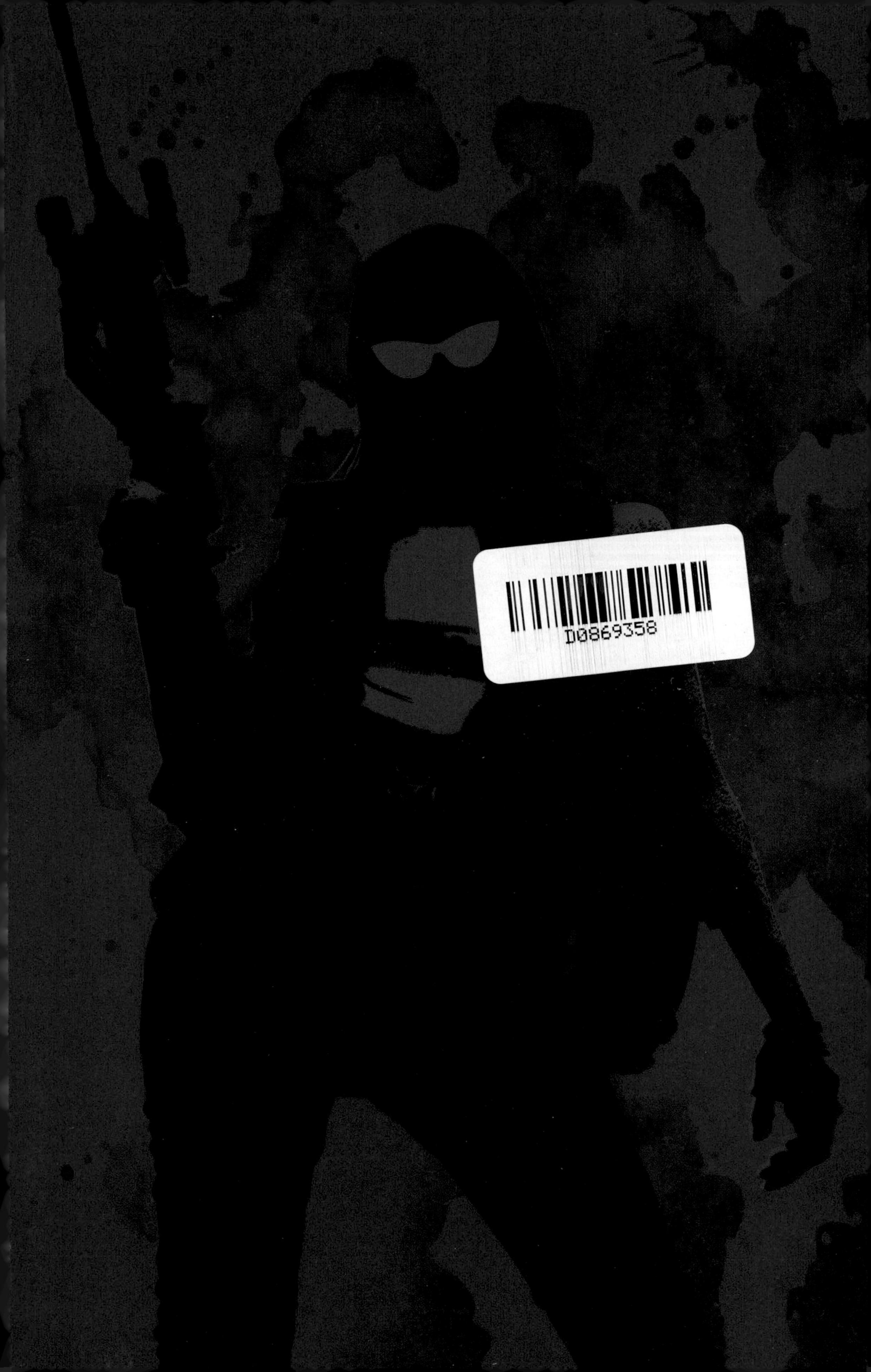

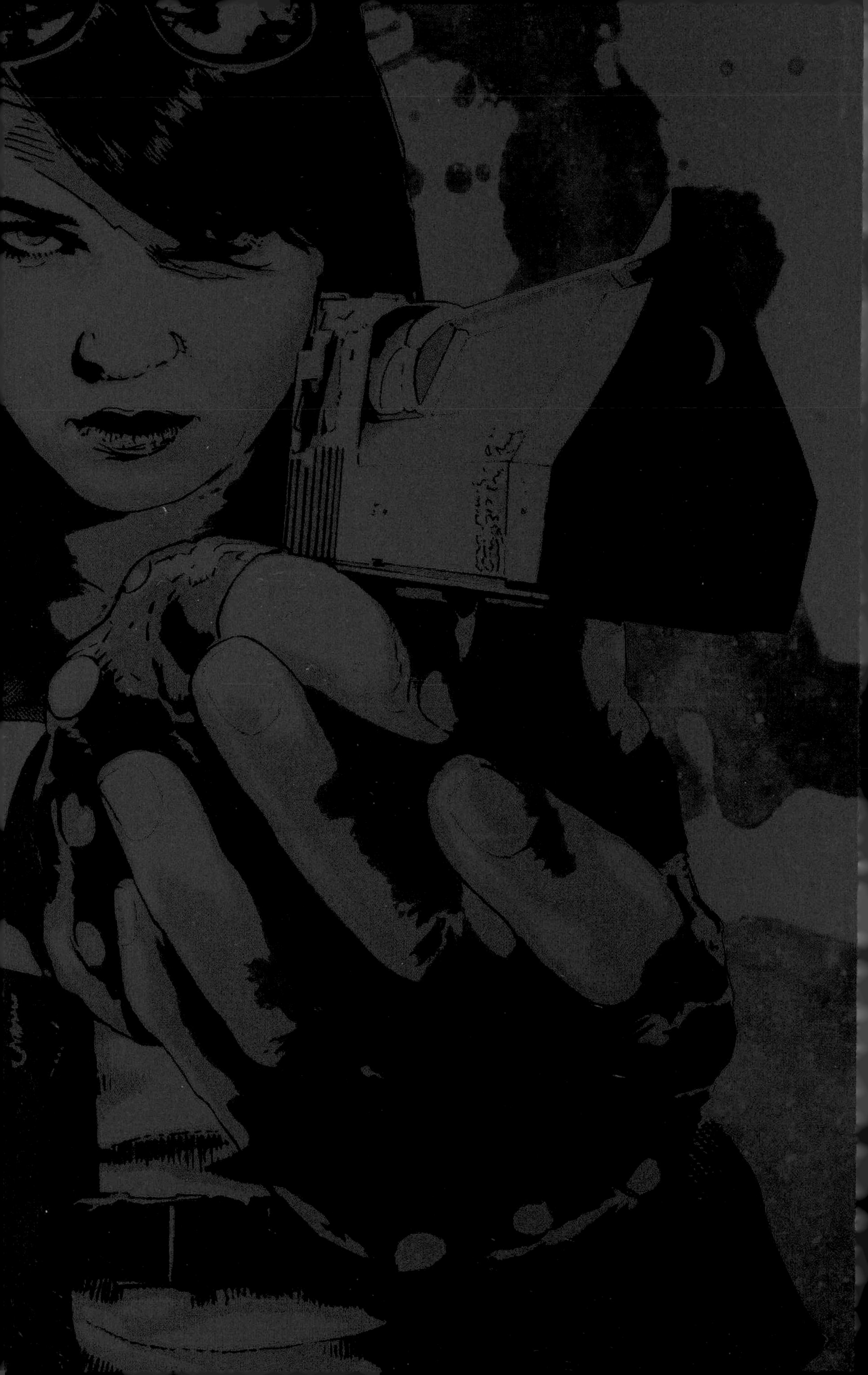

JENNIFER BLOOD

volume 1: A WOMAN'S WORK IS NEVER DONE

written by
GARTH ENNIS

illustrated by
ADRIANO BATISTA (issues 1-3)
MARCOS MARZ (issues 3-4)
KEWBER BAAL (issues 4-6)

colored by
ROMULO FAJARDO JR. (issues 1-4)
INLIGHT STUDIOS (issues 5-6)

lettered by
ROB STEEN

collection cover by
TIM BRADSTREET

collection design by
JASON ULLMEYER

This volume collects issues one through six of the Dynamite Entertainment series, Jennifer Blood.

ISBN-10: 1-60690-261-X   ISBN-13: 978-1-60690-261-5   First Printing   10 9 8 7 6 5 4 3 2 1

JENNIFER BLOOD VOLUME 1: A WOMAN'S WORK IS NEVER DONE. First printing. Contains materials originally published in Jennifer Blood #1-6. Published by Dynamite Entertainment. 155 Ninth Ave. Suite B, Runnemede, NJ 08078. JENNIFER BLOOD © 2012 Spitfire Productions, Ltd. and Dynamite Entertainment. All characters and elements of JENNIFER BLOOD are ™ Spitfire Productions, Ltd. and Dynamite Entertainment. All Rights Reserved.Dynamite, Dynamite Entertainment & The Dynamite Entertainment colophon © 2012 DFI. All Rights Reserved. All names, characters, events, and locales in this publication are entirely fictional. Any resemblance to actual persons (living or dead), events or places, without satiric intent, is coincidental. No portion of this book may be reproduced by any means (digital or print) without the written permission of Dynamite Entertainment except for review purposes. The scanning, uploading and distribution of this book via the internet or via any other means without the permission of the publisher is illegal and punishable by law. Please purchase only authorized electronic editions, and do not participate in or encourage electronic piracy of copyrighted materials. Printed in Canada.

For media rights, foreign rights, promotions, licensing, and advertising: marketing@dynamite.net

DYNAMITE®
ENTERTAINMENT

WWW.DYNAMITE.NET

NICK BARRUCCI • PRESIDENT
JUAN COLLADO • CHIEF OPERATING OFFICER
JOSEPH RYBANDT • EDITOR
JOSH JOHNSON • CREATIVE DIRECTOR
RICH YOUNG • DIRECTOR OF BUSINESS DEVELOPMENT
JASON ULLMEYER • SENIOR DESIGNER
JOSH GREEN • TRAFFIC COORDINATOR
CHRIS CANIANO • PRODUCTION ASSISTANT

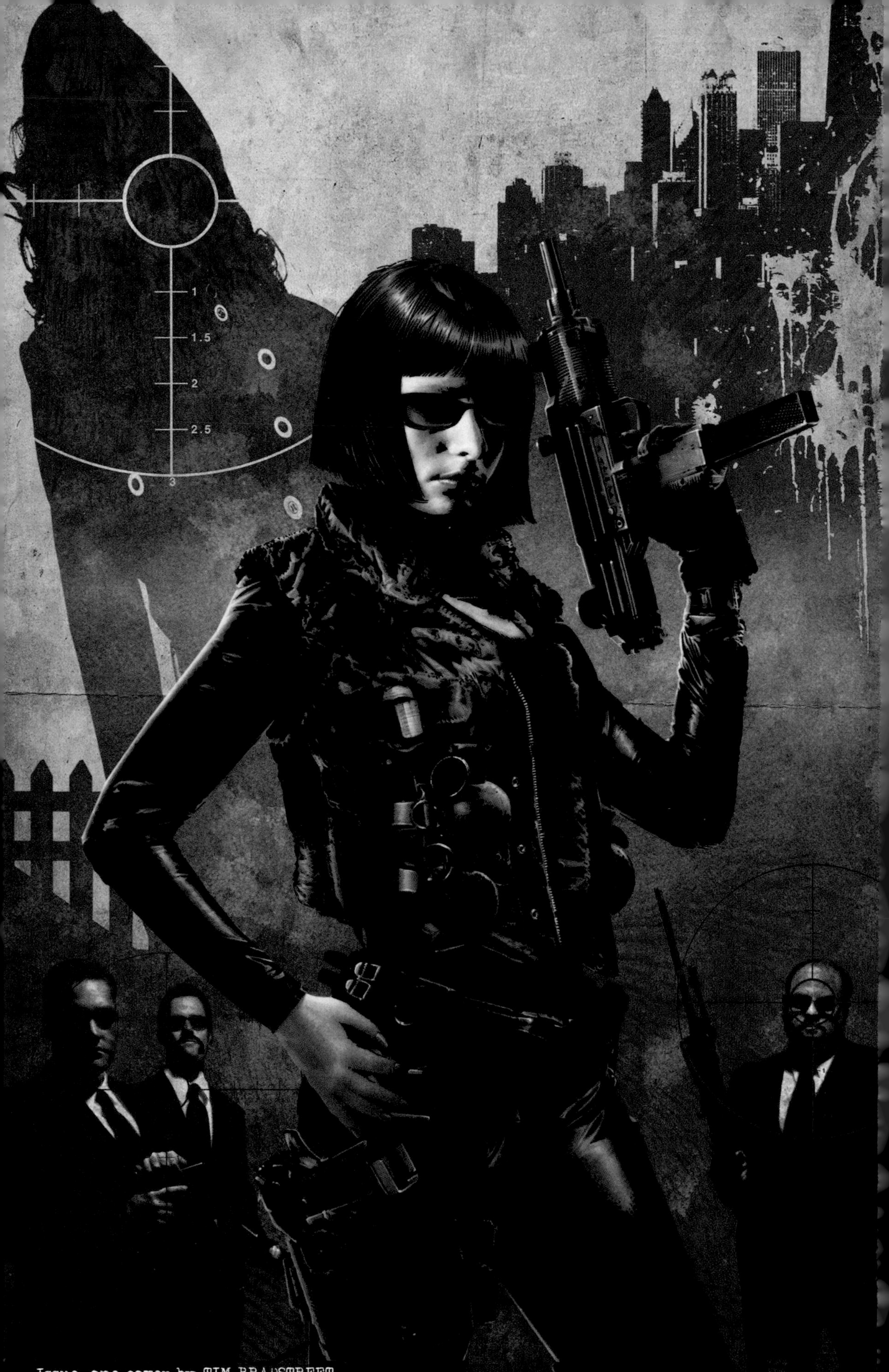
1
1.5
2
2.5
3

Issue one cover by TIM BRADSTREET

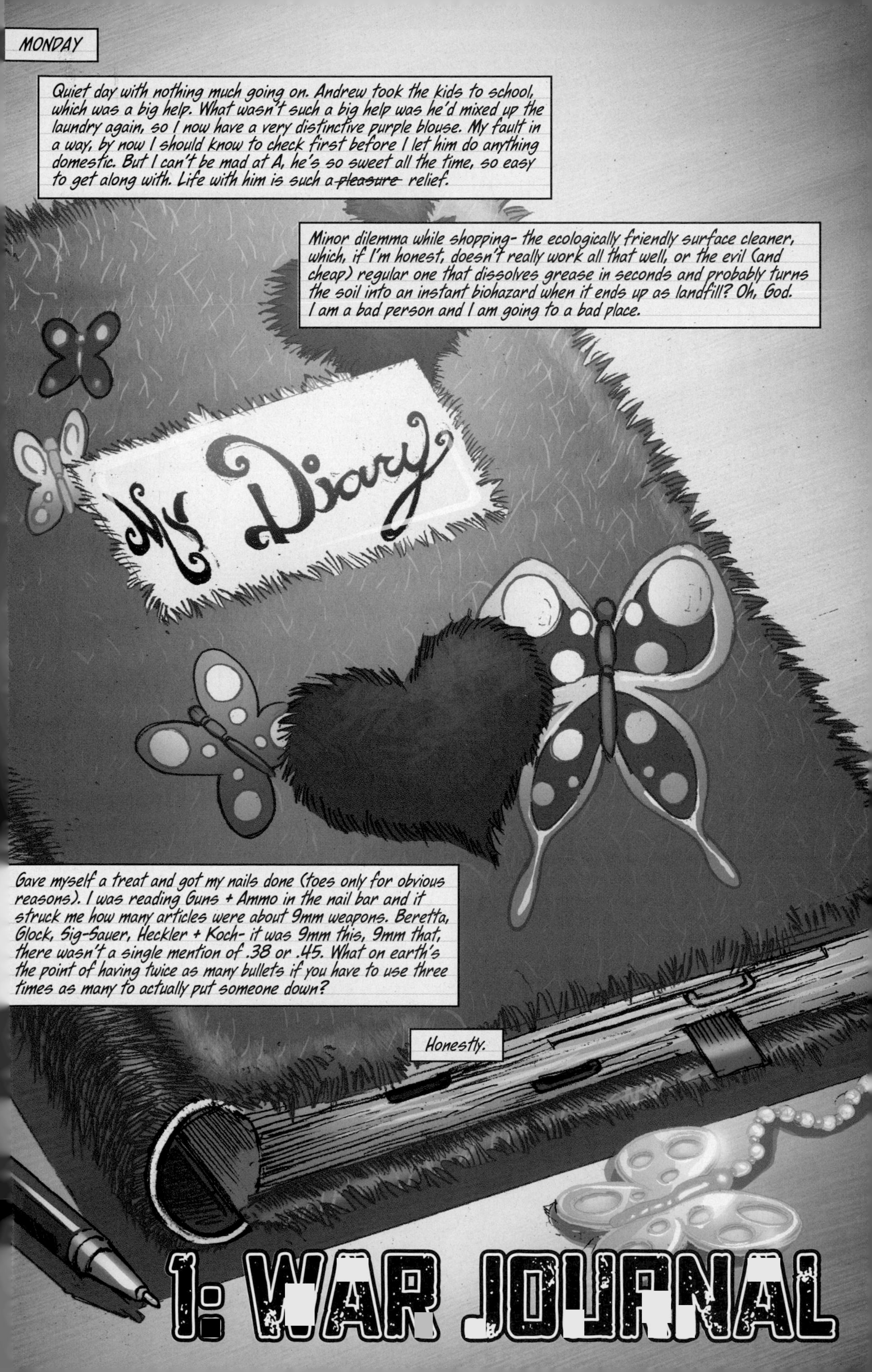
MONDAY
Quiet day with nothing much going on. Andrew took the kids to school, which was a big help. What wasn't such a big help was he'd mixed up the laundry again, so I now have a very distinctive purple blouse. My fault in a way, by now I should know to check first before I let him do anything domestic. But I can't be mad at A, he's so sweet all the time, so easy to get along with. Life with him is such a ~~pleasure~~ relief.
Minor dilemma while shopping- the ecologically friendly surface cleaner, which, if I'm honest, doesn't really work all that well, or the evil (and cheap) regular one that dissolves grease in seconds and probably turns the soil into an instant biohazard when it ends up as landfill? Oh, God. I am a bad person and I am going to a bad place.
My Diary
Gave myself a treat and got my nails done (toes only for obvious reasons). I was reading Guns + Ammo in the nail bar and it struck me how many articles were about 9mm weapons. Beretta, Glock, Sig-Sauer, Heckler + Koch- it was 9mm this, 9mm that, there wasn't a single mention of .38 or .45. What on earth's the point of having twice as many bullets if you have to use three times as many to actually put someone down?
Honestly.
1: WAR JOURNAL

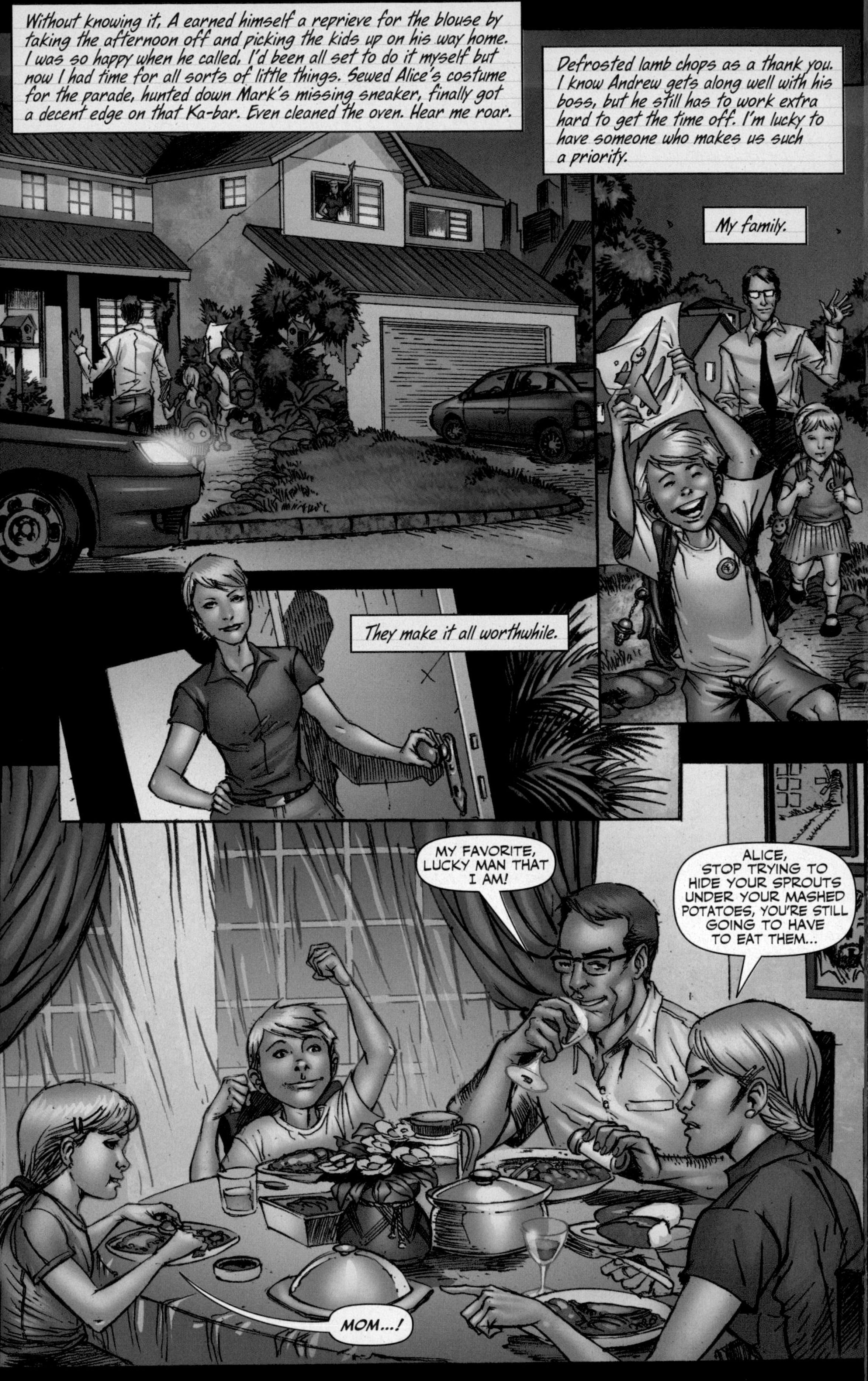
Without knowing it, A earned himself a reprieve for the blouse by taking the afternoon off and picking the kids up on his way home. I was so happy when he called, I'd been all set to do it myself but now I had time for all sorts of little things. Sewed Alice's costume for the parade, hunted down Mark's missing sneaker, finally got a decent edge on that Ka-bar. Even cleaned the oven. Hear me roar.
Defrosted lamb chops as a thank you. I know Andrew gets along well with his boss, but he still has to work extra hard to get the time off. I'm lucky to have someone who makes us such a priority.
My family.
They make it all worthwhile.
MY FAVORITE, LUCKY MAN THAT I AM!
ALICE, STOP TRYING TO HIDE YOUR SPROUTS UNDER YOUR MASHED POTATOES, YOU'RE STILL GOING TO HAVE TO EAT THEM...
MOM...!

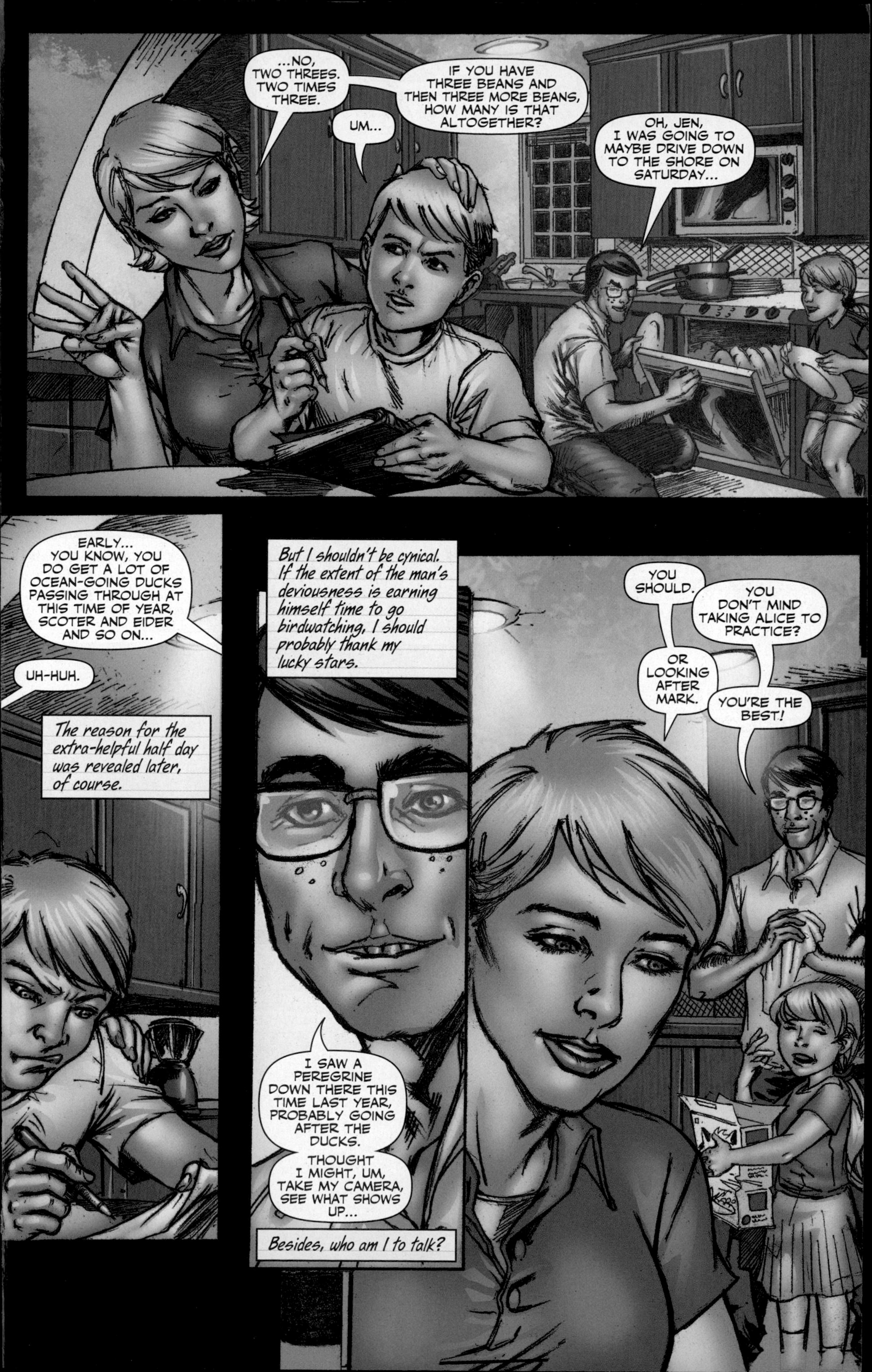

...NO, TWO THREES. TWO TIMES THREE.
IF YOU HAVE THREE BEANS AND THEN THREE MORE BEANS, HOW MANY IS THAT ALTOGETHER?
UM...
OH, JEN, I WAS GOING TO MAYBE DRIVE DOWN TO THE SHORE ON SATURDAY...
EARLY... YOU KNOW, YOU DO GET A LOT OF OCEAN-GOING DUCKS PASSING THROUGH AT THIS TIME OF YEAR, SCOTER AND EIDER AND SO ON...
UH-HUH.
The reason for the extra-helpful half day was revealed later, of course.
But I shouldn't be cynical. If the extent of the man's deviousness is earning himself time to go birdwatching, I should probably thank my lucky stars.
I SAW A PEREGRINE DOWN THERE THIS TIME LAST YEAR, PROBABLY GOING AFTER THE DUCKS.
THOUGHT I MIGHT, UM, TAKE MY CAMERA, SEE WHAT SHOWS UP...
Besides, who am I to talk?
YOU SHOULD.
OR LOOKING AFTER MARK.
YOU DON'T MIND TAKING ALICE TO PRACTICE?
YOU'RE THE BEST!

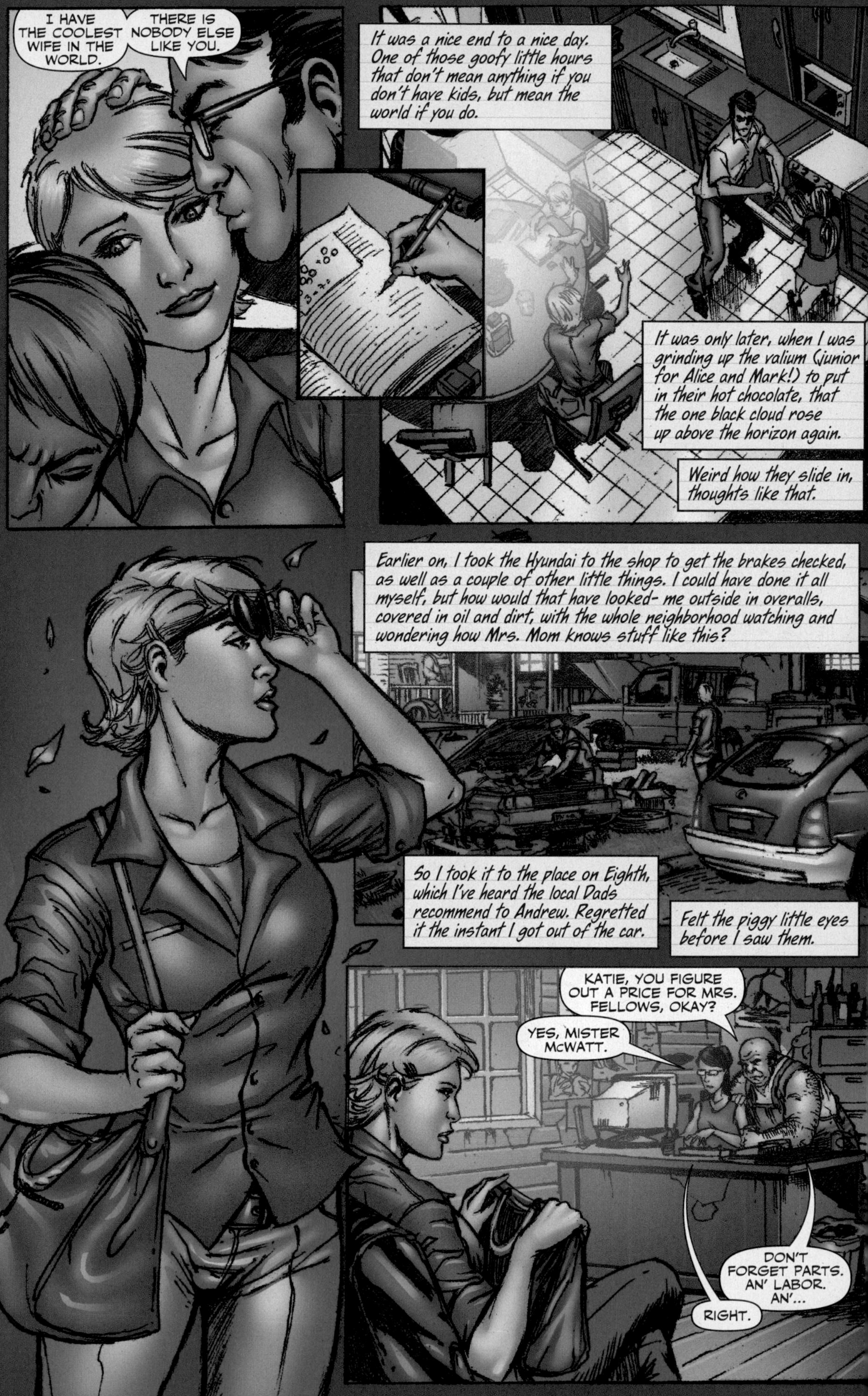
I HAVE THE COOLEST WIFE IN THE WORLD.
THERE IS NOBODY ELSE LIKE YOU.
It was a nice end to a nice day. One of those goofy little hours that don't mean anything if you don't have kids, but mean the world if you do.
It was only later, when I was grinding up the valium (Junior for Alice and Mark!) to put in their hot chocolate, that the one black cloud rose up above the horizon again.
Weird how they slide in, thoughts like that.
Earlier on, I took the Hyundai to the shop to get the brakes checked, as well as a couple of other little things. I could have done it all myself, but how would that have looked- me outside in overalls, covered in oil and dirt, with the whole neighborhood watching and wondering how Mrs. Mom knows stuff like this?
So I took it to the place on Eighth, which I've heard the local Dads recommend to Andrew. Regretted it the instant I got out of the car.
Felt the piggy little eyes before I saw them.
KATIE, YOU FIGURE OUT A PRICE FOR MRS. FELLOWS, OKAY?
YES, MISTER McWATT.
DON'T FORGET PARTS. AN' LABOR. AN'...
RIGHT.

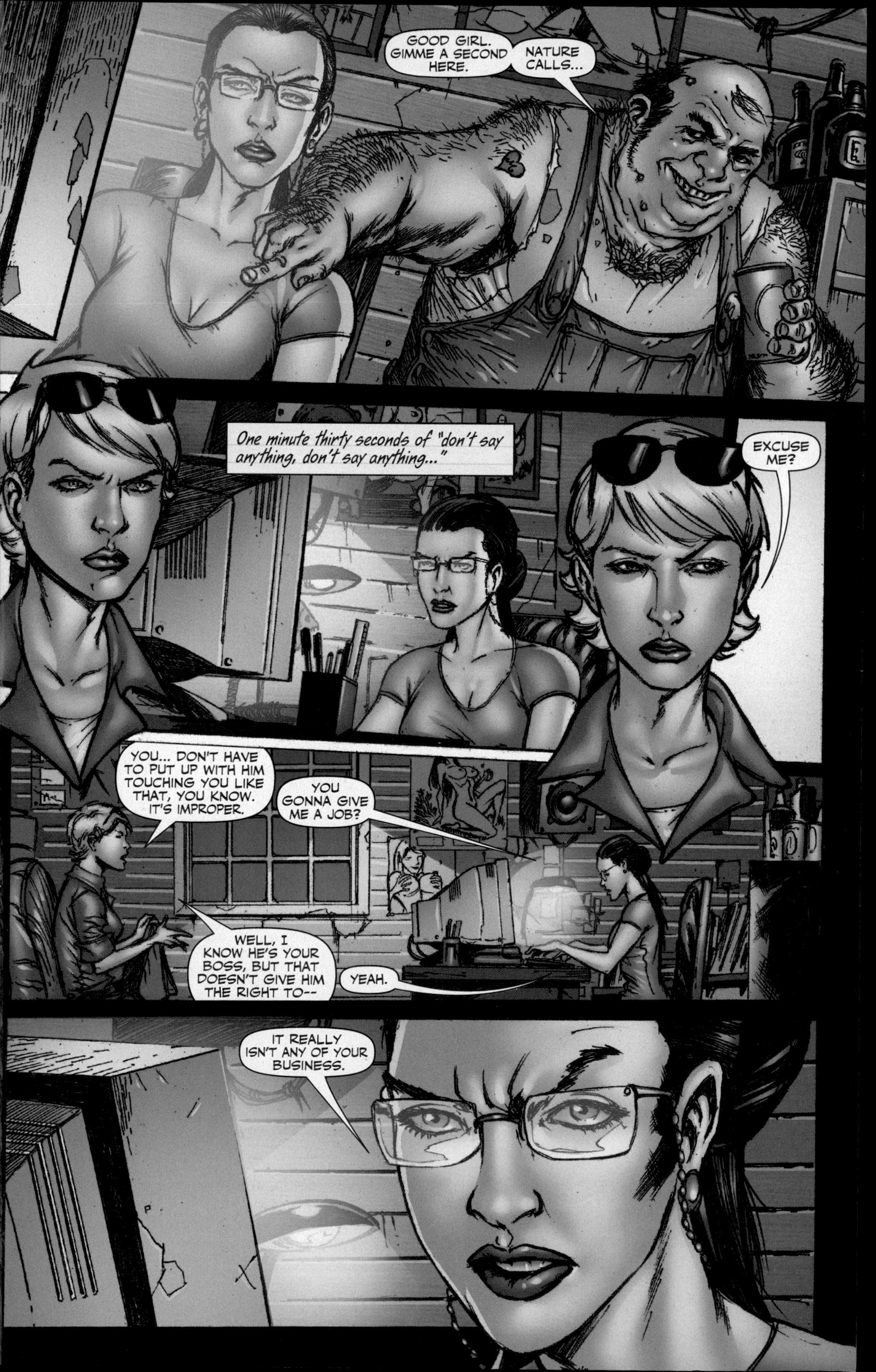
GOOD GIRL. GIMME A SECOND HERE.
NATURE CALLS...
One minute thirty seconds of "don't say anything, don't say anything..."
EXCUSE ME?
YOU... DON'T HAVE TO PUT UP WITH HIM TOUCHING YOU LIKE THAT, YOU KNOW. IT'S IMPROPER.
YOU GONNA GIVE ME A JOB?
WELL, I KNOW HE'S YOUR BOSS, BUT THAT DOESN'T GIVE HIM THE RIGHT TO--
YEAH.
IT REALLY ISN'T ANY OF YOUR BUSINESS.

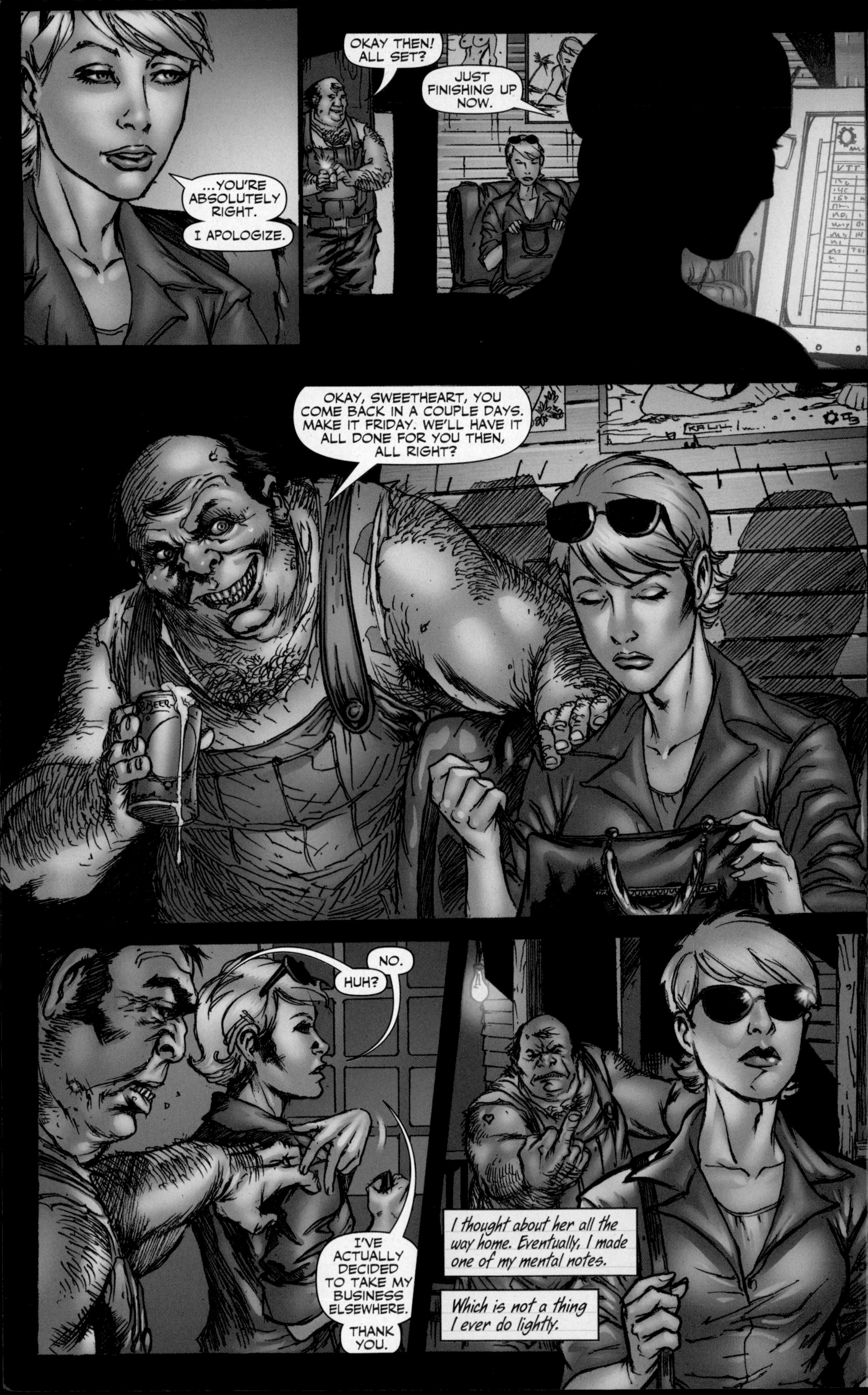
...YOU'RE ABSOLUTELY RIGHT.
I APOLOGIZE.
OKAY THEN! ALL SET?
JUST FINISHING UP NOW.
OKAY, SWEETHEART, YOU COME BACK IN A COUPLE DAYS. MAKE IT FRIDAY. WE'LL HAVE IT ALL DONE FOR YOU THEN, ALL RIGHT?
NO.
HUH?
I'VE ACTUALLY DECIDED TO TAKE MY BUSINESS ELSEWHERE.
THANK YOU.
I thought about her all the way home. Eventually, I made one of my mental notes.
Which is not a thing I ever do lightly.

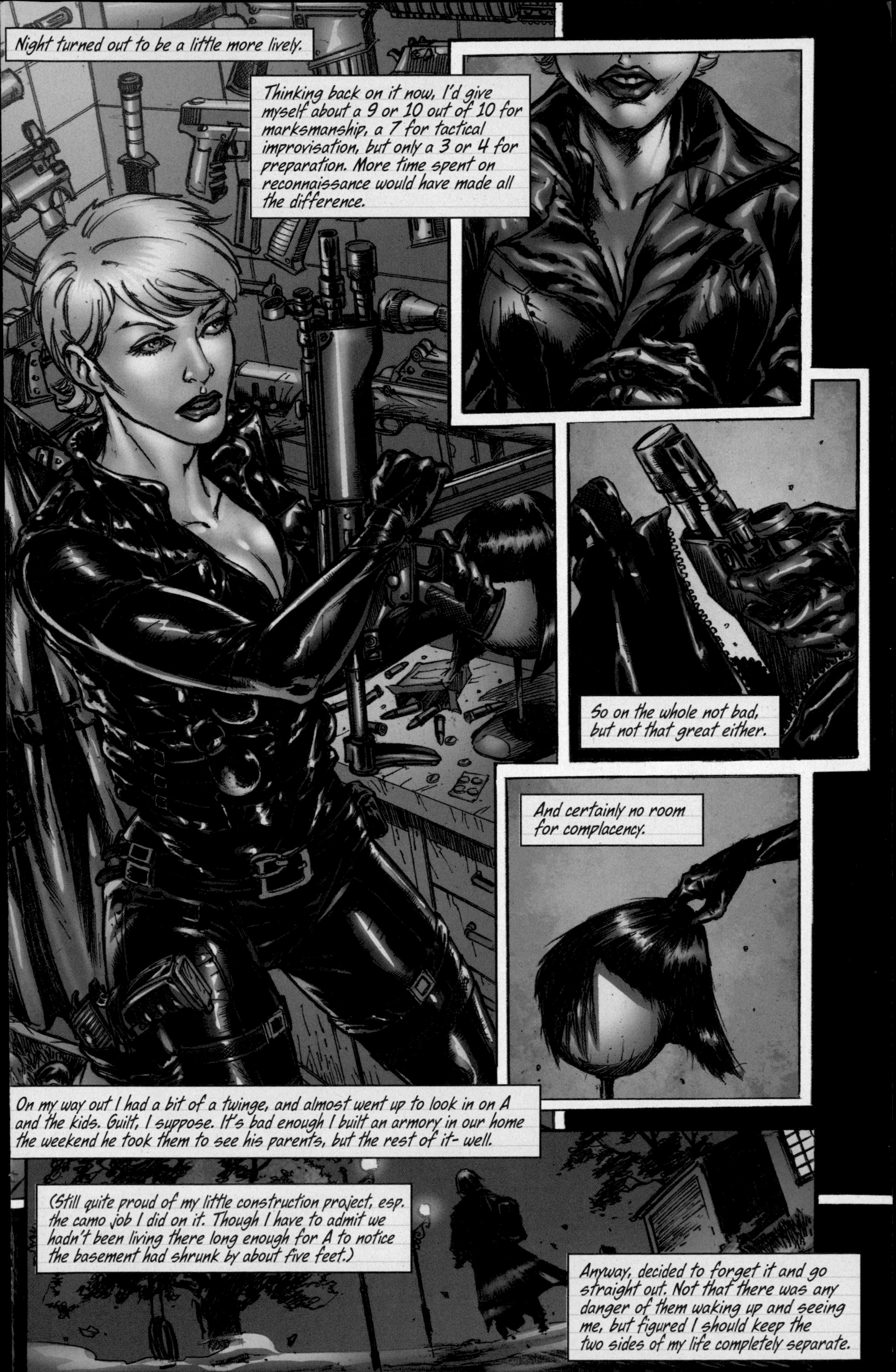
Night turned out to be a little more lively.
Thinking back on it now, I'd give myself about a 9 or 10 out of 10 for marksmanship, a 7 for tactical improvisation, but only a 3 or 4 for preparation. More time spent on reconnaissance would have made all the difference.
So on the whole not bad, but not that great either.
And certainly no room for complacency.
On my way out I had a bit of a twinge, and almost went up to look in on A and the kids. Guilt, I suppose. It's bad enough I built an armory in our home the weekend he took them to see his parents, but the rest of it- well.
(Still quite proud of my little construction project, esp. the camo job I did on it. Though I have to admit we hadn't been living there long enough for A to notice the basement had shrunk by about five feet.)
Anyway, decided to forget it and go straight out. Not that there was any danger of them waking up and seeing me, but figured I should keep the two sides of my life completely separate.

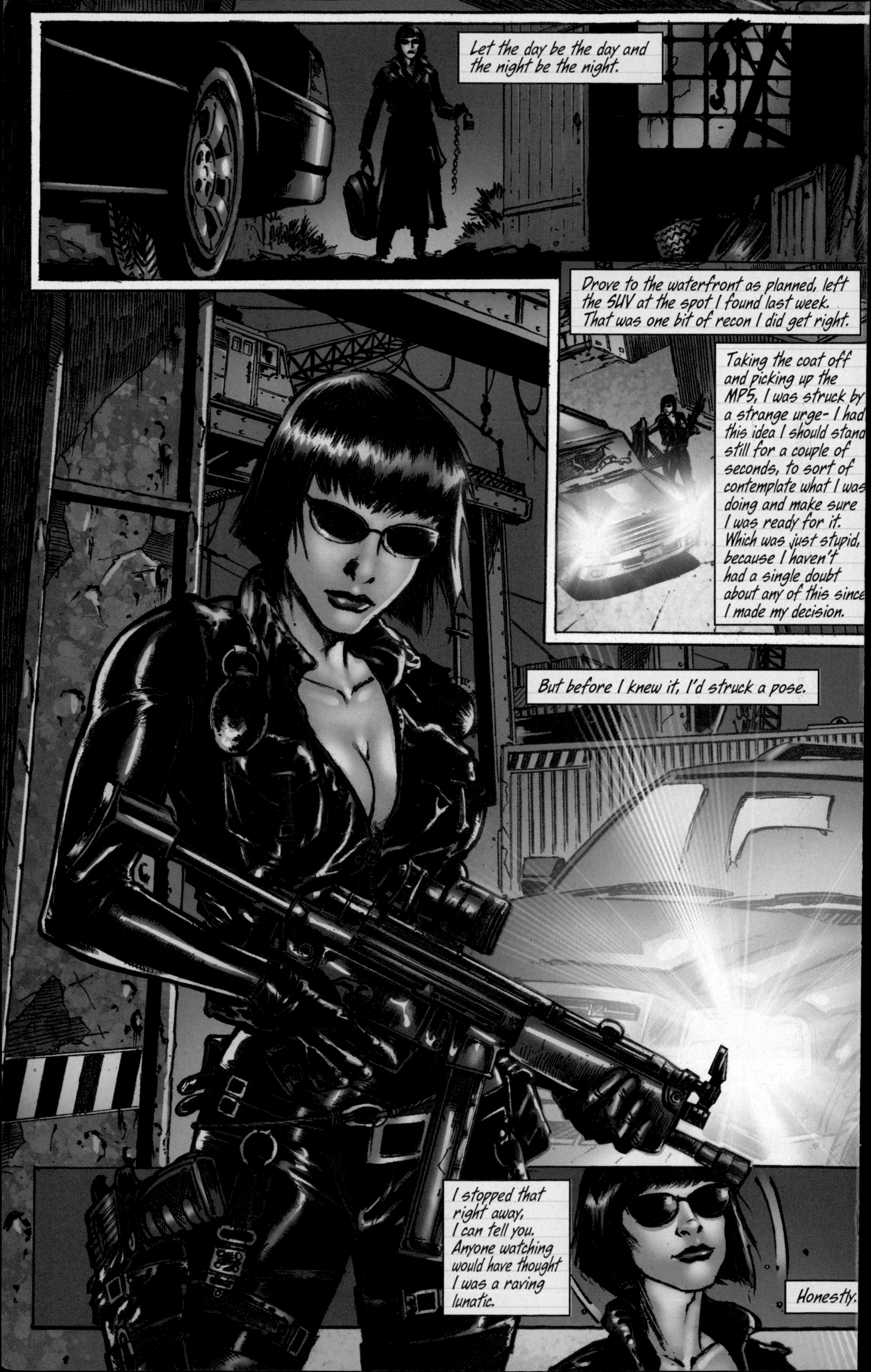
Let the day be the day and the night be the night.
Drove to the waterfront as planned, left the SUV at the spot I found last week. That was one bit of recon I did get right.
Taking the coat off and picking up the MP5, I was struck by a strange urge- I had this idea I should stand still for a couple of seconds, to sort of contemplate what I was doing and make sure I was ready for it. Which was just stupid, because I haven't had a single doubt about any of this since I made my decision.
But before I knew it, I'd struck a pose.
I stopped that right away, I can tell you. Anyone watching would have thought I was a raving lunatic.
Honestly.

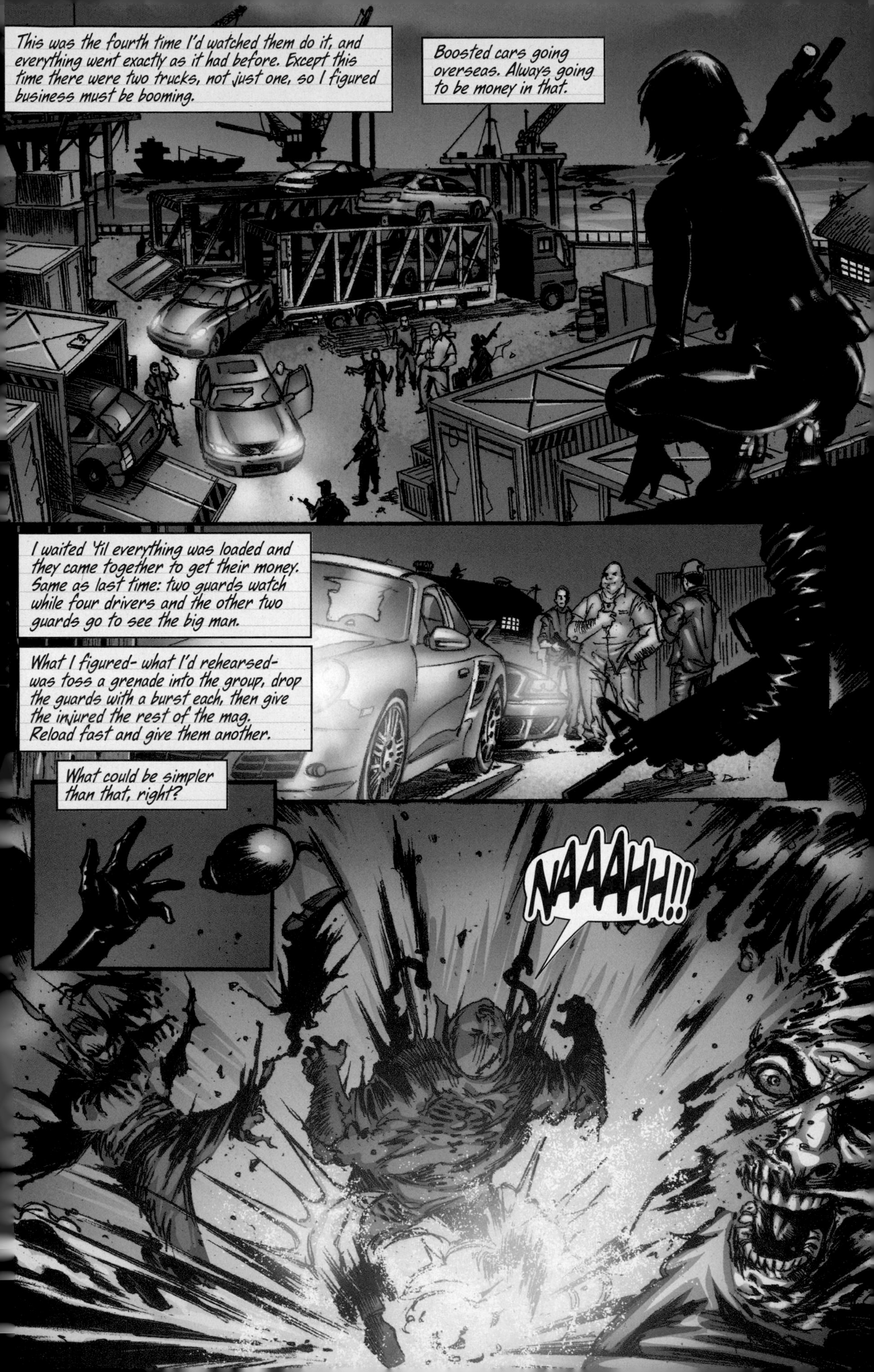
This was the fourth time I'd watched them do it, and everything went exactly as it had before. Except this time there were two trucks, not just one, so I figured business must be booming.
Boosted cars going overseas. Always going to be money in that.
I waited 'til everything was loaded and they came together to get their money. Same as last time: two guards watch while four drivers and the other two guards go to see the big man.
What I figured- what I'd rehearsed- was toss a grenade into the group, drop the guards with a burst each, then give the injured the rest of the mag. Reload fast and give them another.
What could be simpler than that, right?
NAAAHH!!

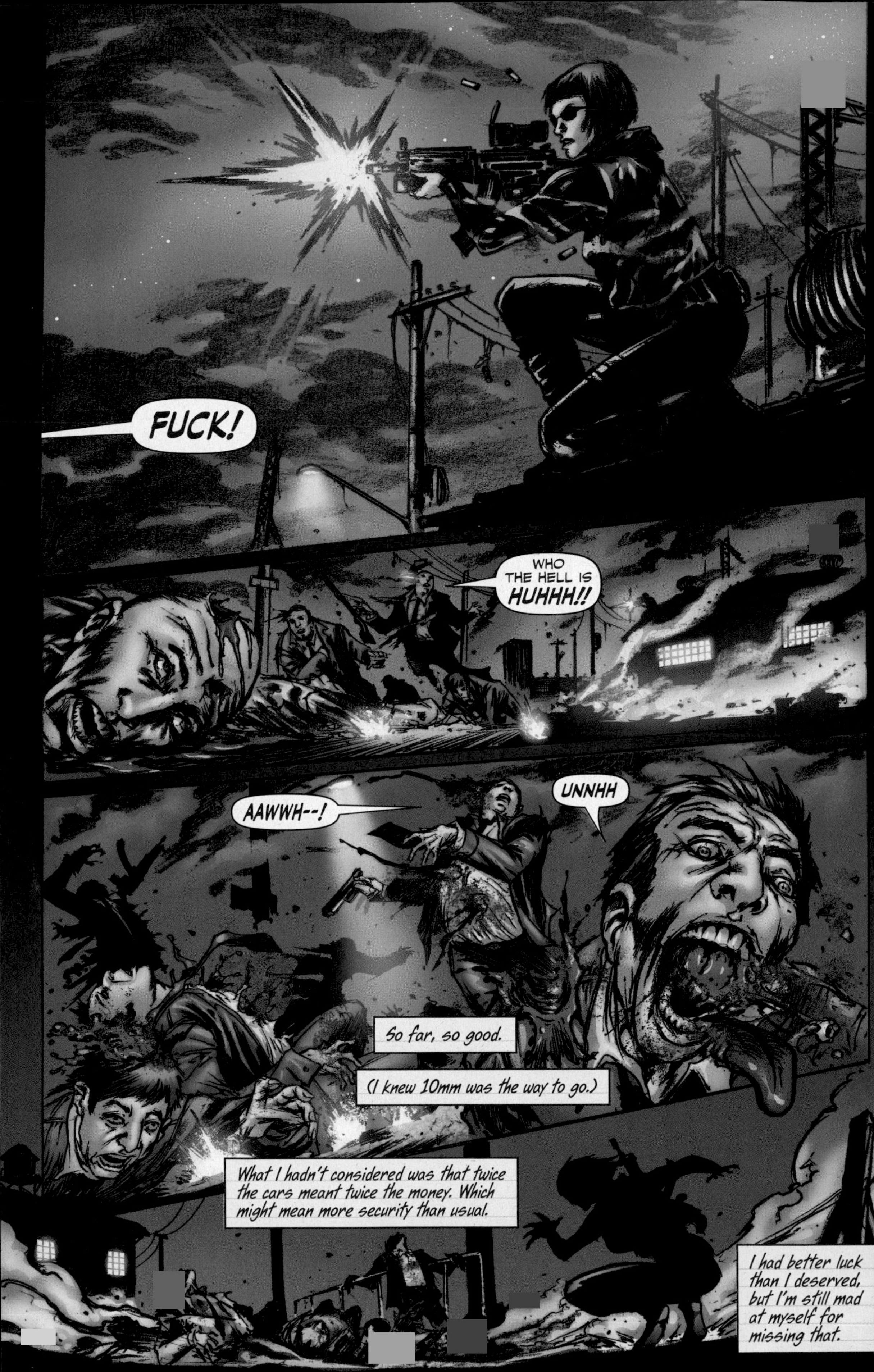
FUCK!
WHO THE HELL IS HUHHH!!
AAWWH--!
UNNHH
So far, so good.
(I knew 10mm was the way to go.)
What I hadn't considered was that twice the cars meant twice the money. Which might mean more security than usual.
I had better luck than I deserved, but I'm still mad at myself for missing that.

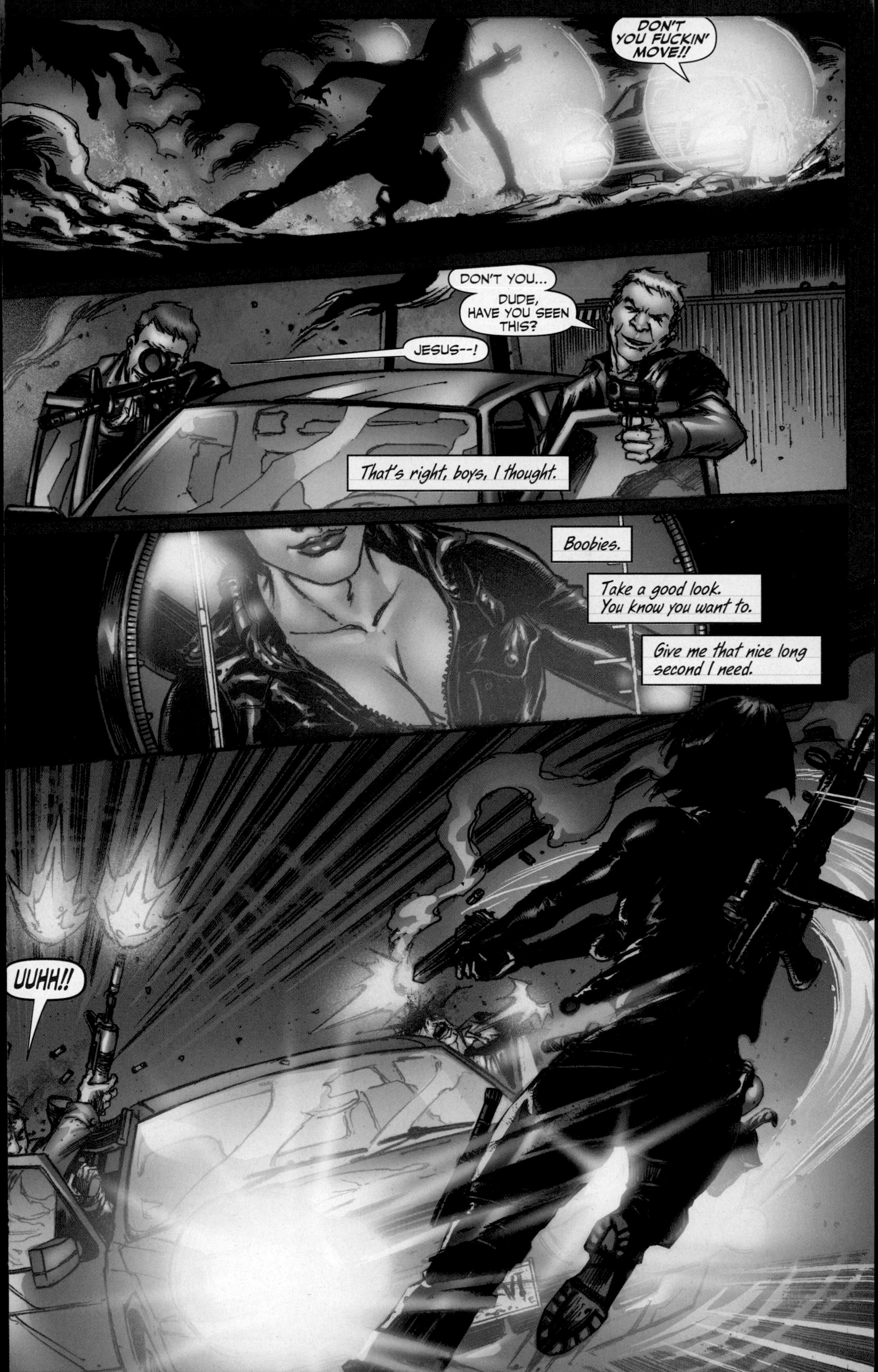
DON'T YOU FUCKIN' MOVE!!
DON'T YOU...
DUDE, HAVE YOU SEEN THIS?
JESUS--!
That's right, boys, I thought.
Boobies.
Take a good look. You know you want to.
Give me that nice long second I need.
UUHH!!

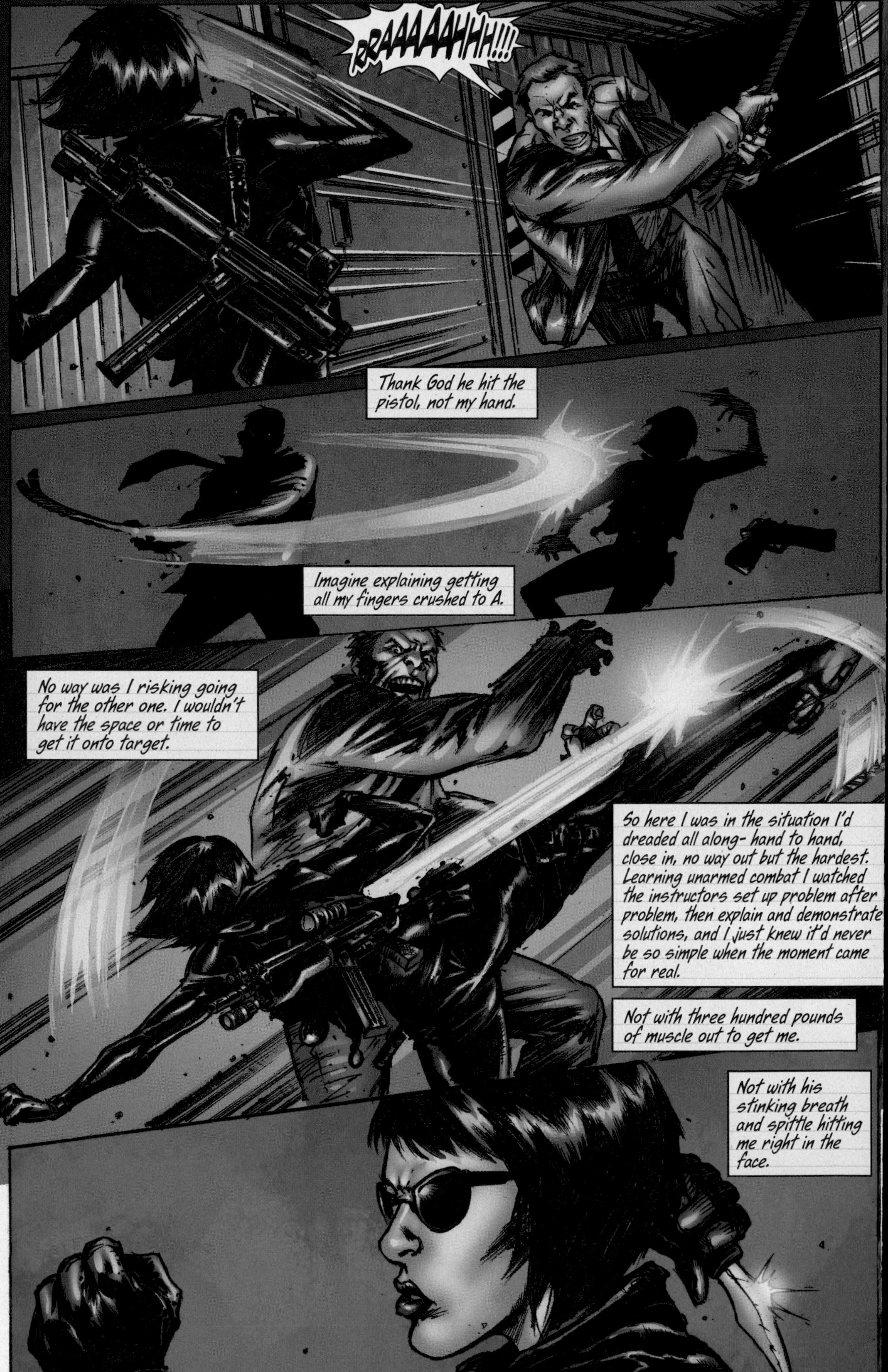
RRAAAAAHHH!!!
Thank God he hit the pistol, not my hand.
Imagine explaining getting all my fingers crushed to A.
No way was I risking going for the other one. I wouldn't have the space or time to get it onto target.
So here I was in the situation I'd dreaded all along- hand to hand, close in, no way out but the hardest. Learning unarmed combat I watched the instructors set up problem after problem, then explain and demonstrate solutions, and I just knew it'd never be so simple when the moment came for real.
Not with three hundred pounds of muscle out to get me.
Not with his stinking breath and spittle hitting me right in the face.

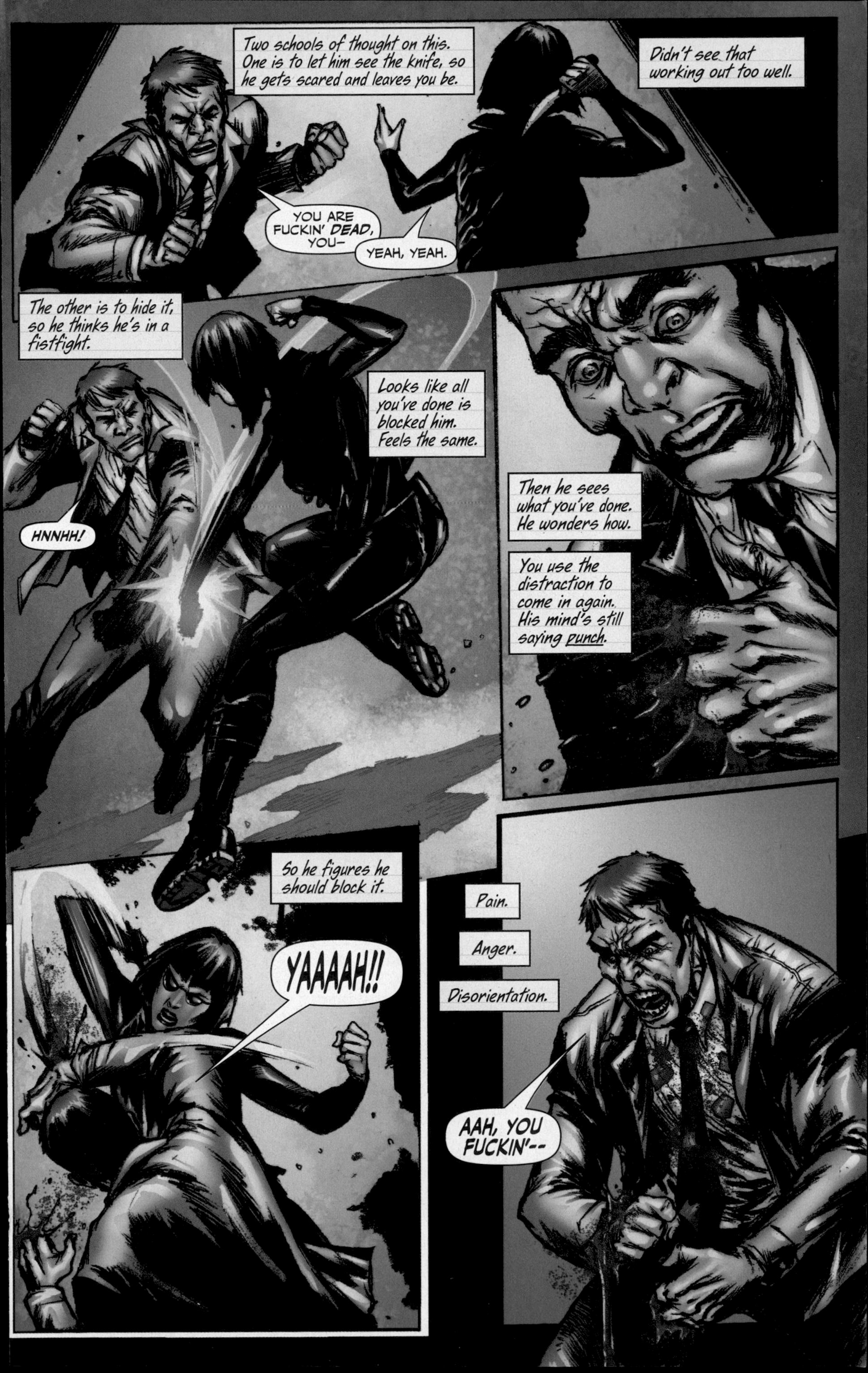
Two schools of thought on this. One is to let him see the knife, so he gets scared and leaves you be.
Didn't see that working out too well.
YOU ARE FUCKIN' DEAD, YOU—
YEAH, YEAH.
The other is to hide it, so he thinks he's in a fistfight.
Looks like all you've done is blocked him. Feels the same.
HNNHH!
Then he sees what you've done. He wonders how.
You use the distraction to come in again. His mind's still saying punch.
So he figures he should block it.
YAAAAH!!
Pain.
Anger.
Disorientation.
AAH, YOU FUCKIN'--

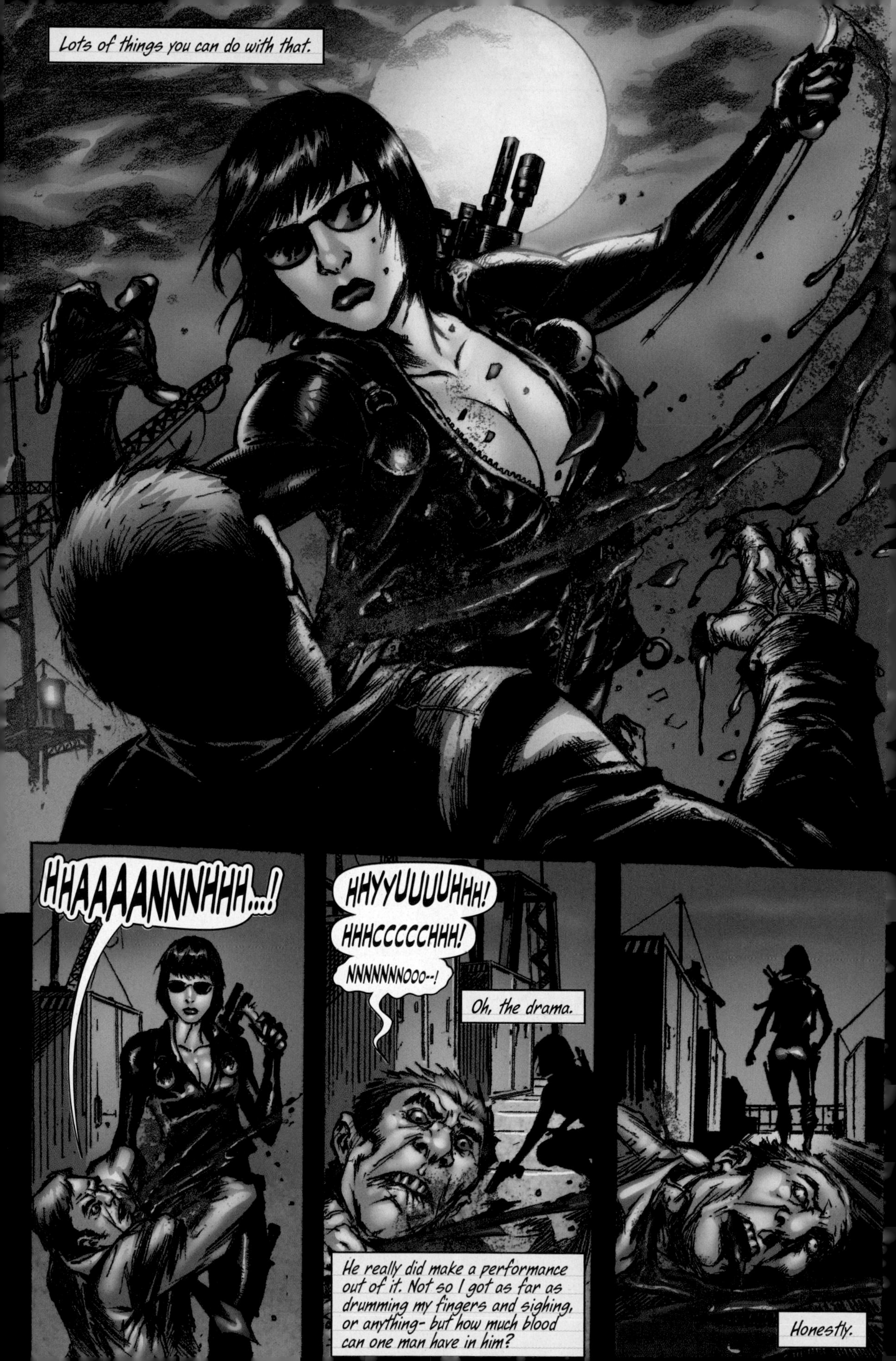
Lots of things you can do with that.
HHAAAAANNNHHH...!
HHYYUUUUHHH!
HHHCCCCCHHH!
NNNNNNNOOO--!
Oh, the drama.
He really did make a performance out of it. Not so I got as far as drumming my fingers and sighing, or anything- but how much blood can one man have in him?
Honestly.

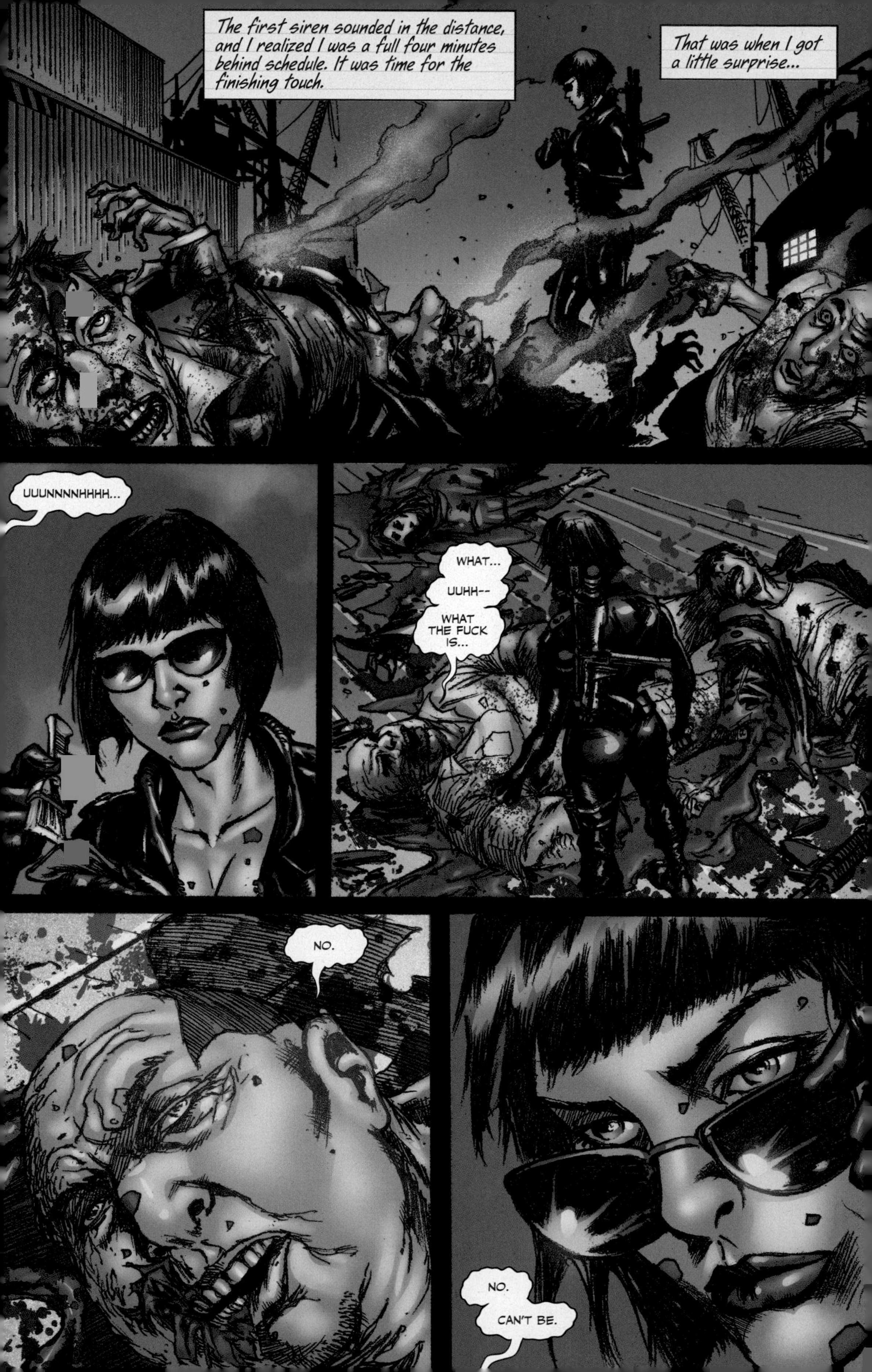
The first siren sounded in the distance, and I realized I was a full four minutes behind schedule. It was time for the finishing touch.
That was when I got a little surprise...
UUUNNNNHHHH...
WHAT...
UUHH--
WHAT THE FUCK IS...
NO.
NO.
CAN'T BE.

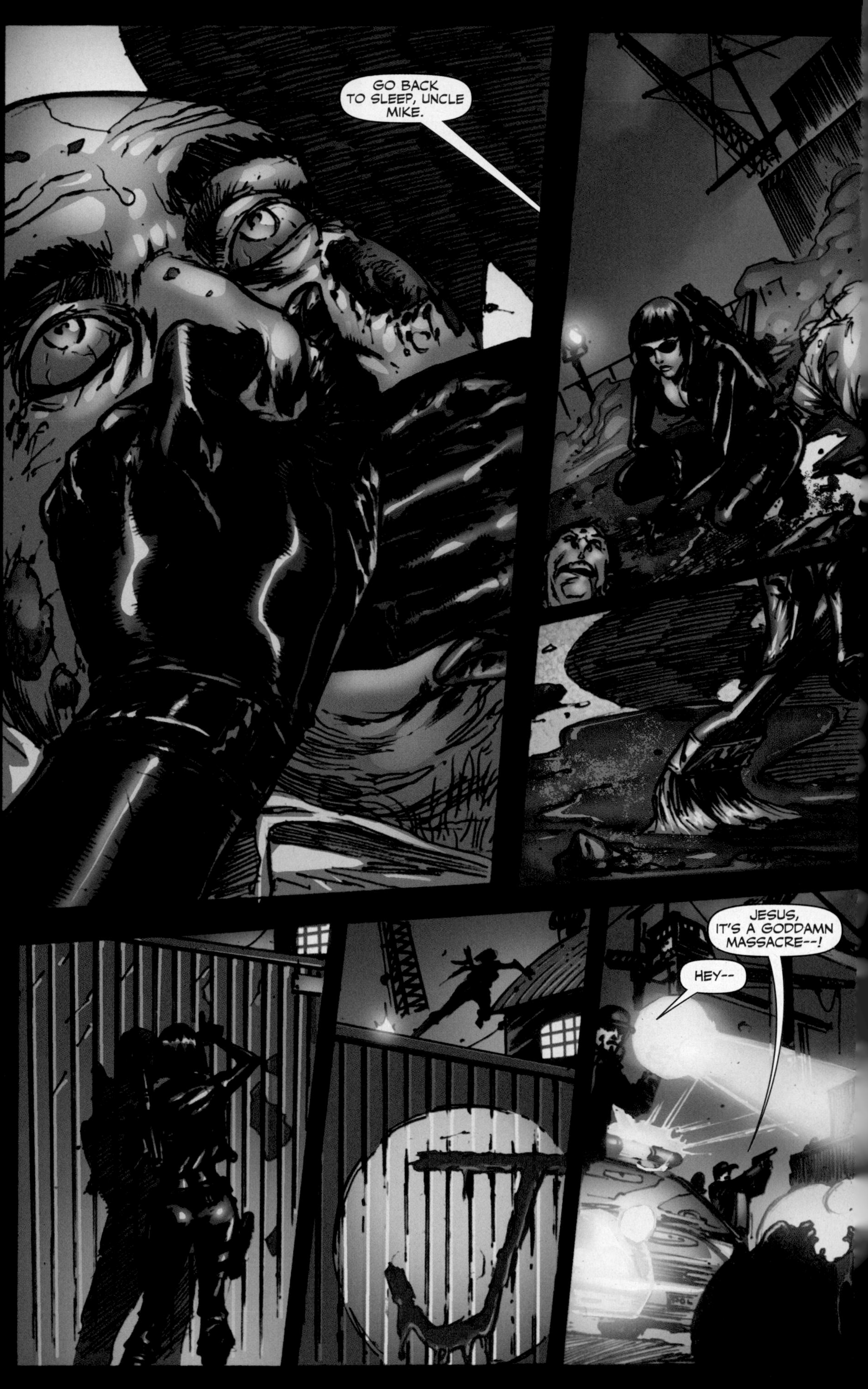
GO BACK TO SLEEP, UNCLE MIKE.
JESUS, IT'S A GODDAMN MASSACRE--!
HEY--

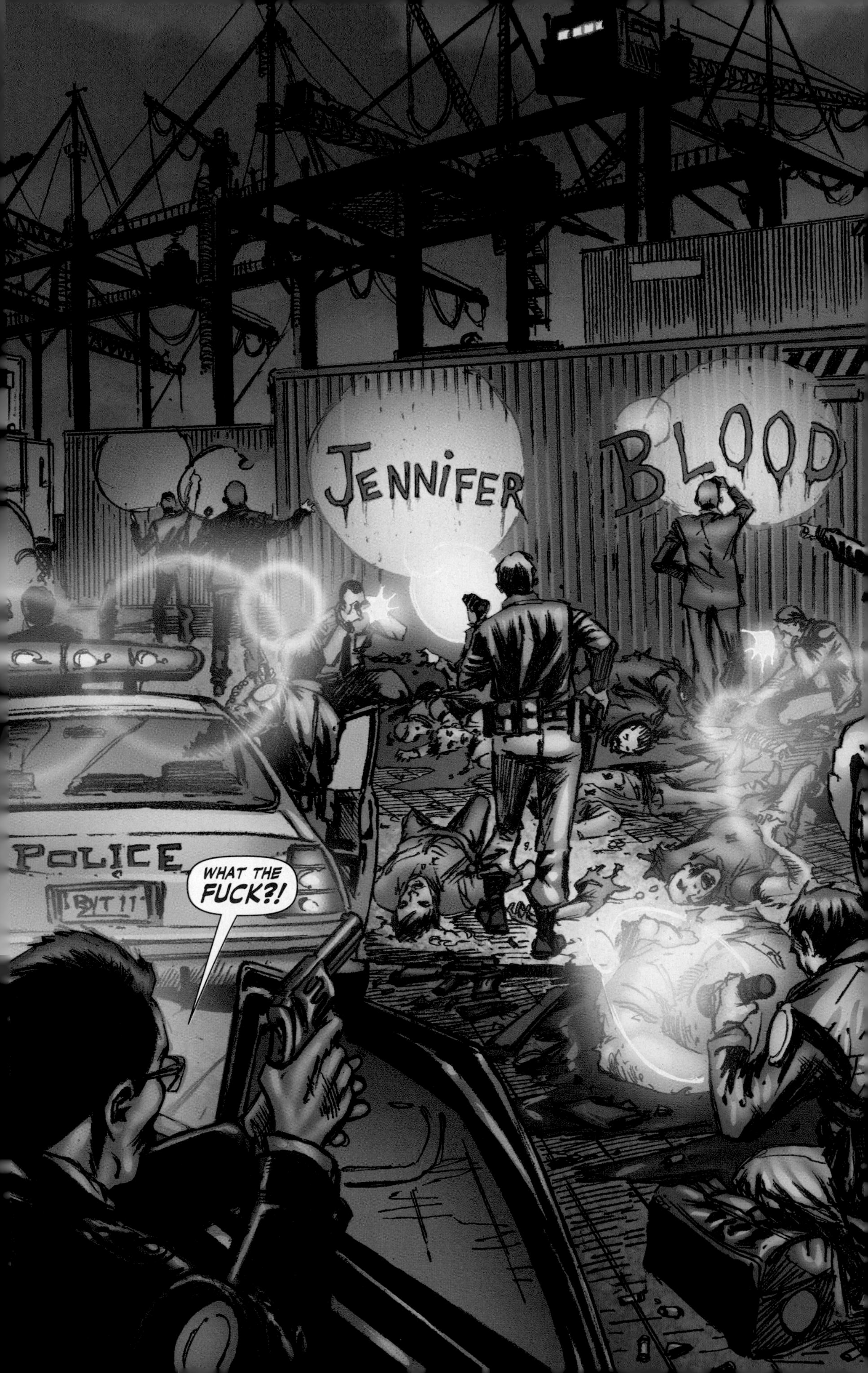
JENNIFER BLOOD
POLICE
WHAT THE FUCK?!

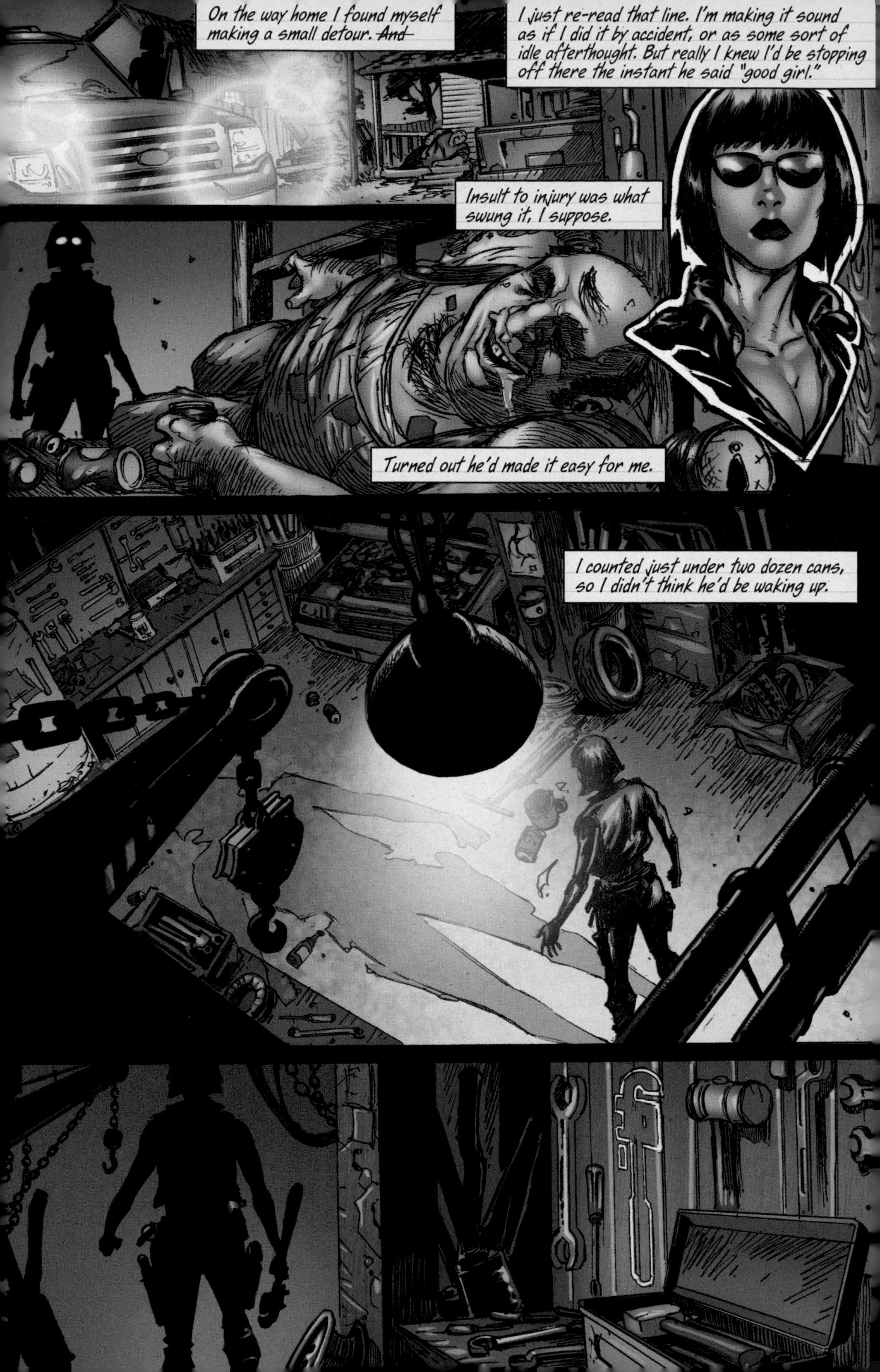

On the way home I found myself making a small detour. ~~And~~
I just re-read that line. I'm making it sound as if I did it by accident, or as some sort of idle afterthought. But really I knew I'd be stopping off there the instant he said "good girl."
Insult to injury was what swung it, I suppose.
Turned out he'd made it easy for me.
I counted just under two dozen cans, so I didn't think he'd be waking up.

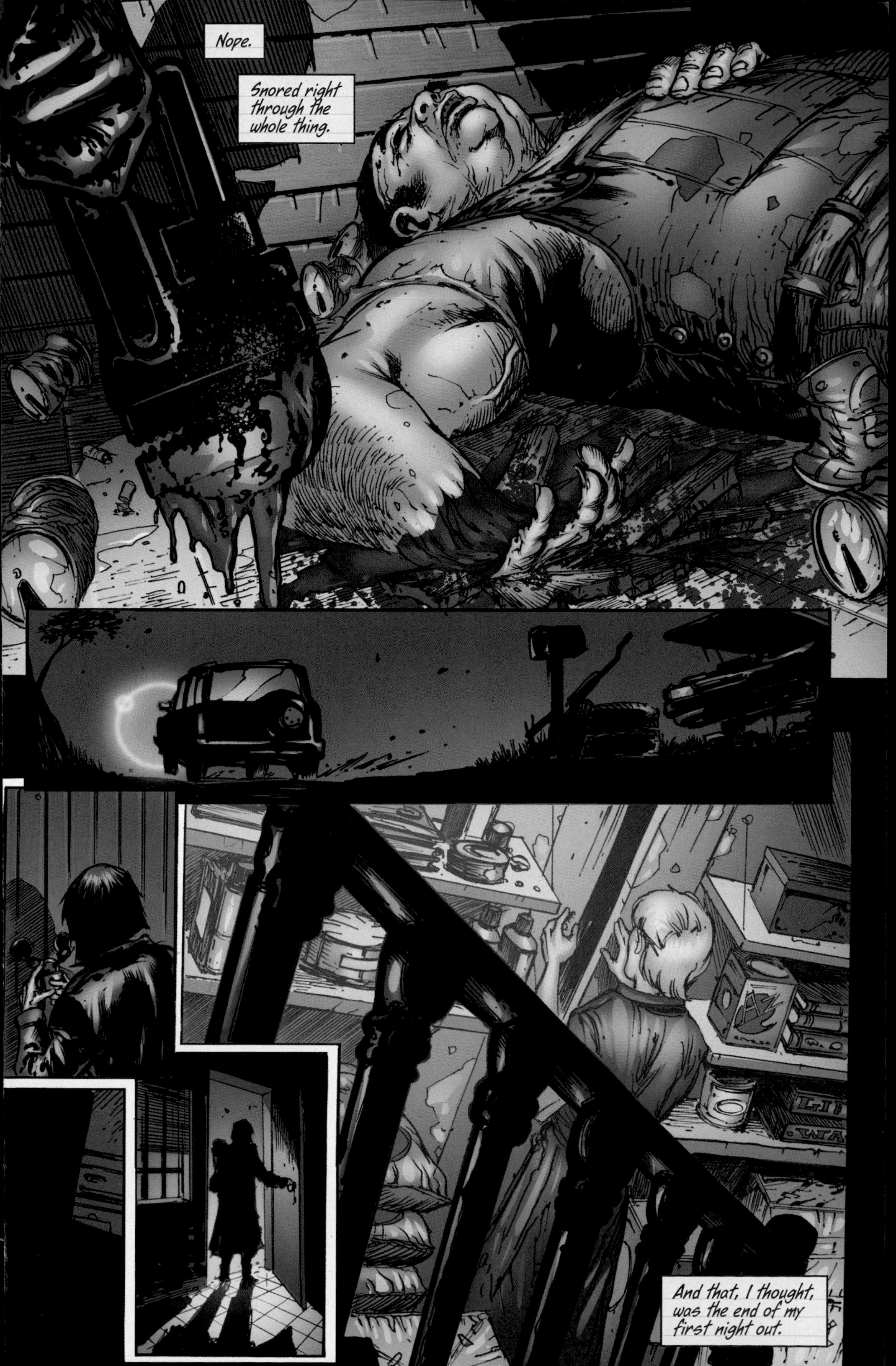
Nope.
Snored right through the whole thing.
And that, I thought, was the end of my first night out.

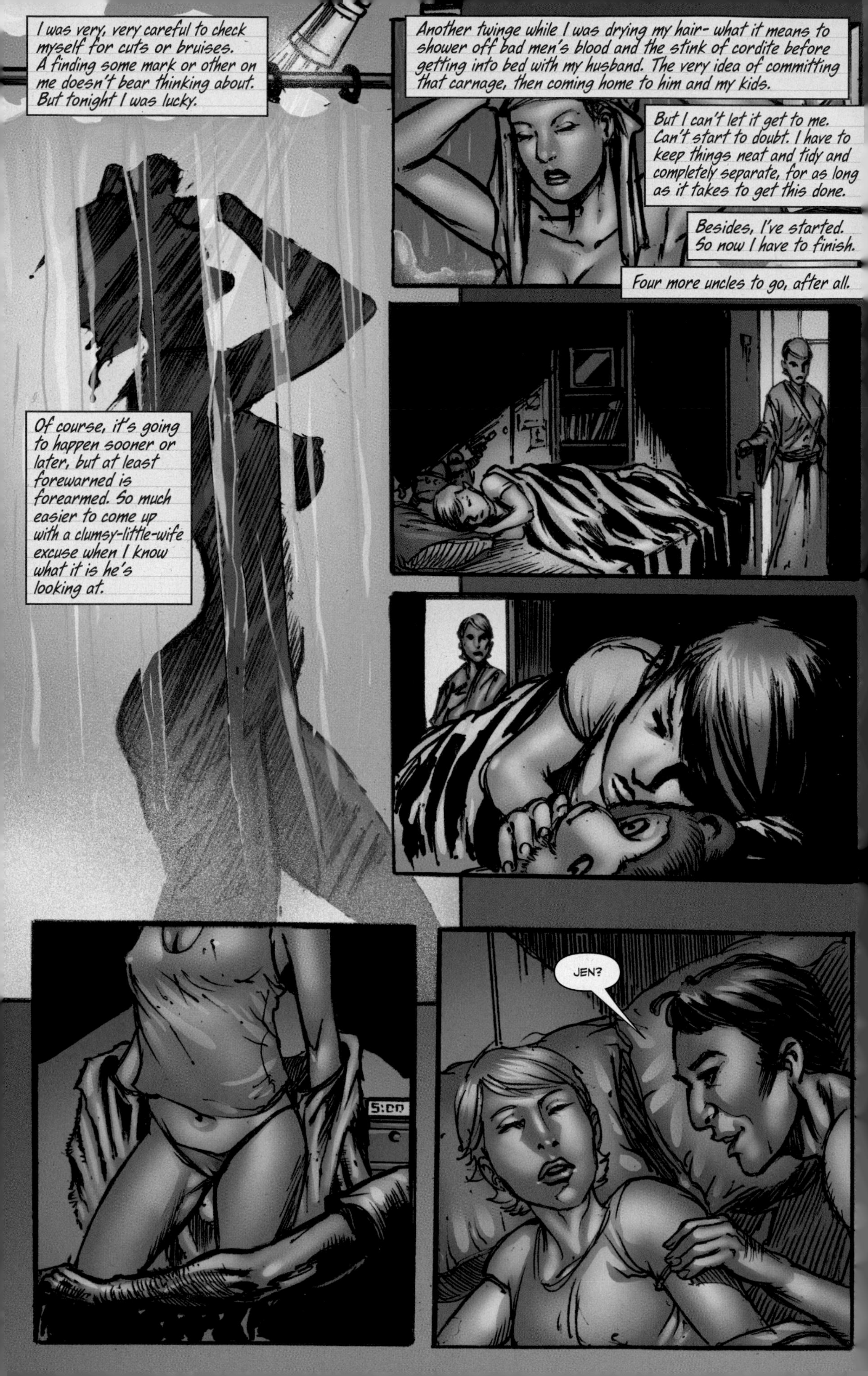
I was very, very careful to check myself for cuts or bruises. A finding some mark or other on me doesn't bear thinking about. But tonight I was lucky.
Of course, it's going to happen sooner or later, but at least forewarned is forearmed. So much easier to come up with a clumsy-little-wife excuse when I know what it is he's looking at.
Another twinge while I was drying my hair- what it means to shower off bad men's blood and the stink of cordite before getting into bed with my husband. The very idea of committing that carnage, then coming home to him and my kids.
But I can't let it get to me. Can't start to doubt. I have to keep things neat and tidy and completely separate, for as long as it takes to get this done.
Besides, I've started. So now I have to finish.
Four more uncles to go, after all.
5:00
JEN?

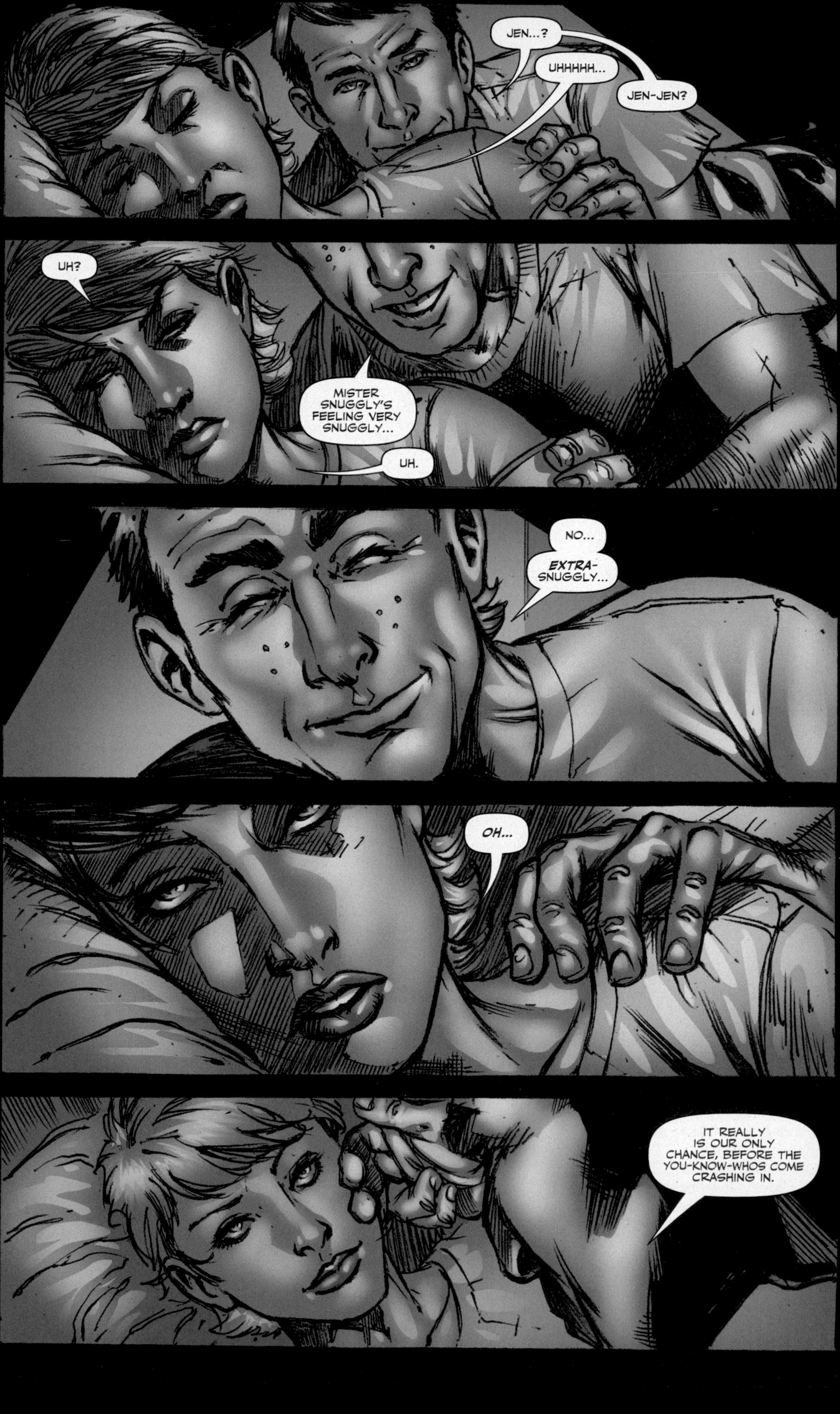
JEN...?
UHHHHH...
JEN-JEN?
UH?
MISTER SNUGGLY'S FEELING VERY SNUGGLY...
UH.
NO... *EXTRA*-SNUGGLY...
OH...
IT REALLY IS OUR ONLY CHANCE, BEFORE THE YOU-KNOW-WHOS COME CRASHING IN.

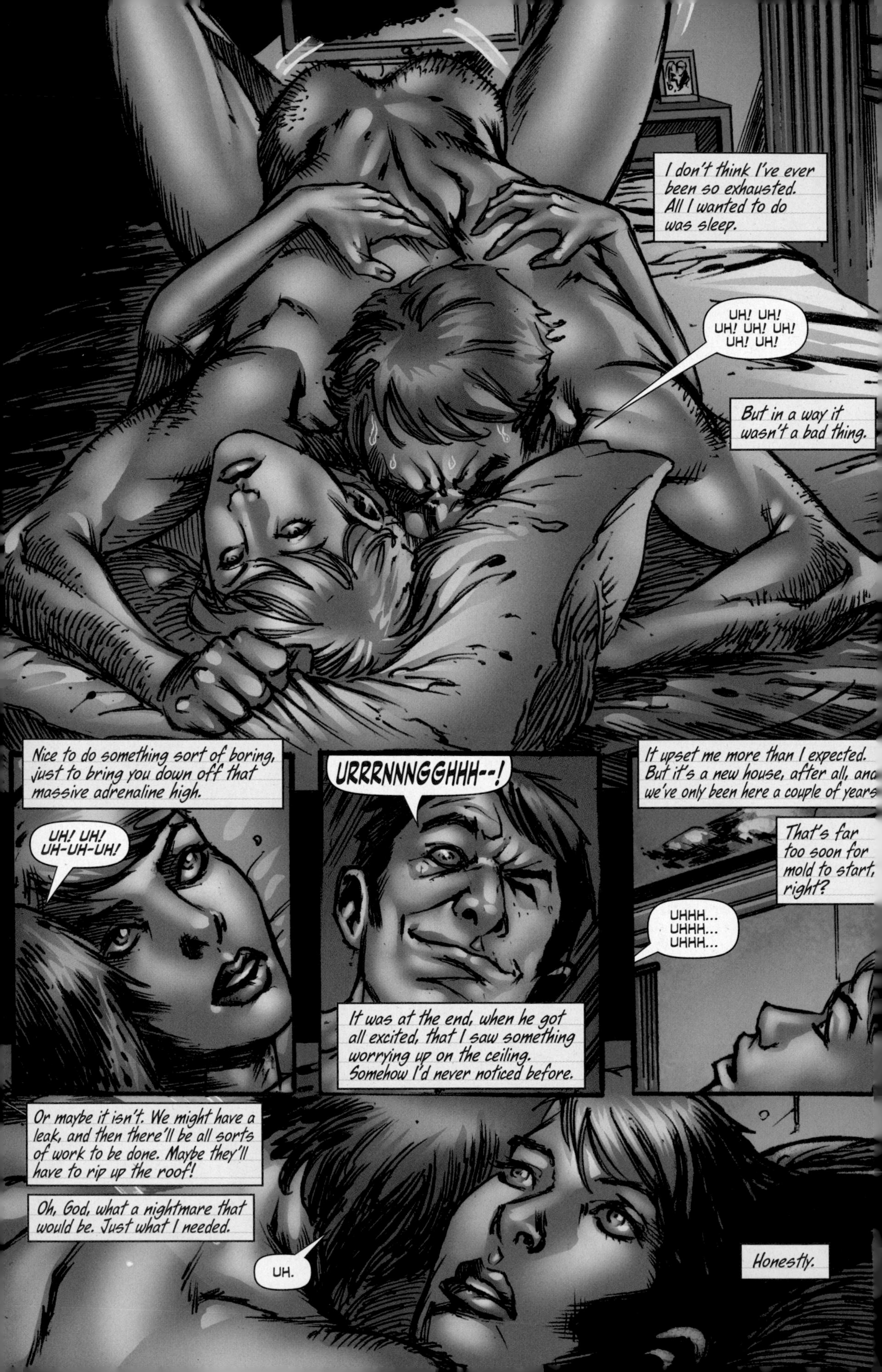
I don't think I've ever been so exhausted. All I wanted to do was sleep.
UH! UH! UH! UH! UH! UH! UH!
But in a way it wasn't a bad thing.
Nice to do something sort of boring, just to bring you down off that massive adrenaline high.
UH! UH! UH-UH-UH!
URRRNNNGGHHH--!
It was at the end, when he got all excited, that I saw something worrying up on the ceiling. Somehow I'd never noticed before.
It upset me more than I expected. But it's a new house, after all, an we've only been here a couple of years
That's far too soon for mold to start, right?
UHHH... UHHH... UHHH...
Or maybe it isn't. We might have a leak, and then there'll be all sorts of work to be done. Maybe they'll have to rip up the roof!
Oh, God, what a nightmare that would be. Just what I needed.
UH.
Honestly.

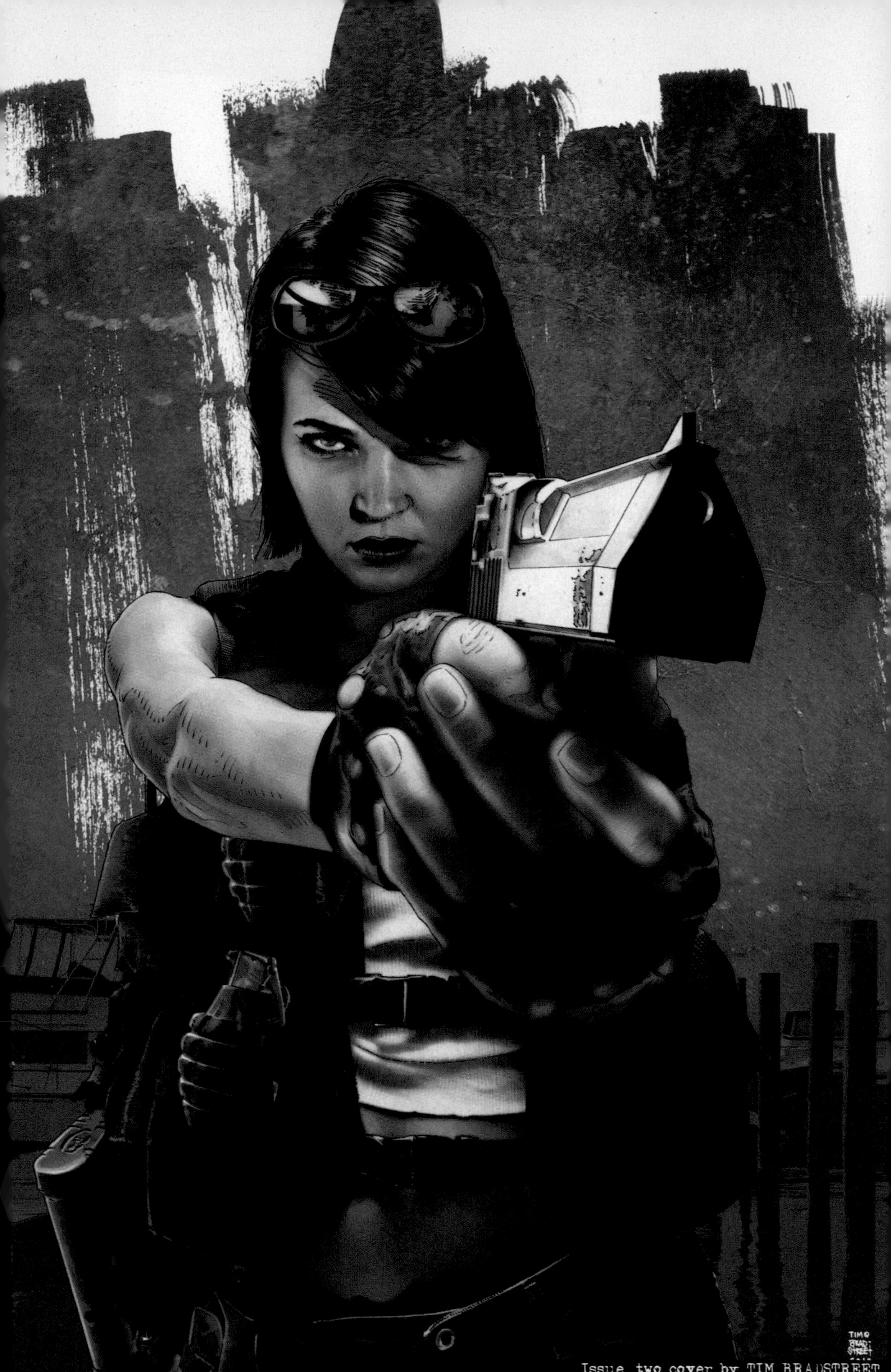

Issue two cover by TIM BRADSTREET

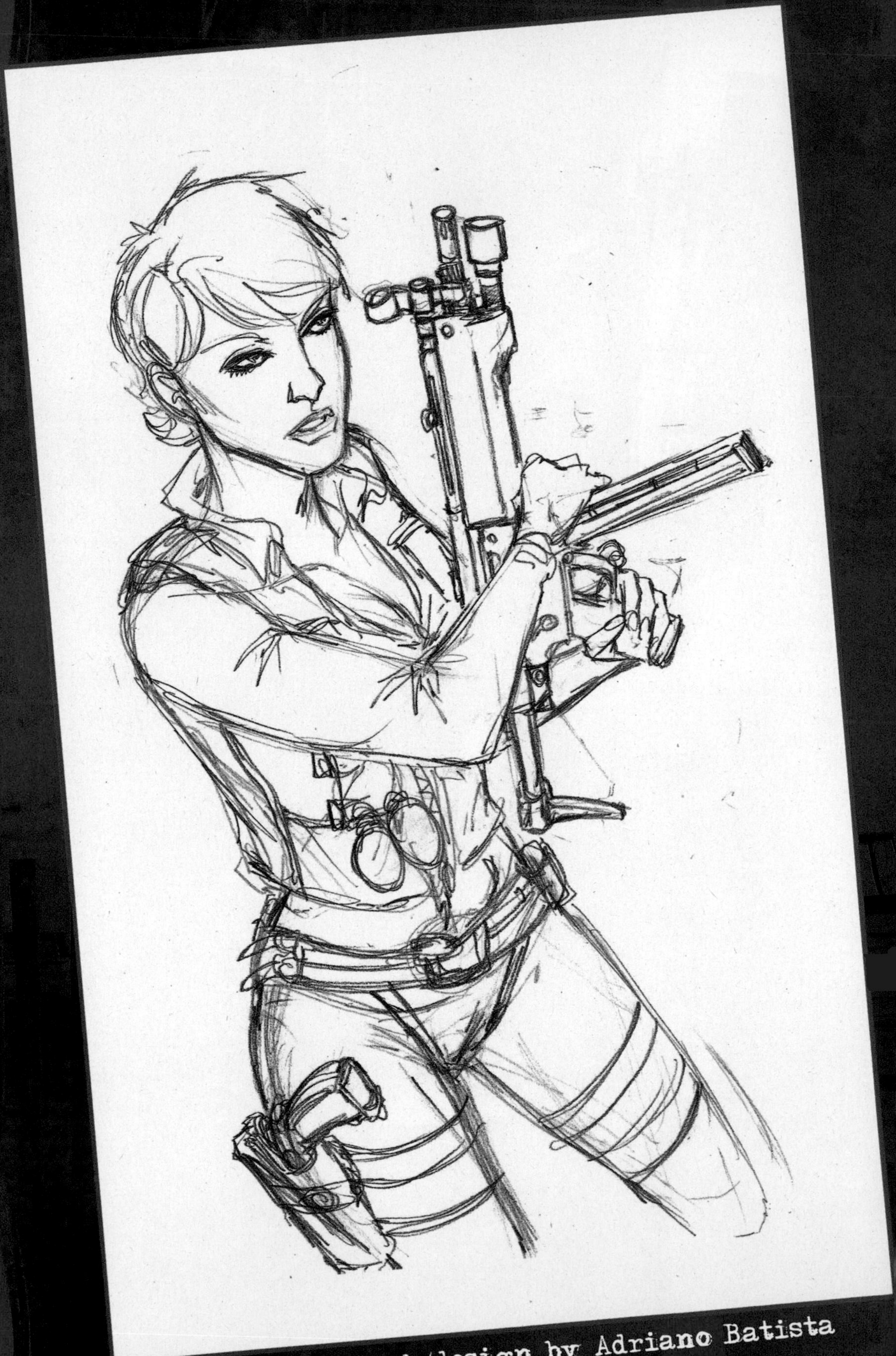

Character sketch/design by Adriano Batista

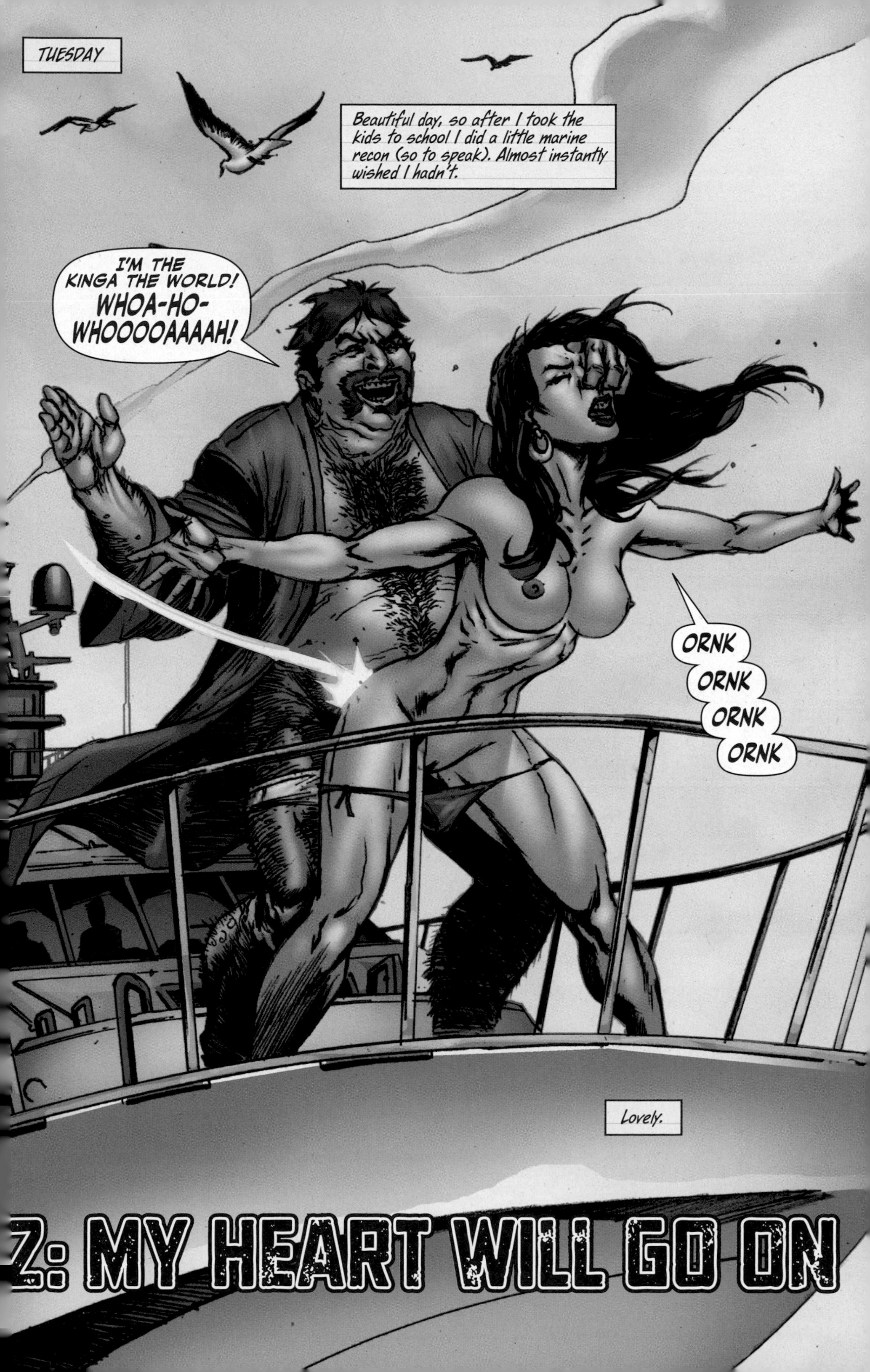
TUESDAY
Beautiful day, so after I took the kids to school I did a little marine recon (so to speak). Almost instantly wished I hadn't.
I'M THE KINGA THE WORLD! WHOA-HO-WHOOOOAAAAH!
ORNK ORNK ORNK ORNK
Lovely.
2: MY HEART WILL GO ON

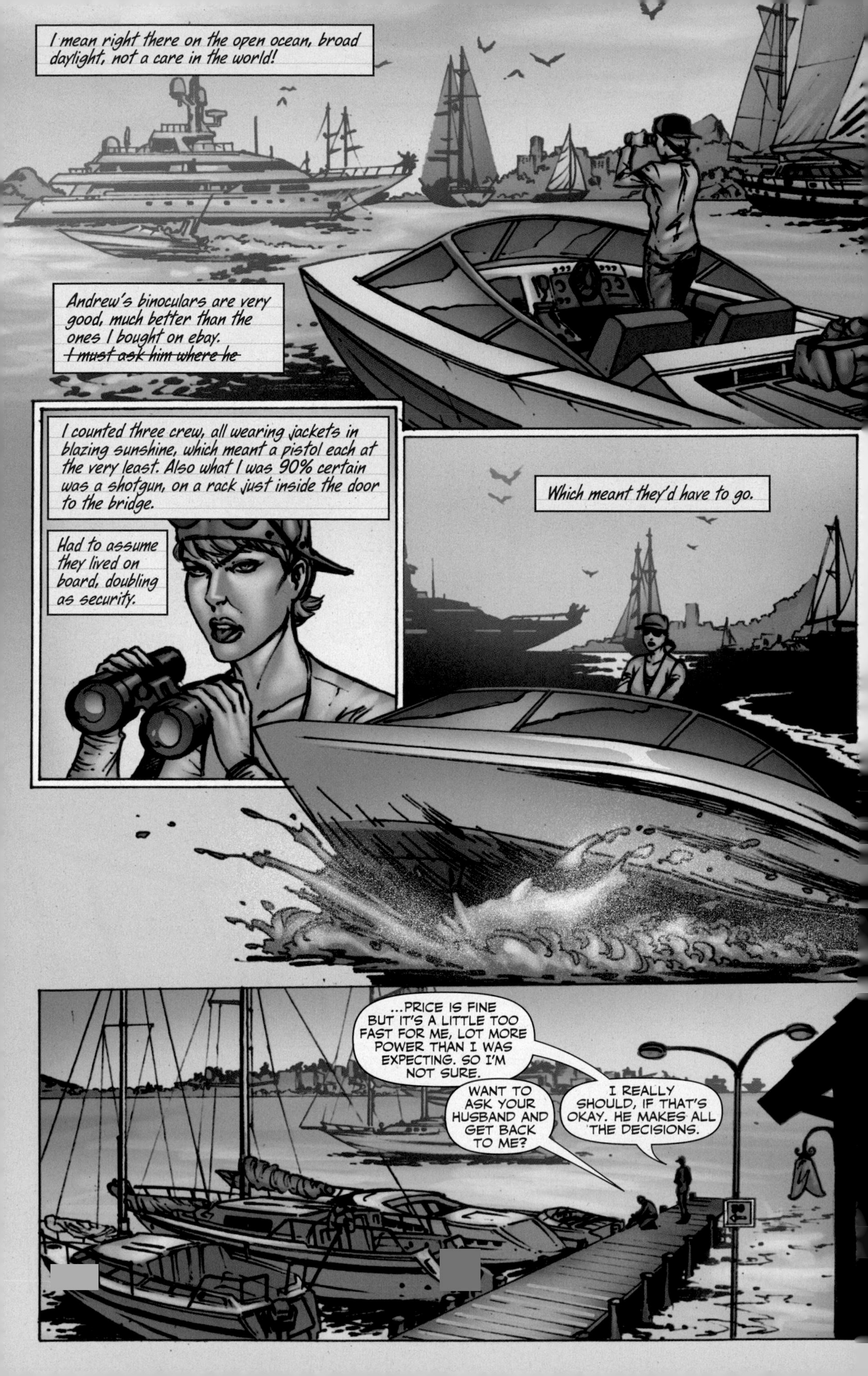
I mean right there on the open ocean, broad daylight, not a care in the world!
Andrew's binoculars are very good, much better than the ones I bought on ebay.
~~I must ask him where he~~
I counted three crew, all wearing jackets in blazing sunshine, which meant a pistol each at the very least. Also what I was 90% certain was a shotgun, on a rack just inside the door to the bridge.
Had to assume they lived on board, doubling as security.
Which meant they'd have to go.
...PRICE IS FINE BUT IT'S A LITTLE TOO FAST FOR ME, LOT MORE POWER THAN I WAS EXPECTING. SO I'M NOT SURE.
WANT TO ASK YOUR HUSBAND AND GET BACK TO ME?
I REALLY SHOULD, IF THAT'S OKAY. HE MAKES ALL THE DECISIONS.

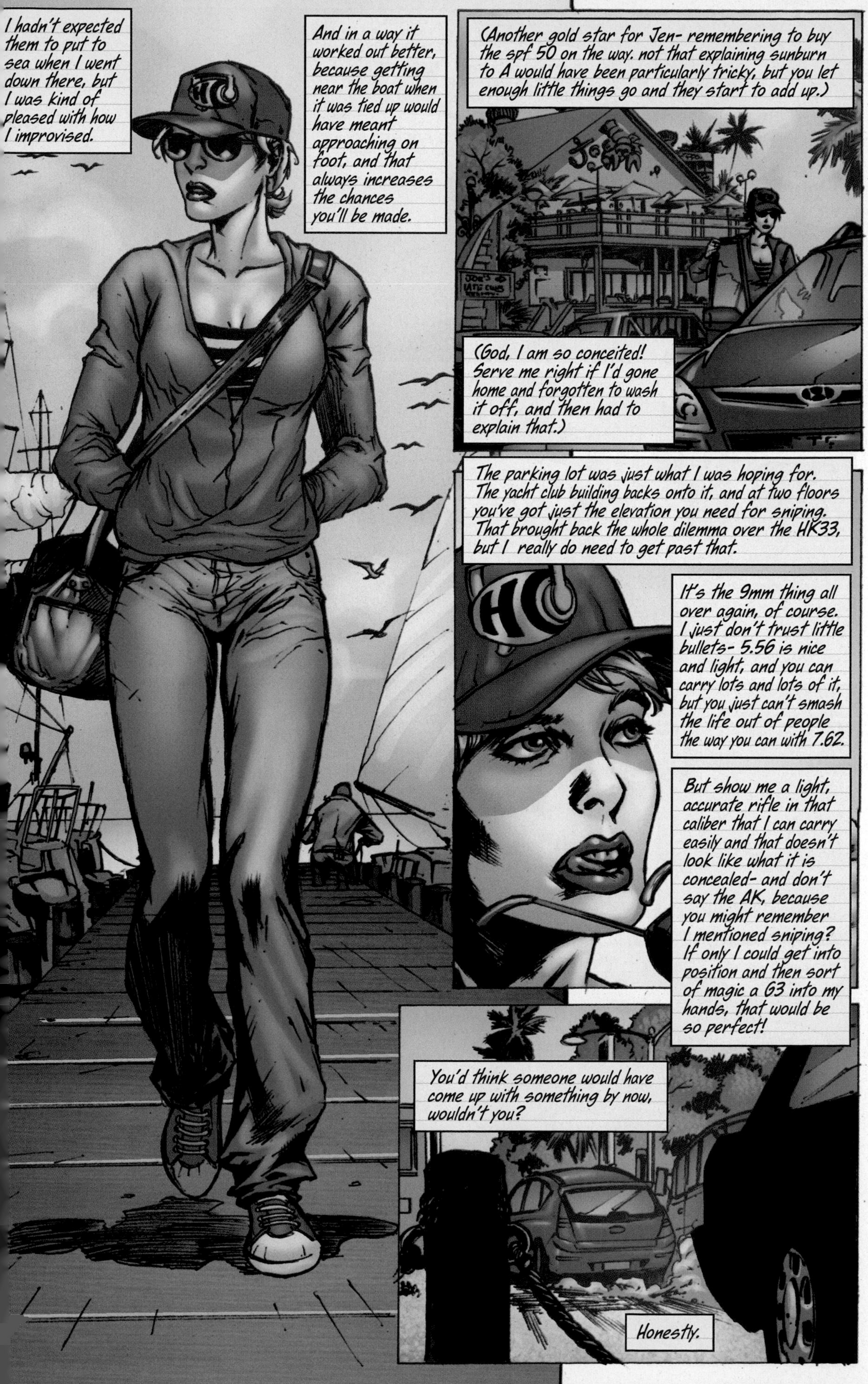
I hadn't expected them to put to sea when I went down there, but I was kind of pleased with how I improvised.
And in a way it worked out better, because getting near the boat when it was tied up would have meant approaching on foot, and that always increases the chances you'll be made.
(Another gold star for Jen- remembering to buy the spf 50 on the way. not that explaining sunburn to A would have been particularly tricky, but you let enough little things go and they start to add up.)
(God, I am so conceited! Serve me right if I'd gone home and forgotten to wash it off, and then had to explain that.)
The parking lot was just what I was hoping for. The yacht club building backs onto it, and at two floors you've got just the elevation you need for sniping. That brought back the whole dilemma over the HK33, but I really do need to get past that.
It's the 9mm thing all over again, of course. I just don't trust little bullets- 5.56 is nice and light, and you can carry lots and lots of it, but you just can't smash the life out of people the way you can with 7.62.
But show me a light, accurate rifle in that caliber that I can carry easily and that doesn't look like what it is concealed- and don't say the AK, because you might remember I mentioned sniping? If only I could get into position and then sort of magic a G3 into my hands, that would be so perfect!
You'd think someone would have come up with something by now, wouldn't you?
Honestly.

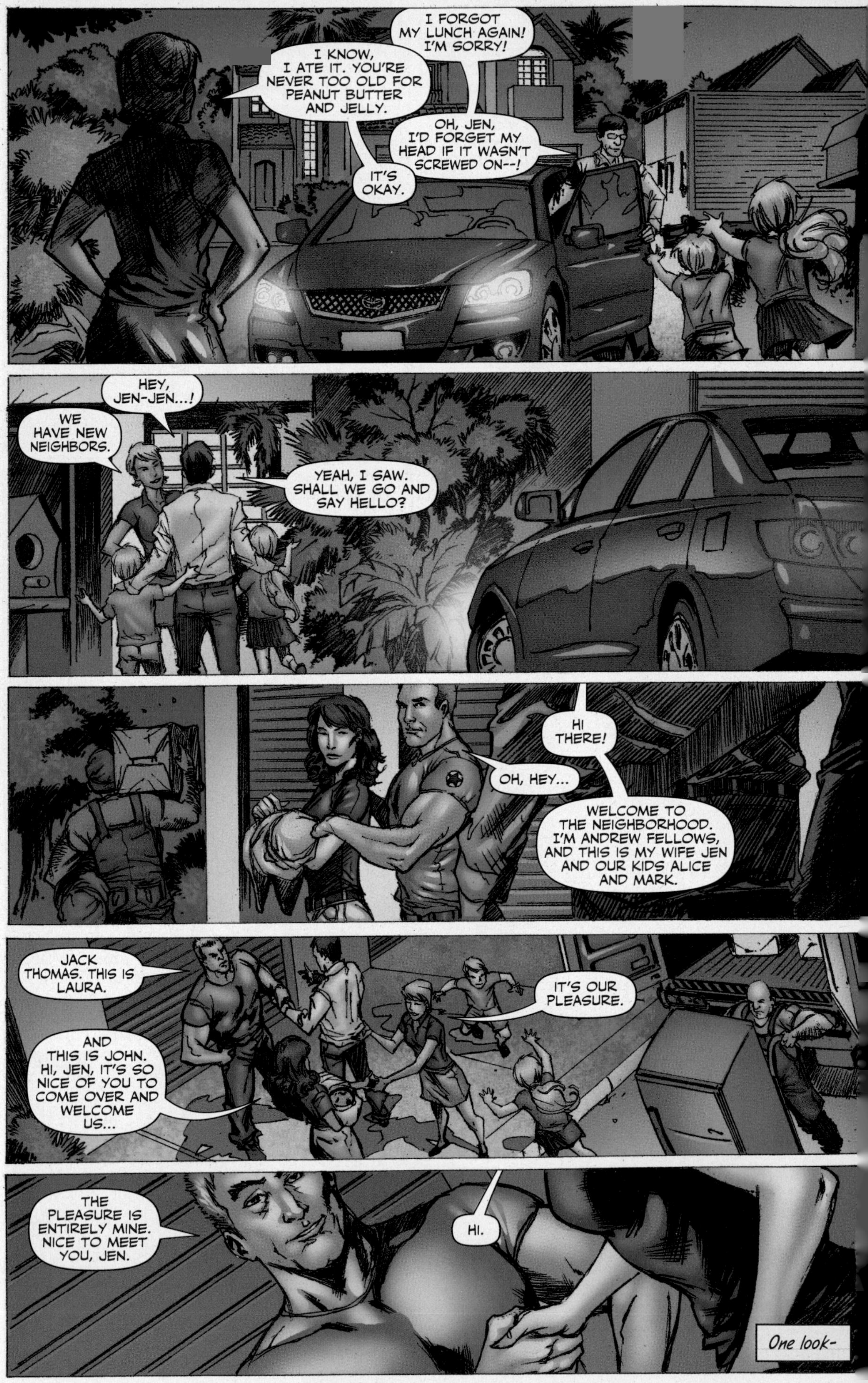
I FORGOT MY LUNCH AGAIN! I'M SORRY!
I KNOW, I ATE IT. YOU'RE NEVER TOO OLD FOR PEANUT BUTTER AND JELLY.
OH, JEN, I'D FORGET MY HEAD IF IT WASN'T SCREWED ON--!
IT'S OKAY.
HEY, JEN-JEN...!
WE HAVE NEW NEIGHBORS.
YEAH, I SAW. SHALL WE GO AND SAY HELLO?
HI THERE!
OH, HEY...
WELCOME TO THE NEIGHBORHOOD. I'M ANDREW FELLOWS, AND THIS IS MY WIFE JEN AND OUR KIDS ALICE AND MARK.
JACK THOMAS. THIS IS LAURA.
IT'S OUR PLEASURE.
AND THIS IS JOHN. HI, JEN, IT'S SO NICE OF YOU TO COME OVER AND WELCOME US...
THE PLEASURE IS ENTIRELY MINE. NICE TO MEET YOU, JEN.
HI.
One look-

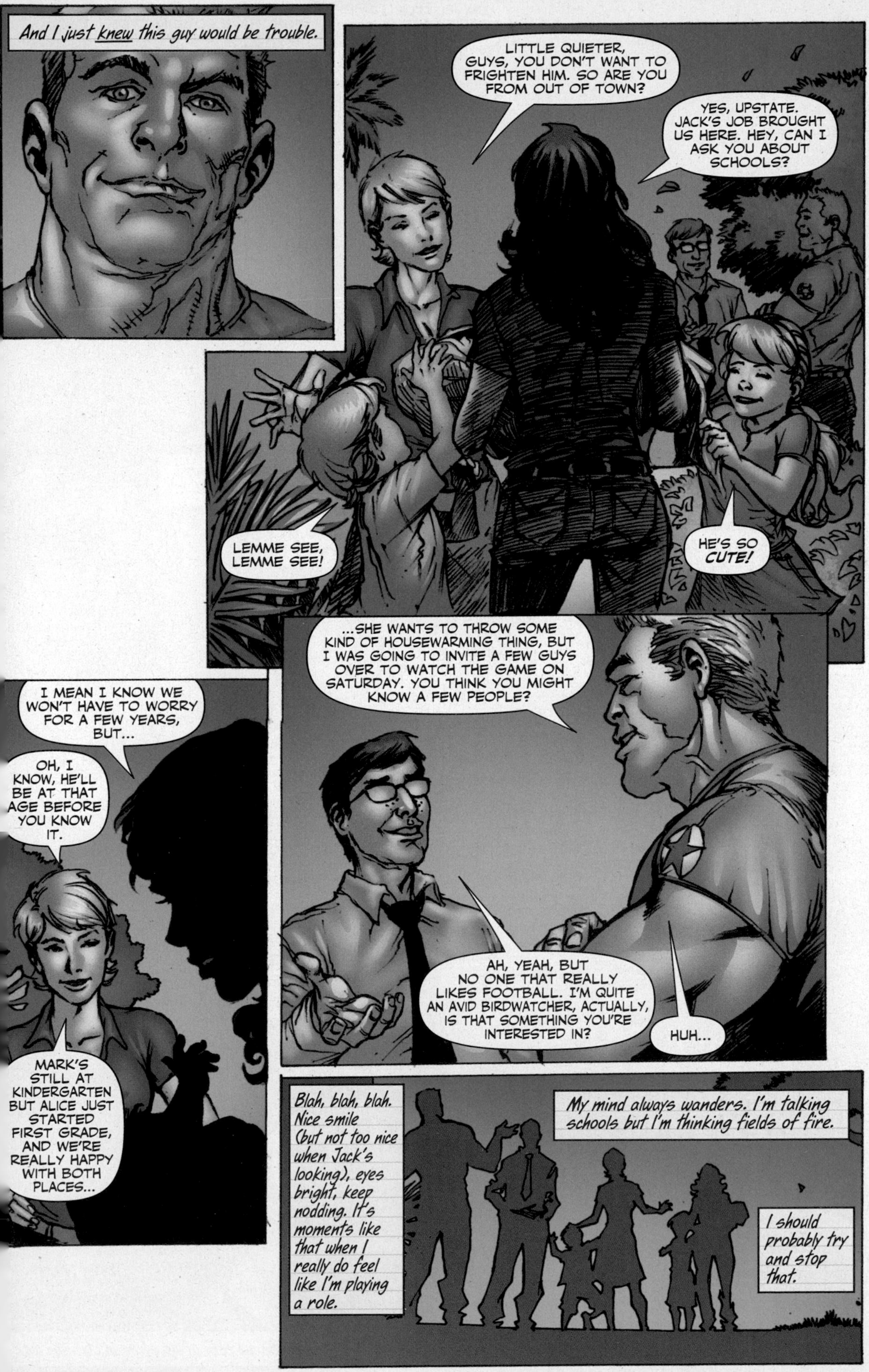

And I just knew this guy would be trouble.
LITTLE QUIETER, GUYS, YOU DON'T WANT TO FRIGHTEN HIM. SO ARE YOU FROM OUT OF TOWN?
YES, UPSTATE. JACK'S JOB BROUGHT US HERE. HEY, CAN I ASK YOU ABOUT SCHOOLS?
LEMME SEE, LEMME SEE!
HE'S SO CUTE!
I MEAN I KNOW WE WON'T HAVE TO WORRY FOR A FEW YEARS, BUT...
OH, I KNOW, HE'LL BE AT THAT AGE BEFORE YOU KNOW IT.
MARK'S STILL AT KINDERGARTEN BUT ALICE JUST STARTED FIRST GRADE, AND WE'RE REALLY HAPPY WITH BOTH PLACES...
...SHE WANTS TO THROW SOME KIND OF HOUSEWARMING THING, BUT I WAS GOING TO INVITE A FEW GUYS OVER TO WATCH THE GAME ON SATURDAY. YOU THINK YOU MIGHT KNOW A FEW PEOPLE?
AH, YEAH, BUT NO ONE THAT REALLY LIKES FOOTBALL. I'M QUITE AN AVID BIRDWATCHER, ACTUALLY, IS THAT SOMETHING YOU'RE INTERESTED IN?
HUH...
Blah, blah, blah. Nice smile (but not too nice when Jack's looking), eyes bright, keep nodding. It's moments like that when I really do feel like I'm playing a role.
My mind always wanders. I'm talking schools but I'm thinking fields of fire.
I should probably try and stop that.

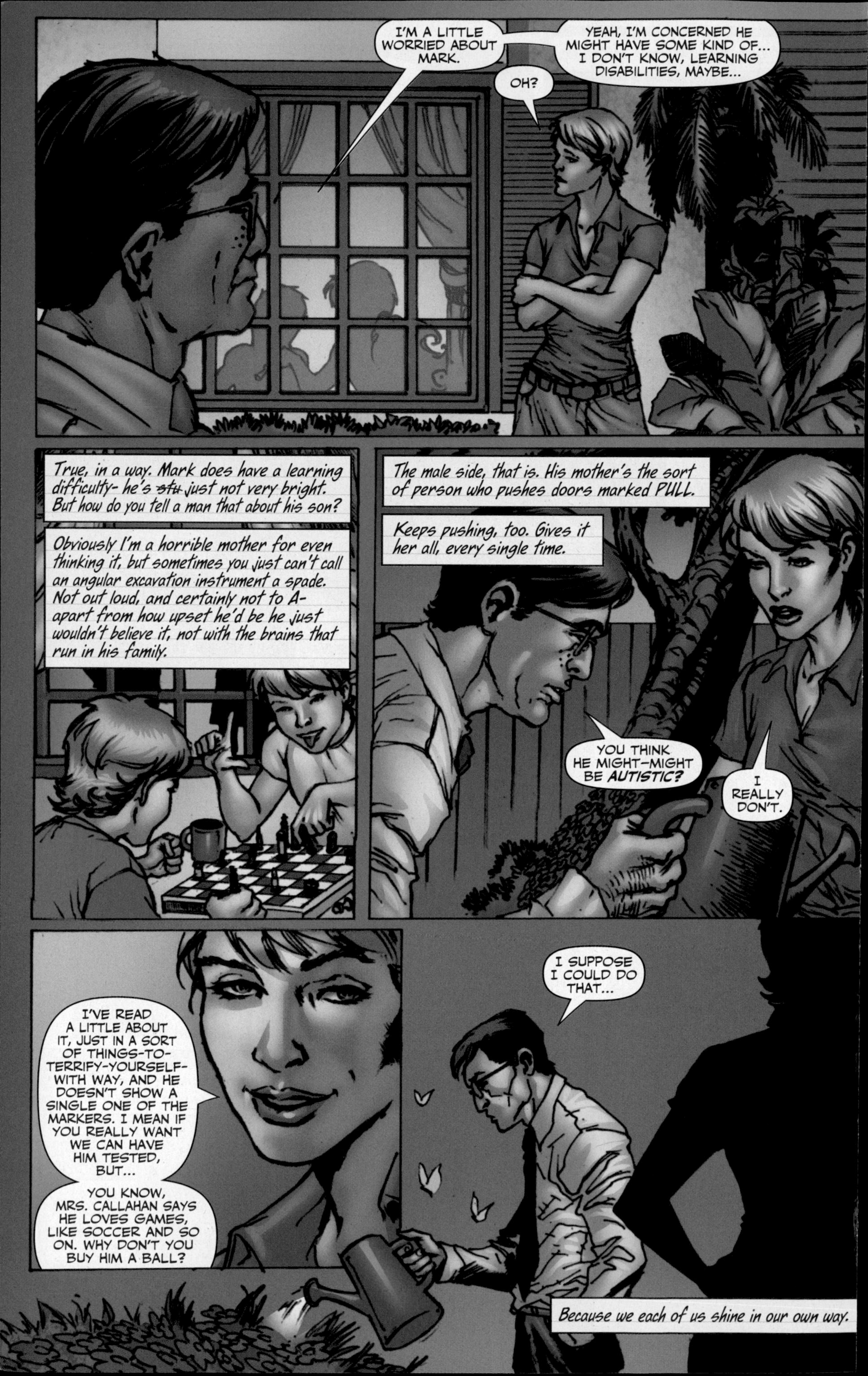

I'M A LITTLE WORRIED ABOUT MARK.
OH?
YEAH, I'M CONCERNED HE MIGHT HAVE SOME KIND OF... I DON'T KNOW, LEARNING DISABILITIES, MAYBE...
True, in a way. Mark does have a learning difficulty- he's ~~stu~~ just not very bright. But how do you tell a man that about his son?
Obviously I'm a horrible mother for even thinking it, but sometimes you just can't call an angular excavation instrument a spade. Not out loud, and certainly not to A- apart from how upset he'd be he just wouldn't believe it, not with the brains that run in his family.
The male side, that is. His mother's the sort of person who pushes doors marked PULL.
Keeps pushing, too. Gives it her all, every single time.
YOU THINK HE MIGHT-MIGHT BE *AUTISTIC?*
I REALLY DON'T.
I'VE READ A LITTLE ABOUT IT, JUST IN A SORT OF THINGS-TO-TERRIFY-YOURSELF-WITH WAY, AND HE DOESN'T SHOW A SINGLE ONE OF THE MARKERS. I MEAN IF YOU REALLY WANT WE CAN HAVE HIM TESTED, BUT...
YOU KNOW, MRS. CALLAHAN SAYS HE LOVES GAMES, LIKE SOCCER AND SO ON. WHY DON'T YOU BUY HIM A BALL?
I SUPPOSE I COULD DO THAT...
Because we each of us shine in our own way.

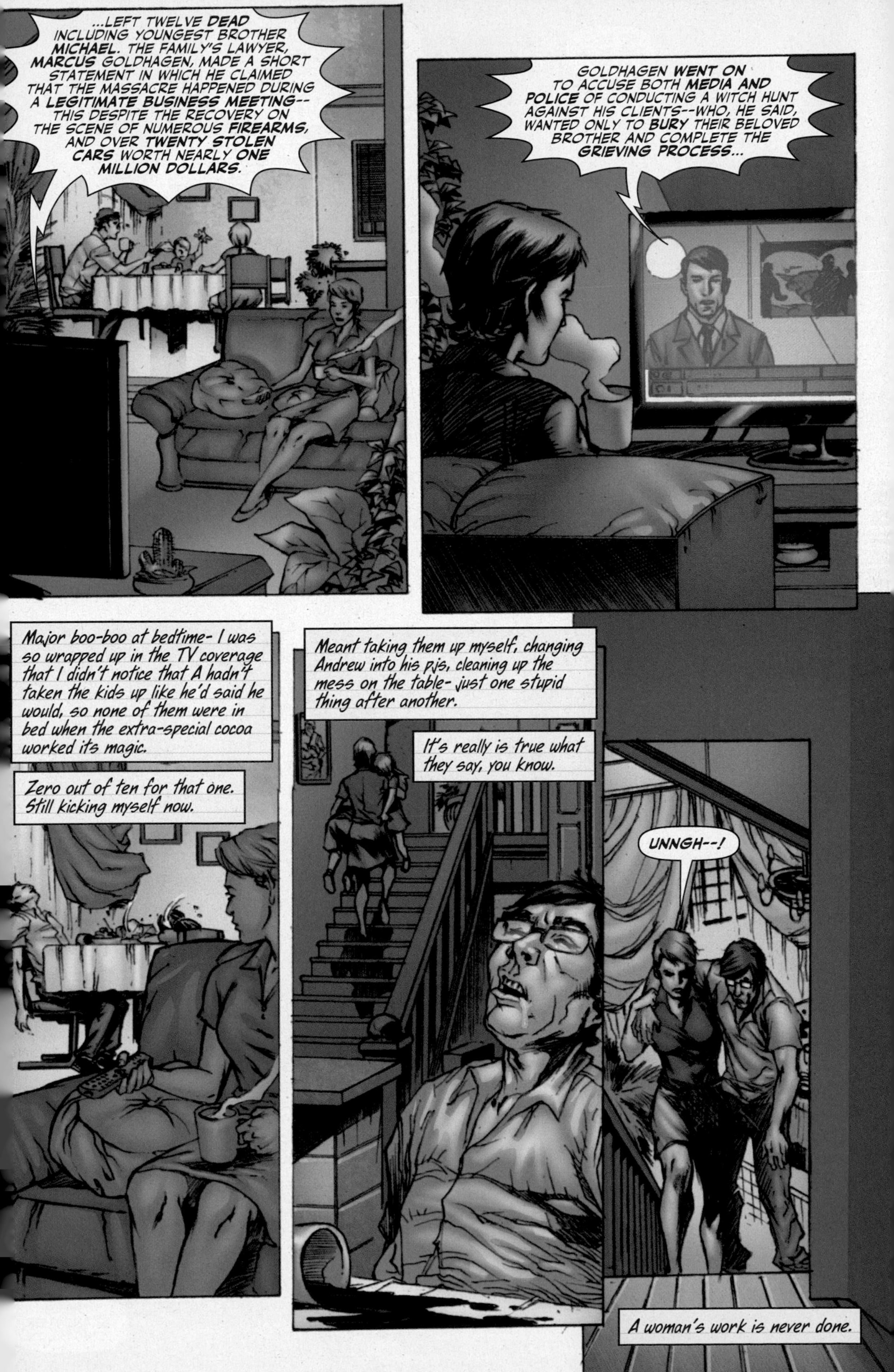
...LEFT TWELVE DEAD INCLUDING YOUNGEST BROTHER MICHAEL. THE FAMILY'S LAWYER, MARCUS GOLDHAGEN, MADE A SHORT STATEMENT IN WHICH HE CLAIMED THAT THE MASSACRE HAPPENED DURING A LEGITIMATE BUSINESS MEETING-- THIS DESPITE THE RECOVERY ON THE SCENE OF NUMEROUS FIREARMS, AND OVER TWENTY STOLEN CARS WORTH NEARLY ONE MILLION DOLLARS.
GOLDHAGEN WENT ON TO ACCUSE BOTH MEDIA AND POLICE OF CONDUCTING A WITCH HUNT AGAINST HIS CLIENTS--WHO, HE SAID, WANTED ONLY TO BURY THEIR BELOVED BROTHER AND COMPLETE THE GRIEVING PROCESS...
Major boo-boo at bedtime- I was so wrapped up in the TV coverage that I didn't notice that A hadn't taken the kids up like he'd said he would, so none of them were in bed when the extra-special cocoa worked its magic.
Zero out of ten for that one. Still kicking myself now.
Meant taking them up myself, changing Andrew into his pjs, cleaning up the mess on the table- just one stupid thing after another.
It's really is true what they say, you know.
UNNGH--!
A woman's work is never done.

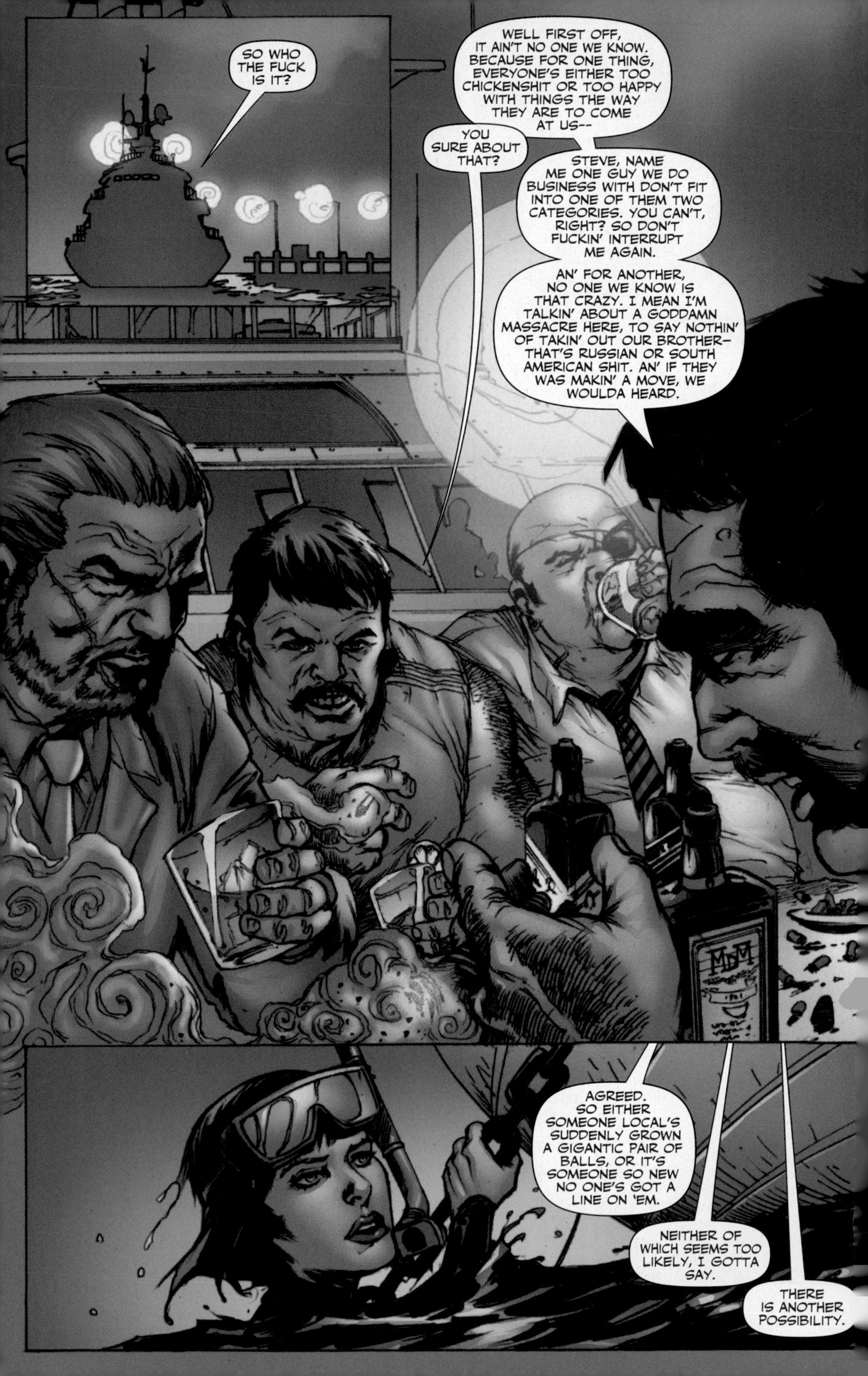
SO WHO THE FUCK IS IT?
WELL FIRST OFF, IT AIN'T NO ONE WE KNOW. BECAUSE FOR ONE THING, EVERYONE'S EITHER TOO CHICKENSHIT OR TOO HAPPY WITH THINGS THE WAY THEY ARE TO COME AT US--
YOU SURE ABOUT THAT?
STEVE, NAME ME ONE GUY WE DO BUSINESS WITH DON'T FIT INTO ONE OF THEM TWO CATEGORIES. YOU CAN'T, RIGHT? SO DON'T FUCKIN' INTERRUPT ME AGAIN.
AN' FOR ANOTHER, NO ONE WE KNOW IS THAT CRAZY. I MEAN I'M TALKIN' ABOUT A GODDAMN MASSACRE HERE, TO SAY NOTHIN' OF TAKIN' OUT OUR BROTHER-- THAT'S RUSSIAN OR SOUTH AMERICAN SHIT. AN' IF THEY WAS MAKIN' A MOVE, WE WOULDA HEARD.
AGREED. SO EITHER SOMEONE LOCAL'S SUDDENLY GROWN A GIGANTIC PAIR OF BALLS, OR IT'S SOMEONE SO NEW NO ONE'S GOT A LINE ON 'EM.
NEITHER OF WHICH SEEMS TOO LIKELY, I GOTTA SAY.
THERE IS ANOTHER POSSIBILITY.

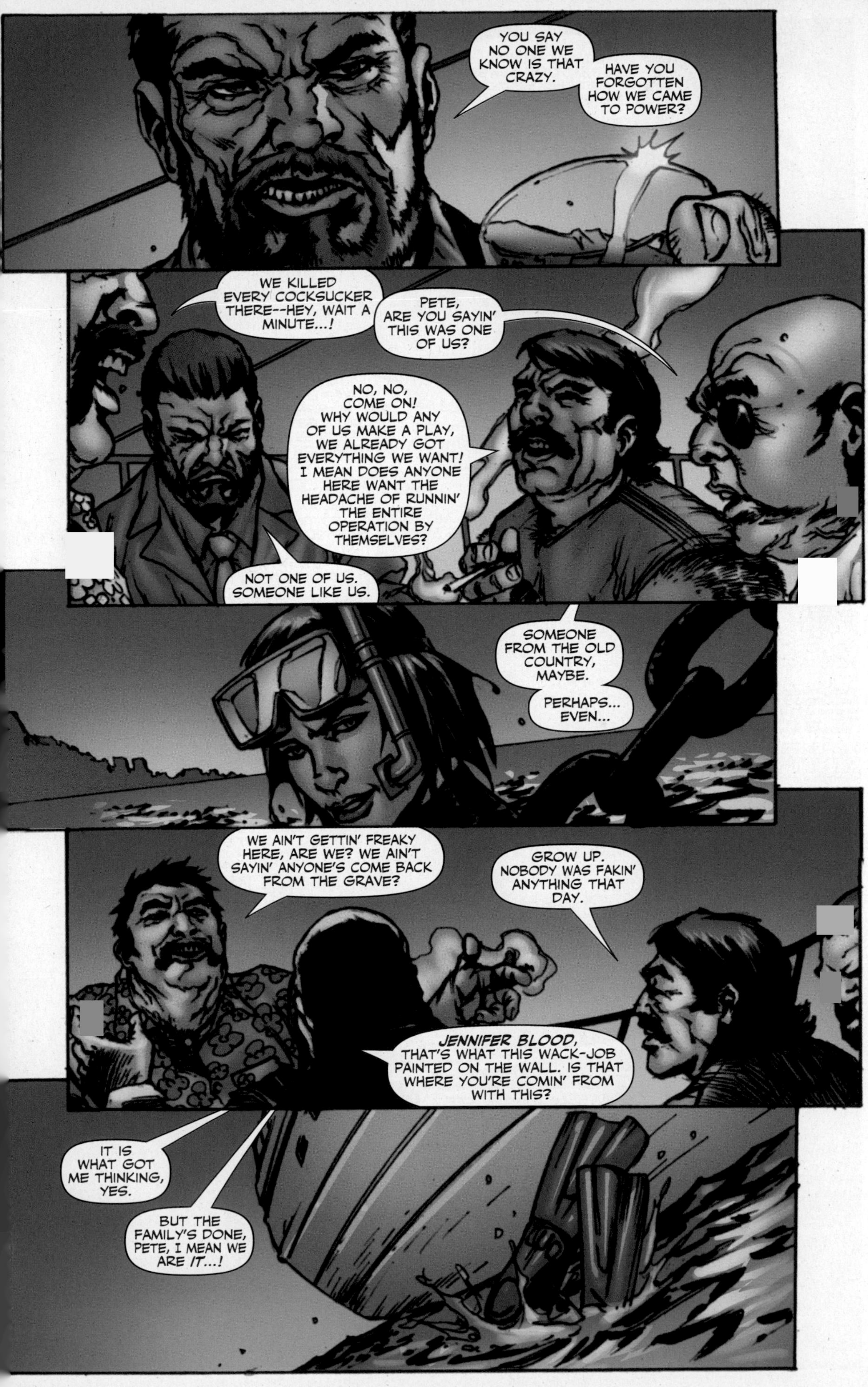
YOU SAY NO ONE WE KNOW IS THAT CRAZY.
HAVE YOU FORGOTTEN HOW WE CAME TO POWER?
WE KILLED EVERY COCKSUCKER THERE--HEY, WAIT A MINUTE...!
PETE, ARE YOU SAYIN' THIS WAS ONE OF US?
NO, NO, COME ON! WHY WOULD ANY OF US MAKE A PLAY, WE ALREADY GOT EVERYTHING WE WANT! I MEAN DOES ANYONE HERE WANT THE HEADACHE OF RUNNIN' THE ENTIRE OPERATION BY THEMSELVES?
NOT ONE OF US. SOMEONE LIKE US.
SOMEONE FROM THE OLD COUNTRY, MAYBE.
PERHAPS... EVEN...
WE AIN'T GETTIN' FREAKY HERE, ARE WE? WE AIN'T SAYIN' ANYONE'S COME BACK FROM THE GRAVE?
GROW UP. NOBODY WAS FAKIN' ANYTHING THAT DAY.
JENNIFER BLOOD, THAT'S WHAT THIS WACK-JOB PAINTED ON THE WALL. IS THAT WHERE YOU'RE COMIN' FROM WITH THIS?
IT IS WHAT GOT ME THINKING, YES.
BUT THE FAMILY'S DONE, PETE, I MEAN WE ARE *IT*...!

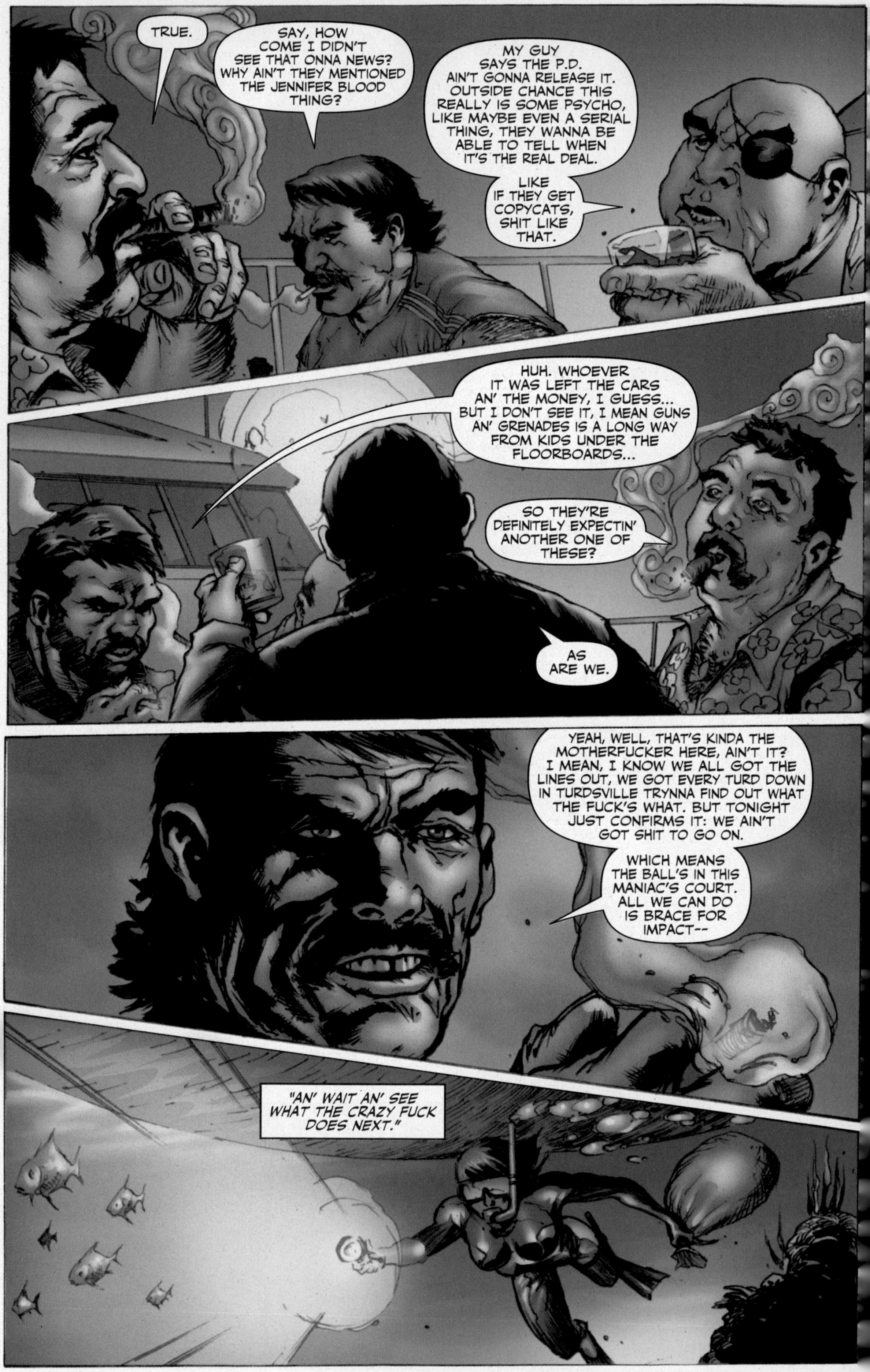
TRUE.
SAY, HOW COME I DIDN'T SEE THAT ONNA NEWS? WHY AIN'T THEY MENTIONED THE JENNIFER BLOOD THING?
MY GUY SAYS THE P.D. AIN'T GONNA RELEASE IT. OUTSIDE CHANCE THIS REALLY IS SOME PSYCHO, LIKE MAYBE EVEN A SERIAL THING, THEY WANNA BE ABLE TO TELL WHEN IT'S THE REAL DEAL.
LIKE IF THEY GET COPYCATS, SHIT LIKE THAT.
HUH. WHOEVER IT WAS LEFT THE CARS AN' THE MONEY, I GUESS... BUT I DON'T SEE IT, I MEAN GUNS AN' GRENADES IS A LONG WAY FROM KIDS UNDER THE FLOORBOARDS...
SO THEY'RE DEFINITELY EXPECTIN' ANOTHER ONE OF THESE?
AS ARE WE.
YEAH, WELL, THAT'S KINDA THE MOTHERFUCKER HERE, AIN'T IT? I MEAN, I KNOW WE ALL GOT THE LINES OUT, WE GOT EVERY TURD DOWN IN TURDSVILLE TRYNNA FIND OUT WHAT THE FUCK'S WHAT. BUT TONIGHT JUST CONFIRMS IT: WE AIN'T GOT SHIT TO GO ON.
WHICH MEANS THE BALL'S IN THIS MANIAC'S COURT. ALL WE CAN DO IS BRACE FOR IMPACT--
"AN' WAIT AN' SEE WHAT THE CRAZY FUCK DOES NEXT."

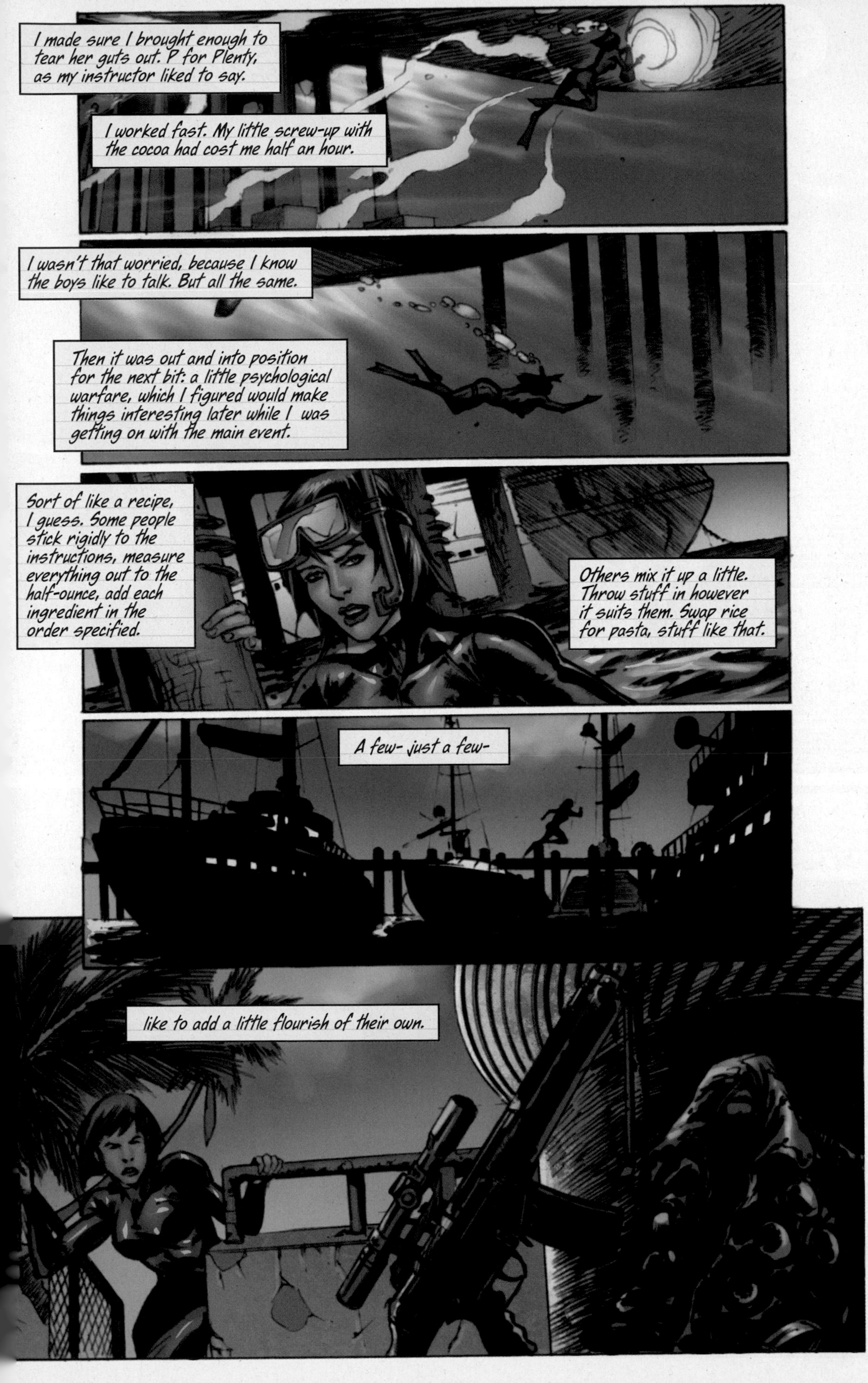

I made sure I brought enough to tear her guts out. P for Plenty, as my instructor liked to say.
I worked fast. My little screw-up with the cocoa had cost me half an hour.
I wasn't that worried, because I know the boys like to talk. But all the same.
Then it was out and into position for the next bit: a little psychological warfare, which I figured would make things interesting later while I was getting on with the main event.
Sort of like a recipe, I guess. Some people stick rigidly to the instructions, measure everything out to the half-ounce, add each ingredient in the order specified.
Others mix it up a little. Throw stuff in however it suits them. Swap rice for pasta, stuff like that.
A few- just a few-
like to add a little flourish of their own.

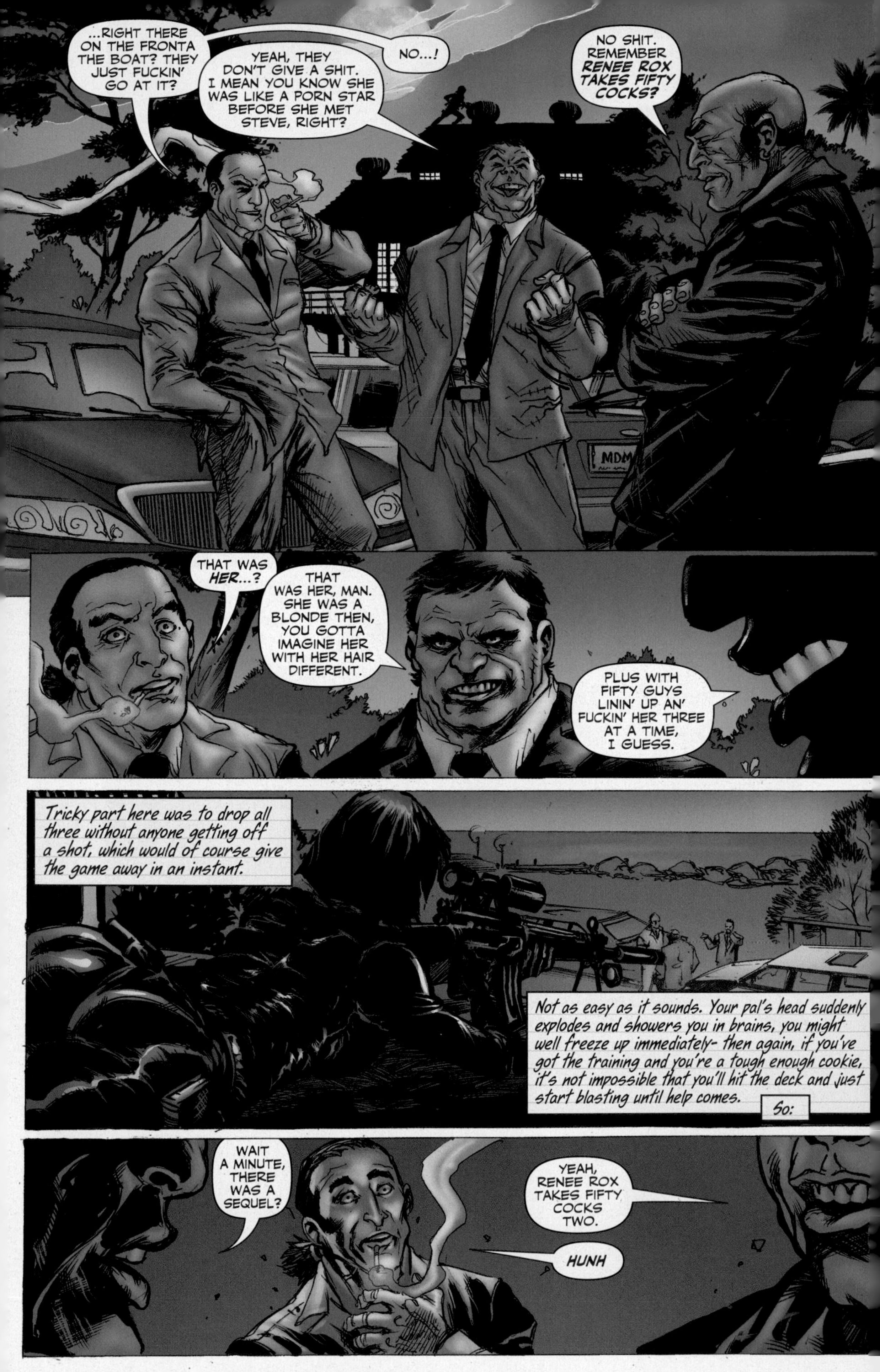
...RIGHT THERE ON THE FRONTA THE BOAT? THEY JUST FUCKIN' GO AT IT?
YEAH, THEY DON'T GIVE A SHIT. I MEAN YOU KNOW SHE WAS LIKE A PORN STAR BEFORE SHE MET STEVE, RIGHT?
NO...!
NO SHIT. REMEMBER RENEE ROX TAKES FIFTY COCKS?
MDM
THAT WAS HER...?
THAT WAS HER, MAN. SHE WAS A BLONDE THEN, YOU GOTTA IMAGINE HER WITH HER HAIR DIFFERENT.
PLUS WITH FIFTY GUYS LININ' UP AN' FUCKIN' HER THREE AT A TIME, I GUESS.
Tricky part here was to drop all three without anyone getting off a shot, which would of course give the game away in an instant.
Not as easy as it sounds. Your pal's head suddenly explodes and showers you in brains, you might well freeze up immediately- then again, if you've got the training and you're a tough enough cookie, it's not impossible that you'll hit the deck and just start blasting until help comes.
So:
WAIT A MINUTE, THERE WAS A SEQUEL?
YEAH, RENEE ROX TAKES FIFTY COCKS TWO.
HUNH

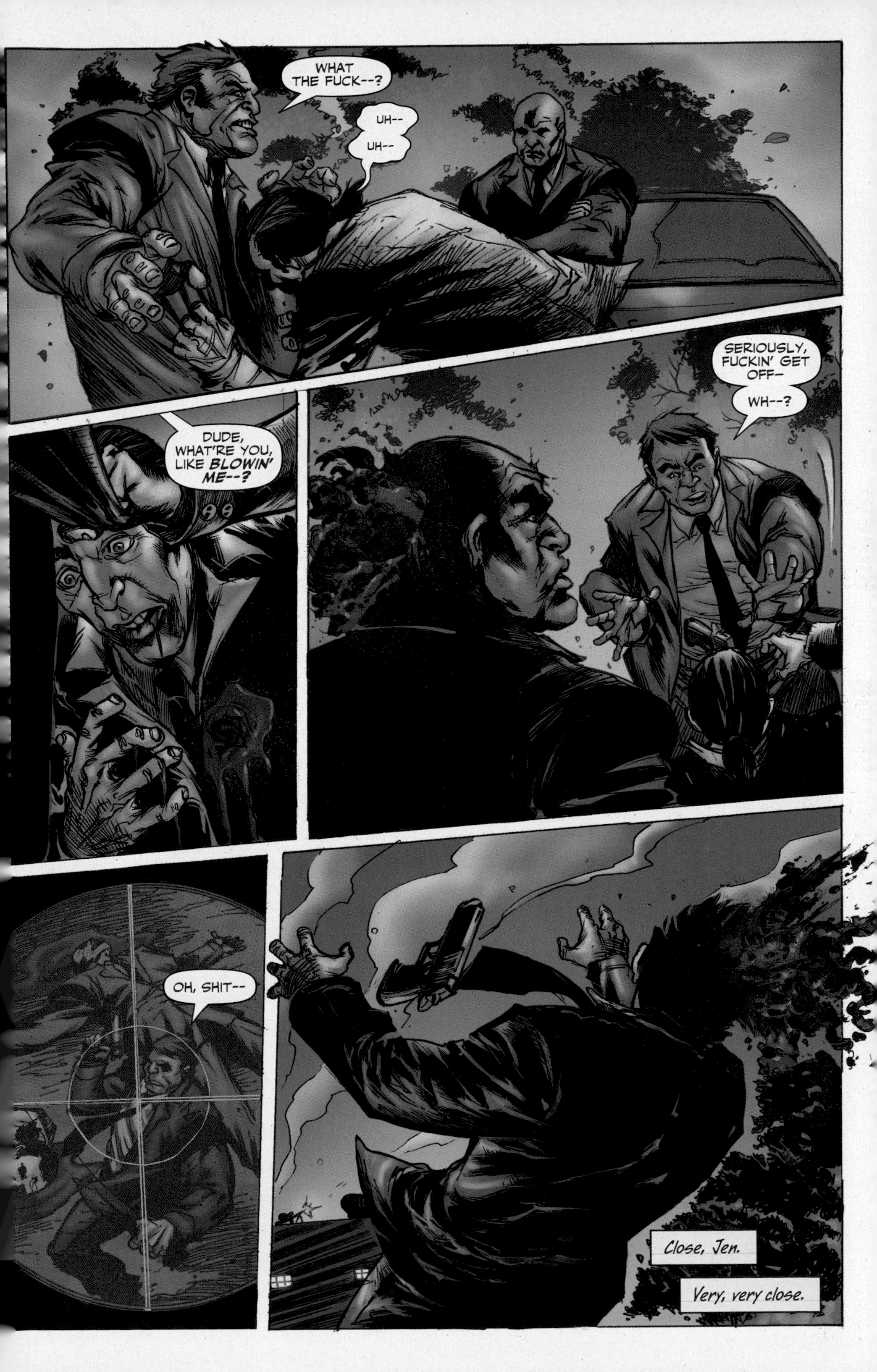
WHAT THE FUCK--?
UH--
UH--
SERIOUSLY, FUCKIN' GET OFF--
WH--?
DUDE, WHAT'RE YOU, LIKE **BLOWIN' ME**--?
OH, SHIT--
Close, Jen.
Very, very close.

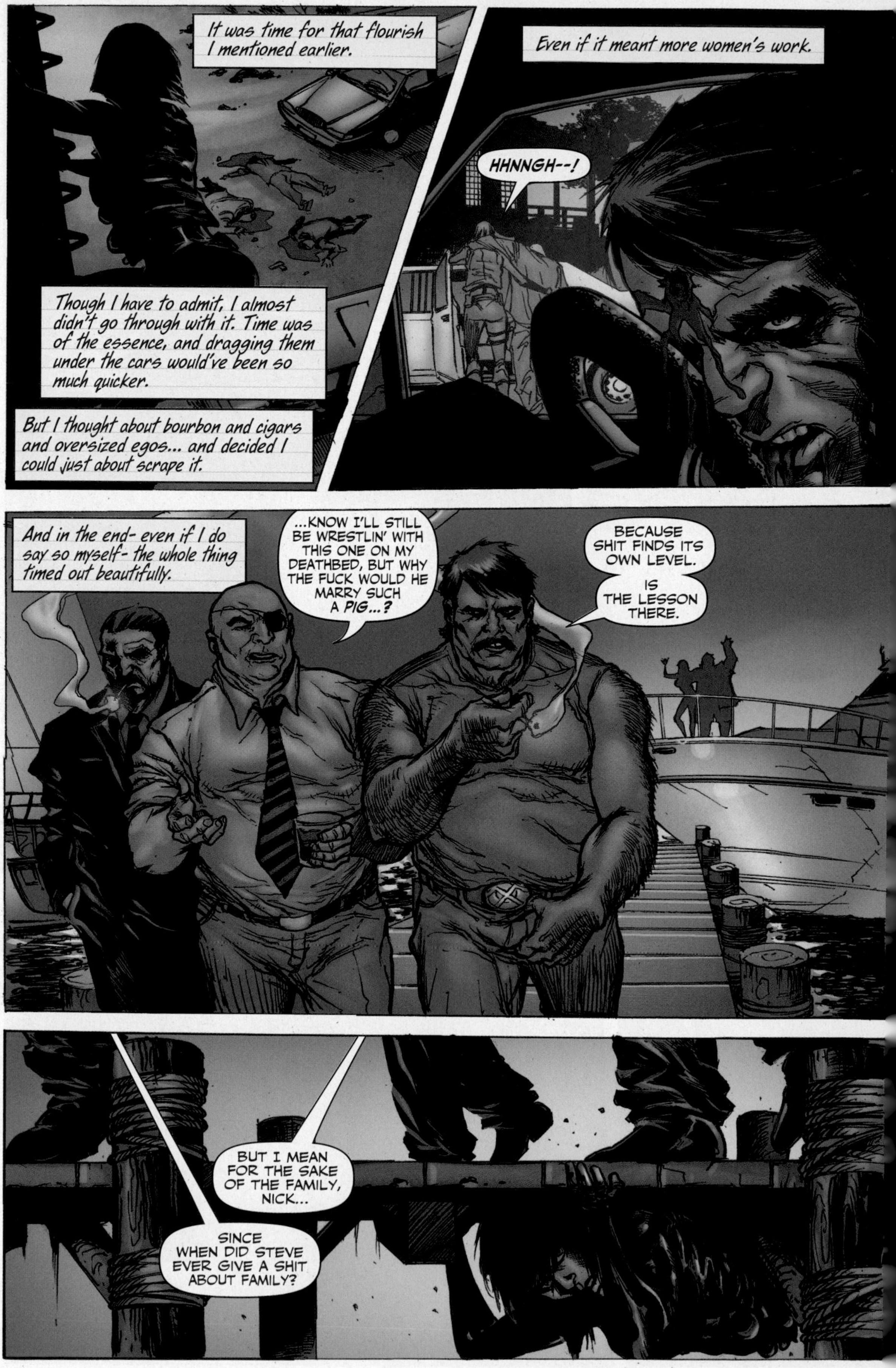
It was time for that flourish I mentioned earlier.
Though I have to admit, I almost didn't go through with it. Time was of the essence, and dragging them under the cars would've been so much quicker.
But I thought about bourbon and cigars and oversized egos... and decided I could just about scrape it.
Even if it meant more women's work.
HHNNGH--!
And in the end- even if I do say so myself- the whole thing timed out beautifully.
...KNOW I'LL STILL BE WRESTLIN' WITH THIS ONE ON MY DEATHBED, BUT WHY THE FUCK WOULD HE MARRY SUCH A PIG...?
BECAUSE SHIT FINDS ITS OWN LEVEL.
IS THE LESSON THERE.
BUT I MEAN FOR THE SAKE OF THE FAMILY, NICK...
SINCE WHEN DID STEVE EVER GIVE A SHIT ABOUT FAMILY?

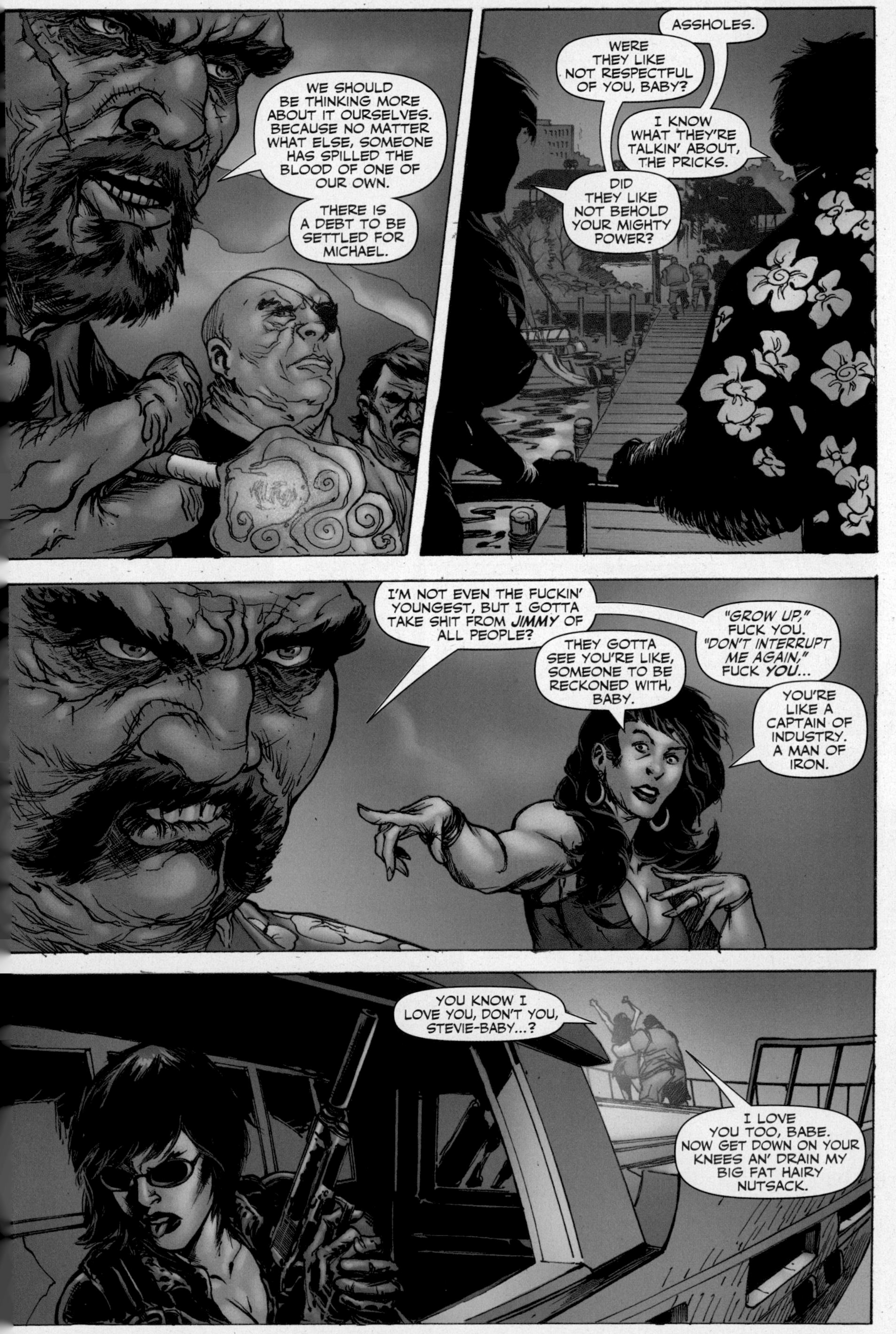
WE SHOULD BE THINKING MORE ABOUT IT OURSELVES. BECAUSE NO MATTER WHAT ELSE, SOMEONE HAS SPILLED THE BLOOD OF ONE OF OUR OWN.
THERE IS A DEBT TO BE SETTLED FOR MICHAEL.
ASSHOLES.
WERE THEY LIKE NOT RESPECTFUL OF YOU, BABY?
I KNOW WHAT THEY'RE TALKIN' ABOUT, THE PRICKS.
DID THEY LIKE NOT BEHOLD YOUR MIGHTY POWER?
I'M NOT EVEN THE FUCKIN' YOUNGEST, BUT I GOTTA TAKE SHIT FROM JIMMY OF ALL PEOPLE?
THEY GOTTA SEE YOU'RE LIKE, SOMEONE TO BE RECKONED WITH, BABY.
"GROW UP," FUCK YOU. "DON'T INTERRUPT ME AGAIN," FUCK YOU...
YOU'RE LIKE A CAPTAIN OF INDUSTRY. A MAN OF IRON.
YOU KNOW I LOVE YOU, DON'T YOU, STEVIE-BABY...?
I LOVE YOU TOO, BABE. NOW GET DOWN ON YOUR KNEES AN' DRAIN MY BIG FAT HAIRY NUTSACK.

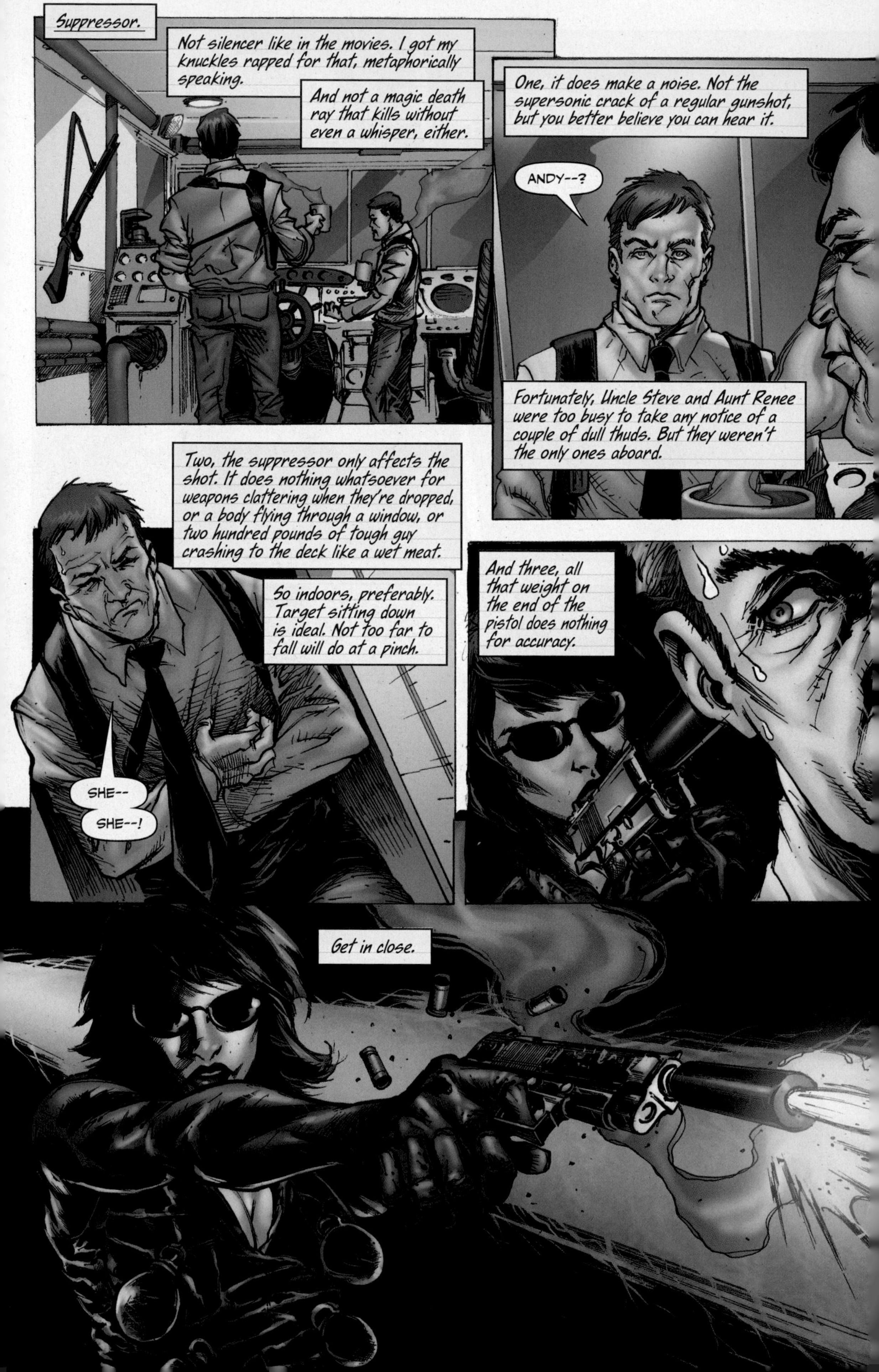
Suppressor.
Not silencer like in the movies. I got my knuckles rapped for that, metaphorically speaking.
And not a magic death ray that kills without even a whisper, either.
One, it does make a noise. Not the supersonic crack of a regular gunshot, but you better believe you can hear it.
ANDY--?
Fortunately, Uncle Steve and Aunt Renee were too busy to take any notice of a couple of dull thuds. But they weren't the only ones aboard.
Two, the suppressor only affects the shot. It does nothing whatsoever for weapons clattering when they're dropped, or a body flying through a window, or two hundred pounds of tough guy crashing to the deck like a wet meat.
So indoors, preferably. Target sitting down is ideal. Not too far to fall will do at a pinch.
SHE--
SHE--!
And three, all that weight on the end of the pistol does nothing for accuracy.
Get in close.

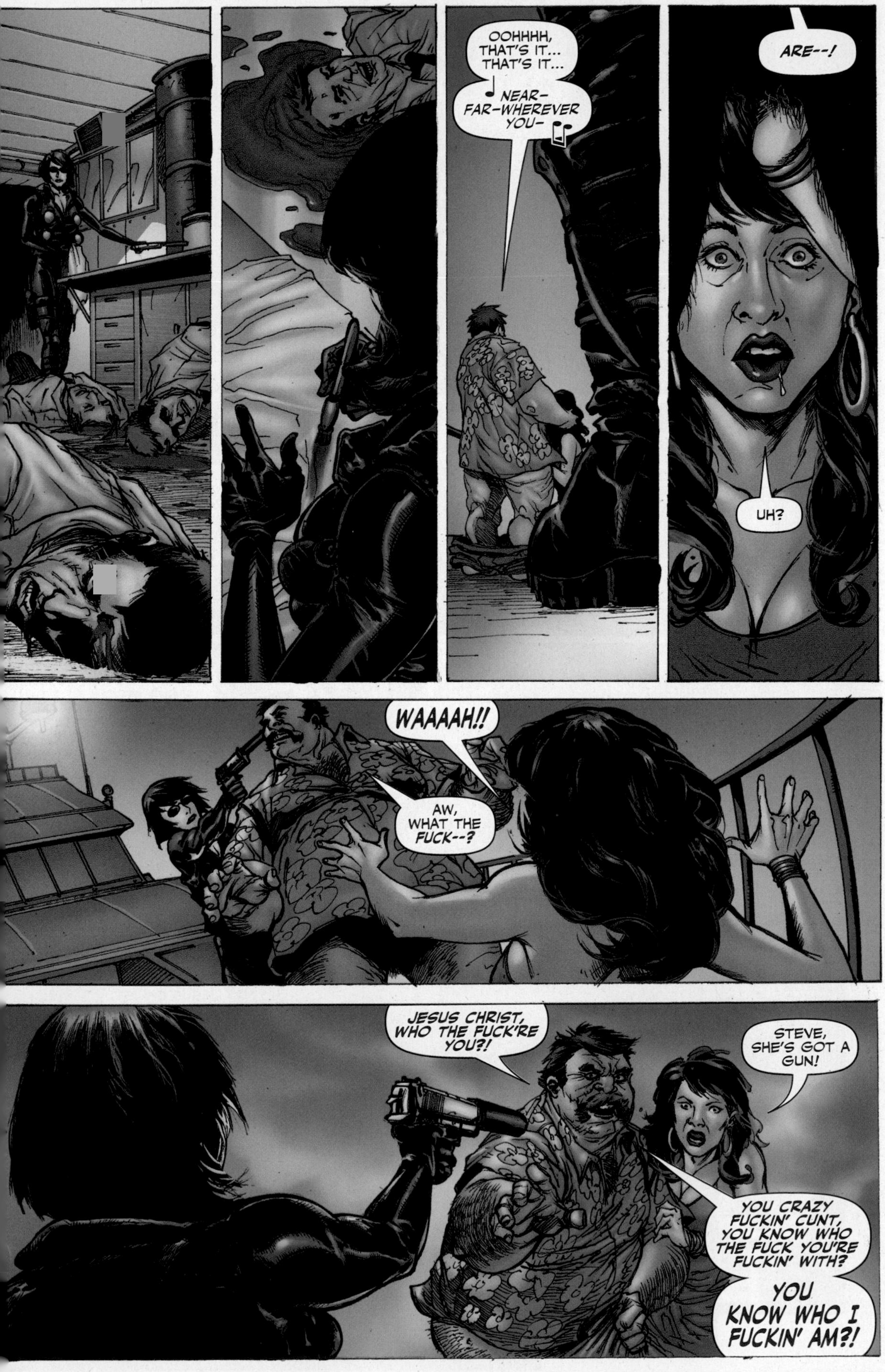

OOHHHH, THAT'S IT... THAT'S IT...
NEAR-FAR-WHEREVER YOU-
ARE--!
UH?
WAAAAH!!
AW, WHAT THE FUCK--?
JESUS CHRIST, WHO THE FUCK'RE YOU?!
STEVE, SHE'S GOT A GUN!
YOU CRAZY FUCKIN' CUNT, YOU KNOW WHO THE FUCK YOU'RE FUCKIN' WITH?
YOU KNOW WHO I FUCKIN' AM?!

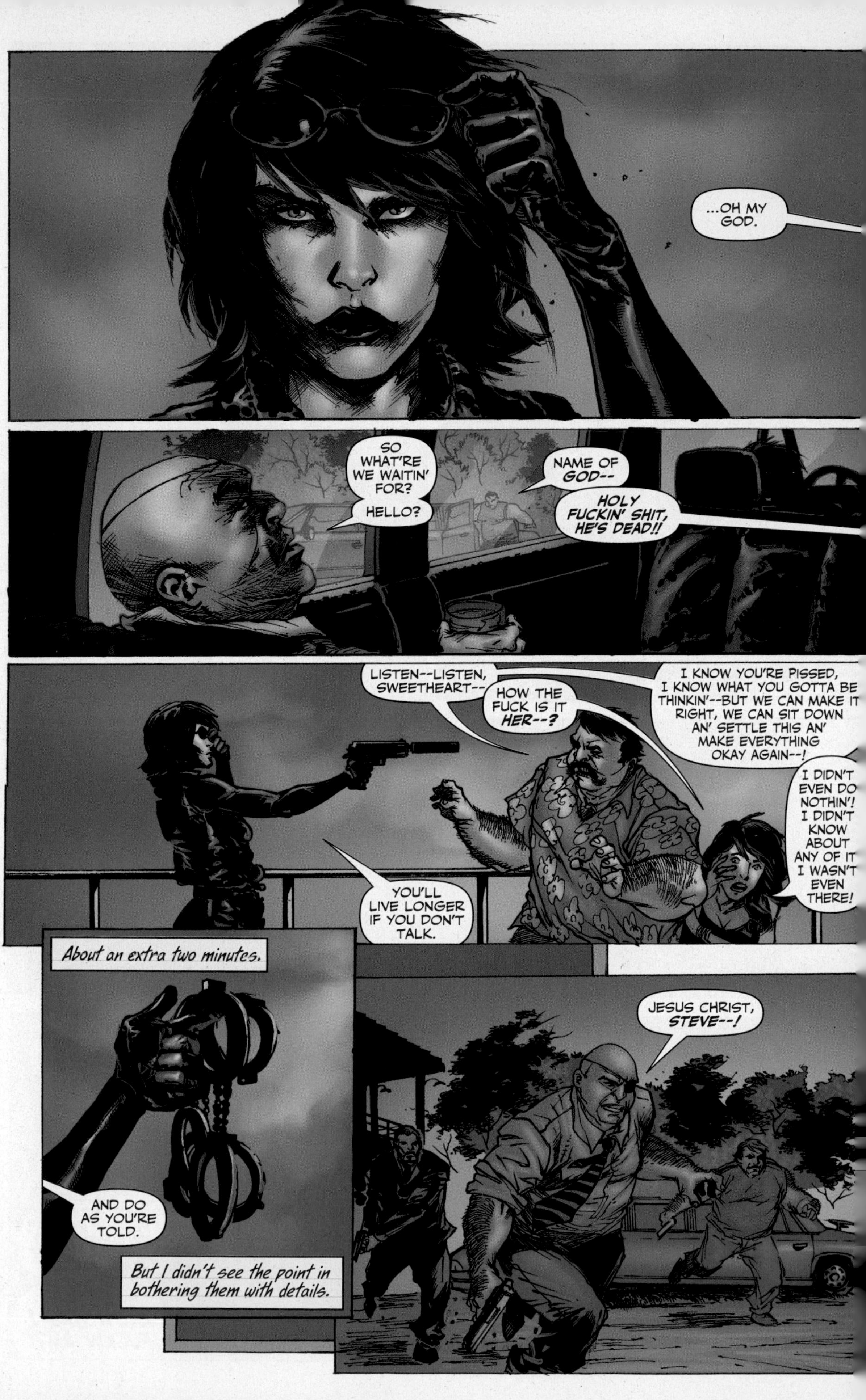
...OH MY GOD.
SO WHAT'RE WE WAITIN' FOR?
HELLO?
NAME OF GOD--
HOLY FUCKIN' SHIT, HE'S DEAD!!
LISTEN--LISTEN, SWEETHEART--
HOW THE FUCK IS IT HER--?
I KNOW YOU'RE PISSED, I KNOW WHAT YOU GOTTA BE THINKIN'--BUT WE CAN MAKE IT RIGHT, WE CAN SIT DOWN AN' SETTLE THIS AN' MAKE EVERYTHING OKAY AGAIN--!
I DIDN'T EVEN DO NOTHIN'! I DIDN'T KNOW ABOUT ANY OF IT I WASN'T EVEN THERE!
YOU'LL LIVE LONGER IF YOU DON'T TALK.
About an extra two minutes.
AND DO AS YOU'RE TOLD.
But I didn't see the point in bothering them with details.
JESUS CHRIST, STEVE--!

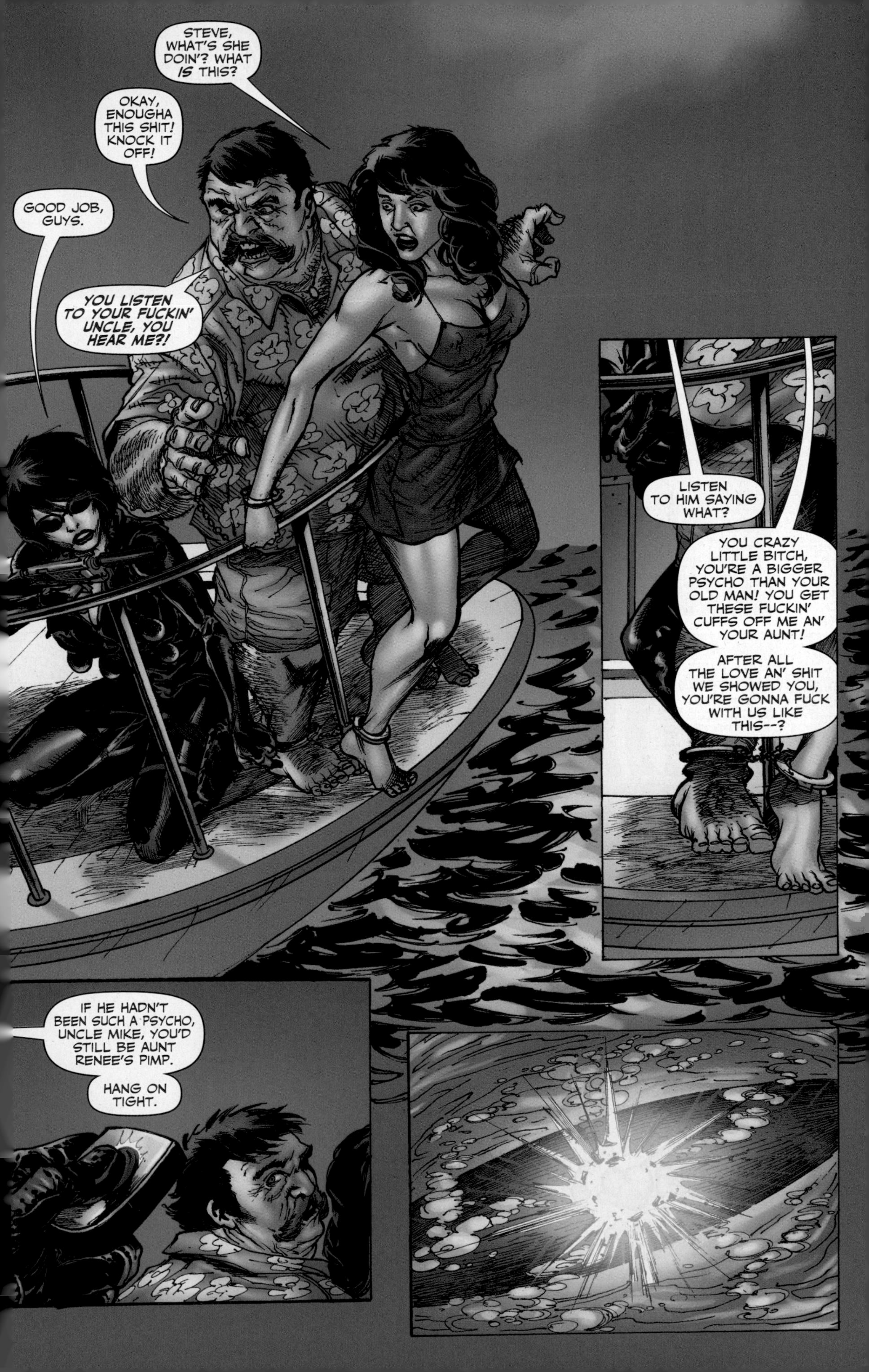
STEVE, WHAT'S SHE DOIN'? WHAT *IS* THIS?
OKAY, ENOUGHA THIS SHIT! KNOCK IT OFF!
GOOD JOB, GUYS.
YOU LISTEN TO YOUR FUCKIN' UNCLE, YOU HEAR ME?!
LISTEN TO HIM SAYING WHAT?
YOU CRAZY LITTLE BITCH, YOU'RE A BIGGER PSYCHO THAN YOUR OLD MAN! YOU GET THESE FUCKIN' CUFFS OFF ME AN' YOUR AUNT!
AFTER ALL THE LOVE AN' SHIT WE SHOWED YOU, YOU'RE GONNA FUCK WITH US LIKE THIS--?
IF HE HADN'T BEEN SUCH A PSYCHO, UNCLE MIKE, YOU'D STILL BE AUNT RENEE'S PIMP.
HANG ON TIGHT.

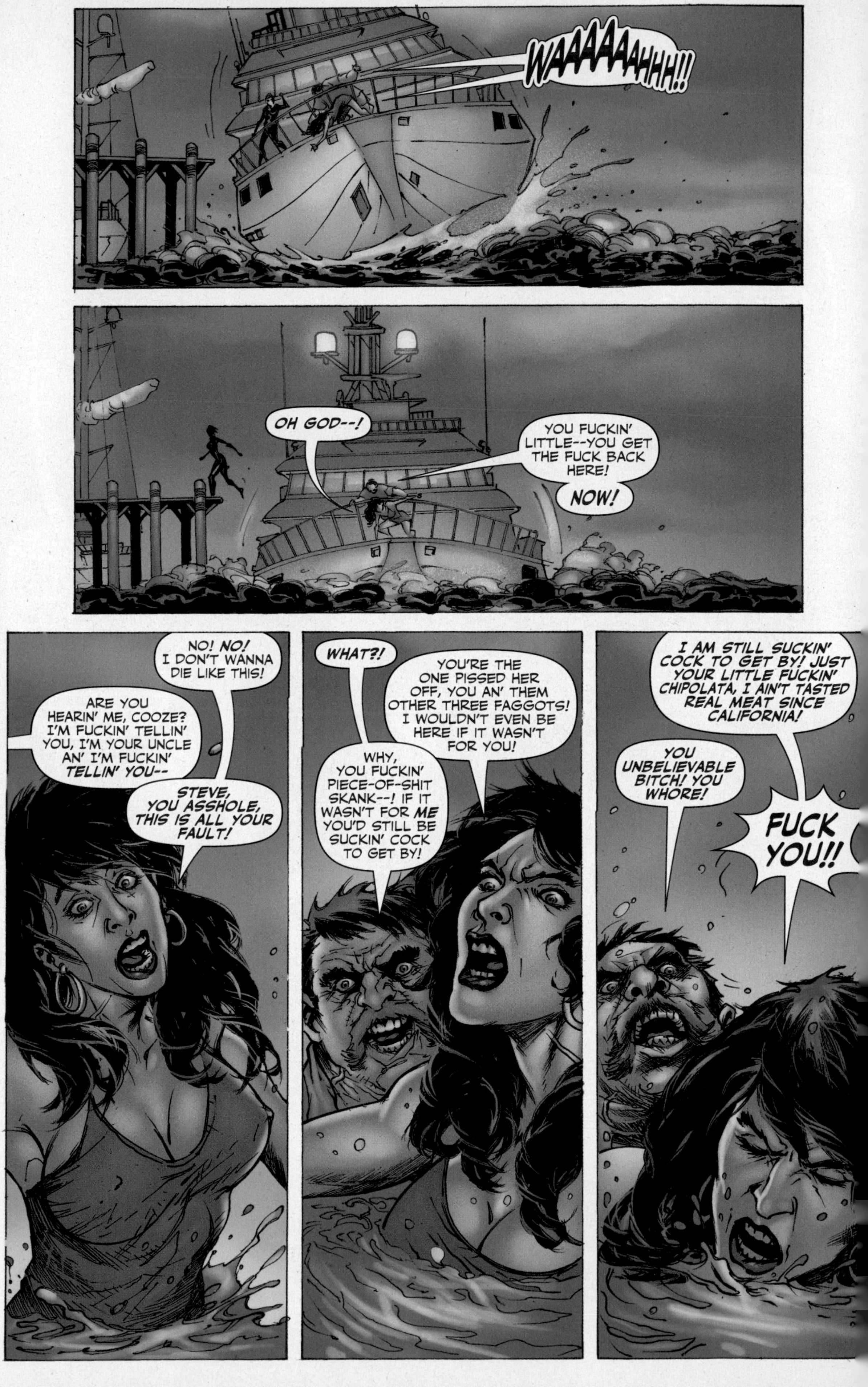
WAAAAAAHHH!!
OH GOD--!
YOU FUCKIN' LITTLE--YOU GET THE FUCK BACK HERE!
NOW!
NO! NO! I DON'T WANNA DIE LIKE THIS!
ARE YOU HEARIN' ME, COOZE? I'M FUCKIN' TELLIN' YOU, I'M YOUR UNCLE AN' I'M FUCKIN' TELLIN' YOU--
STEVE, YOU ASSHOLE, THIS IS ALL YOUR FAULT!
WHAT?!
YOU'RE THE ONE PISSED HER OFF, YOU AN' THEM OTHER THREE FAGGOTS! I WOULDN'T EVEN BE HERE IF IT WASN'T FOR YOU!
WHY, YOU FUCKIN' PIECE-OF-SHIT SKANK--! IF IT WASN'T FOR ME YOU'D STILL BE SUCKIN' COCK TO GET BY!
I AM STILL SUCKIN' COCK TO GET BY! JUST YOUR LITTLE FUCKIN' CHIPOLATA, I AIN'T TASTED REAL MEAT SINCE CALIFORNIA!
YOU UNBELIEVABLE BITCH! YOU WHORE!
FUCK YOU!!

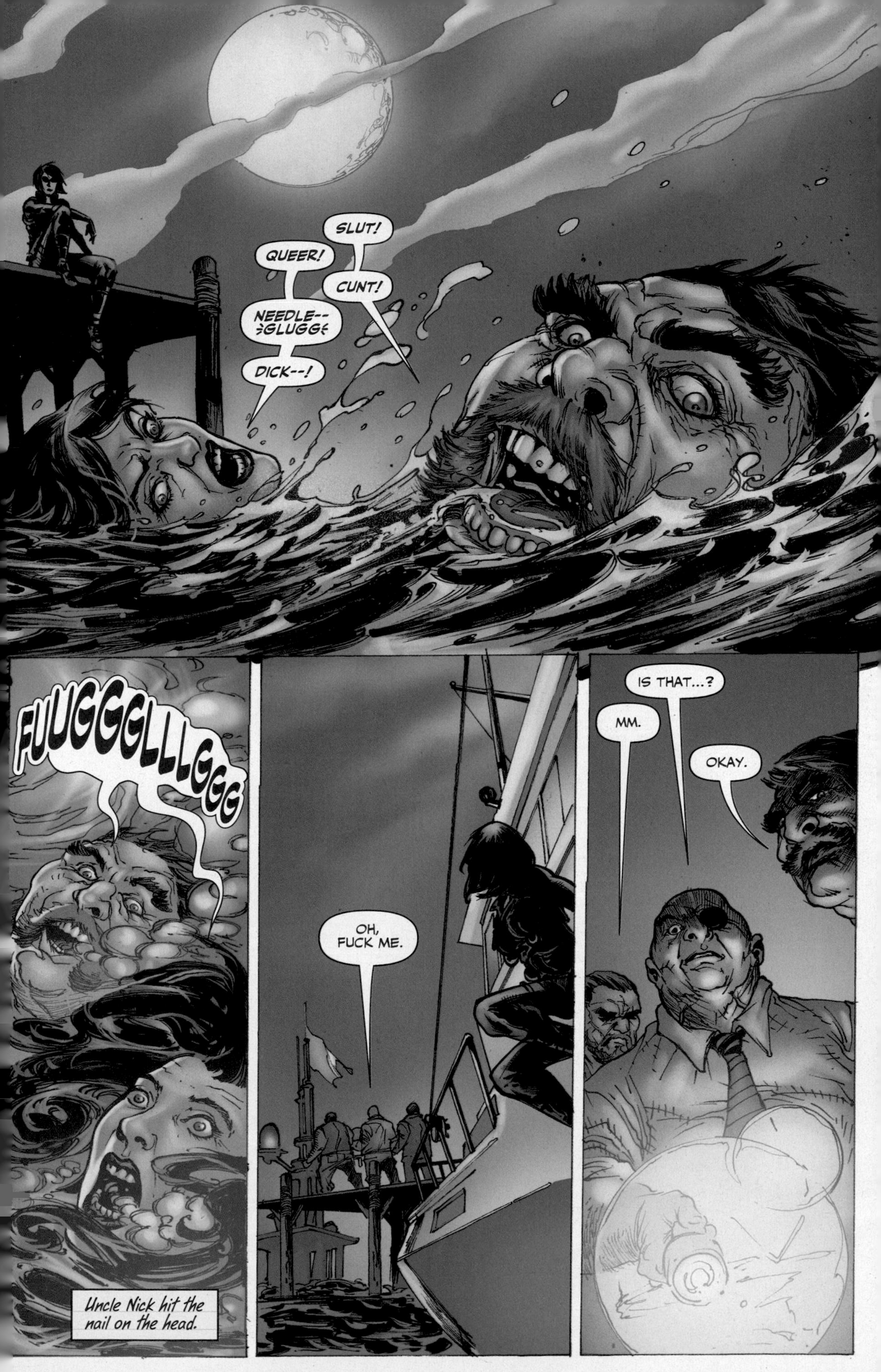
SLUT!
QUEER!
CUNT!
NEEDLE-- GLUGG
DICK--!
FUUGGGLLLGGG
Uncle Nick hit the nail on the head.
OH, FUCK ME.
IS THAT...?
MM.
OKAY.

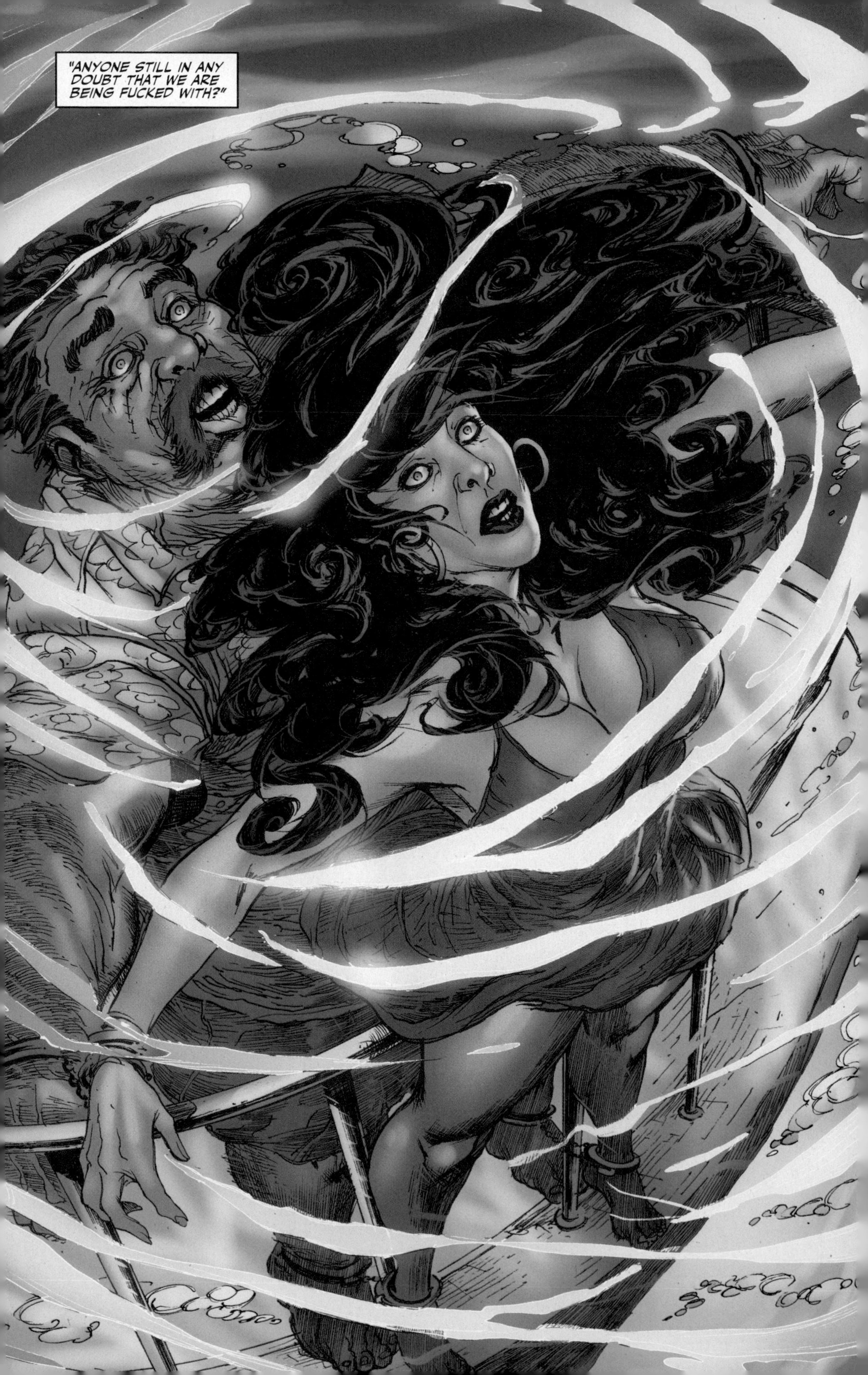
"ANYONE STILL IN ANY DOUBT THAT WE ARE BEING FUCKED WITH?"

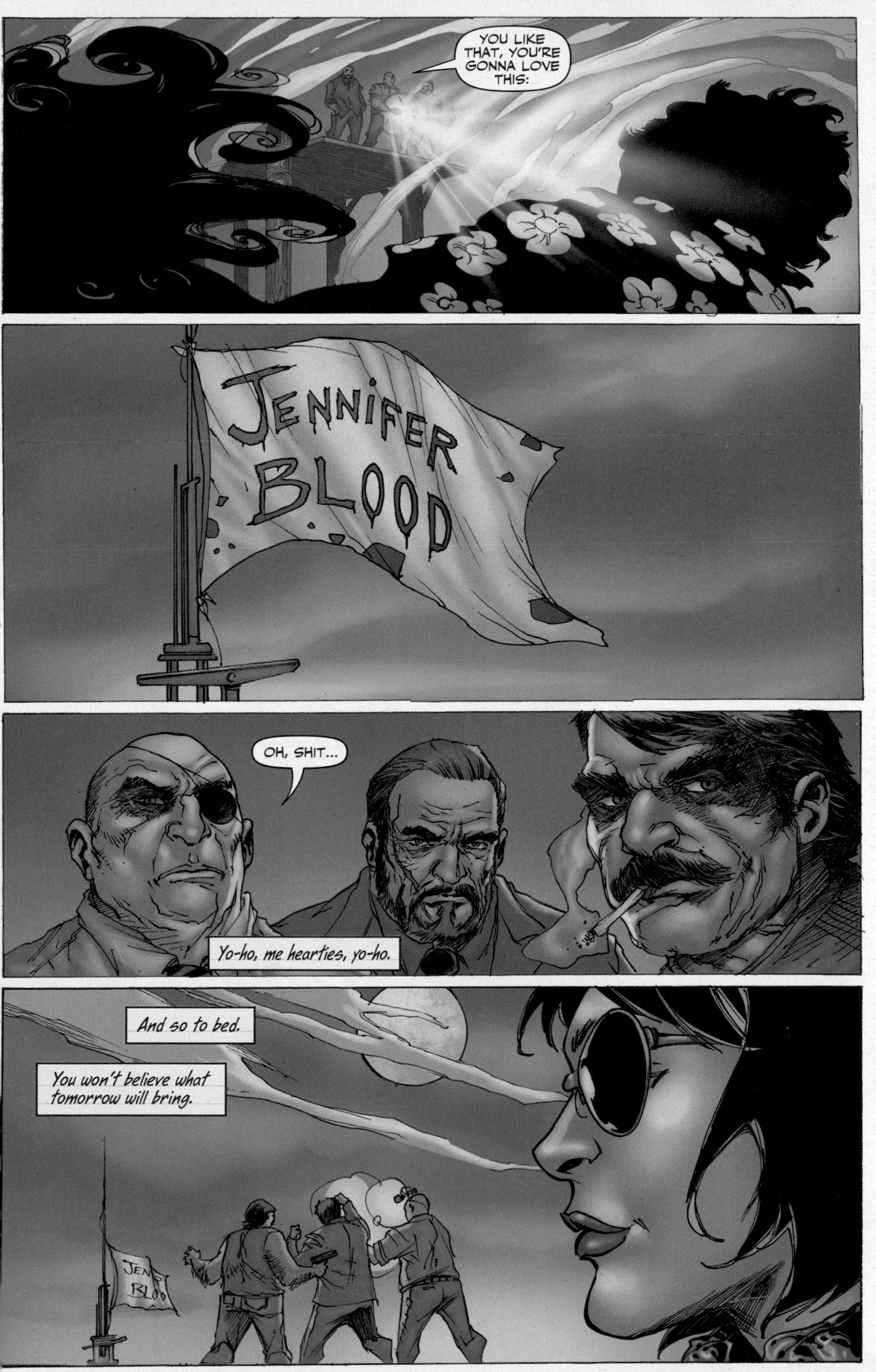
YOU LIKE THAT, YOU'RE GONNA LOVE THIS:
JENNIFER BLOOD
OH, SHIT...
Yo-ho, me hearties, yo-ho.
And so to bed.
You won't believe what tomorrow will bring.
JENNIFER BLOOD

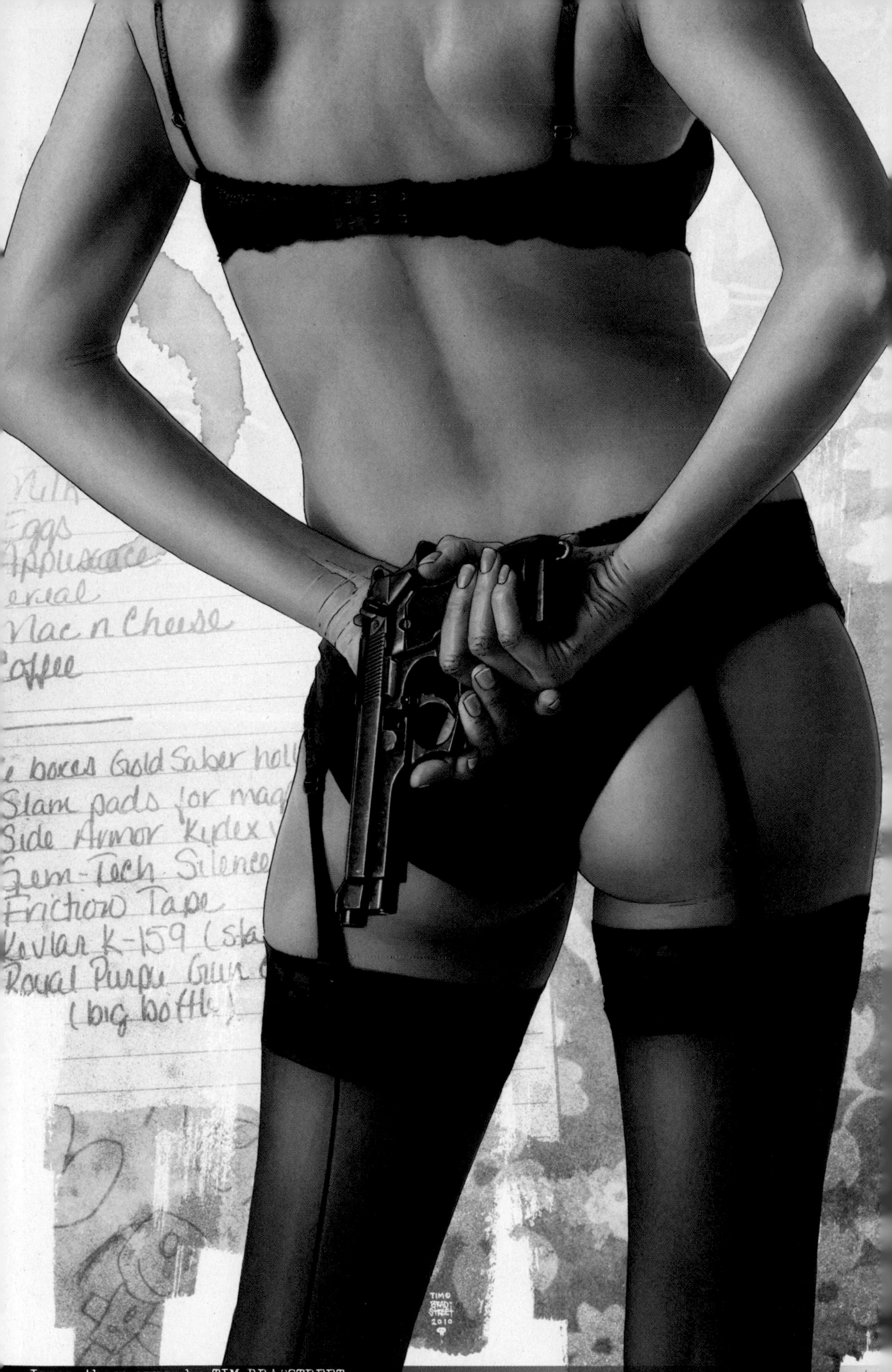
Eggs
Mac n Cheese
Coffee
boxes Gold Saber holl
Slam pads for mag
Side Armor Kydex
Gem-Tech Silence
Friction Tape
Kevlar K-159
Royal Purple Gun
(big bottle)
TIM BRADSTREET 2010

Issue three cover by TIM BRADSTREET

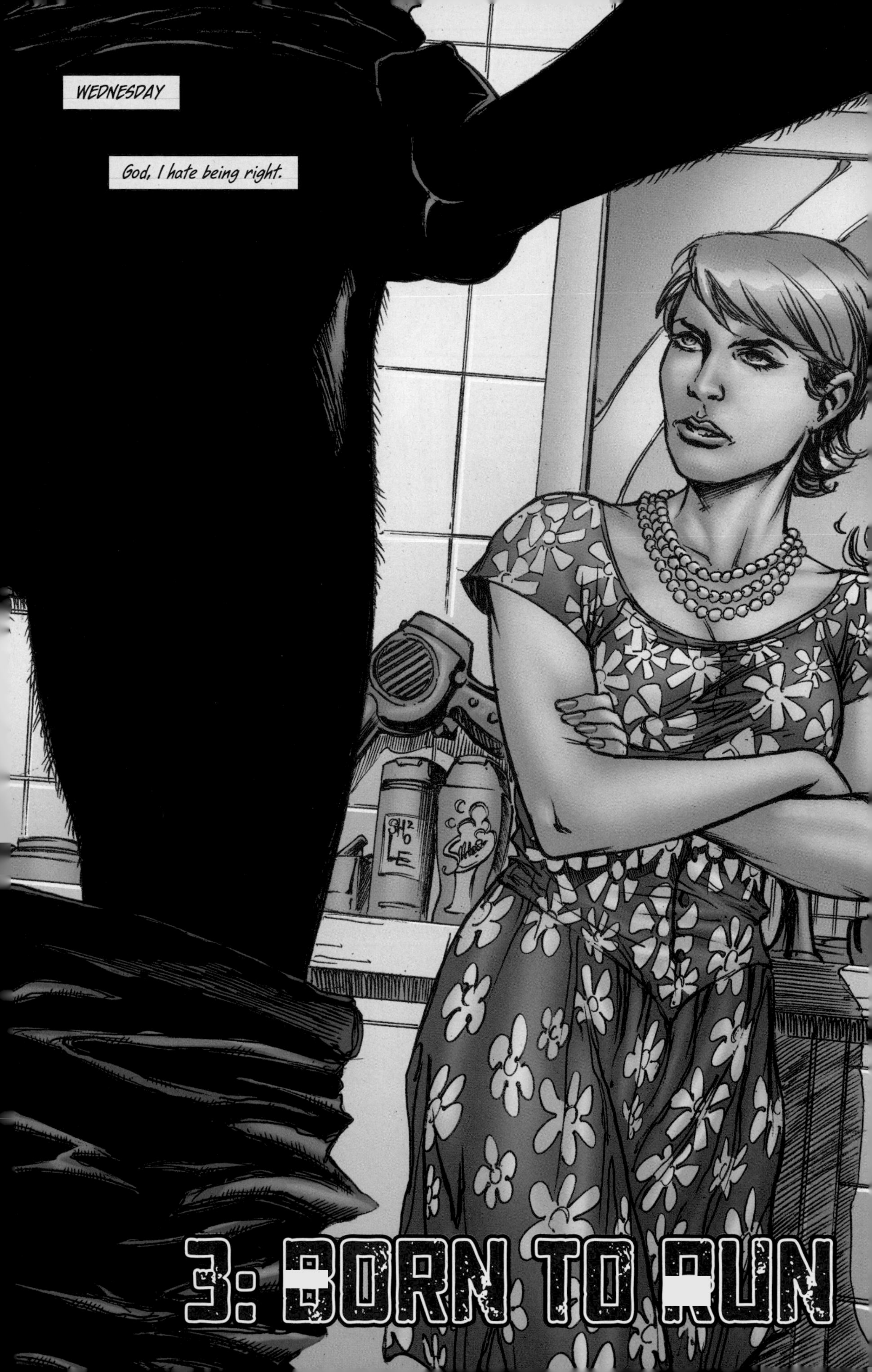
WEDNESDAY
God, I hate being right.
3: BORN TO RUN

JACK, WHAT ARE YOU DOING...?

CAN'T YOU TELL?

THIS IS YOUR HOUSEWARMING PARTY, YOUR WIFE'S GOING TO WONDER WHERE YOU ARE.

COME ON, DON'T ACT ALL INNOCENT WITH ME--!

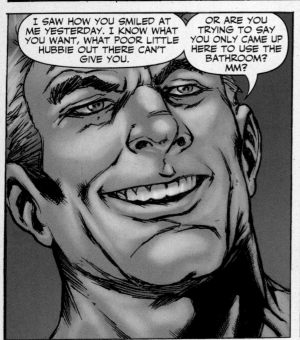

I SAW HOW YOU SMILED AT ME YESTERDAY. I KNOW WHAT YOU WANT, WHAT POOR LITTLE HUBBIE OUT THERE CAN'T GIVE YOU.

OR ARE YOU TRYING TO SAY YOU ONLY CAME UP HERE TO USE THE BATHROOM? MM?

ALL YOU SAW WAS ME SEEING YOU THINKING THAT.

I'M NOT INTERESTED IN SOME KIND OF EXTRA-MARITAL STUPIDITY WITH THE GUY ACROSS THE STREET, JACK. I DON'T WANT TO BETRAY MY HUSBAND AT ALL.

PLEASE MOVE.

OH, YOU'RE A COLD ONE, AREN'T YOU? YOU THINK YOU'RE TOO GOOD FOR ME OR SOMETHING?

OR ARE YOU MAYBE JUST PLAYING HARD TO GET...?

Trouble. As predicted by moi.

The problem was I had no idea how to deal with him.

By which I mean I don't know any of those funny little moves they teach in women's self-defense classes, where you twist wrists or yank fingers backwards or whatever- the idea being that you safely incapacitate your attacker before running for it.

I never learned any of that.

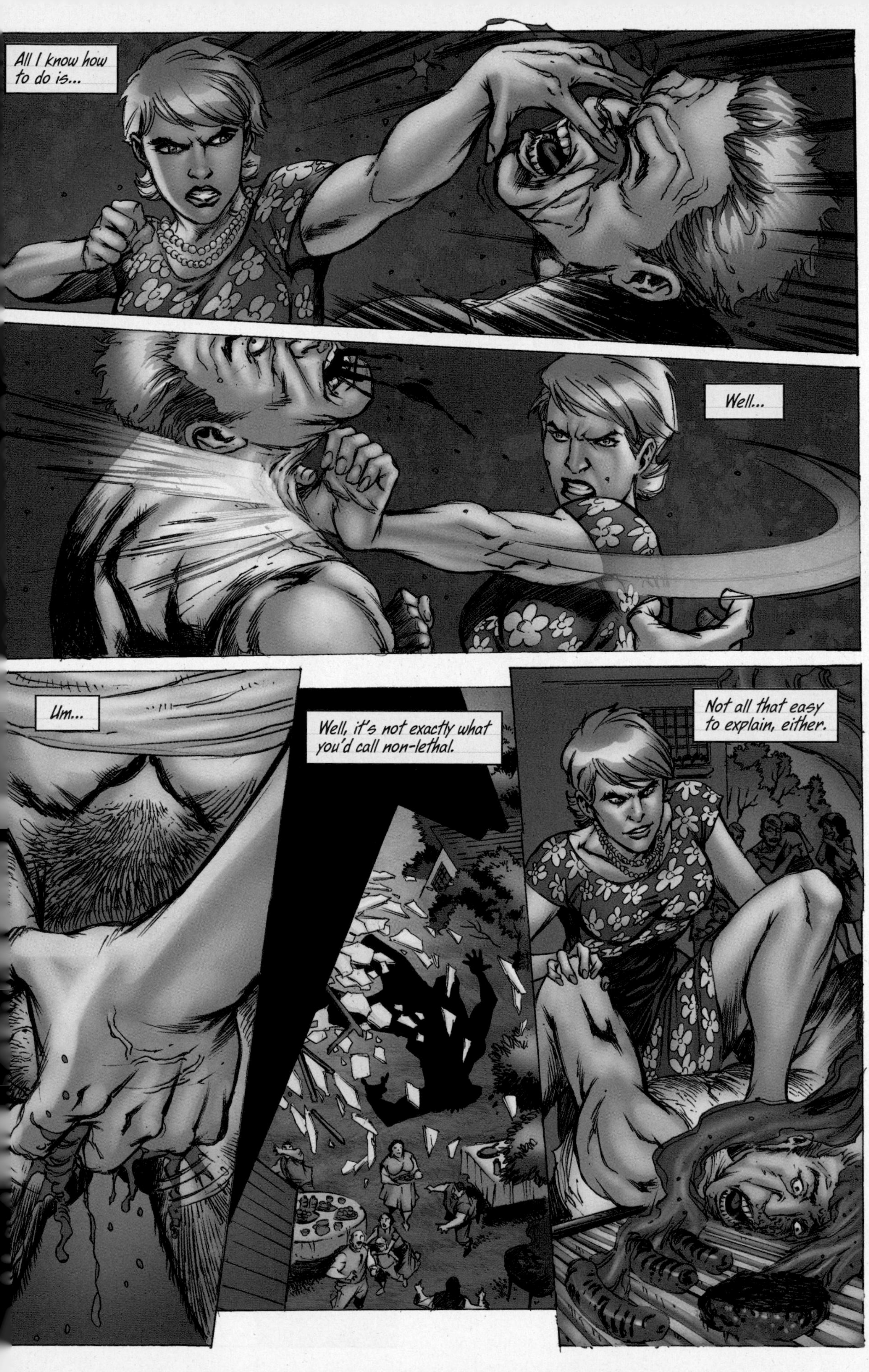
All I know how to do is...
Well...
Um...
Well, it's not exactly what you'd call non-lethal.
Not all that easy to explain, either.

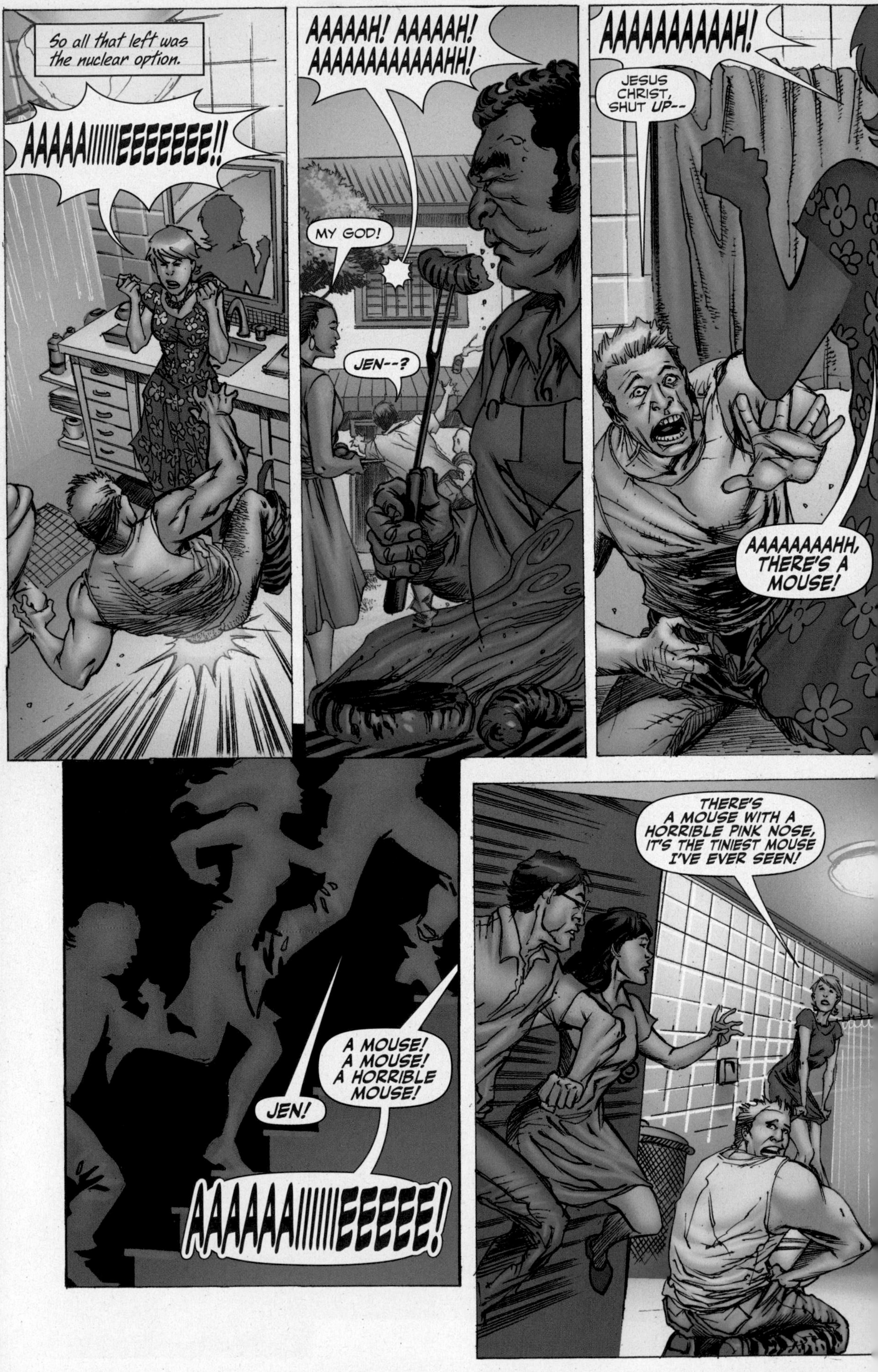
So all that left was the nuclear option.
AAAAAIIIIIIEEEEEEE!!
AAAAAH! AAAAAH! AAAAAAAAAAAAHH!
MY GOD!
JEN--?
AAAAAAAAAAH!
JESUS CHRIST, SHUT UP--
AAAAAAAAHH, THERE'S A MOUSE!
JEN!
A MOUSE! A MOUSE! A HORRIBLE MOUSE!
AAAAAAIIIIIIEEEEE!
THERE'S A MOUSE WITH A HORRIBLE PINK NOSE, IT'S THE TINIEST MOUSE I'VE EVER SEEN!

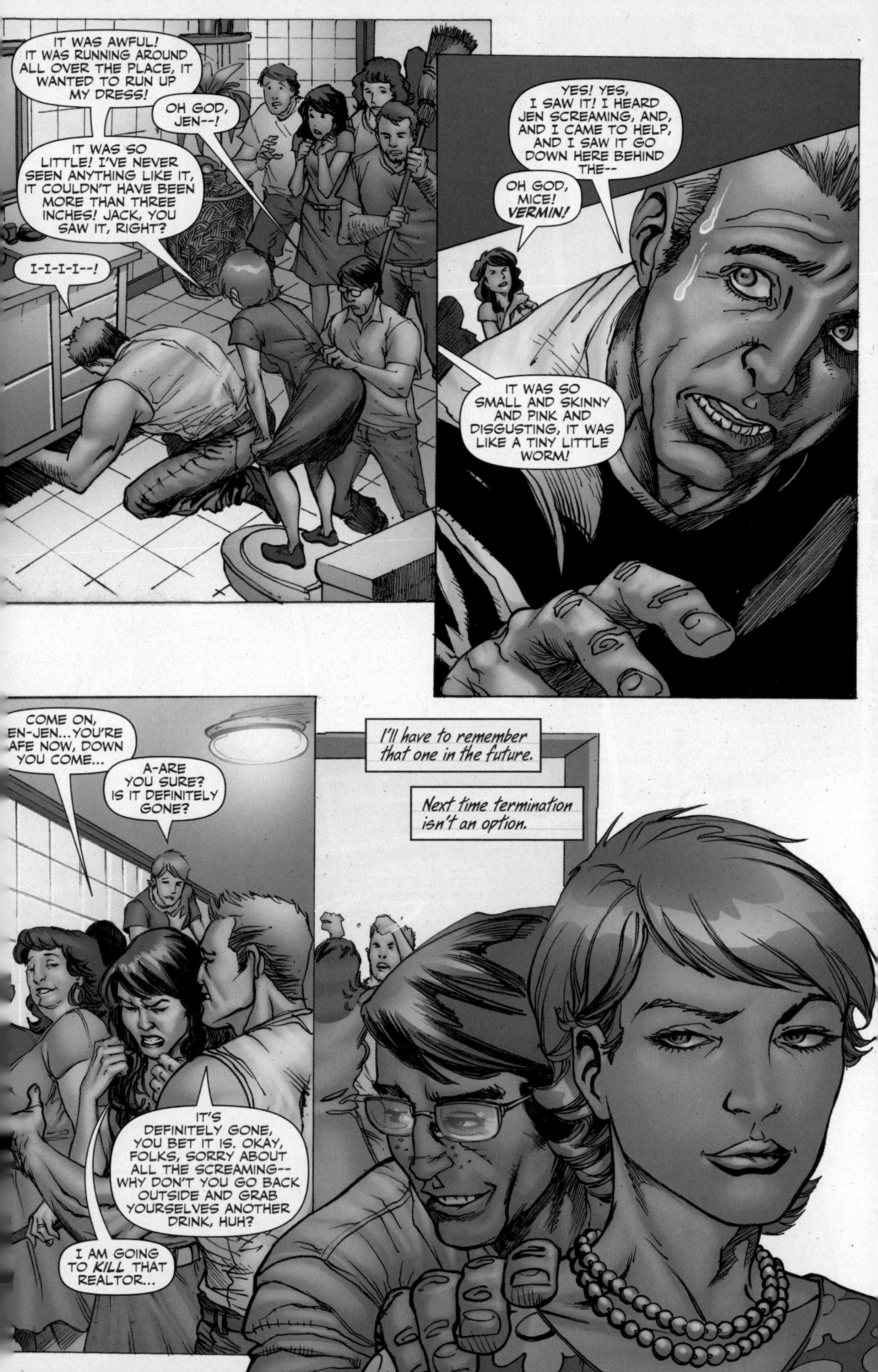
IT WAS AWFUL! IT WAS RUNNING AROUND ALL OVER THE PLACE, IT WANTED TO RUN UP MY DRESS!
OH GOD, JEN--!
IT WAS SO LITTLE! I'VE NEVER SEEN ANYTHING LIKE IT, IT COULDN'T HAVE BEEN MORE THAN THREE INCHES! JACK, YOU SAW IT, RIGHT?
I-I-I-I--!
YES! YES, I SAW IT! I HEARD JEN SCREAMING, AND, AND I CAME TO HELP, AND I SAW IT GO DOWN HERE BEHIND THE--
OH GOD, MICE! VERMIN!
IT WAS SO SMALL AND SKINNY AND PINK AND DISGUSTING, IT WAS LIKE A TINY LITTLE WORM!
COME ON, EN-JEN...YOU'RE AFE NOW, DOWN YOU COME...
A-ARE YOU SURE? IS IT DEFINITELY GONE?
I'll have to remember that one in the future.
Next time termination isn't an option.
IT'S DEFINITELY GONE, YOU BET IT IS. OKAY, FOLKS, SORRY ABOUT ALL THE SCREAMING-- WHY DON'T YOU GO BACK OUTSIDE AND GRAB YOURSELVES ANOTHER DRINK, HUH?
I AM GOING TO KILL THAT REALTOR...

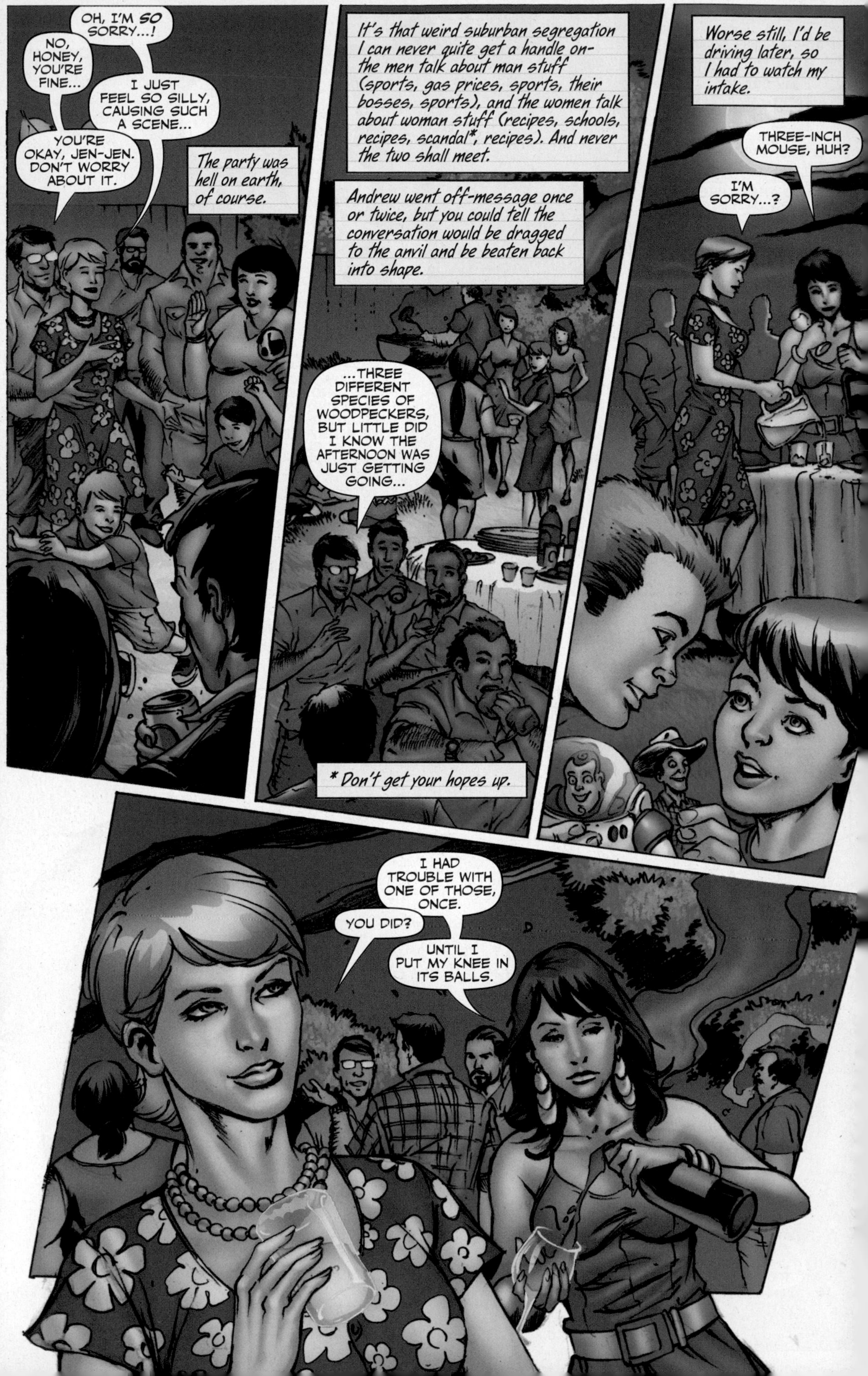
OH, I'M SO SORRY...!
NO, HONEY, YOU'RE FINE...
I JUST FEEL SO SILLY, CAUSING SUCH A SCENE...
YOU'RE OKAY, JEN-JEN. DON'T WORRY ABOUT IT.
The party was hell on earth, of course.
It's that weird suburban segregation I can never quite get a handle on- the men talk about man stuff (sports, gas prices, sports, their bosses, sports), and the women talk about woman stuff (recipes, schools, recipes, scandal*, recipes). And never the two shall meet.
Andrew went off-message once or twice, but you could tell the conversation would be dragged to the anvil and be beaten back into shape.
...THREE DIFFERENT SPECIES OF WOODPECKERS, BUT LITTLE DID I KNOW THE AFTERNOON WAS JUST GETTING GOING...
* Don't get your hopes up.
Worse still, I'd be driving later, so I had to watch my intake.
THREE-INCH MOUSE, HUH?
I'M SORRY...?
I HAD TROUBLE WITH ONE OF THOSE, ONCE.
YOU DID?
UNTIL I PUT MY KNEE IN ITS BALLS.

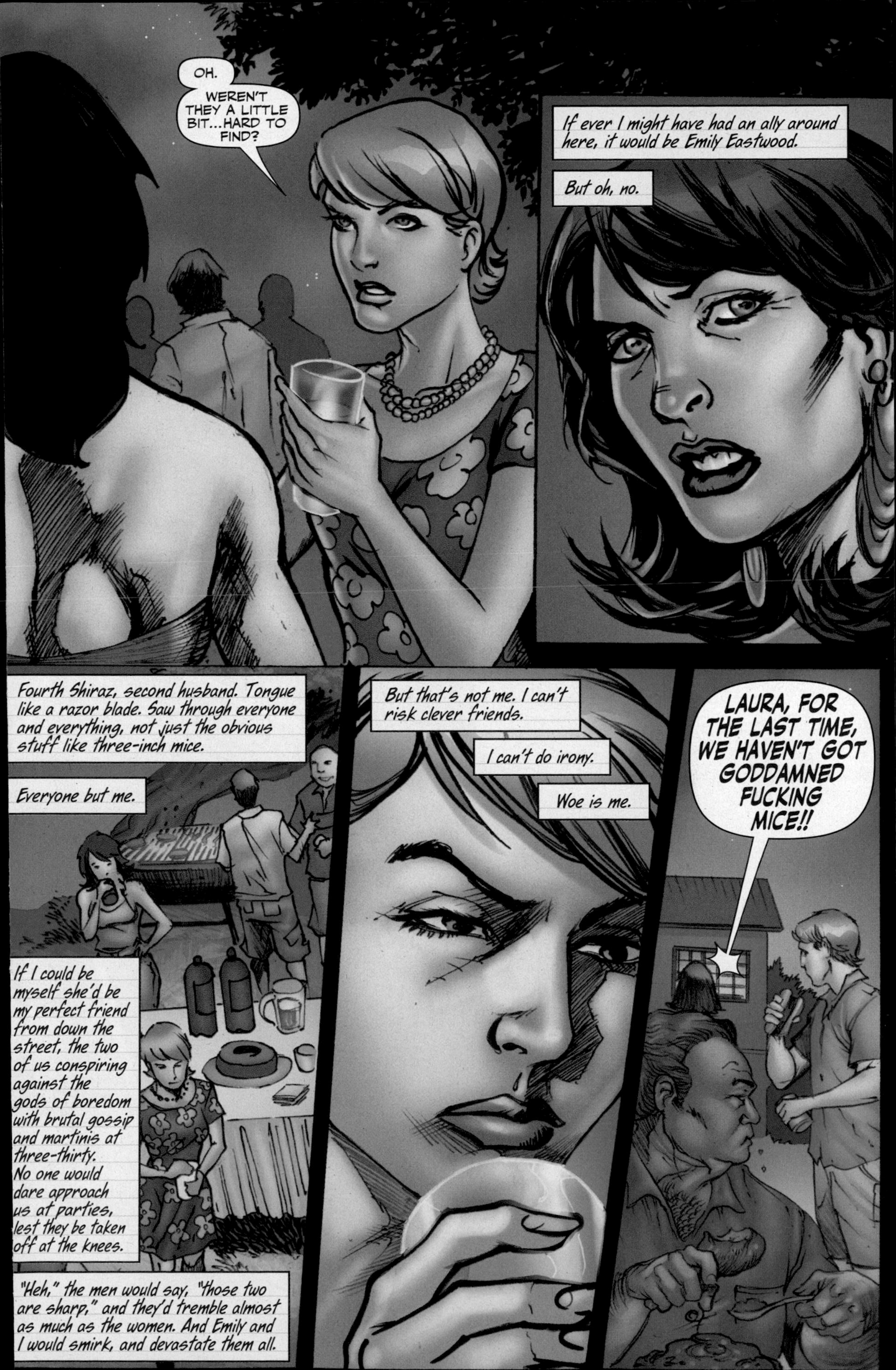
OH.
WEREN'T THEY A LITTLE BIT...HARD TO FIND?
If ever I might have had an ally around here, it would be Emily Eastwood.
But oh, no.
Fourth Shiraz, second husband. Tongue like a razor blade. Saw through everyone and everything, not just the obvious stuff like three-inch mice.
Everyone but me.
If I could be myself she'd be my perfect friend from down the street, the two of us conspiring against the gods of boredom with brutal gossip and martinis at three-thirty. No one would dare approach us at parties, lest they be taken off at the knees.
"Heh," the men would say, "those two are sharp," and they'd tremble almost as much as the women. And Emily and I would smirk, and devastate them all.
But that's not me. I can't risk clever friends.
I can't do irony.
Woe is me.
LAURA, FOR THE LAST TIME, WE HAVEN'T GOT GODDAMNED FUCKING MICE!!

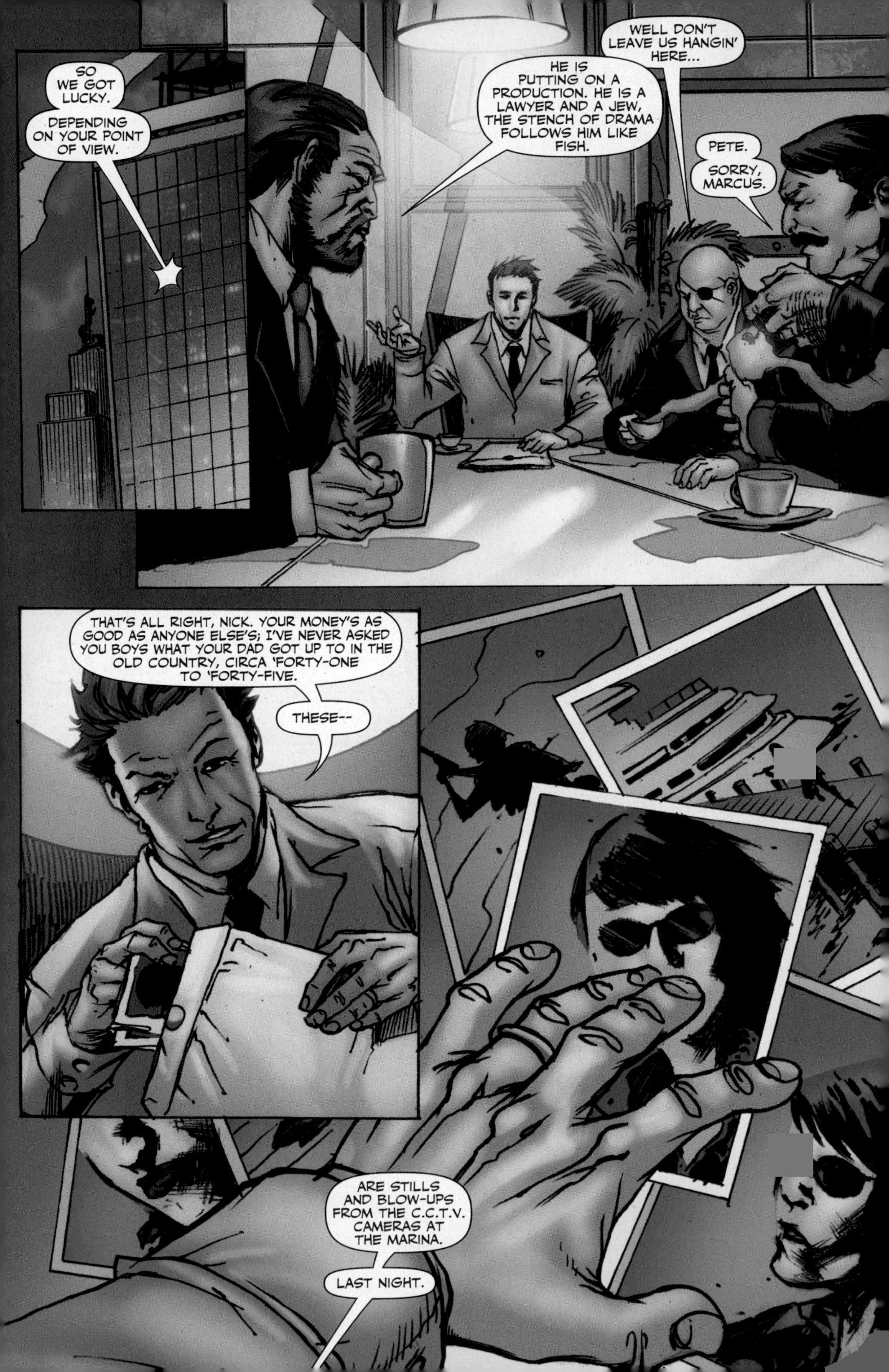
SO WE GOT LUCKY.
DEPENDING ON YOUR POINT OF VIEW.
HE IS PUTTING ON A PRODUCTION. HE IS A LAWYER AND A JEW, THE STENCH OF DRAMA FOLLOWS HIM LIKE FISH.
WELL DON'T LEAVE US HANGIN' HERE...
PETE.
SORRY, MARCUS.
THAT'S ALL RIGHT, NICK. YOUR MONEY'S AS GOOD AS ANYONE ELSE'S; I'VE NEVER ASKED YOU BOYS WHAT YOUR DAD GOT UP TO IN THE OLD COUNTRY, CIRCA 'FORTY-ONE TO 'FORTY-FIVE.
THESE--
ARE STILLS AND BLOW-UPS FROM THE C.C.T.V. CAMERAS AT THE MARINA.
LAST NIGHT.

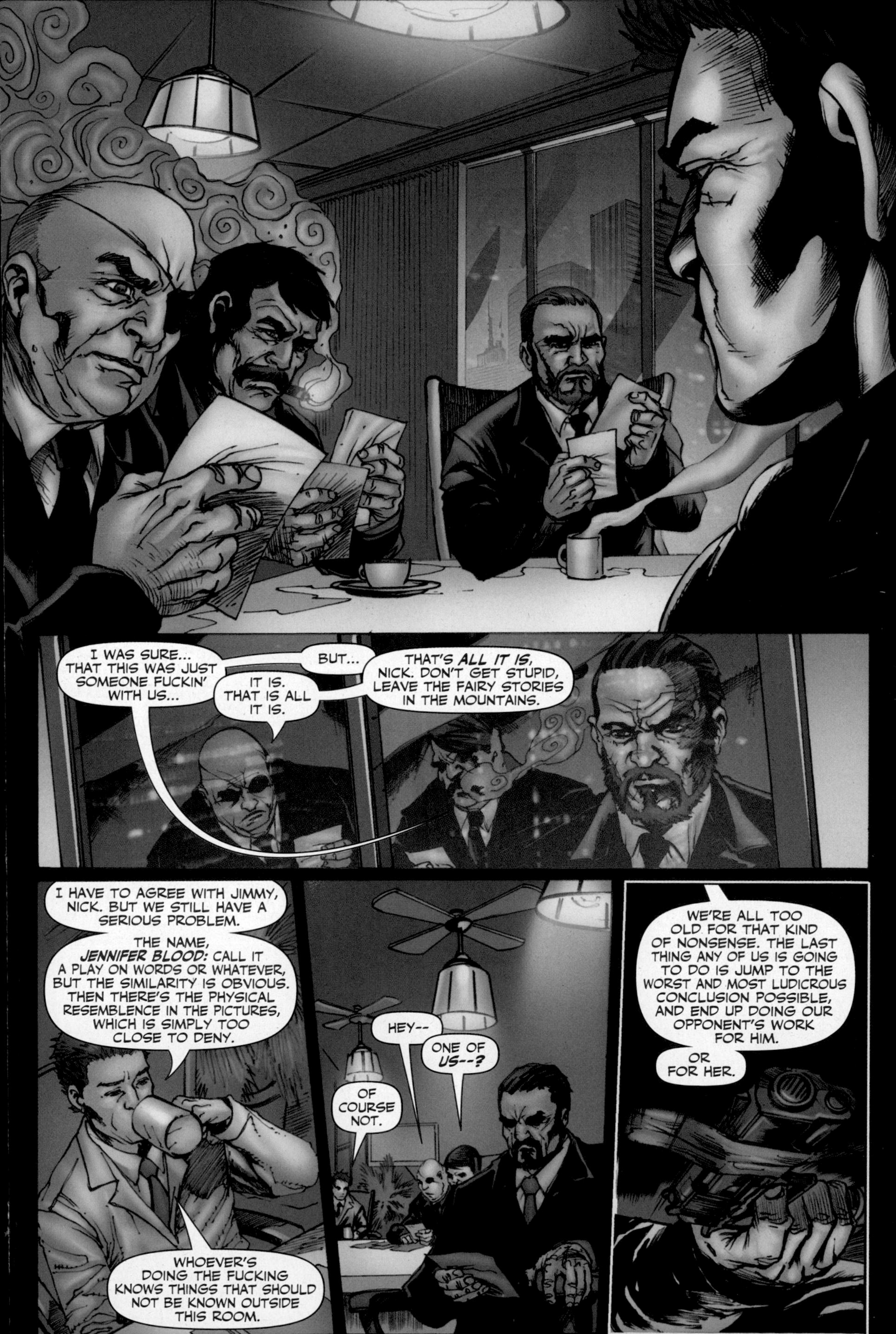
I WAS SURE... THAT THIS WAS JUST SOMEONE FUCKIN' WITH US...
BUT...
IT IS. THAT IS ALL IT IS.
THAT'S *ALL IT IS,* NICK. DON'T GET STUPID, LEAVE THE FAIRY STORIES IN THE MOUNTAINS.
I HAVE TO AGREE WITH JIMMY, NICK. BUT WE STILL HAVE A SERIOUS PROBLEM.
THE NAME, *JENNIFER BLOOD:* CALL IT A PLAY ON WORDS OR WHATEVER, BUT THE SIMILARITY IS OBVIOUS. THEN THERE'S THE PHYSICAL RESEMBLENCE IN THE PICTURES, WHICH IS SIMPLY TOO CLOSE TO DENY.
WHOEVER'S DOING THE FUCKING KNOWS THINGS THAT SHOULD NOT BE KNOWN OUTSIDE THIS ROOM.
HEY--
ONE OF *US--?*
OF COURSE NOT.
WE'RE ALL TOO OLD FOR THAT KIND OF NONSENSE. THE LAST THING ANY OF US IS GOING TO DO IS JUMP TO THE WORST AND MOST LUDICROUS CONCLUSION POSSIBLE, AND END UP DOING OUR OPPONENT'S WORK FOR HIM.
OR FOR HER.

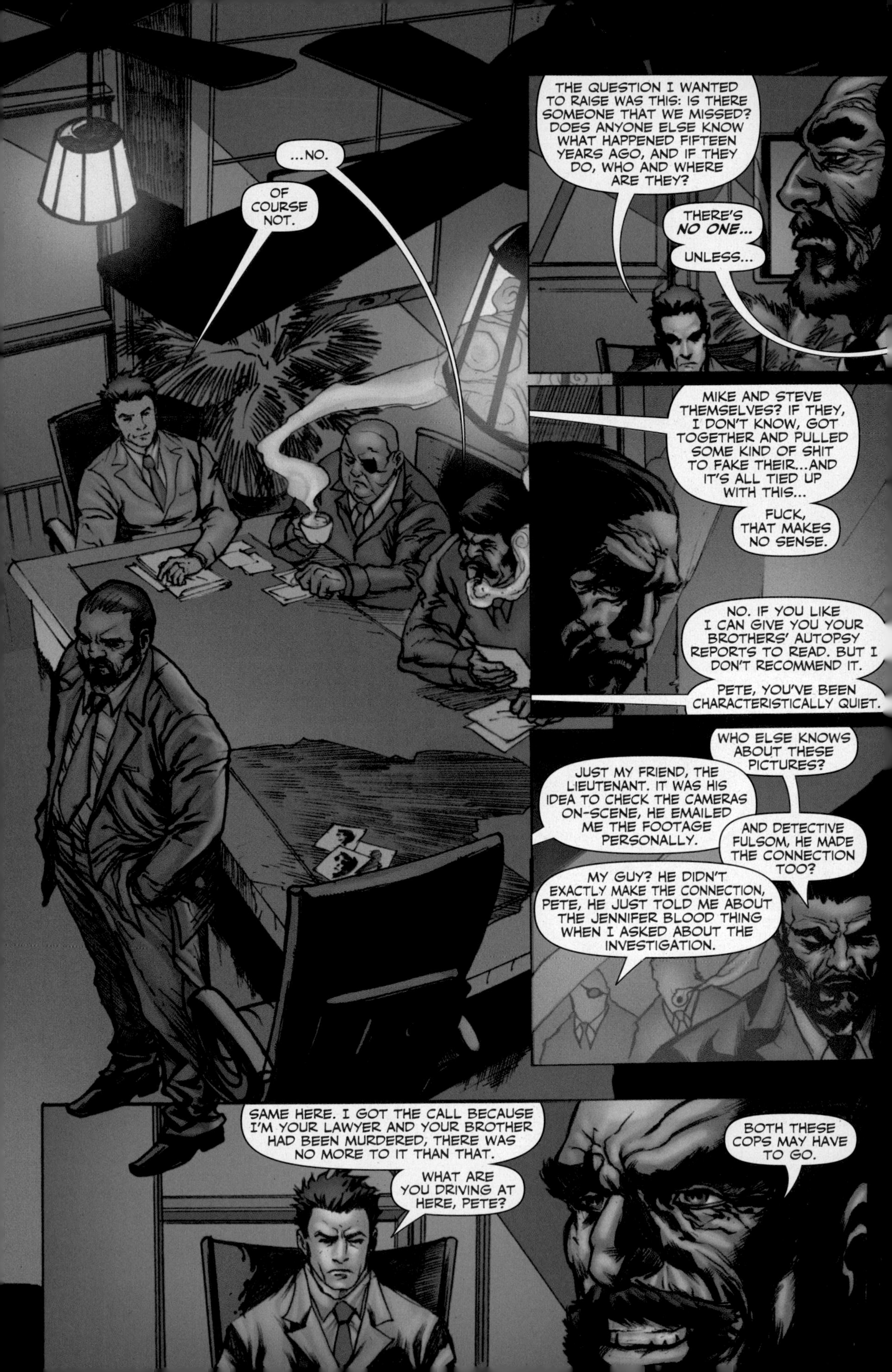
...NO.
OF COURSE NOT.
THE QUESTION I WANTED TO RAISE WAS THIS: IS THERE SOMEONE THAT WE MISSED? DOES ANYONE ELSE KNOW WHAT HAPPENED FIFTEEN YEARS AGO, AND IF THEY DO, WHO AND WHERE ARE THEY?
THERE'S NO ONE...
UNLESS...
MIKE AND STEVE THEMSELVES? IF THEY, I DON'T KNOW, GOT TOGETHER AND PULLED SOME KIND OF SHIT TO FAKE THEIR...AND IT'S ALL TIED UP WITH THIS...
FUCK, THAT MAKES NO SENSE.
NO. IF YOU LIKE I CAN GIVE YOU YOUR BROTHERS' AUTOPSY REPORTS TO READ. BUT I DON'T RECOMMEND IT.
PETE, YOU'VE BEEN CHARACTERISTICALLY QUIET.
WHO ELSE KNOWS ABOUT THESE PICTURES?
JUST MY FRIEND, THE LIEUTENANT. IT WAS HIS IDEA TO CHECK THE CAMERAS ON-SCENE, HE EMAILED ME THE FOOTAGE PERSONALLY.
AND DETECTIVE FULSOM, HE MADE THE CONNECTION TOO?
MY GUY? HE DIDN'T EXACTLY MAKE THE CONNECTION, PETE, HE JUST TOLD ME ABOUT THE JENNIFER BLOOD THING WHEN I ASKED ABOUT THE INVESTIGATION.
SAME HERE. I GOT THE CALL BECAUSE I'M YOUR LAWYER AND YOUR BROTHER HAD BEEN MURDERED, THERE WAS NO MORE TO IT THAN THAT.
WHAT ARE YOU DRIVING AT HERE, PETE?
BOTH THESE COPS MAY HAVE TO GO.

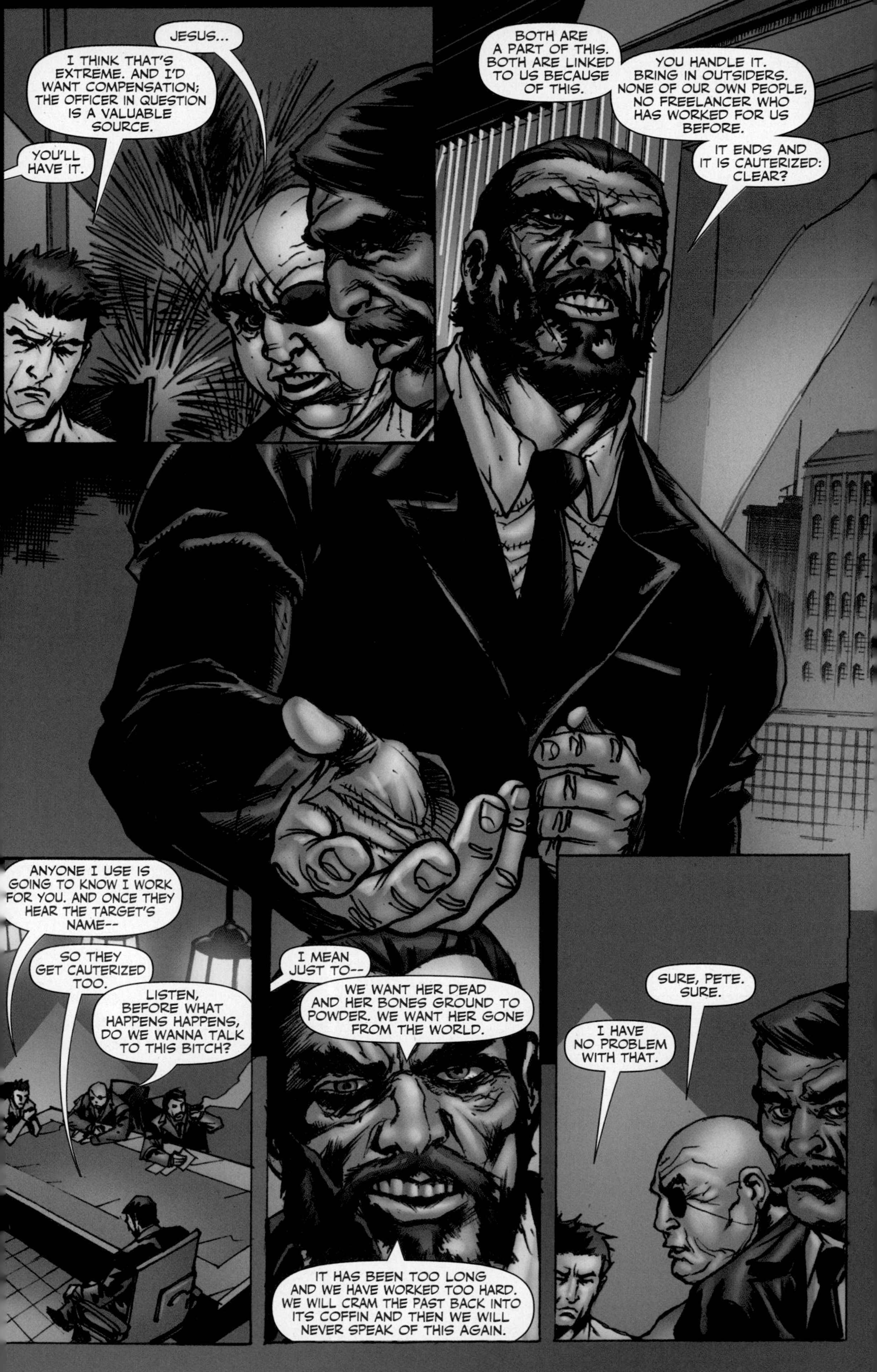
JESUS...
I THINK THAT'S EXTREME. AND I'D WANT COMPENSATION; THE OFFICER IN QUESTION IS A VALUABLE SOURCE.
YOU'LL HAVE IT.
BOTH ARE A PART OF THIS. BOTH ARE LINKED TO US BECAUSE OF THIS.
YOU HANDLE IT. BRING IN OUTSIDERS. NONE OF OUR OWN PEOPLE, NO FREELANCER WHO HAS WORKED FOR US BEFORE.
IT ENDS AND IT IS CAUTERIZED: CLEAR?
ANYONE I USE IS GOING TO KNOW I WORK FOR YOU. AND ONCE THEY HEAR THE TARGET'S NAME--
SO THEY GET CAUTERIZED TOO.
LISTEN, BEFORE WHAT HAPPENS HAPPENS, DO WE WANNA TALK TO THIS BITCH?
I MEAN JUST TO--
WE WANT HER DEAD AND HER BONES GROUND TO POWDER. WE WANT HER GONE FROM THE WORLD.
IT HAS BEEN TOO LONG AND WE HAVE WORKED TOO HARD. WE WILL CRAM THE PAST BACK INTO ITS COFFIN AND THEN WE WILL NEVER SPEAK OF THIS AGAIN.
SURE, PETE. SURE.
I HAVE NO PROBLEM WITH THAT.

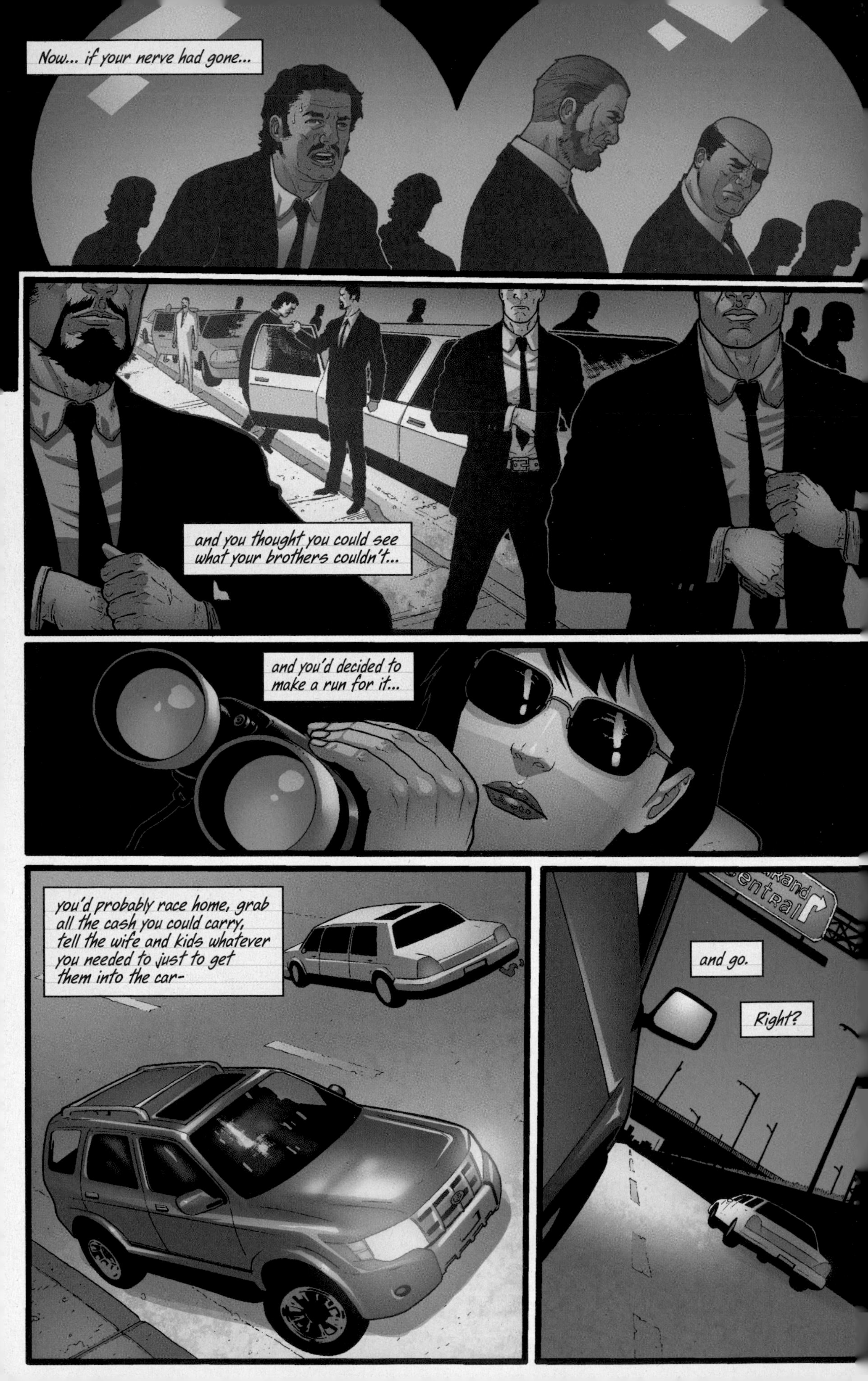
Now... if your nerve had gone...
and you thought you could see what your brothers couldn't...
and you'd decided to make a run for it...
you'd probably race home, grab all the cash you could carry, tell the wife and kids whatever you needed to just to get them into the car-
Grand Central
and go.
Right?

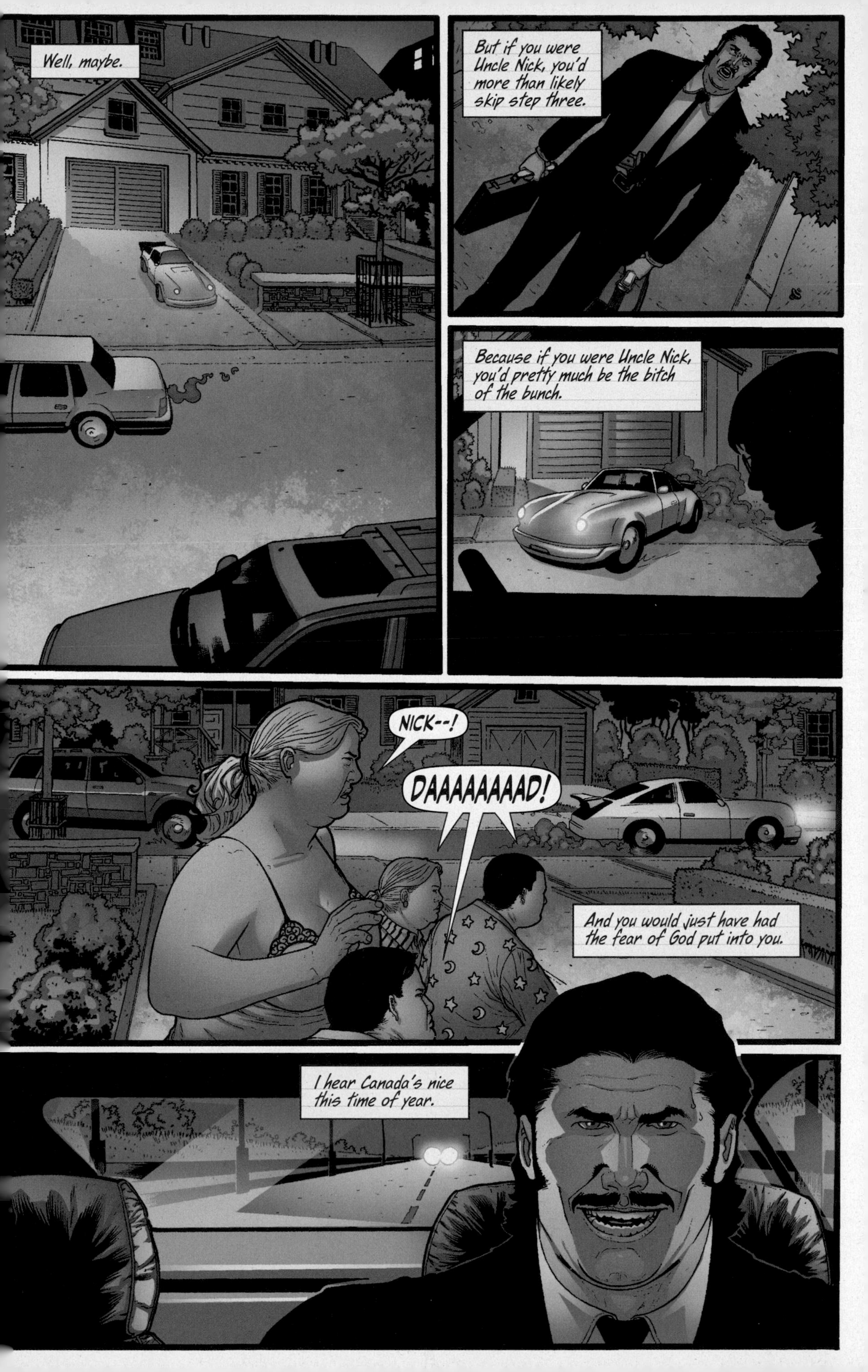
Well, maybe.
But if you were Uncle Nick, you'd more than likely skip step three.
Because if you were Uncle Nick, you'd pretty much be the bitch of the bunch.
NICK--!
DAAAAAAAAD!
And you would just have had the fear of God put into you.
I hear Canada's nice this time of year.

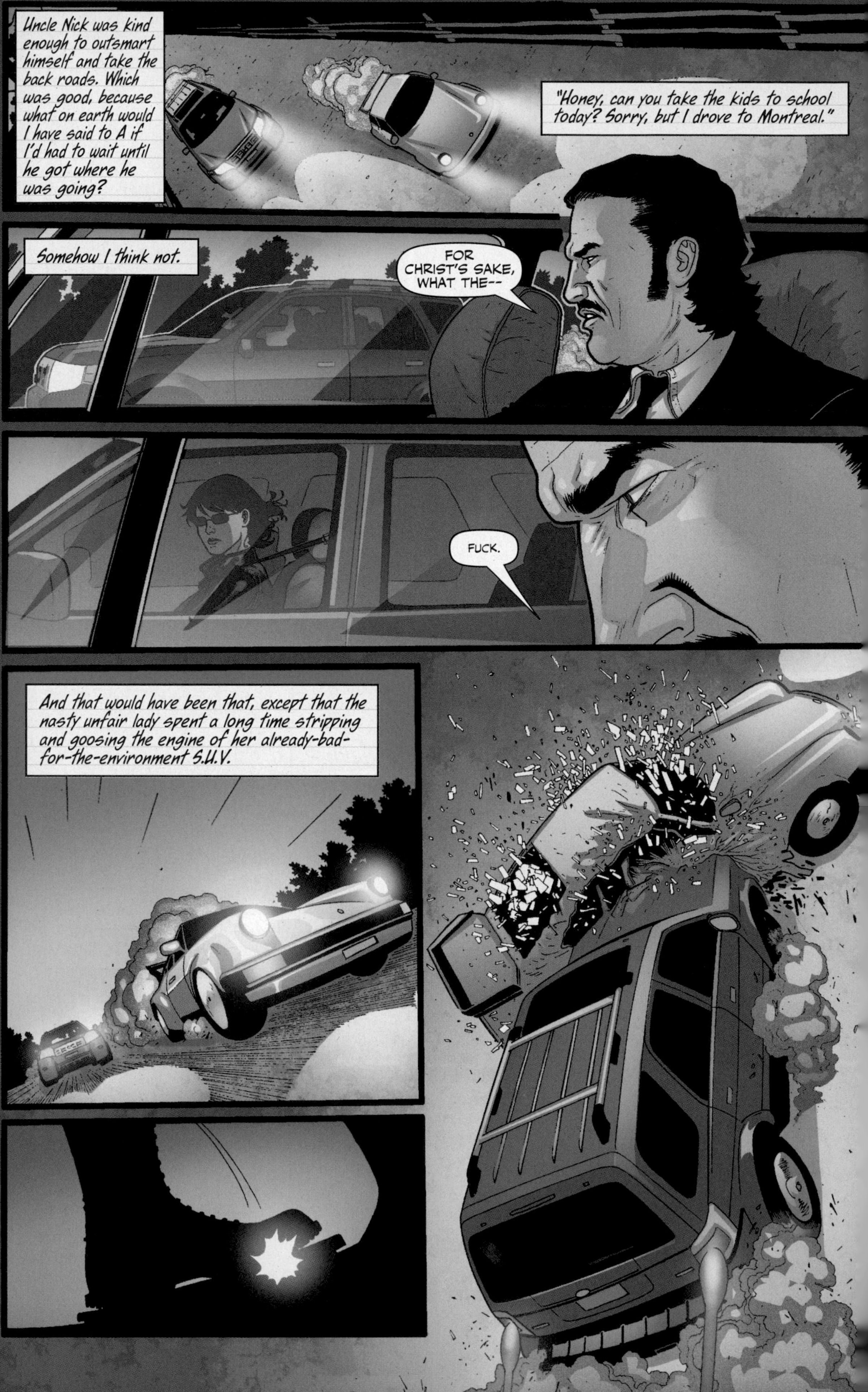
Uncle Nick was kind enough to outsmart himself and take the back roads. Which was good, because what on earth would I have said to A if I'd had to wait until he got where he was going?
"Honey, can you take the kids to school today? Sorry, but I drove to Montreal."
Somehow I think not.
FOR CHRIST'S SAKE, WHAT THE--
FUCK.
And that would have been that, except that the nasty unfair lady spent a long time stripping and goosing the engine of her already-bad-for-the-environment S.U.V.

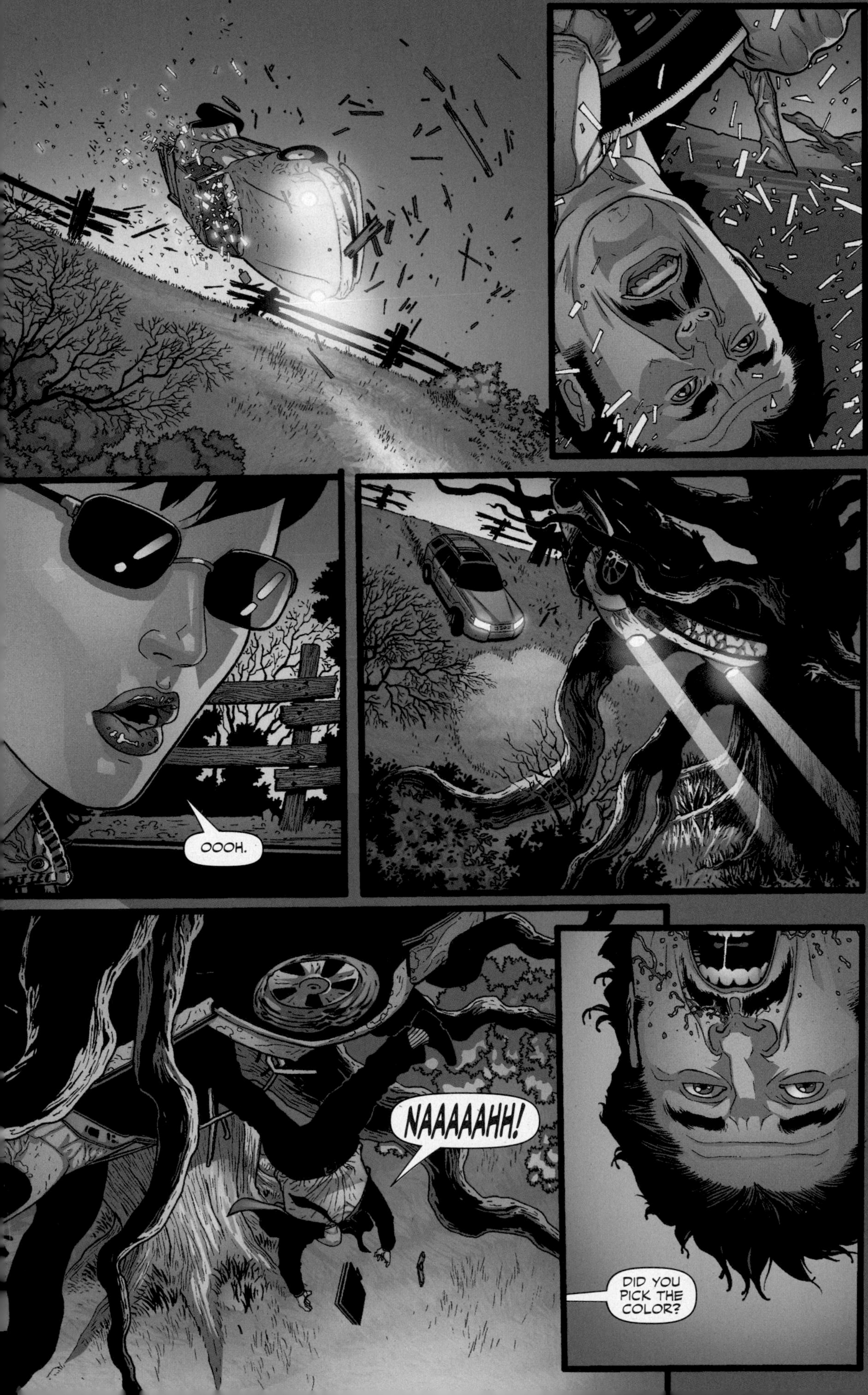
OOOH.
NAAAAAHH!
DID YOU PICK THE COLOR?

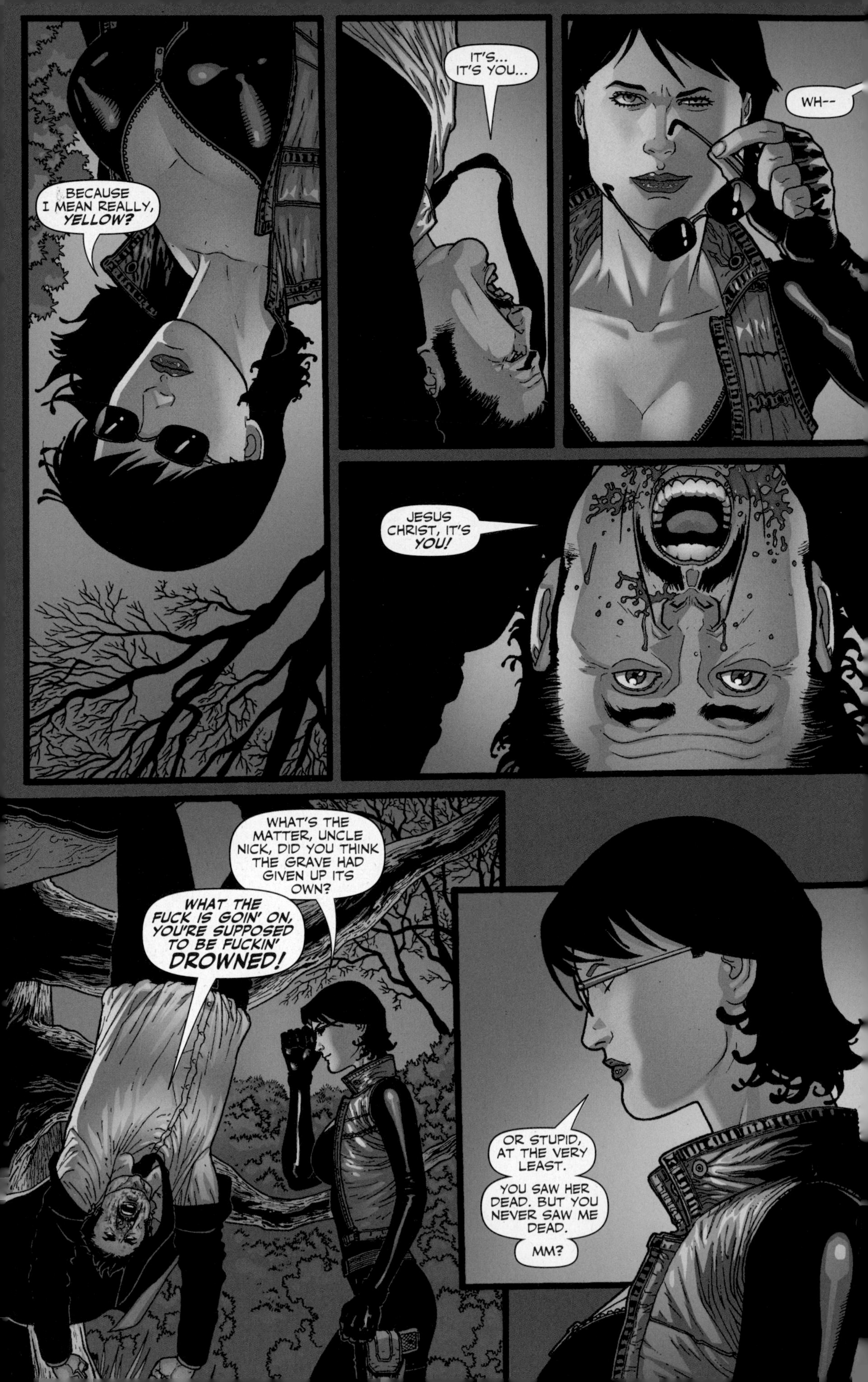
BECAUSE I MEAN REALLY, *YELLOW?*
IT'S... IT'S YOU...
WH--
JESUS CHRIST, IT'S *YOU!*
WHAT'S THE MATTER, UNCLE NICK, DID YOU THINK THE GRAVE HAD GIVEN UP ITS OWN?
WHAT THE FUCK IS GOIN' ON, YOU'RE SUPPOSED TO BE FUCKIN' DROWNED!
OR STUPID, AT THE VERY LEAST.
YOU SAW HER DEAD. BUT YOU NEVER SAW ME DEAD.
MM?

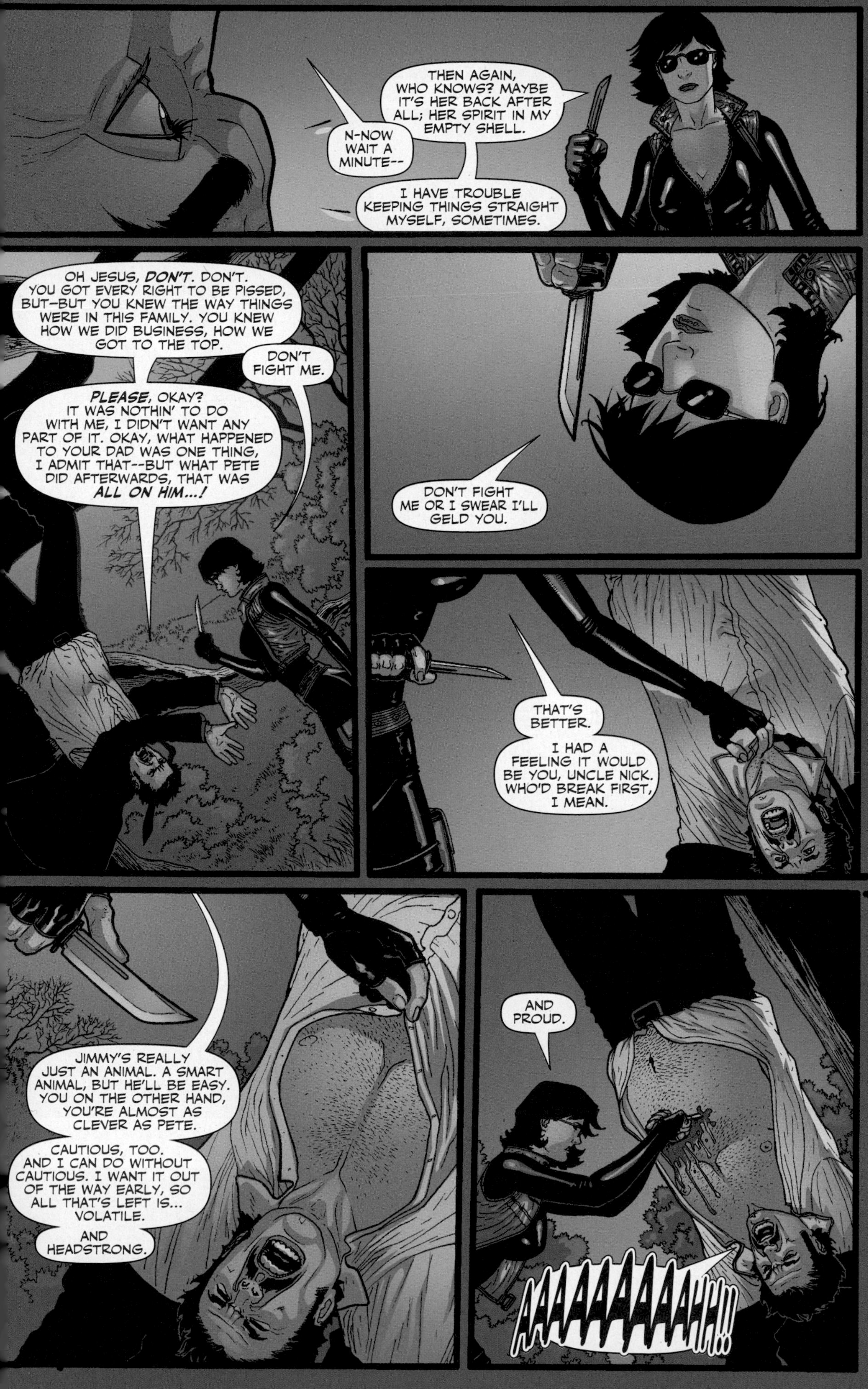
THEN AGAIN, WHO KNOWS? MAYBE IT'S HER BACK AFTER ALL; HER SPIRIT IN MY EMPTY SHELL.
N-NOW WAIT A MINUTE--
I HAVE TROUBLE KEEPING THINGS STRAIGHT MYSELF, SOMETIMES.
OH JESUS, DON'T. DON'T. YOU GOT EVERY RIGHT TO BE PISSED, BUT--BUT YOU KNEW THE WAY THINGS WERE IN THIS FAMILY. YOU KNEW HOW WE DID BUSINESS, HOW WE GOT TO THE TOP.
DON'T FIGHT ME.
PLEASE, OKAY? IT WAS NOTHIN' TO DO WITH ME, I DIDN'T WANT ANY PART OF IT. OKAY, WHAT HAPPENED TO YOUR DAD WAS ONE THING, I ADMIT THAT--BUT WHAT PETE DID AFTERWARDS, THAT WAS ALL ON HIM...!
DON'T FIGHT ME OR I SWEAR I'LL GELD YOU.
THAT'S BETTER.
I HAD A FEELING IT WOULD BE YOU, UNCLE NICK. WHO'D BREAK FIRST, I MEAN.
JIMMY'S REALLY JUST AN ANIMAL. A SMART ANIMAL, BUT HE'LL BE EASY. YOU ON THE OTHER HAND, YOU'RE ALMOST AS CLEVER AS PETE.
CAUTIOUS, TOO. AND I CAN DO WITHOUT CAUTIOUS. I WANT IT OUT OF THE WAY EARLY, SO ALL THAT'S LEFT IS... VOLATILE.
AND HEADSTRONG.
AND PROUD.
AAAAAAAAAAHH!!

For my next trick I needed about thirty feet of intestine, but Uncle Nick could barely oblige me with ten. I don't even think it was his fault, unless he was tensing up or something- which I have to admit is fairly unlikely.

That was when I had kind of a brainwave.

Try as I might I couldn't make any more headway. It was slippery work, too, and before long I'd pretty much exhausted myself.

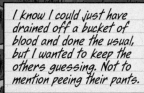

I know I could just have drained off a bucket of blood and done the usual, but I wanted to keep the others guessing. Not to mention peeing their pants.

OH MY GOD, YOU FUCKING INHUMAN CUNT--

AAAAIIIIEEEEE!!

But that would have been a little disgusting.

In the end I had to compromise anyway. The original plan was to cut it up, make thirteen letters out of the pieces-

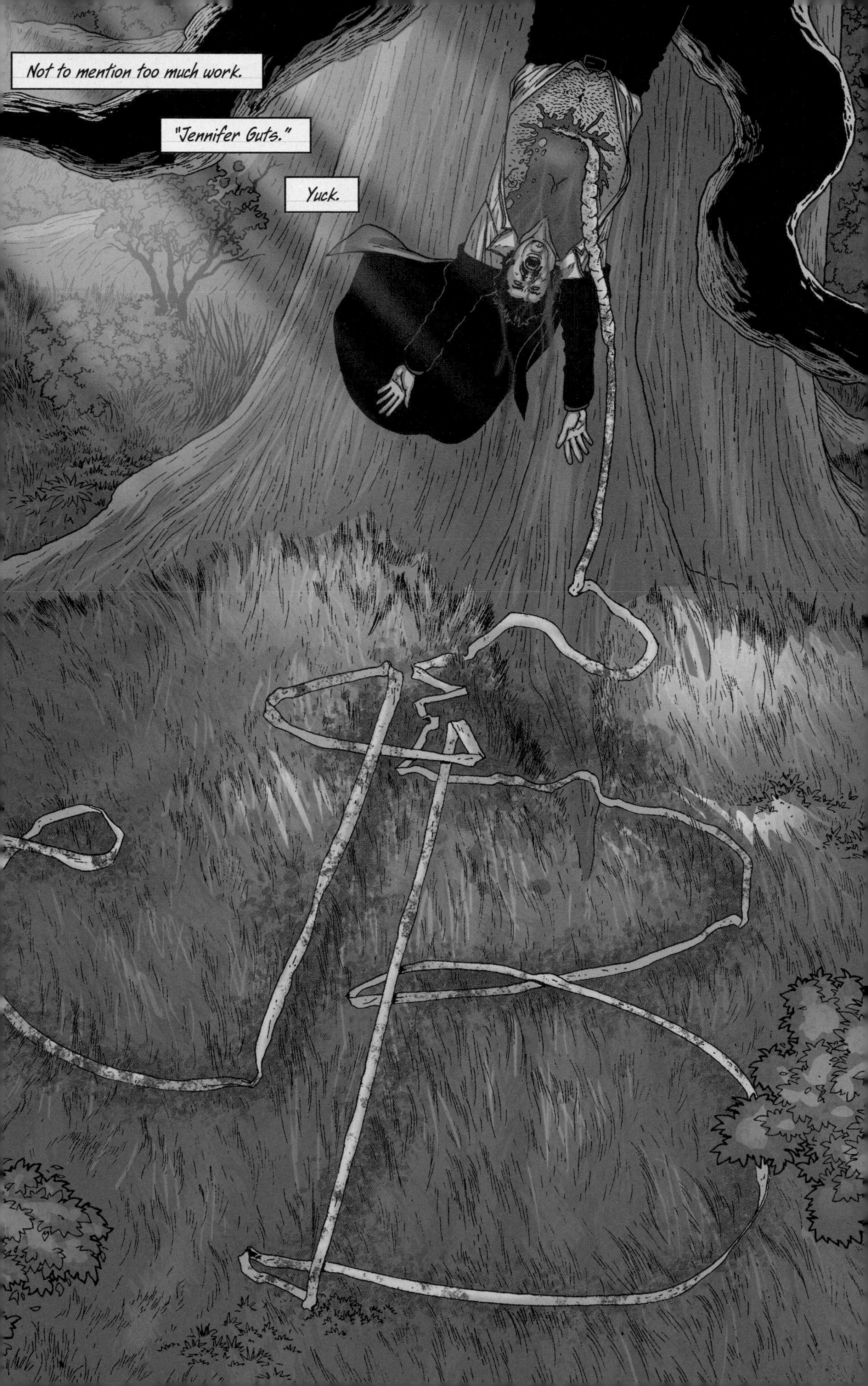
Not to mention too much work.
"Jennifer Guts."
Yuck.

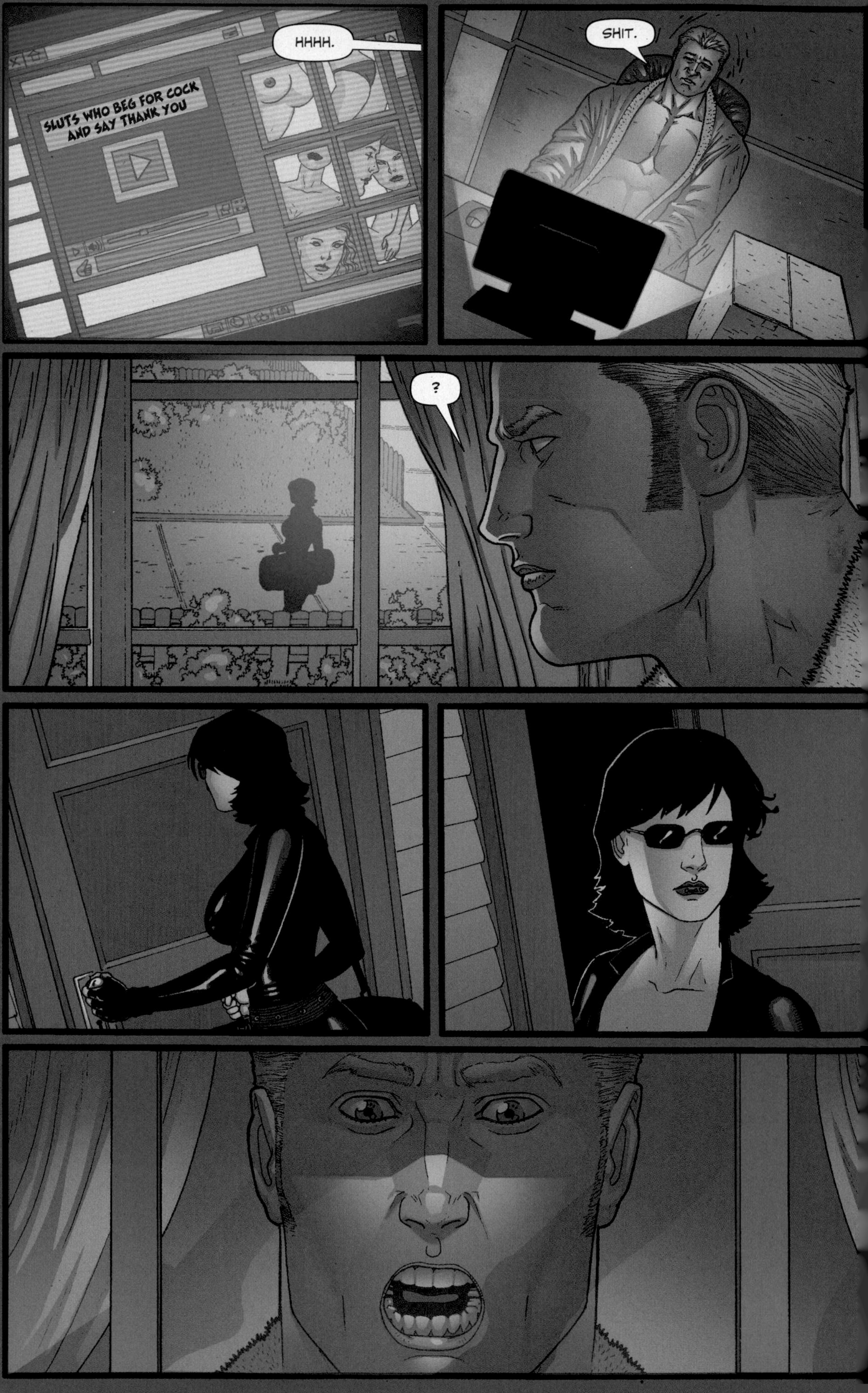

SLUTS WHO BEG FOR COCK AND SAY THANK YOU
HHHH.
SHIT.
?

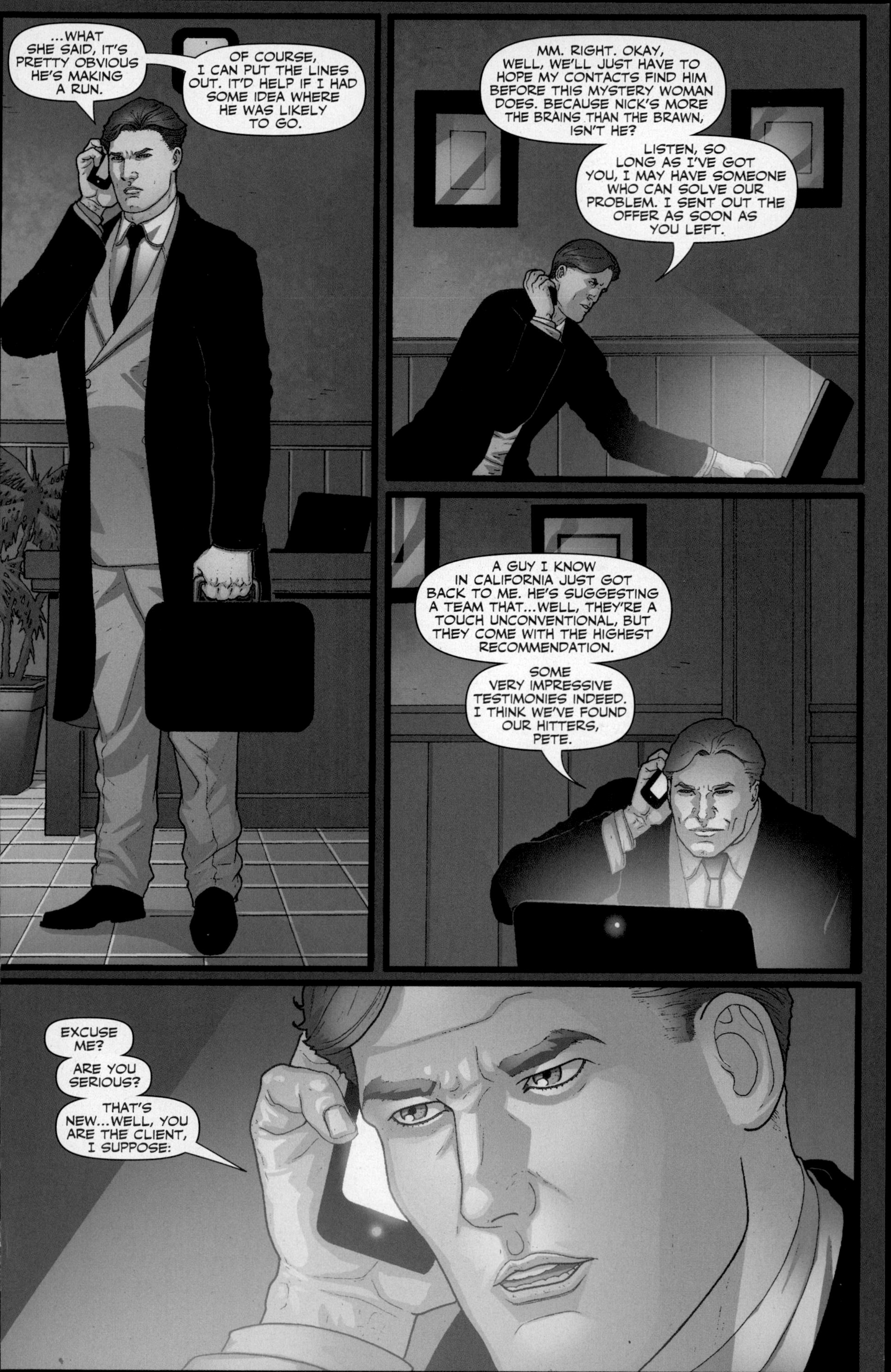
...WHAT SHE SAID, IT'S PRETTY OBVIOUS HE'S MAKING A RUN.
OF COURSE, I CAN PUT THE LINES OUT. IT'D HELP IF I HAD SOME IDEA WHERE HE WAS LIKELY TO GO.
MM. RIGHT. OKAY, WELL, WE'LL JUST HAVE TO HOPE MY CONTACTS FIND HIM BEFORE THIS MYSTERY WOMAN DOES. BECAUSE NICK'S MORE THE BRAINS THAN THE BRAWN, ISN'T HE?
LISTEN, SO LONG AS I'VE GOT YOU, I MAY HAVE SOMEONE WHO CAN SOLVE OUR PROBLEM. I SENT OUT THE OFFER AS SOON AS YOU LEFT.
A GUY I KNOW IN CALIFORNIA JUST GOT BACK TO ME. HE'S SUGGESTING A TEAM THAT...WELL, THEY'RE A TOUCH UNCONVENTIONAL, BUT THEY COME WITH THE HIGHEST RECOMMENDATION.
SOME VERY IMPRESSIVE TESTIMONIES INDEED. I THINK WE'VE FOUND OUR HITTERS, PETE.
EXCUSE ME?
ARE YOU SERIOUS?
THAT'S NEW...WELL, YOU ARE THE CLIENT, I SUPPOSE:

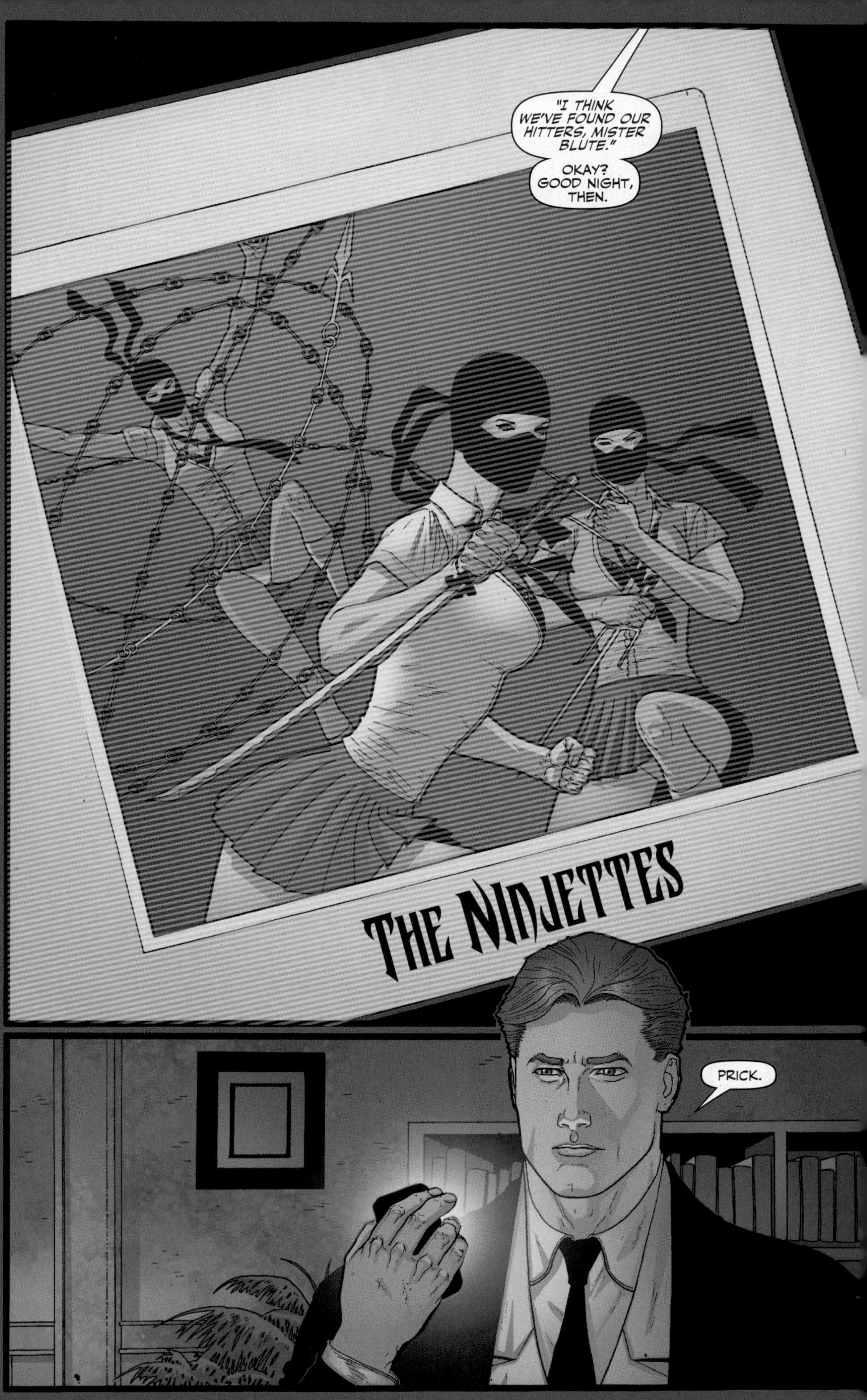
"I THINK WE'VE FOUND OUR HITTERS, MISTER BLUTE."
OKAY? GOOD NIGHT, THEN.
THE NINJETTES
PRICK.

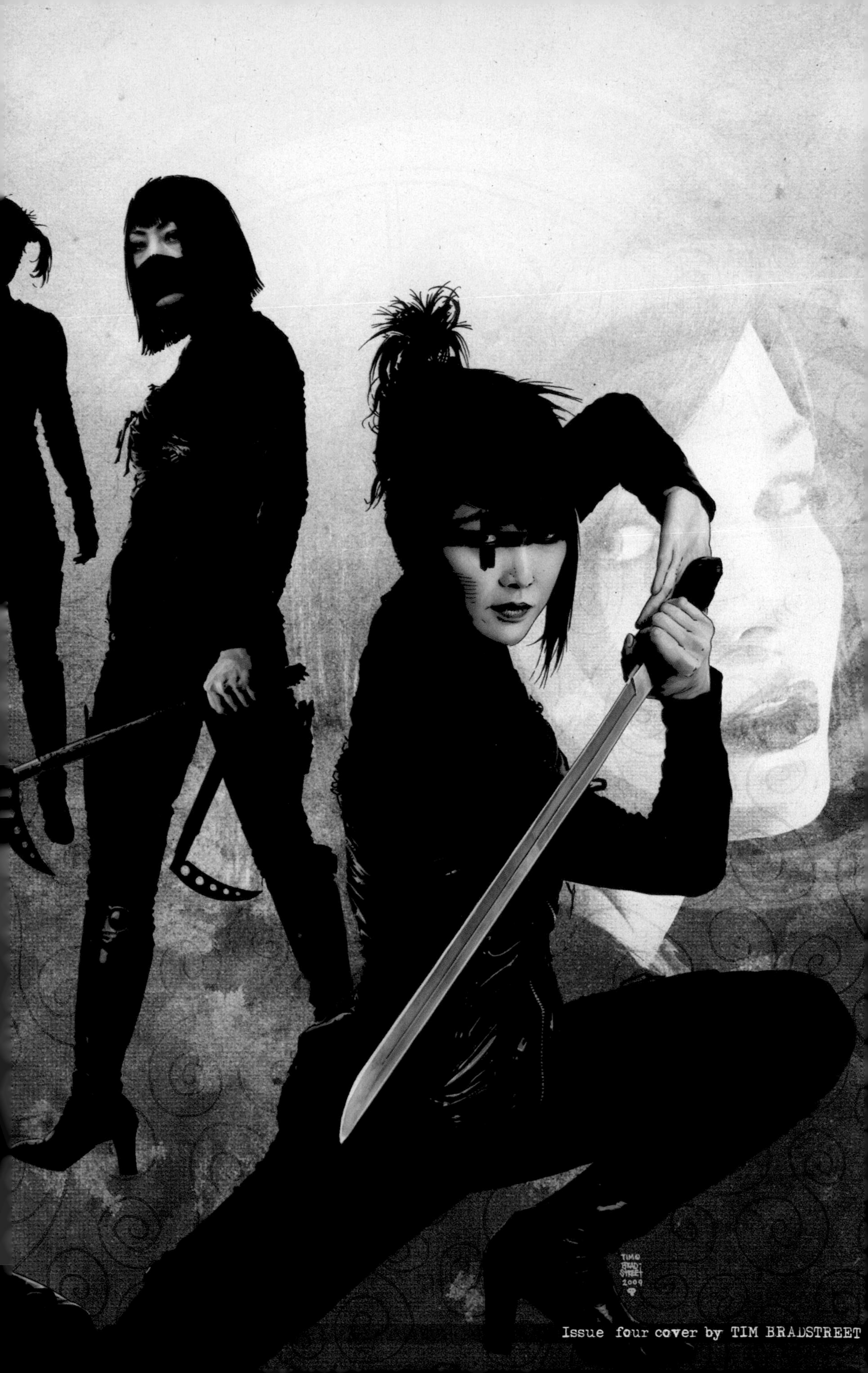
TIM BRADSTREET 2009

Issue four cover by TIM BRADSTREET

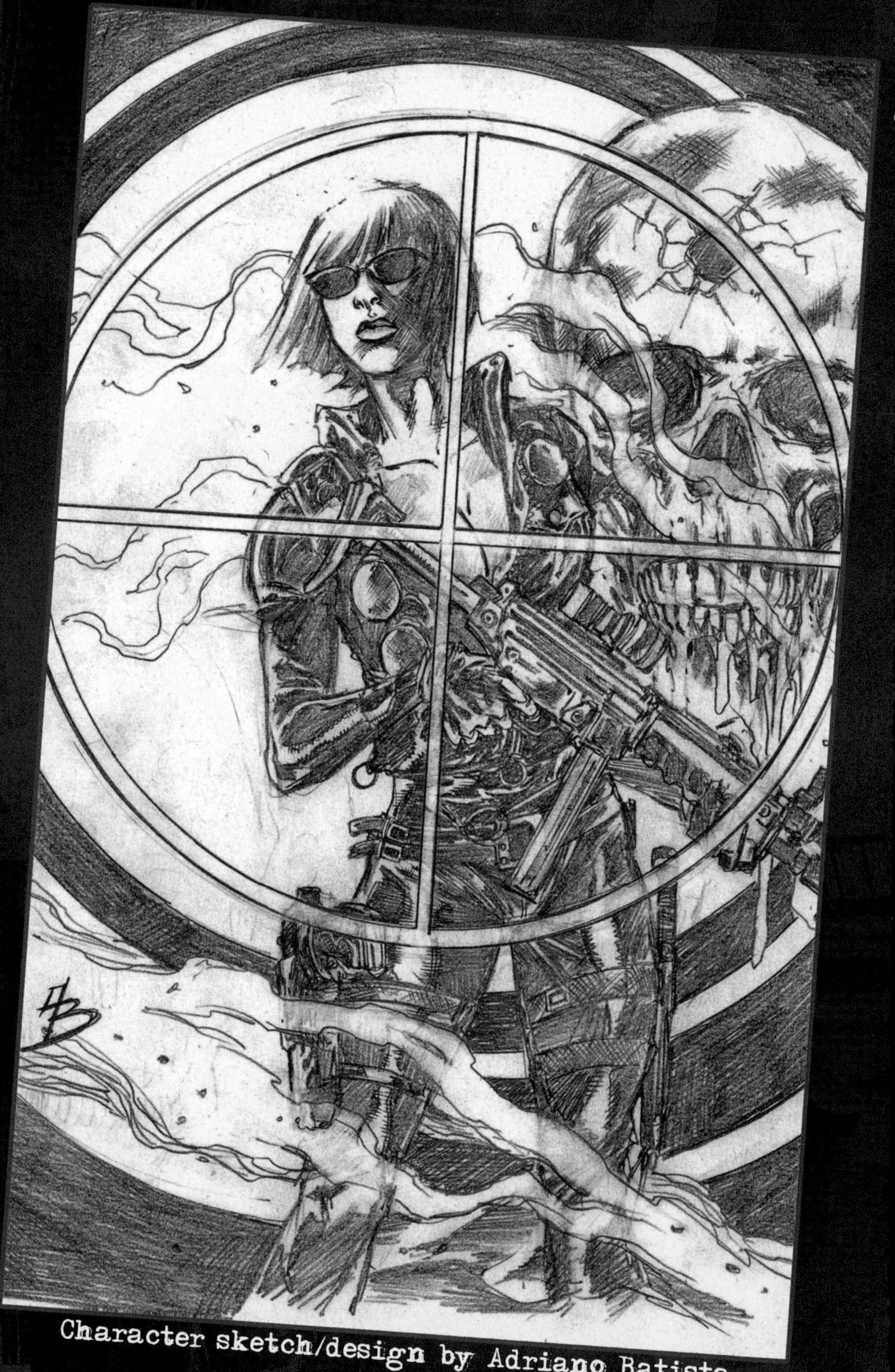

Character sketch/design by Adriano Batista

THURSDAY
HEE HEEHEEHEE HEE!
YOU BET! NINJETTES!
OH YES, WE KILL THIS JENNIFER BLOOD FOR YOU! WE DO GOOD JOB!
4: THREE LITTLE GIRLS FROM SCHOOL ARE WE

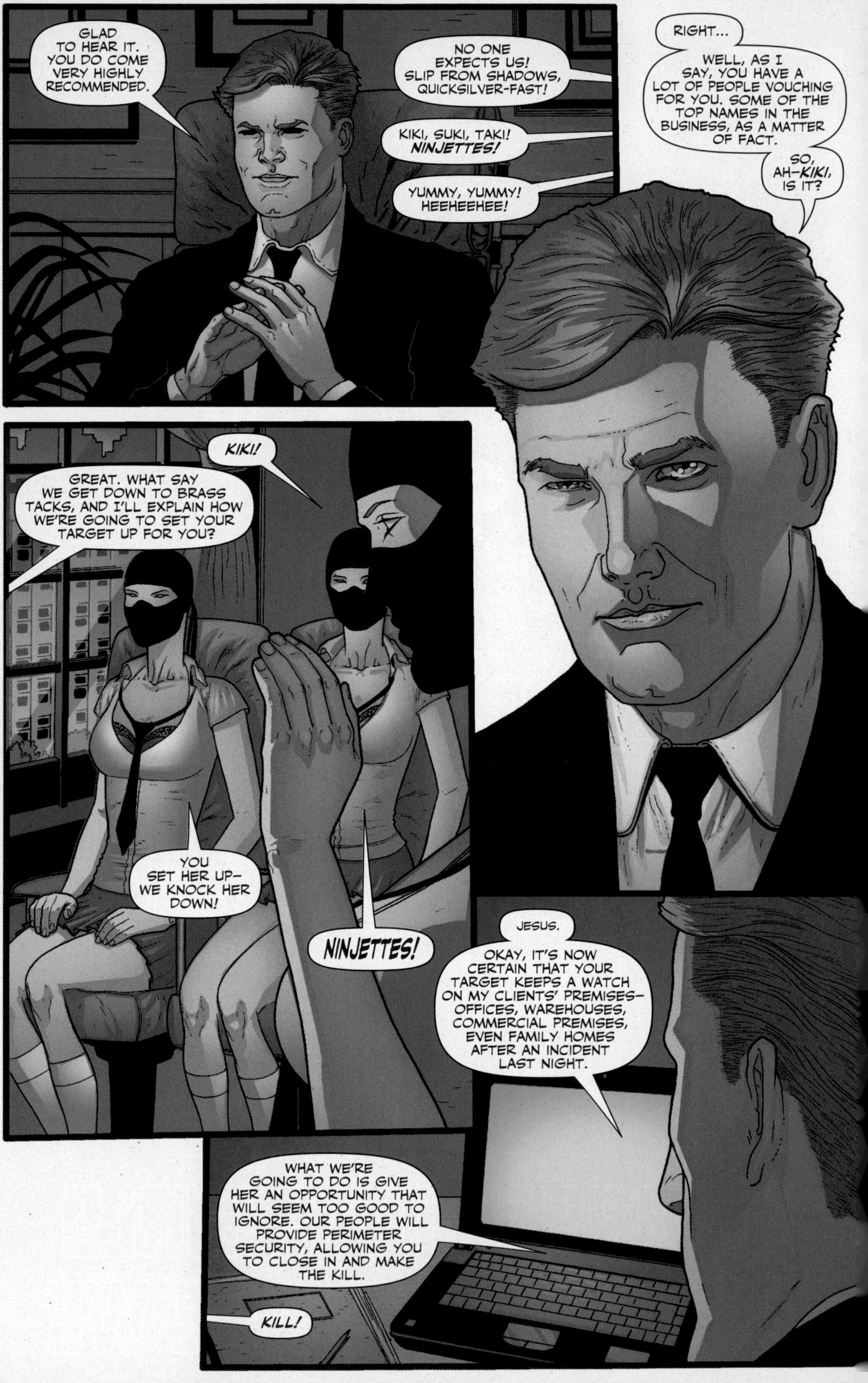
GLAD TO HEAR IT. YOU DO COME VERY HIGHLY RECOMMENDED.
NO ONE EXPECTS US! SLIP FROM SHADOWS, QUICKSILVER-FAST!
KIKI, SUKI, TAKI! *NINJETTES!*
YUMMY, YUMMY! HEEHEEHEE!
RIGHT...
WELL, AS I SAY, YOU HAVE A LOT OF PEOPLE VOUCHING FOR YOU. SOME OF THE TOP NAMES IN THE BUSINESS, AS A MATTER OF FACT.
SO, AH--*KIKI*, IS IT?
KIKI!
GREAT. WHAT SAY WE GET DOWN TO BRASS TACKS, AND I'LL EXPLAIN HOW WE'RE GOING TO SET YOUR TARGET UP FOR YOU?
YOU SET HER UP-- WE KNOCK HER DOWN!
NINJETTES!
JESUS.
OKAY, IT'S NOW CERTAIN THAT YOUR TARGET KEEPS A WATCH ON MY CLIENTS' PREMISES-- OFFICES, WAREHOUSES, COMMERCIAL PREMISES, EVEN FAMILY HOMES AFTER AN INCIDENT LAST NIGHT.
WHAT WE'RE GOING TO DO IS GIVE HER AN OPPORTUNITY THAT WILL SEEM TOO GOOD TO IGNORE. OUR PEOPLE WILL PROVIDE PERIMETER SECURITY, ALLOWING YOU TO CLOSE IN AND MAKE THE KILL.
KILL!

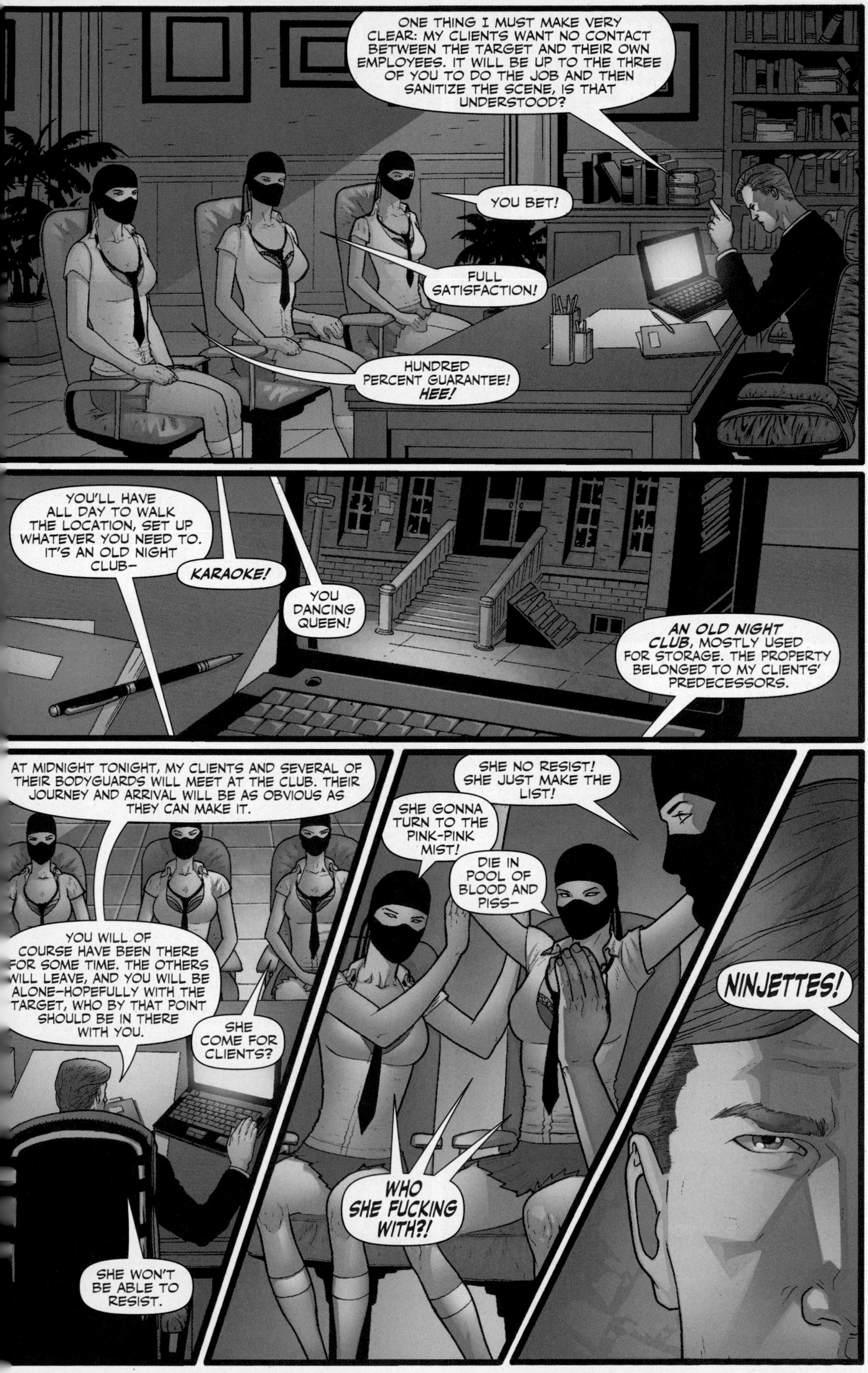

ONE THING I MUST MAKE VERY CLEAR: MY CLIENTS WANT NO CONTACT BETWEEN THE TARGET AND THEIR OWN EMPLOYEES. IT WILL BE UP TO THE THREE OF YOU TO DO THE JOB AND THEN SANITIZE THE SCENE, IS THAT UNDERSTOOD?
YOU BET!
FULL SATISFACTION!
HUNDRED PERCENT GUARANTEE! HEE!
YOU'LL HAVE ALL DAY TO WALK THE LOCATION, SET UP WHATEVER YOU NEED TO. IT'S AN OLD NIGHT CLUB–
KARAOKE!
YOU DANCING QUEEN!
AN OLD NIGHT CLUB, MOSTLY USED FOR STORAGE. THE PROPERTY BELONGED TO MY CLIENTS' PREDECESSORS.
AT MIDNIGHT TONIGHT, MY CLIENTS AND SEVERAL OF THEIR BODYGUARDS WILL MEET AT THE CLUB. THEIR JOURNEY AND ARRIVAL WILL BE AS OBVIOUS AS THEY CAN MAKE IT.
YOU WILL OF COURSE HAVE BEEN THERE FOR SOME TIME. THE OTHERS WILL LEAVE, AND YOU WILL BE ALONE–HOPEFULLY WITH THE TARGET, WHO BY THAT POINT SHOULD BE IN THERE WITH YOU.
SHE COME FOR CLIENTS?
SHE WON'T BE ABLE TO RESIST.
SHE NO RESIST! SHE JUST MAKE THE LIST!
SHE GONNA TURN TO THE PINK-PINK MIST!
DIE IN POOL OF BLOOD AND PISS–
WHO SHE FUCKING WITH?!
NINJETTES!

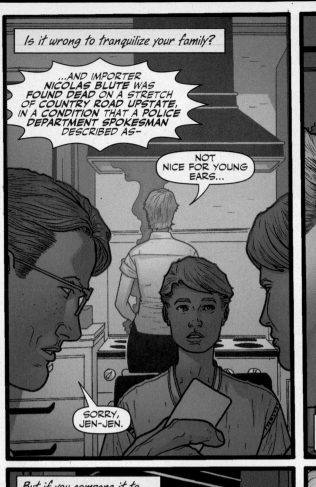

Is it wrong to tranquilize your family?

...AND IMPORTER NICOLAS BLUTE WAS FOUND DEAD ON A STRETCH OF COUNTRY ROAD UPSTATE, IN A CONDITION THAT A POLICE DEPARTMENT SPOKESMAN DESCRIBED AS—

NOT NICE FOR YOUNG EARS...

SORRY, JEN-JEN.

SEE, MARK, THE BEST THING TO DO IS CONCENTRATE ON ONE OR TWO COLORS—LIKE ALICE, SHE'S GOT ALL THE REDS AND ALL THE GREENS.

YOU'VE GOT ONE BLUE, ONE ORANGE, ONE PINK, ONE YELLOW. IF YOU DON'T COMPLETE A SET YOU CAN'T BUILD ANY HOUSES...

BUT I LIKE IT, IT'S A RAINBOW...!

I suppose it is, yes. Kind of wrong. It's been bothering me a little bit.

But if you compare it to, say, a sustained campaign of murder and terror resulting in the deaths of dozens of people— well, then it doesn't seem quite so bad.

And seeing as the whole point of doping the family is to prevent them finding out about the murder and terror- specifically that you're the one responsible- then you could almost call it positive.

And it is only temporary.

And they do get a good night's sleep.

So scale of one to ten, where ten is gutting your uncle and using his viscera to spell out your initials?

READY...!

YAY!

Barely even two, if you ask me.

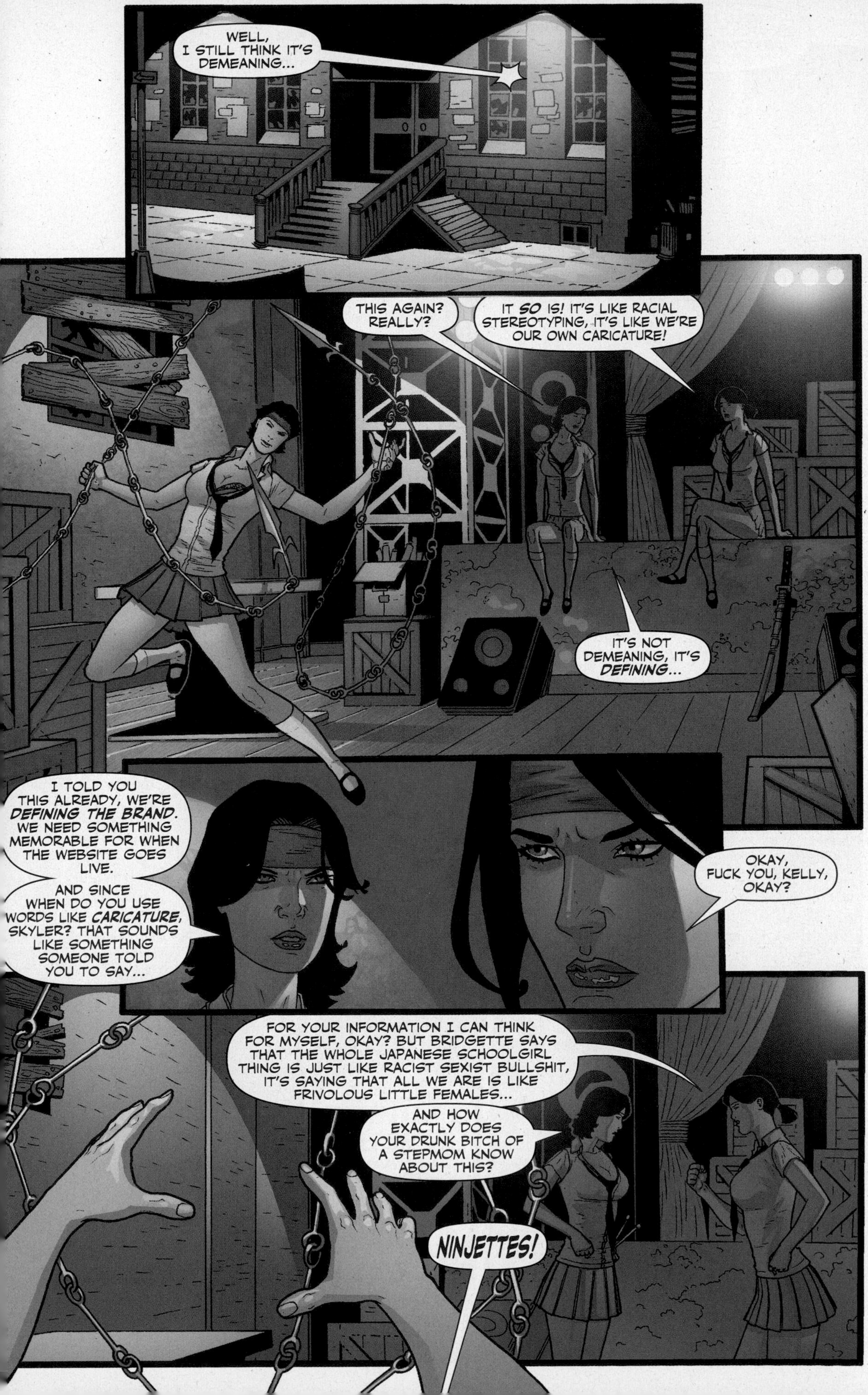
WELL, I STILL THINK IT'S DEMEANING...
THIS AGAIN? REALLY?
IT *SO* IS! IT'S LIKE RACIAL STEREOTYPING, IT'S LIKE WE'RE OUR OWN CARICATURE!
IT'S NOT DEMEANING, IT'S *DEFINING*...
I TOLD YOU THIS ALREADY, WE'RE ***DEFINING THE BRAND***. WE NEED SOMETHING MEMORABLE FOR WHEN THE WEBSITE GOES LIVE.
AND SINCE WHEN DO YOU USE WORDS LIKE *CARICATURE*, SKYLER? THAT SOUNDS LIKE SOMETHING SOMEONE TOLD YOU TO SAY...
OKAY, FUCK YOU, KELLY, OKAY?
FOR YOUR INFORMATION I CAN THINK FOR MYSELF, OKAY? BUT BRIDGETTE SAYS THAT THE WHOLE JAPANESE SCHOOLGIRL THING IS JUST LIKE RACIST SEXIST BULLSHIT, IT'S SAYING THAT ALL WE ARE IS LIKE FRIVOLOUS LITTLE FEMALES...
AND HOW EXACTLY DOES YOUR DRUNK BITCH OF A STEPMOM KNOW ABOUT THIS?
NINJETTES!

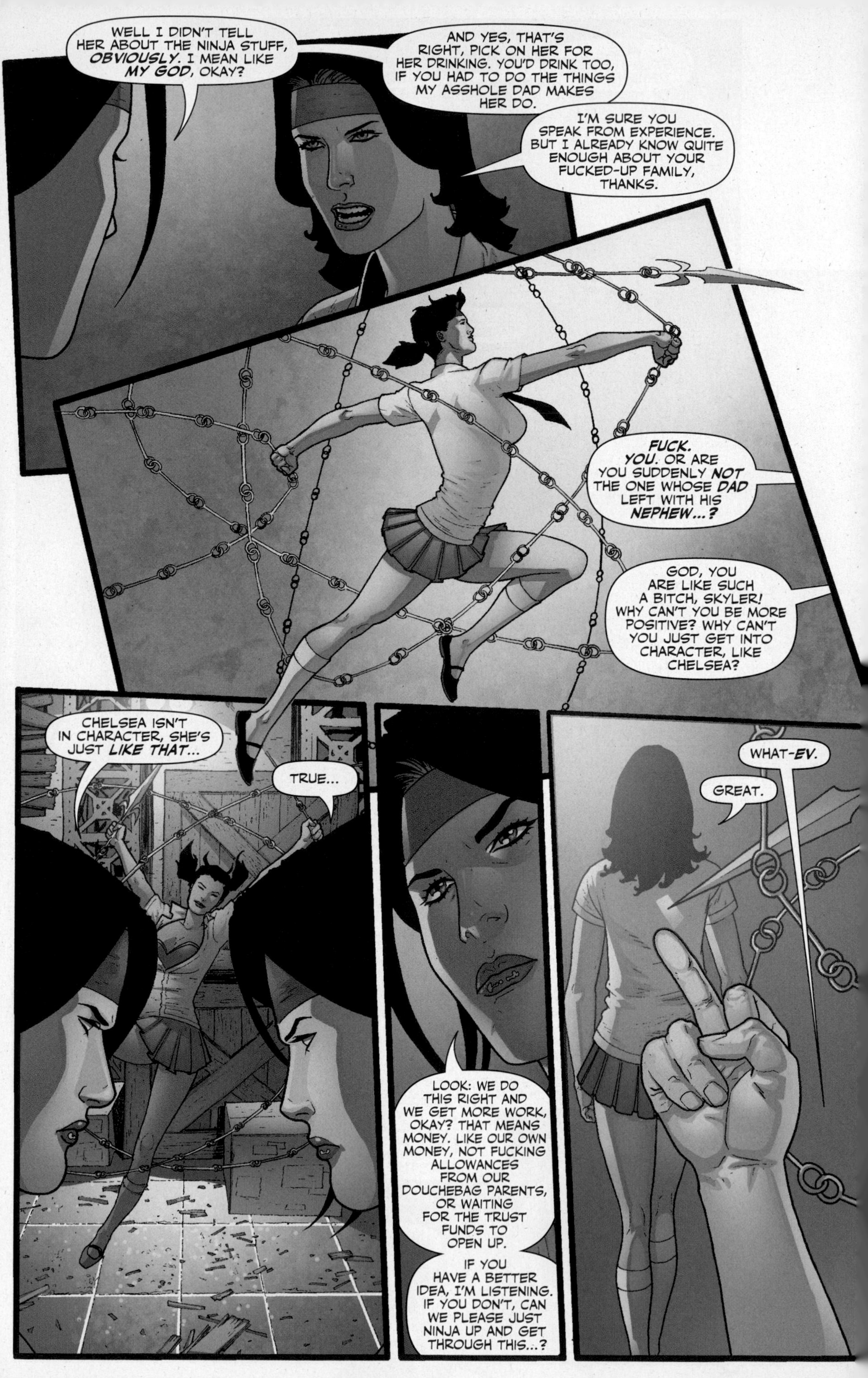
WELL I DIDN'T TELL HER ABOUT THE NINJA STUFF, *OBVIOUSLY*. I MEAN LIKE *MY GOD*, OKAY?
AND YES, THAT'S RIGHT, PICK ON HER FOR HER DRINKING. YOU'D DRINK TOO, IF YOU HAD TO DO THE THINGS MY ASSHOLE DAD MAKES HER DO.
I'M SURE YOU SPEAK FROM EXPERIENCE. BUT I ALREADY KNOW QUITE ENOUGH ABOUT YOUR FUCKED-UP FAMILY, THANKS.
FUCK. YOU. OR ARE YOU SUDDENLY *NOT* THE ONE WHOSE *DAD* LEFT WITH HIS *NEPHEW...?*
GOD, YOU ARE LIKE SUCH A BITCH, SKYLER! WHY CAN'T YOU BE MORE POSITIVE? WHY CAN'T YOU JUST GET INTO CHARACTER, LIKE CHELSEA?
CHELSEA ISN'T IN CHARACTER, SHE'S JUST *LIKE THAT*...
TRUE...
LOOK: WE DO THIS RIGHT AND WE GET MORE WORK, OKAY? THAT MEANS MONEY. LIKE OUR OWN MONEY, NOT FUCKING ALLOWANCES FROM OUR DOUCHEBAG PARENTS, OR WAITING FOR THE TRUST FUNDS TO OPEN UP.
IF YOU HAVE A BETTER IDEA, I'M LISTENING. IF YOU DON'T, CAN WE PLEASE JUST NINJA UP AND GET THROUGH THIS...?
WHAT-*EV*.
GREAT.

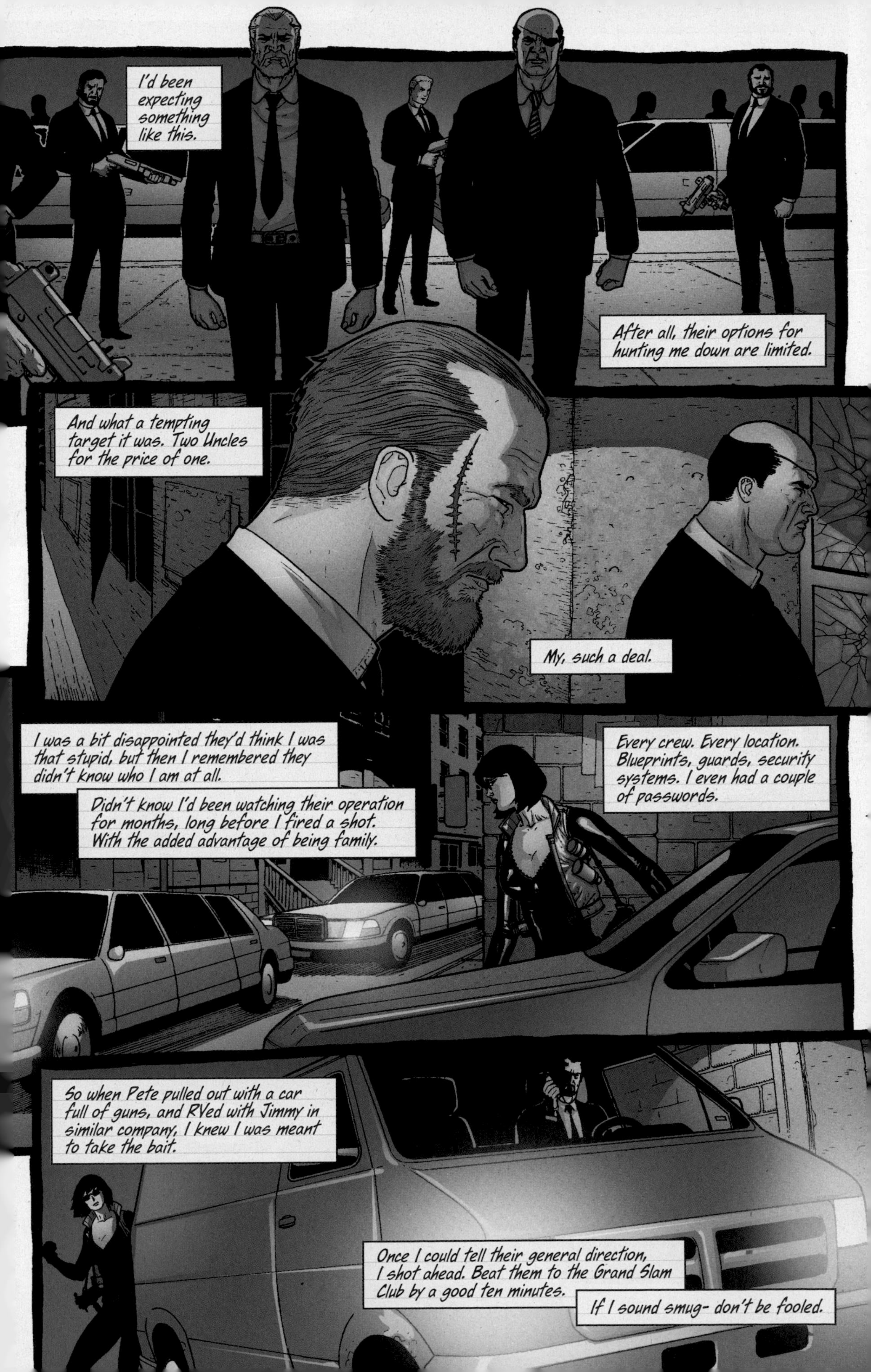
I'd been expecting something like this.
After all, their options for hunting me down are limited.
And what a tempting target it was. Two Uncles for the price of one.
My, such a deal.
I was a bit disappointed they'd think I was that stupid, but then I remembered they didn't know who I am at all.
Didn't know I'd been watching their operation for months, long before I fired a shot. With the added advantage of being family.
Every crew. Every location. Blueprints, guards, security systems. I even had a couple of passwords.
So when Pete pulled out with a car full of guns, and RVed with Jimmy in similar company, I knew I was meant to take the bait.
Once I could tell their general direction, I shot ahead. Beat them to the Grand Slam Club by a good ten minutes.
If I sound smug- don't be fooled.

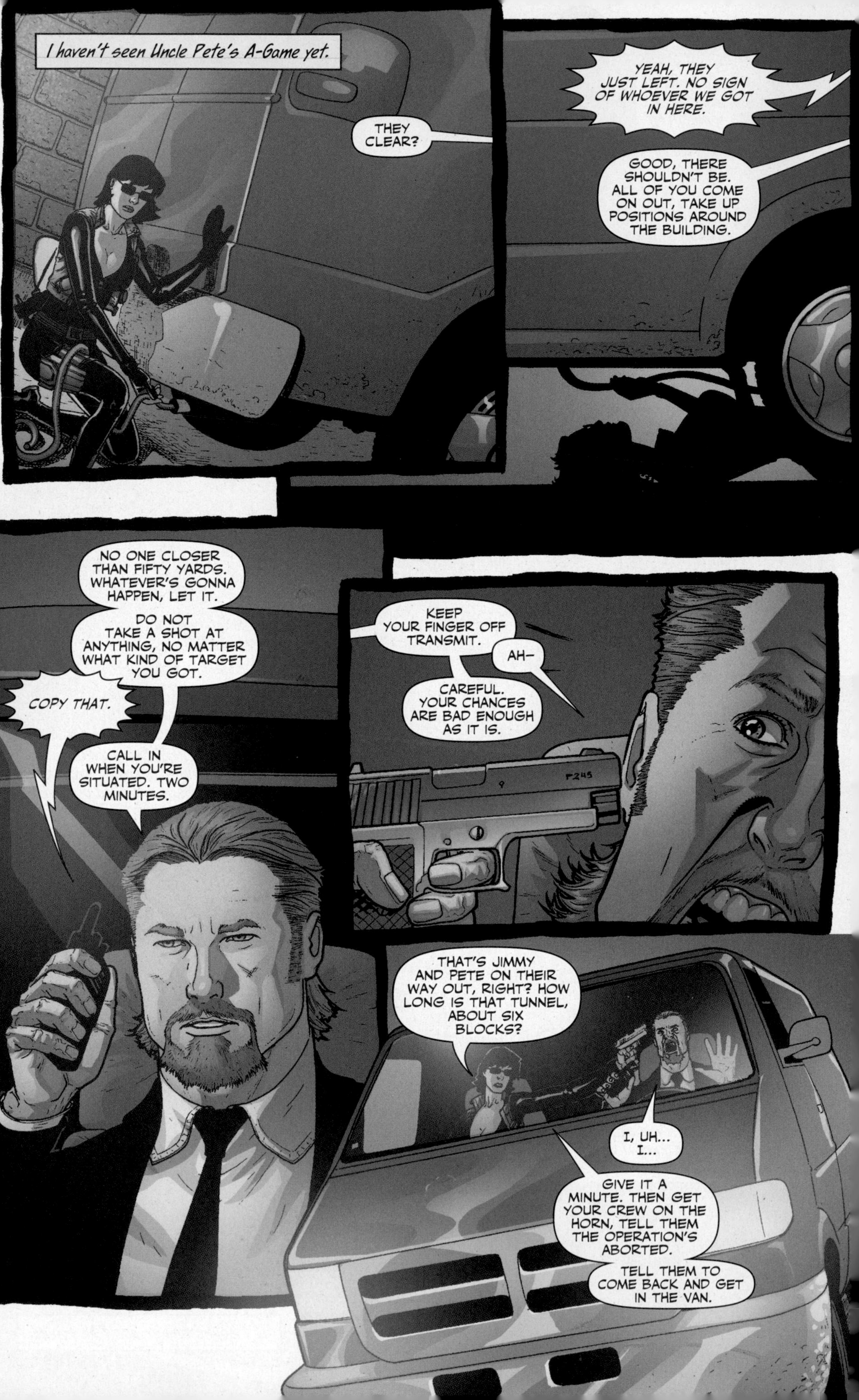
I haven't seen Uncle Pete's A-Game yet.
THEY CLEAR?
YEAH, THEY JUST LEFT. NO SIGN OF WHOEVER WE GOT IN HERE.
GOOD, THERE SHOULDN'T BE. ALL OF YOU COME ON OUT, TAKE UP POSITIONS AROUND THE BUILDING.
NO ONE CLOSER THAN FIFTY YARDS. WHATEVER'S GONNA HAPPEN, LET IT.
DO NOT TAKE A SHOT AT ANYTHING, NO MATTER WHAT KIND OF TARGET YOU GOT.
COPY THAT.
CALL IN WHEN YOU'RE SITUATED. TWO MINUTES.
KEEP YOUR FINGER OFF TRANSMIT.
AH–
CAREFUL. YOUR CHANCES ARE BAD ENOUGH AS IT IS.
THAT'S JIMMY AND PETE ON THEIR WAY OUT, RIGHT? HOW LONG IS THAT TUNNEL, ABOUT SIX BLOCKS?
I, UH... I...
GIVE IT A MINUTE. THEN GET YOUR CREW ON THE HORN, TELL THEM THE OPERATION'S ABORTED.
TELL THEM TO COME BACK AND GET IN THE VAN.

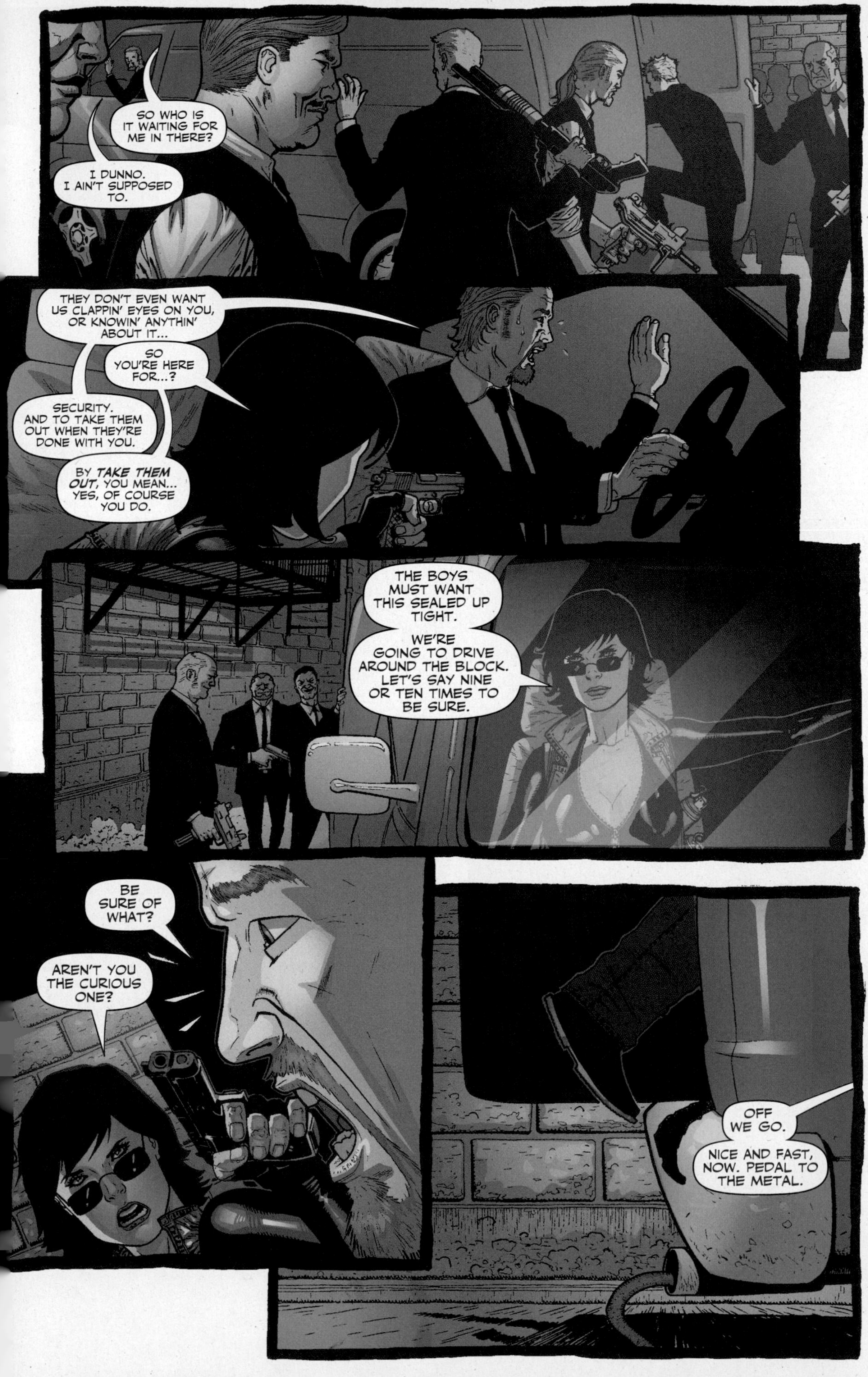
SO WHO IS IT WAITING FOR ME IN THERE?
I DUNNO. I AIN'T SUPPOSED TO.
THEY DON'T EVEN WANT US CLAPPIN' EYES ON YOU, OR KNOWIN' ANYTHIN' ABOUT IT...
SO YOU'RE HERE FOR...?
SECURITY. AND TO TAKE THEM OUT WHEN THEY'RE DONE WITH YOU.
BY *TAKE THEM OUT*, YOU MEAN... YES, OF COURSE YOU DO.
THE BOYS MUST WANT THIS SEALED UP TIGHT.
WE'RE GOING TO DRIVE AROUND THE BLOCK. LET'S SAY NINE OR TEN TIMES TO BE SURE.
BE SURE OF WHAT?
AREN'T YOU THE CURIOUS ONE?
OFF WE GO.
NICE AND FAST, NOW. PEDAL TO THE METAL.

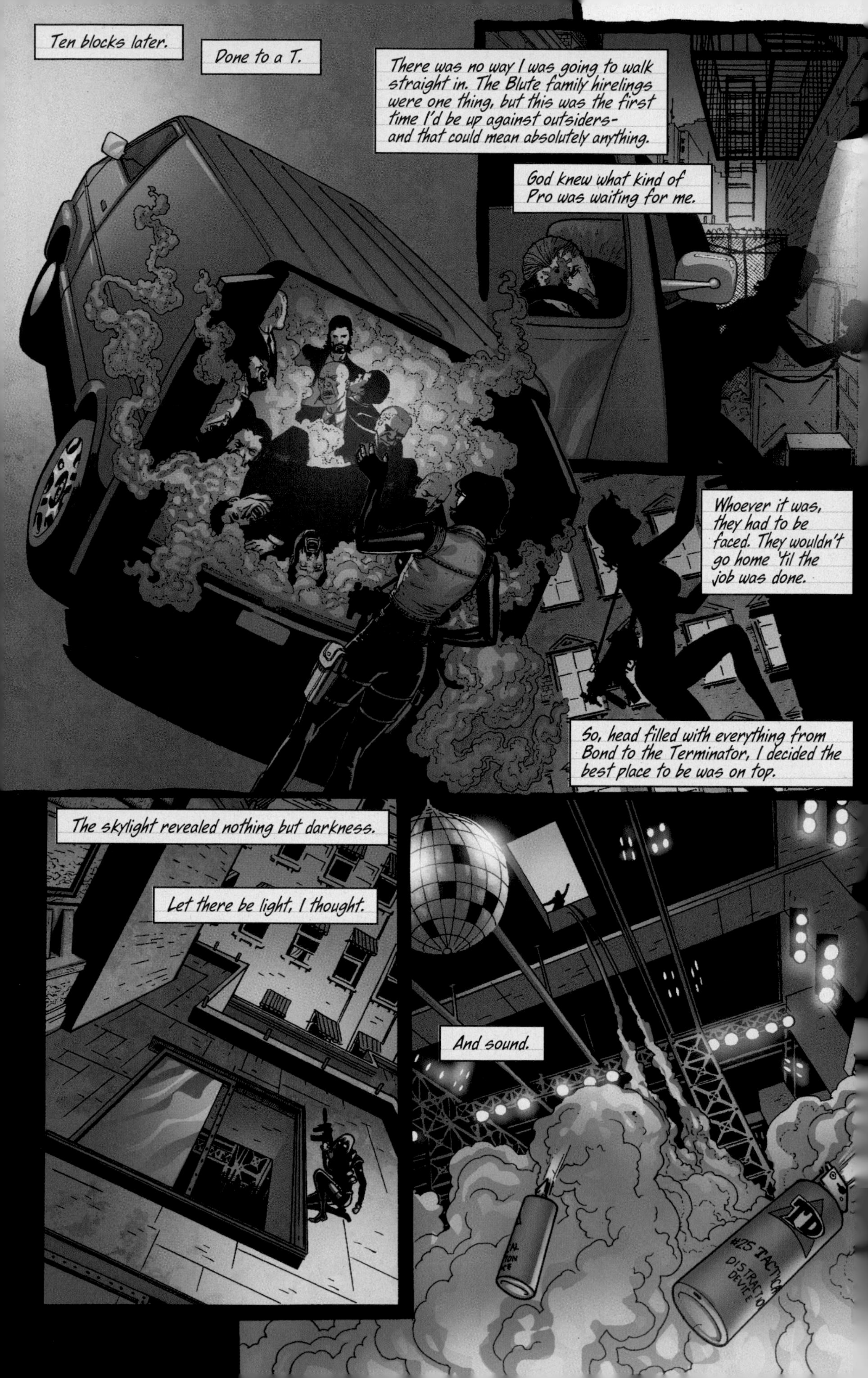
Ten blocks later.
Done to a T.
There was no way I was going to walk straight in. The Blute family hirelings were one thing, but this was the first time I'd be up against outsiders- and that could mean absolutely anything.
God knew what kind of Pro was waiting for me.
Whoever it was, they had to be faced. They wouldn't go home 'til the job was done.
So, head filled with everything from Bond to the Terminator, I decided the best place to be was on top.
The skylight revealed nothing but darkness.
Let there be light, I thought.
And sound.

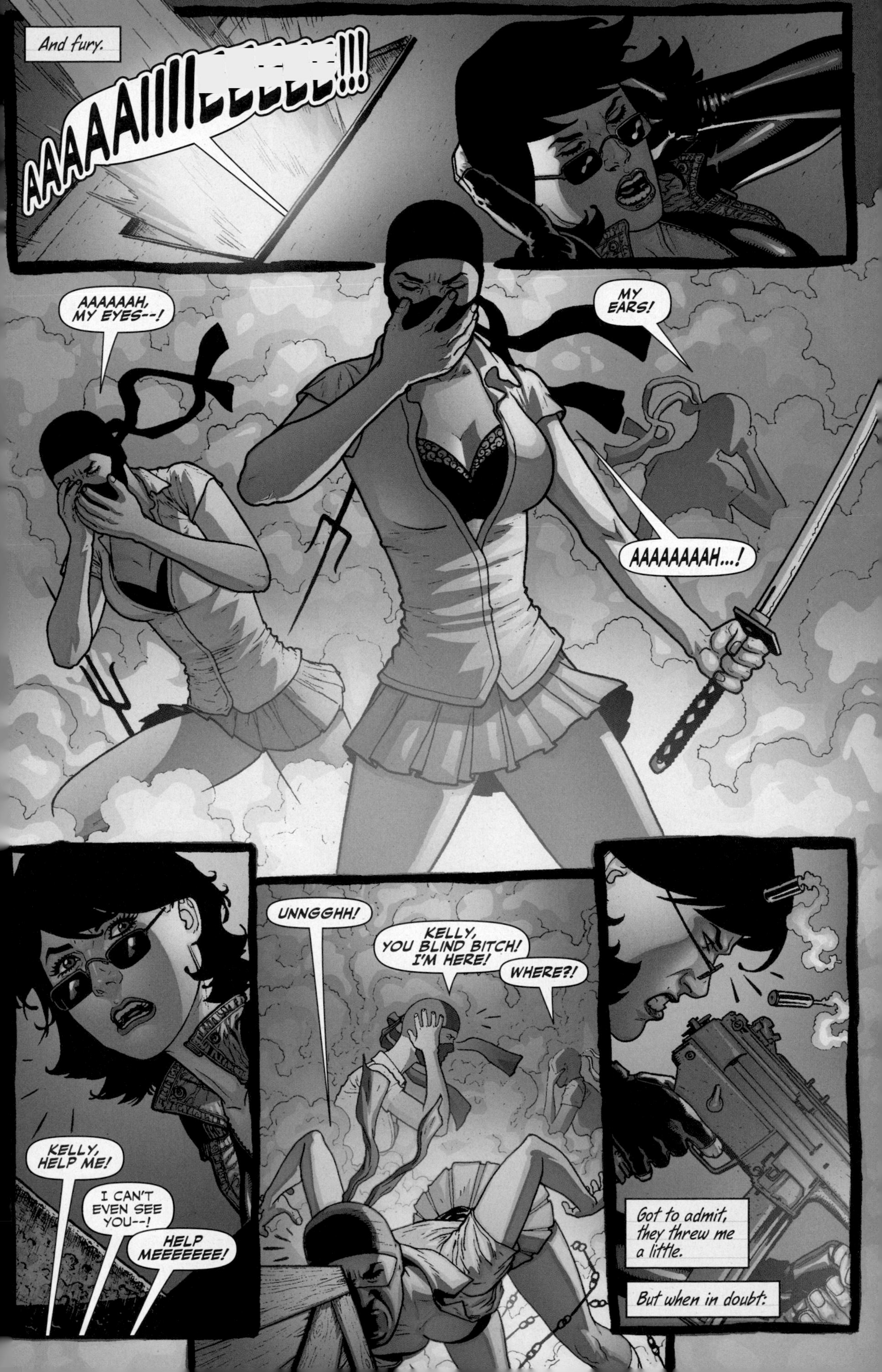
And fury.
AAAAAIIIII
AAAAAAH, MY EYES--!
MY EARS!
AAAAAAAAH...!
KELLY, HELP ME!
I CAN'T EVEN SEE YOU--!
HELP MEEEEEEE!
UNNGGHH!
KELLY, YOU BLIND BITCH! I'M HERE!
WHERE?!
Got to admit, they threw me a little.
But when in doubt:

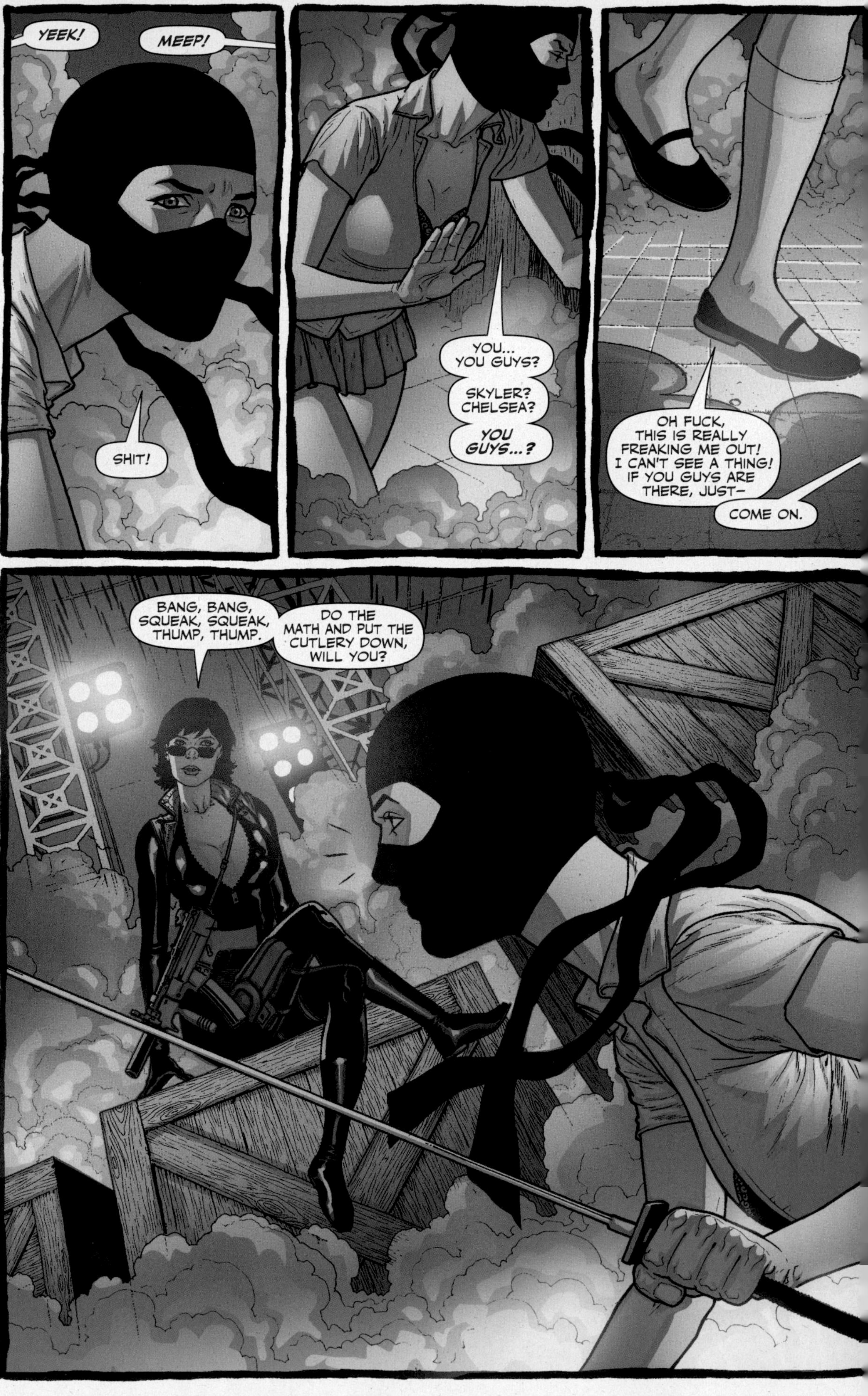
YEEK!
MEEP!
SHIT!
YOU... YOU GUYS?
SKYLER? CHELSEA?
YOU GUYS...?
OH FUCK, THIS IS REALLY FREAKING ME OUT! I CAN'T SEE A THING! IF YOU GUYS ARE THERE, JUST–
COME ON.
BANG, BANG, SQUEAK, SQUEAK, THUMP, THUMP.
DO THE MATH AND PUT THE CUTLERY DOWN, WILL YOU?

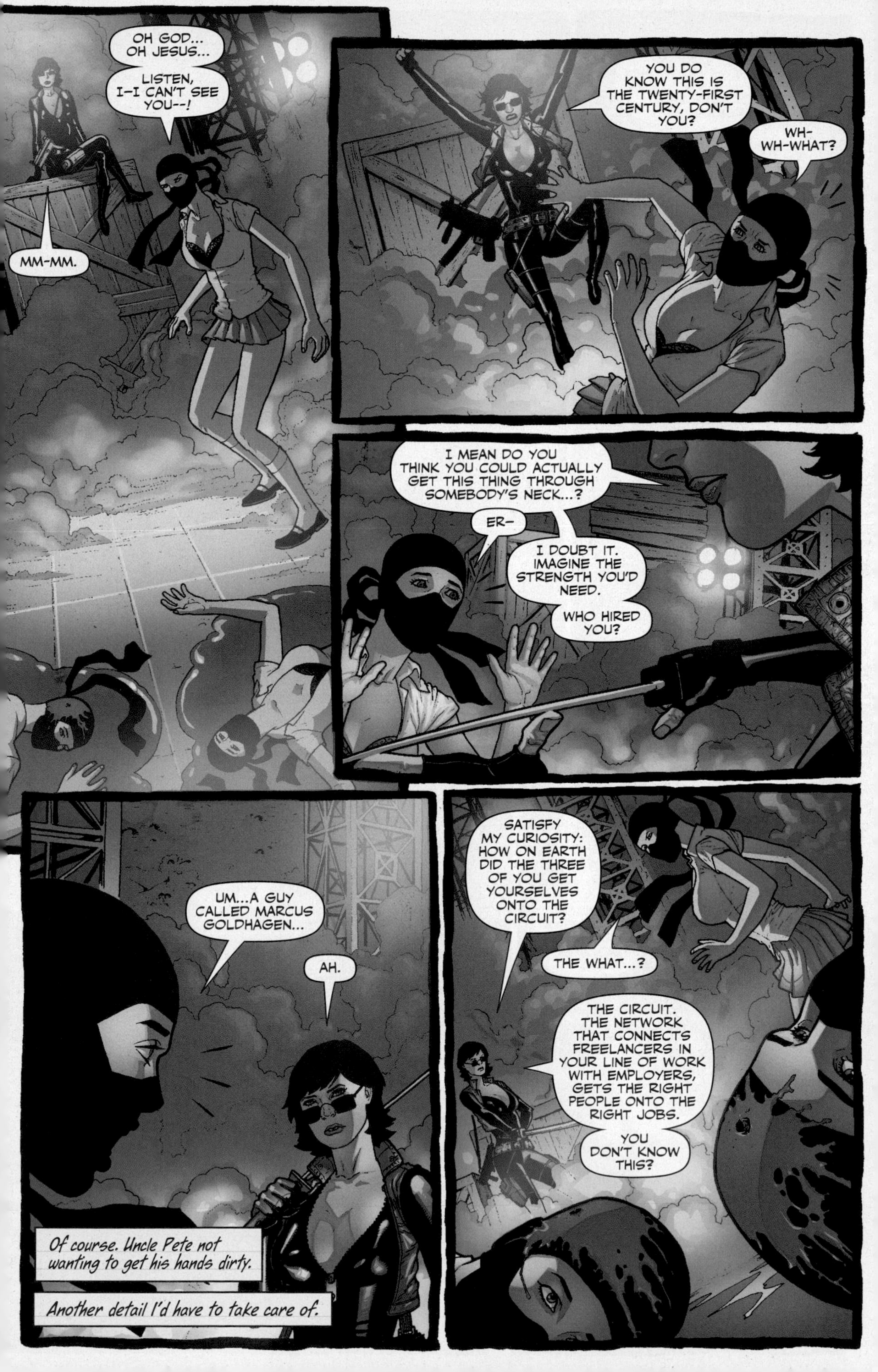
OH GOD... OH JESUS...
LISTEN, I--I CAN'T SEE YOU--!
MM-MM.
YOU DO KNOW THIS IS THE TWENTY-FIRST CENTURY, DON'T YOU?
WH- WH-WHAT?
I MEAN DO YOU THINK YOU COULD ACTUALLY GET THIS THING THROUGH SOMEBODY'S NECK...?
ER-
I DOUBT IT. IMAGINE THE STRENGTH YOU'D NEED.
WHO HIRED YOU?
UM...A GUY CALLED MARCUS GOLDHAGEN...
AH.
Of course. Uncle Pete not wanting to get his hands dirty.
Another detail I'd have to take care of.
SATISFY MY CURIOSITY: HOW ON EARTH DID THE THREE OF YOU GET YOURSELVES ONTO THE CIRCUIT?
THE WHAT...?
THE CIRCUIT. THE NETWORK THAT CONNECTS FREELANCERS IN YOUR LINE OF WORK WITH EMPLOYERS, GETS THE RIGHT PEOPLE ONTO THE RIGHT JOBS.
YOU DON'T KNOW THIS?

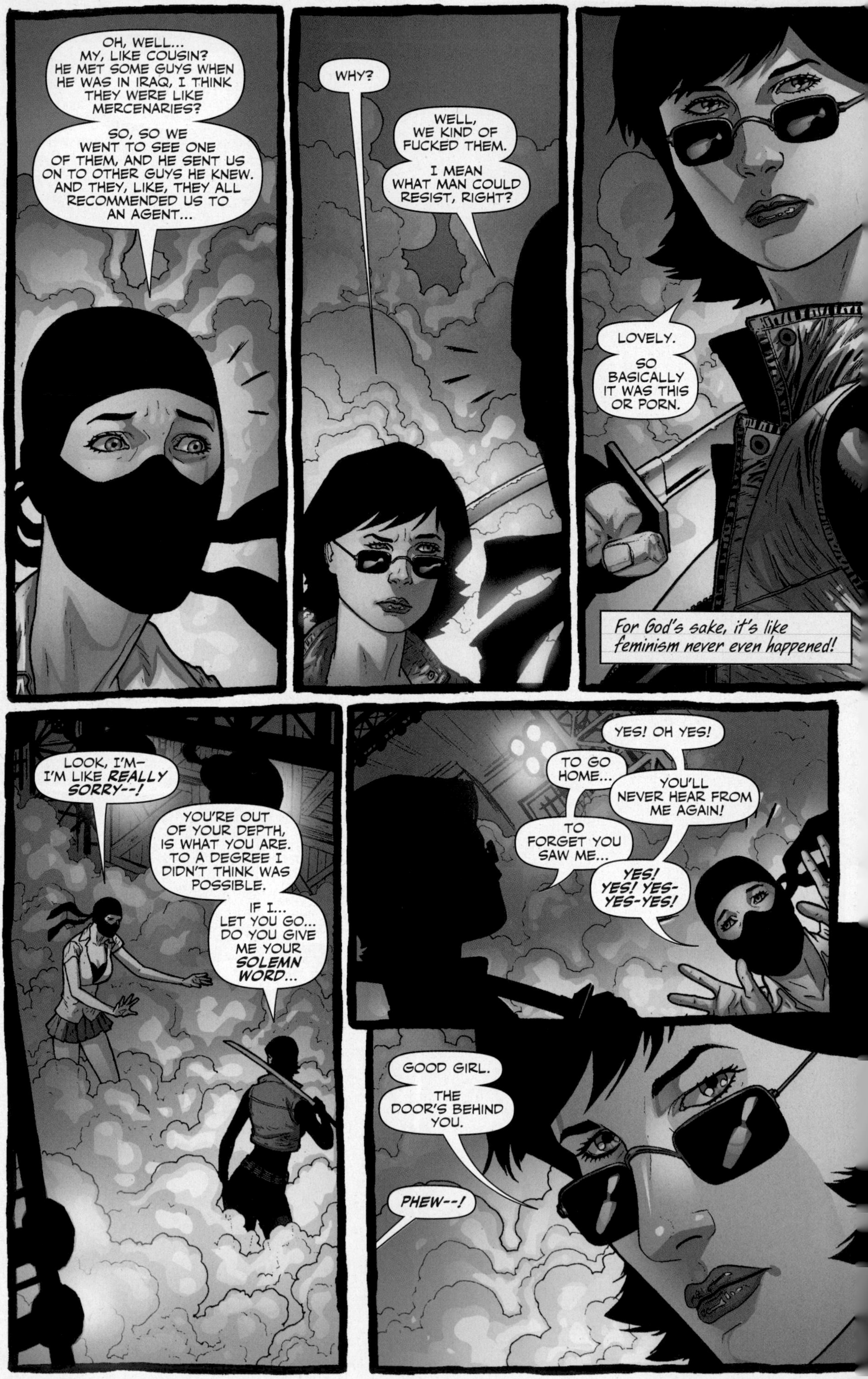
OH, WELL... MY, LIKE COUSIN? HE MET SOME GUYS WHEN HE WAS IN IRAQ, I THINK THEY WERE LIKE MERCENARIES?
SO, SO WE WENT TO SEE ONE OF THEM, AND HE SENT US ON TO OTHER GUYS HE KNEW. AND THEY, LIKE, THEY ALL RECOMMENDED US TO AN AGENT...
WHY?
WELL, WE KIND OF FUCKED THEM.
I MEAN WHAT MAN COULD RESIST, RIGHT?
LOVELY.
SO BASICALLY IT WAS THIS OR PORN.
For God's sake, it's like feminism never even happened!
LOOK, I'M– I'M LIKE REALLY SORRY--!
YOU'RE OUT OF YOUR DEPTH, IS WHAT YOU ARE. TO A DEGREE I DIDN'T THINK WAS POSSIBLE.
IF I... LET YOU GO... DO YOU GIVE ME YOUR SOLEMN WORD...
YES! OH YES!
TO GO HOME...
YOU'LL NEVER HEAR FROM ME AGAIN!
TO FORGET YOU SAW ME...
YES! YES! YES-YES-YES!
GOOD GIRL.
THE DOOR'S BEHIND YOU.
PHEW--!

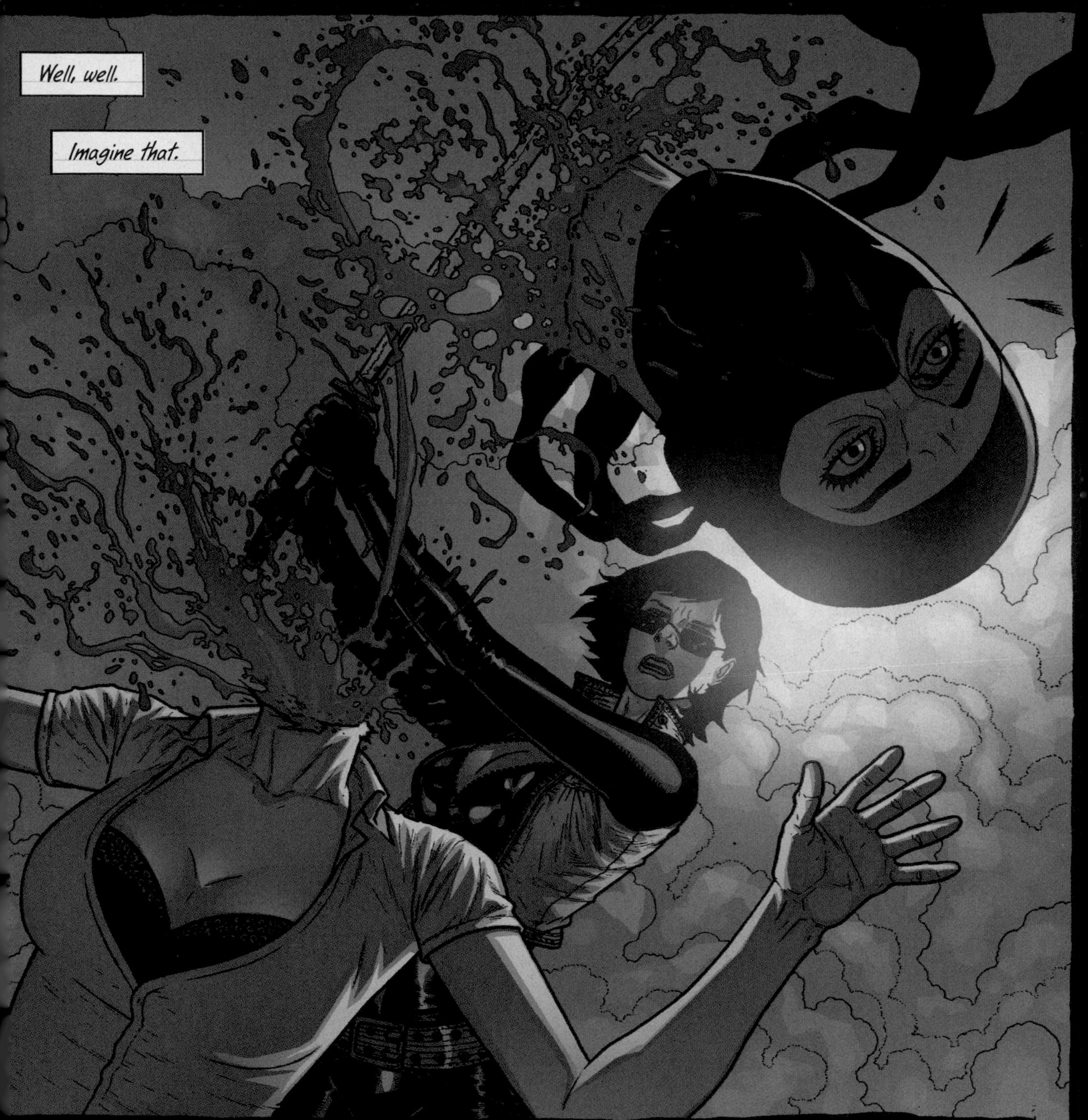
Well, well.
Imagine that.
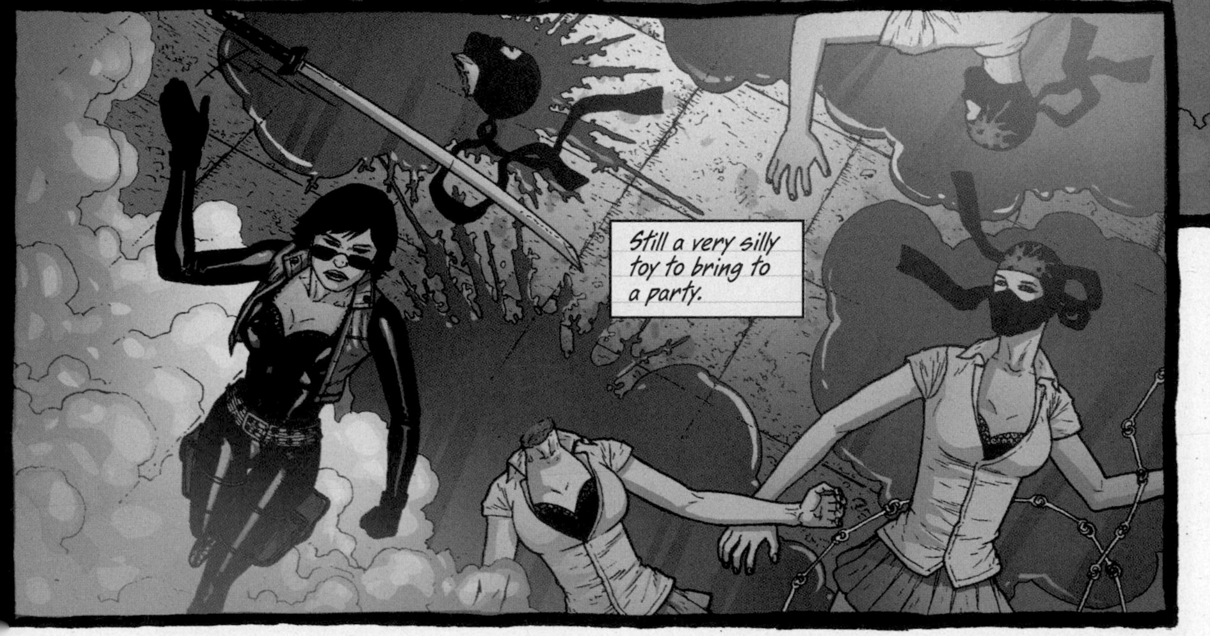
Still a very silly toy to bring to a party.

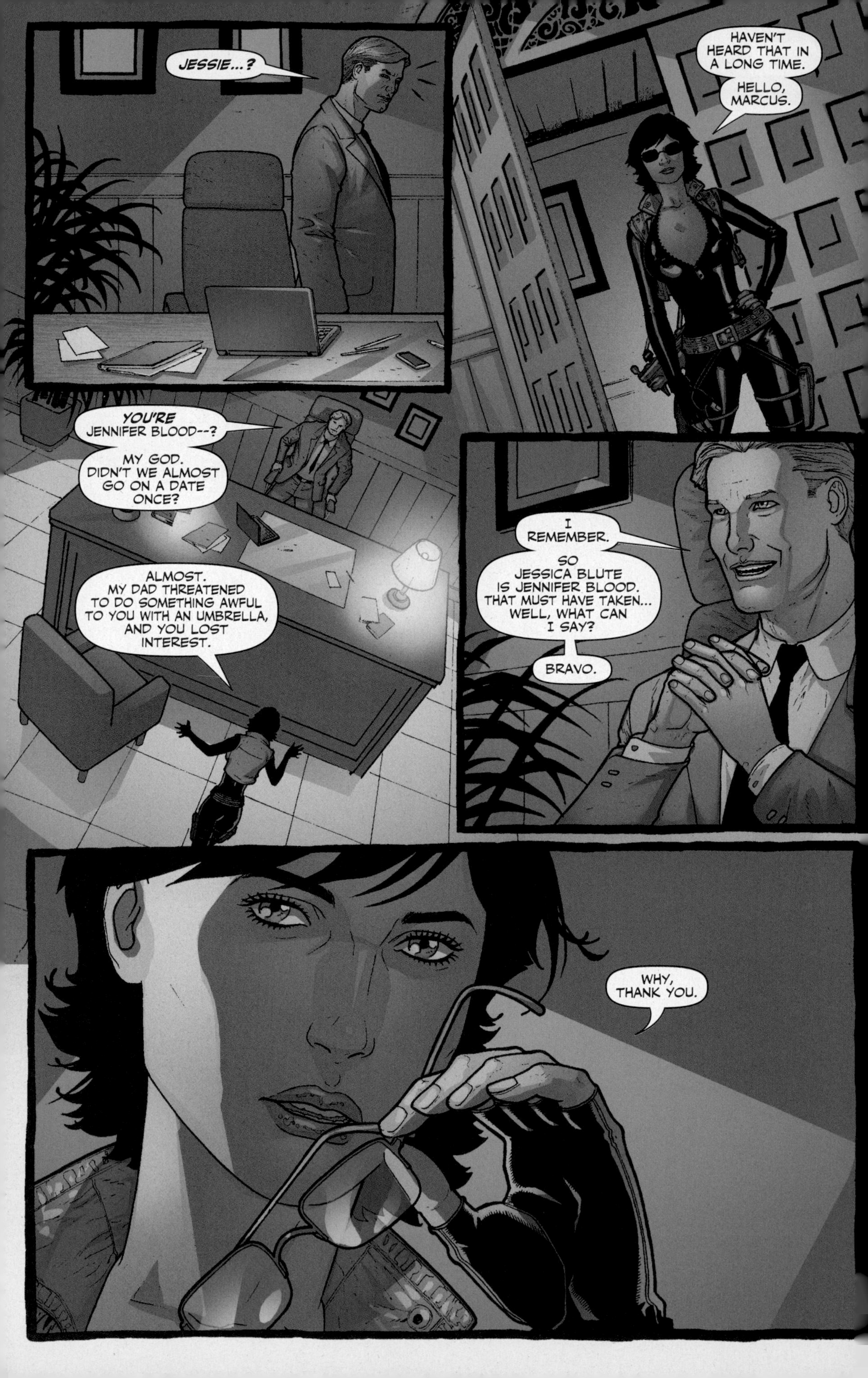
JESSIE...?
HAVEN'T HEARD THAT IN A LONG TIME.
HELLO, MARCUS.
YOU'RE JENNIFER BLOOD--?
MY GOD. DIDN'T WE ALMOST GO ON A DATE ONCE?
ALMOST. MY DAD THREATENED TO DO SOMETHING AWFUL TO YOU WITH AN UMBRELLA, AND YOU LOST INTEREST.
I REMEMBER.
SO JESSICA BLUTE IS JENNIFER BLOOD. THAT MUST HAVE TAKEN... WELL, WHAT CAN I SAY?
BRAVO.
WHY, THANK YOU.

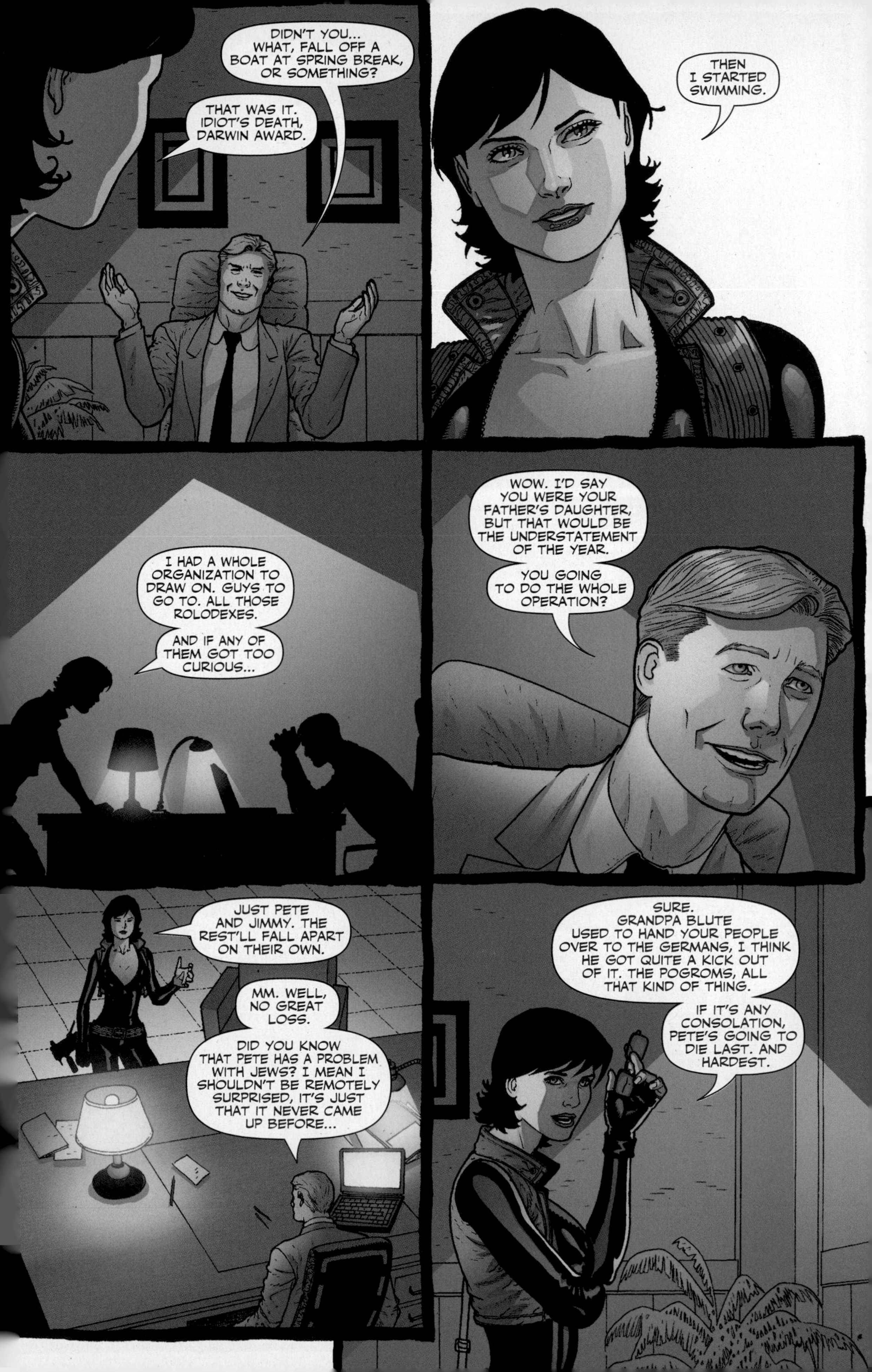
DIDN'T YOU... WHAT, FALL OFF A BOAT AT SPRING BREAK, OR SOMETHING?
THAT WAS IT. IDIOT'S DEATH, DARWIN AWARD.
THEN I STARTED SWIMMING.
I HAD A WHOLE ORGANIZATION TO DRAW ON. GUYS TO GO TO. ALL THOSE ROLODEXES.
AND IF ANY OF THEM GOT TOO CURIOUS...
WOW. I'D SAY YOU WERE YOUR FATHER'S DAUGHTER, BUT THAT WOULD BE THE UNDERSTATEMENT OF THE YEAR.
YOU GOING TO DO THE WHOLE OPERATION?
JUST PETE AND JIMMY. THE REST'LL FALL APART ON THEIR OWN.
MM. WELL, NO GREAT LOSS.
DID YOU KNOW THAT PETE HAS A PROBLEM WITH JEWS? I MEAN I SHOULDN'T BE REMOTELY SURPRISED, IT'S JUST THAT IT NEVER CAME UP BEFORE...
SURE. GRANDPA BLUTE USED TO HAND YOUR PEOPLE OVER TO THE GERMANS, I THINK HE GOT QUITE A KICK OUT OF IT. THE POGROMS, ALL THAT KIND OF THING.
IF IT'S ANY CONSOLATION, PETE'S GOING TO DIE LAST. AND HARDEST.

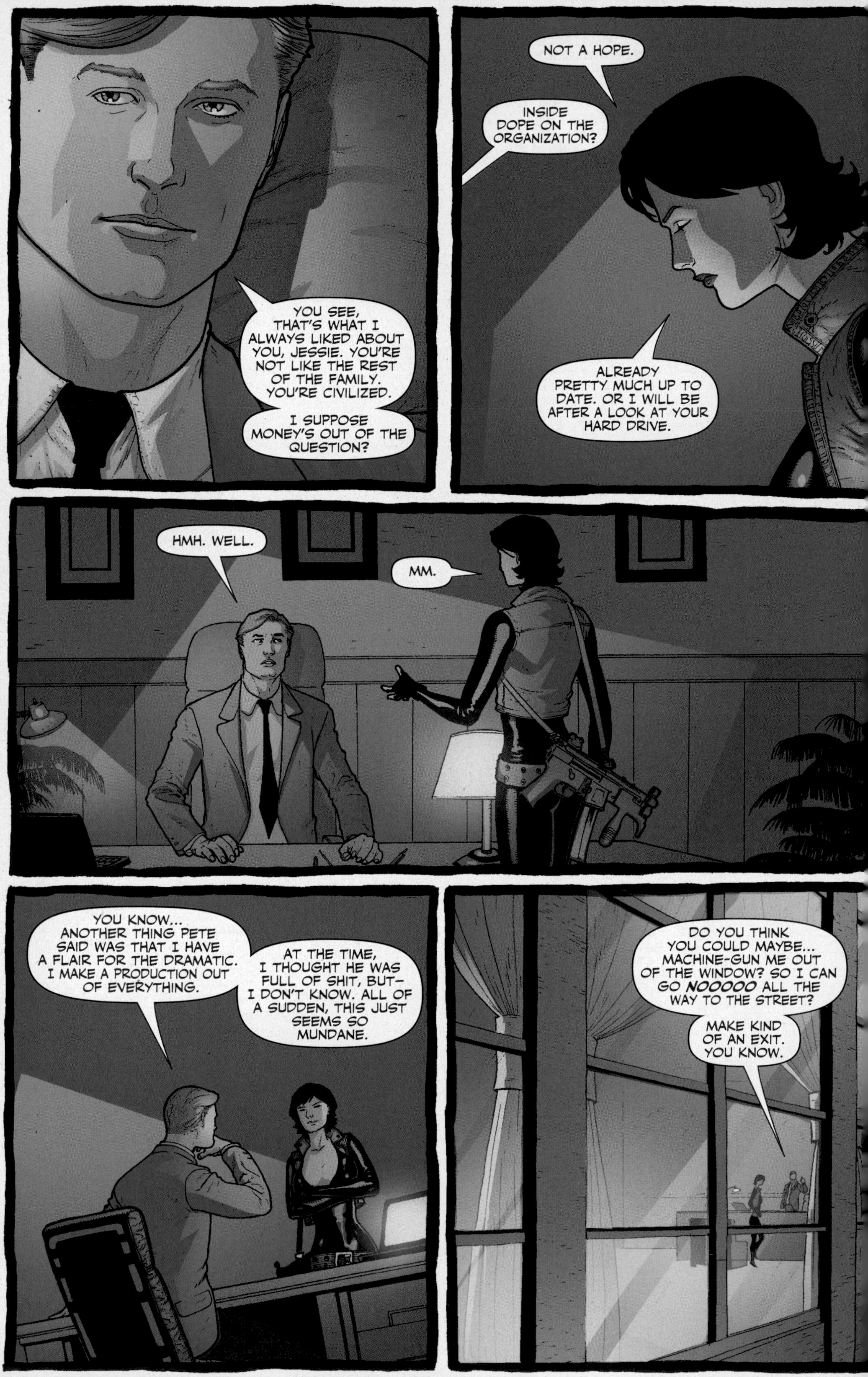
YOU SEE, THAT'S WHAT I ALWAYS LIKED ABOUT YOU, JESSIE. YOU'RE NOT LIKE THE REST OF THE FAMILY. YOU'RE CIVILIZED.
I SUPPOSE MONEY'S OUT OF THE QUESTION?
NOT A HOPE.
INSIDE DOPE ON THE ORGANIZATION?
ALREADY PRETTY MUCH UP TO DATE. OR I WILL BE AFTER A LOOK AT YOUR HARD DRIVE.
HMH. WELL.
MM.
YOU KNOW... ANOTHER THING PETE SAID WAS THAT I HAVE A FLAIR FOR THE DRAMATIC. I MAKE A PRODUCTION OUT OF EVERYTHING.
AT THE TIME, I THOUGHT HE WAS FULL OF SHIT, BUT– I DON'T KNOW. ALL OF A SUDDEN, THIS JUST SEEMS SO MUNDANE.
DO YOU THINK YOU COULD MAYBE... MACHINE-GUN ME OUT OF THE WINDOW? SO I CAN GO *NOOOOO* ALL THE WAY TO THE STREET?
MAKE KIND OF AN EXIT. YOU KNOW.

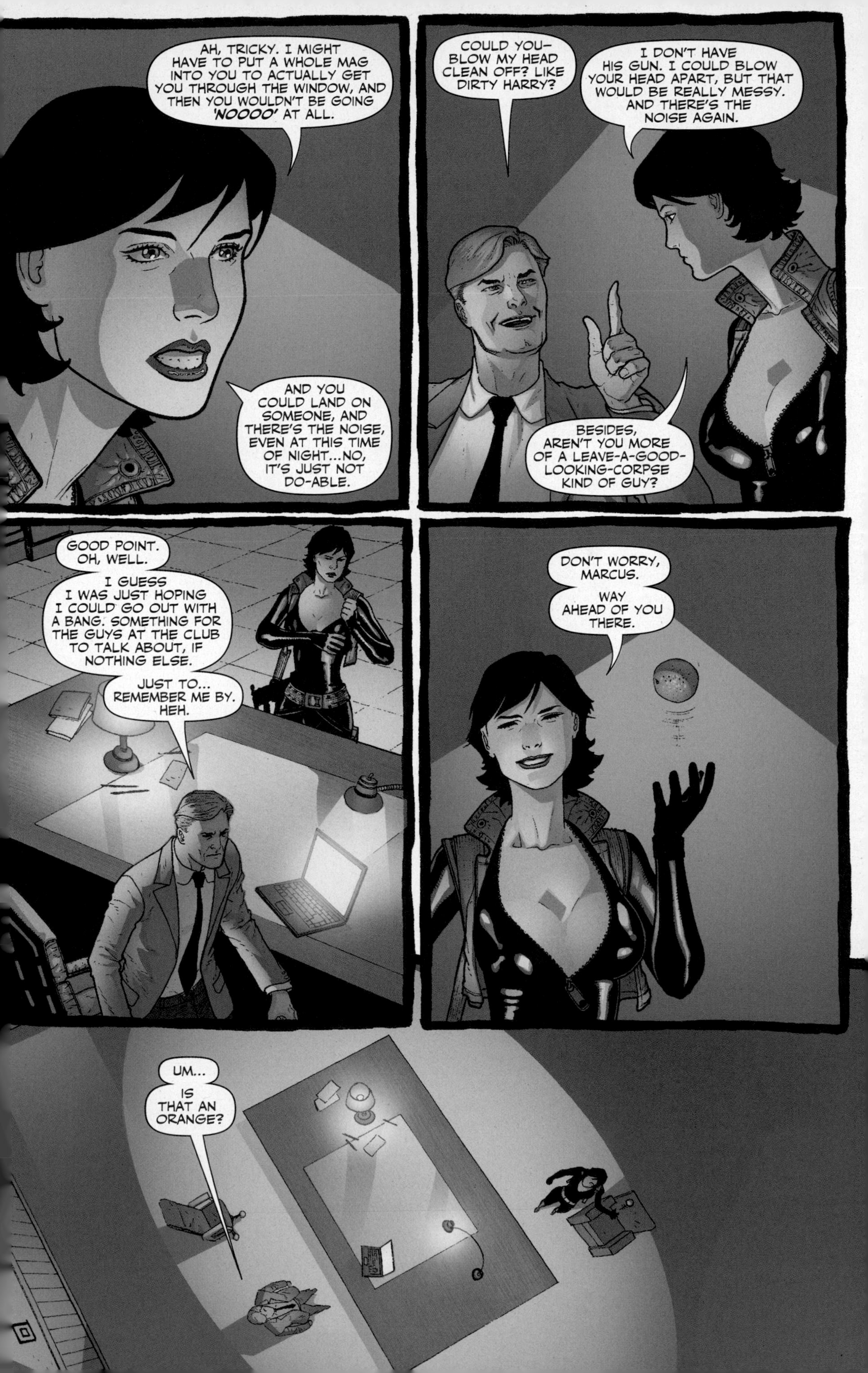
AH, TRICKY. I MIGHT HAVE TO PUT A WHOLE MAG INTO YOU TO ACTUALLY GET YOU THROUGH THE WINDOW, AND THEN YOU WOULDN'T BE GOING *'NOOOO'* AT ALL.
AND YOU COULD LAND ON SOMEONE, AND THERE'S THE NOISE, EVEN AT THIS TIME OF NIGHT...NO, IT'S JUST NOT DO-ABLE.
COULD YOU— BLOW MY HEAD CLEAN OFF? LIKE DIRTY HARRY?
I DON'T HAVE HIS GUN. I COULD BLOW YOUR HEAD APART, BUT THAT WOULD BE REALLY MESSY. AND THERE'S THE NOISE AGAIN.
BESIDES, AREN'T YOU MORE OF A LEAVE-A-GOOD-LOOKING-CORPSE KIND OF GUY?
GOOD POINT. OH, WELL.
I GUESS I WAS JUST HOPING I COULD GO OUT WITH A BANG. SOMETHING FOR THE GUYS AT THE CLUB TO TALK ABOUT, IF NOTHING ELSE.
JUST TO... REMEMBER ME BY. HEH.
DON'T WORRY, MARCUS.
WAY AHEAD OF YOU THERE.
UM...
IS THAT AN ORANGE?

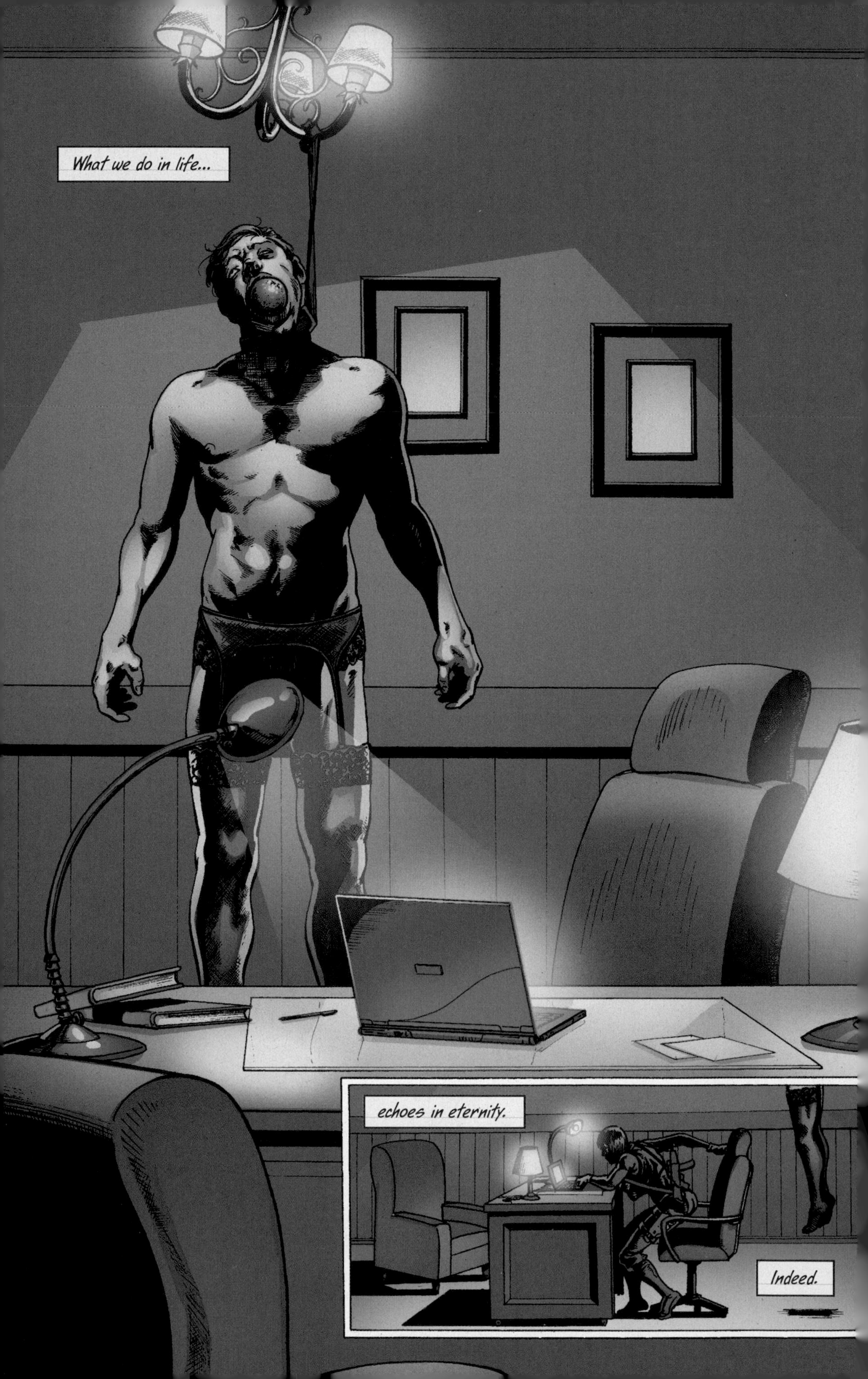
What we do in life...
echoes in eternity.
Indeed.

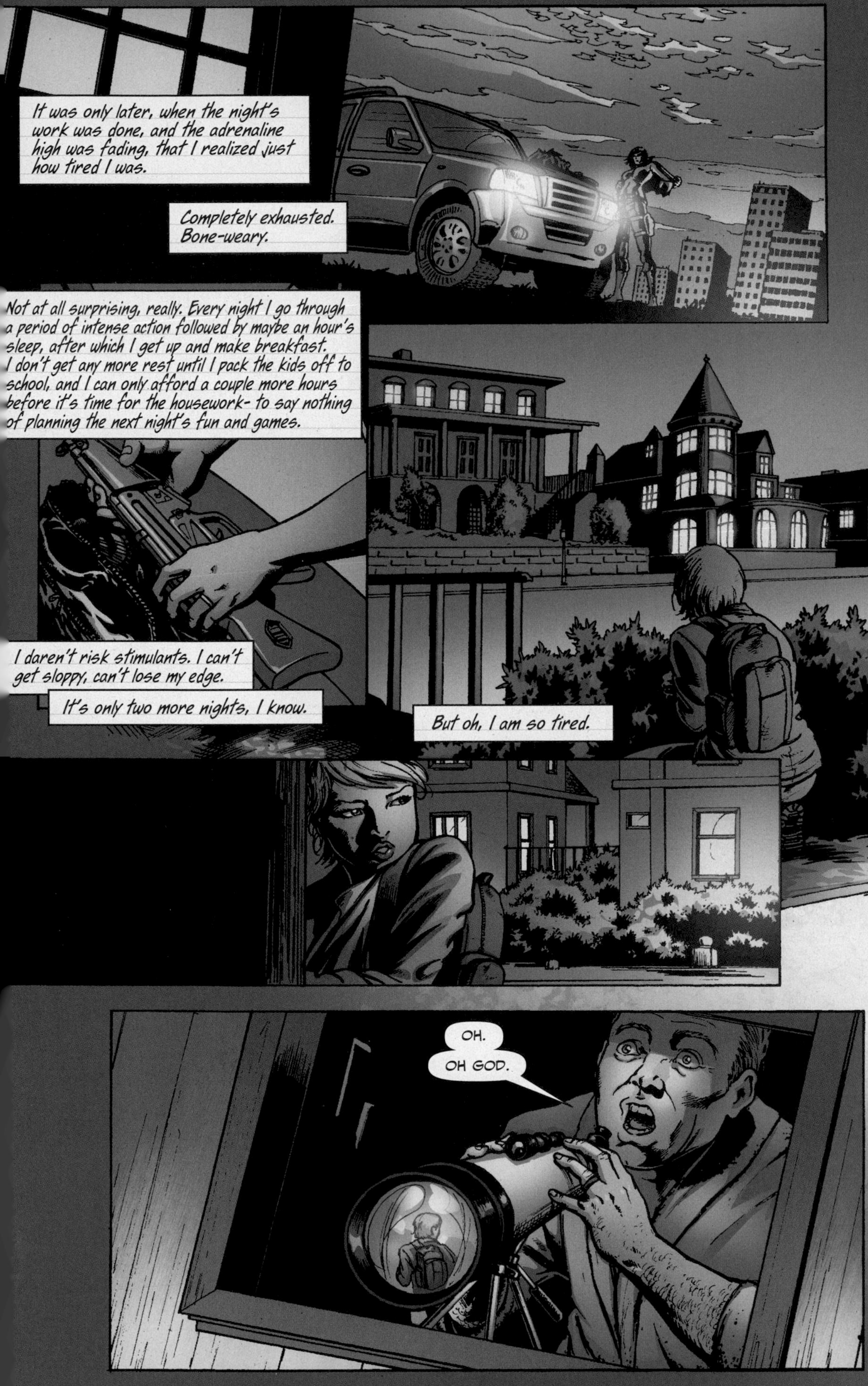
It was only later, when the night's work was done, and the adrenaline high was fading, that I realized just how tired I was.
Completely exhausted. Bone-weary.
Not at all surprising, really. Every night I go through a period of intense action followed by maybe an hour's sleep, after which I get up and make breakfast. I don't get any more rest until I pack the kids off to school, and I can only afford a couple more hours before it's time for the housework- to say nothing of planning the next night's fun and games.
I daren't risk stimulants. I can't get sloppy, can't lose my edge.
It's only two more nights, I know.
But oh, I am so tired.
OH.
OH GOD.

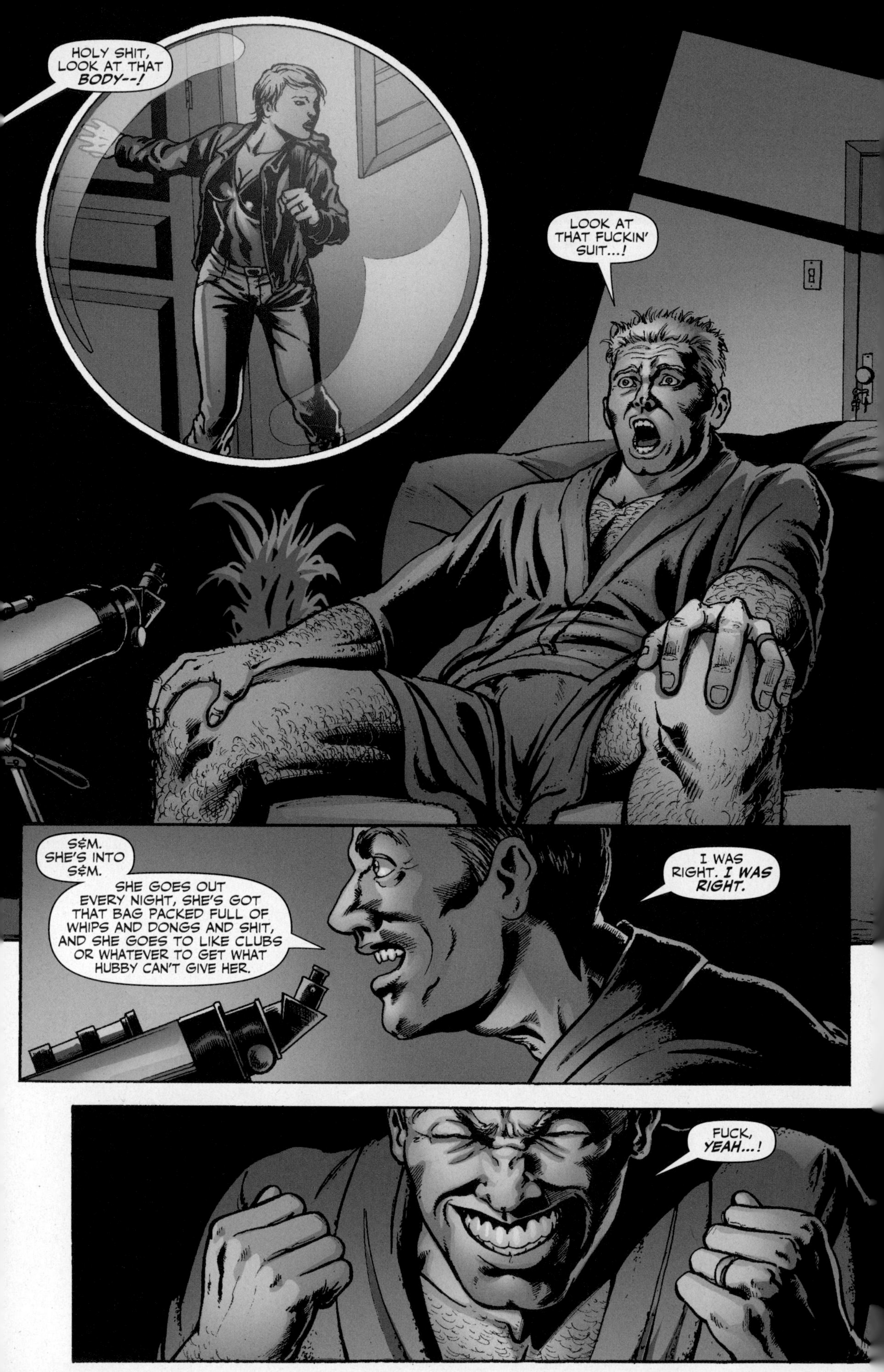
HOLY SHIT, LOOK AT THAT BODY--!
LOOK AT THAT FUCKIN' SUIT...!
S&M. SHE'S INTO S&M.
SHE GOES OUT EVERY NIGHT, SHE'S GOT THAT BAG PACKED FULL OF WHIPS AND DONGS AND SHIT, AND SHE GOES TO LIKE CLUBS OR WHATEVER TO GET WHAT HUBBY CAN'T GIVE HER.
I WAS RIGHT. I WAS RIGHT.
FUCK, YEAH...!

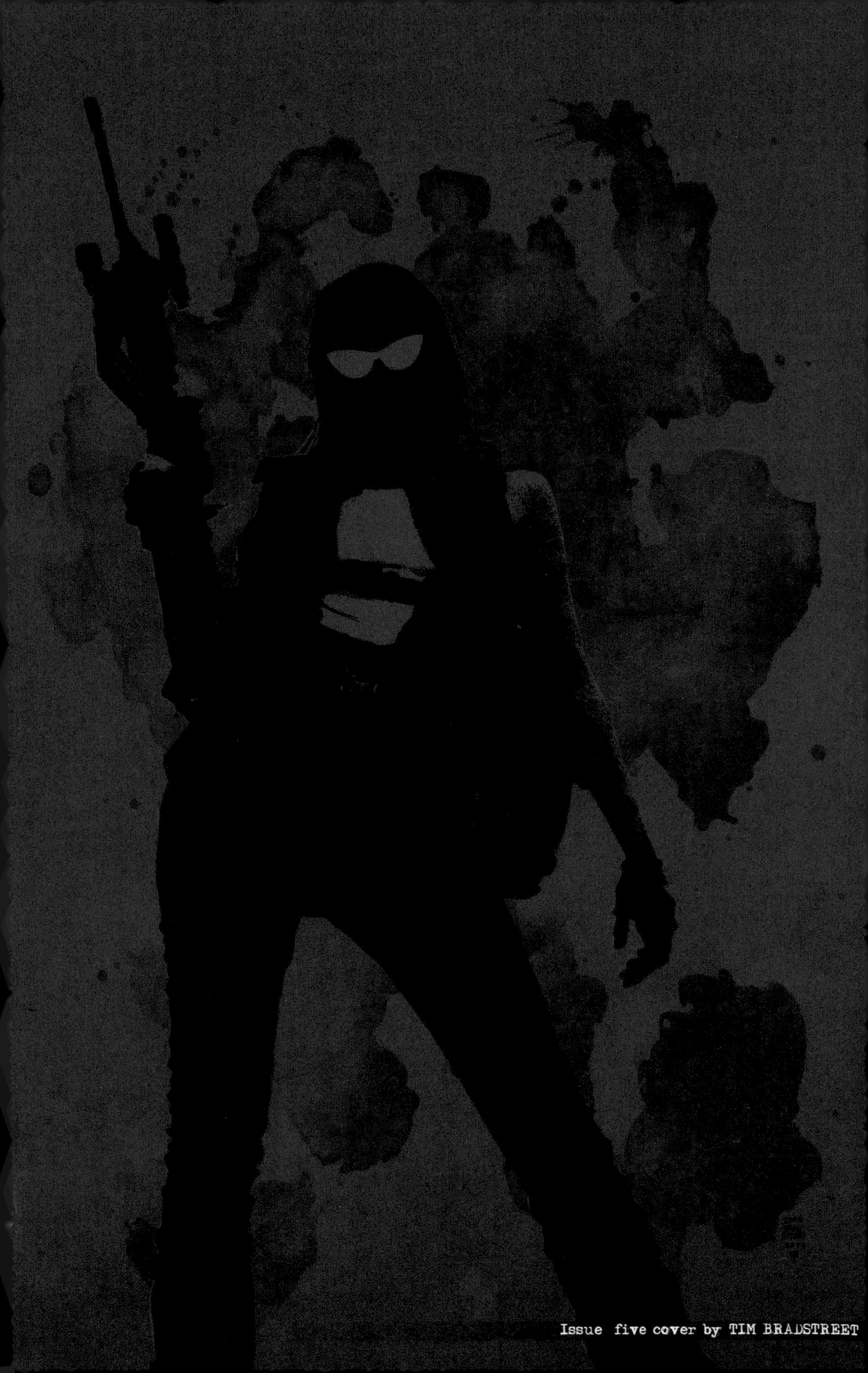

Issue five cover by TIM BRADSTREET

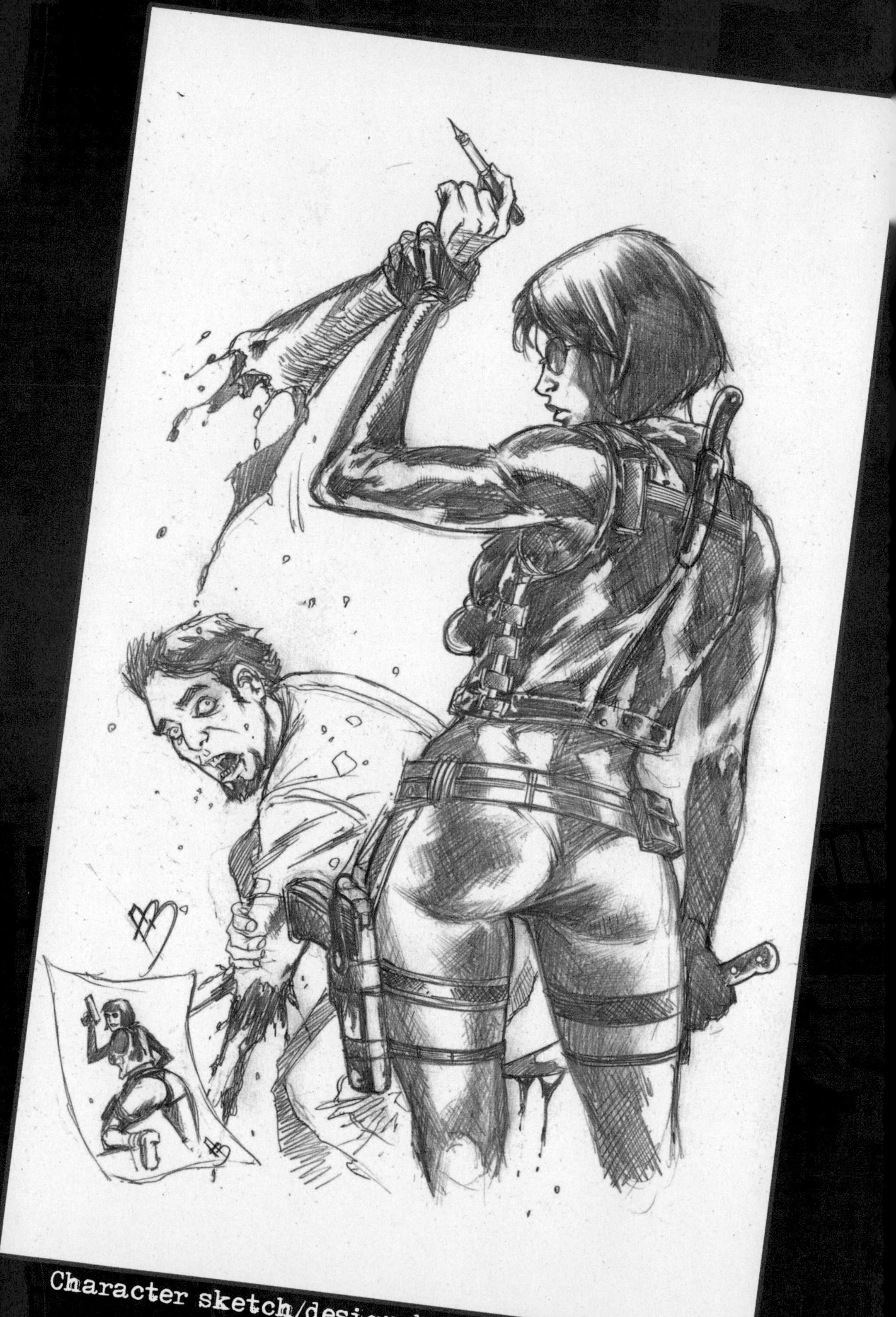

Character sketch/design by Adriano Batista

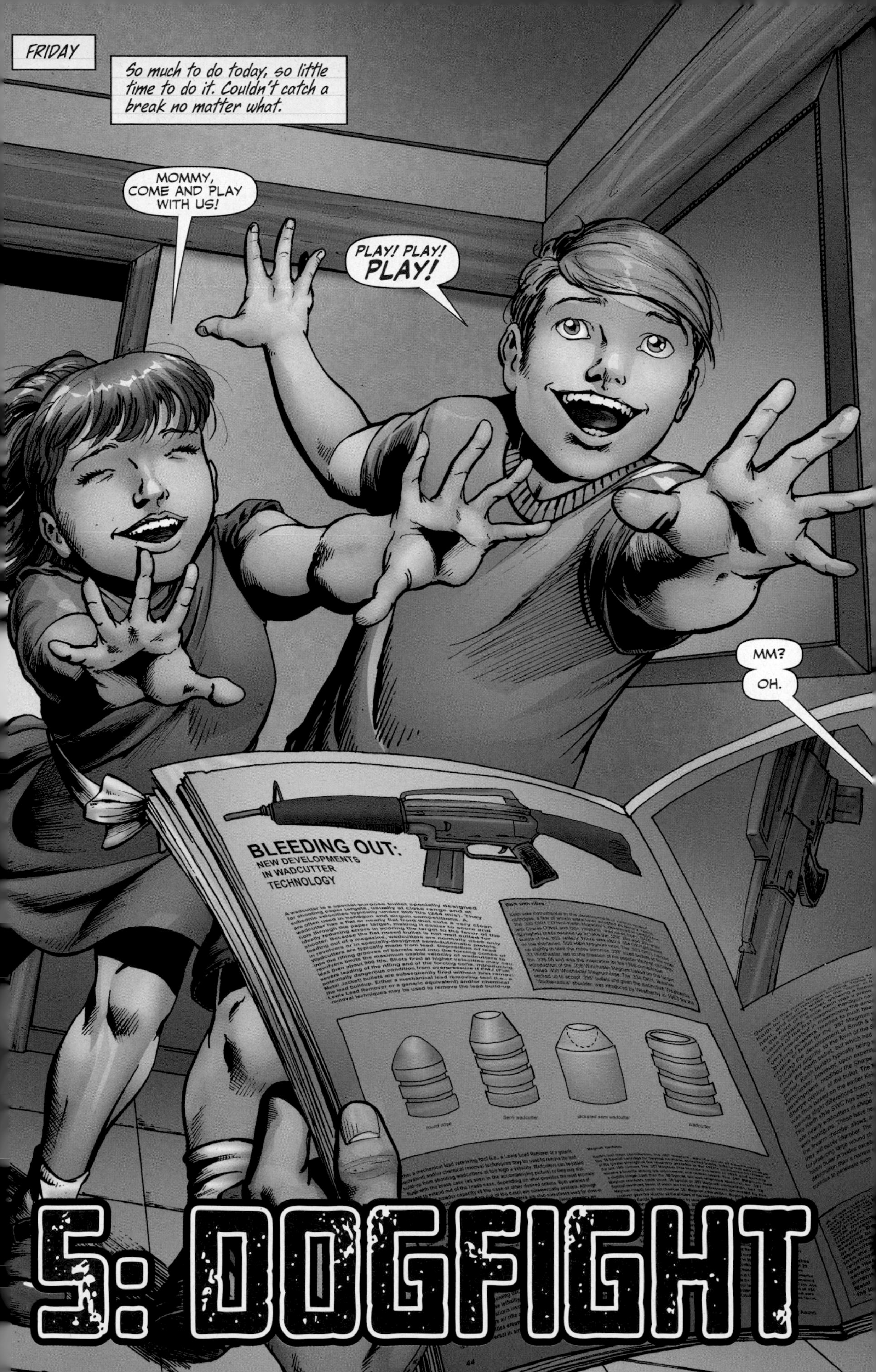
FRIDAY
So much to do today, so little time to do it. Couldn't catch a break no matter what.
MOMMY, COME AND PLAY WITH US!
PLAY! PLAY! PLAY!
MM?
OH.
BLEEDING OUT: NEW DEVELOPMENTS IN WADCUTTER TECHNOLOGY
5: DOGFIGHT

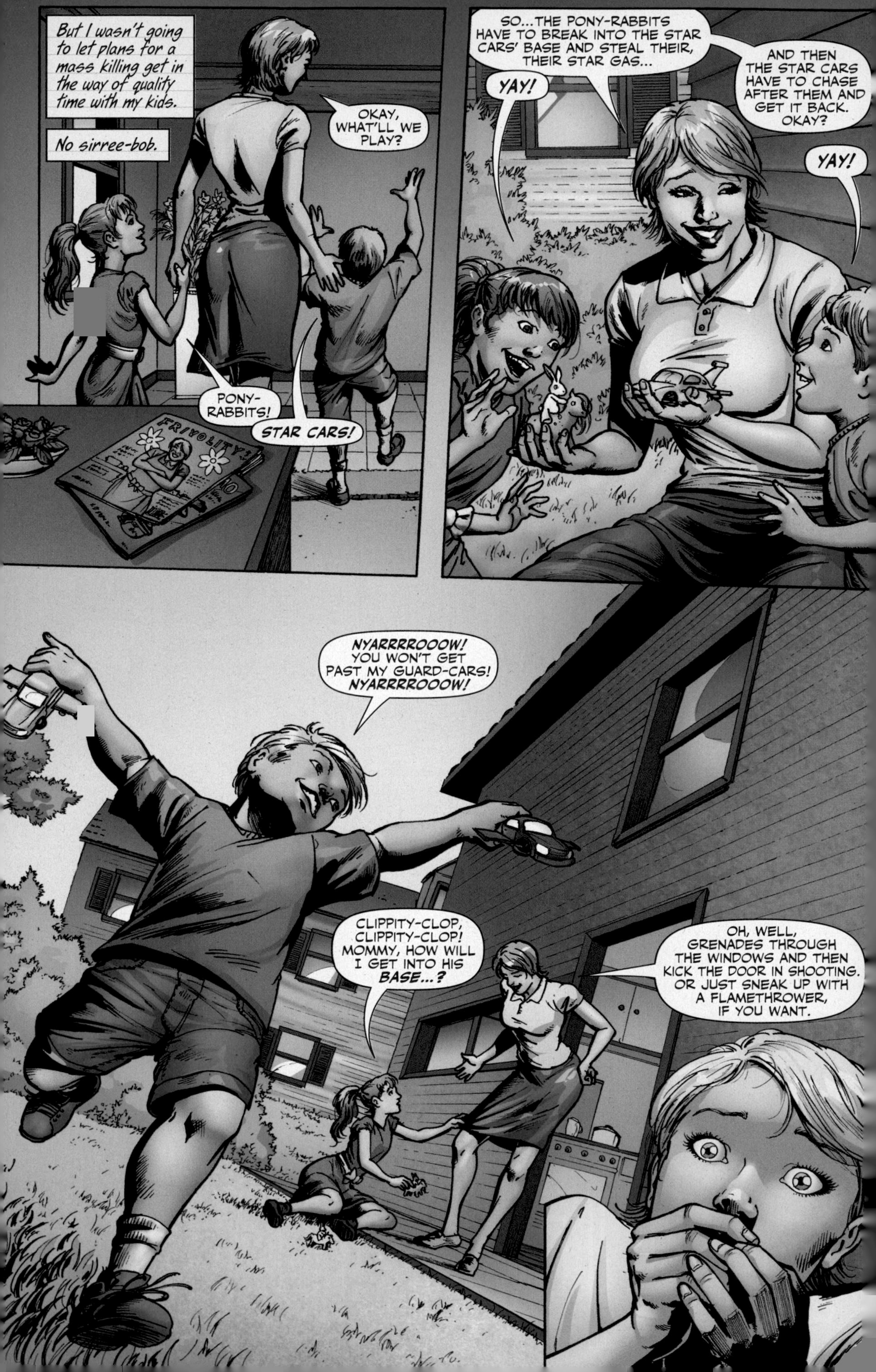

But I wasn't going to let plans for a mass killing get in the way of quality time with my kids.
No sirree-bob.
OKAY, WHAT'LL WE PLAY?
PONY-RABBITS!
STAR CARS!
FRIVOLITY
SO...THE PONY-RABBITS HAVE TO BREAK INTO THE STAR CARS' BASE AND STEAL THEIR, THEIR STAR GAS...
YAY!
AND THEN THE STAR CARS HAVE TO CHASE AFTER THEM AND GET IT BACK. OKAY?
YAY!
NYARRRROOOW! YOU WON'T GET PAST MY GUARD-CARS! NYARRRROOOW!
CLIPPITY-CLOP, CLIPPITY-CLOP! MOMMY, HOW WILL I GET INTO HIS BASE...?
OH, WELL, GRENADES THROUGH THE WINDOWS AND THEN KICK THE DOOR IN SHOOTING. OR JUST SNEAK UP WITH A FLAMETHROWER, IF YOU WANT.

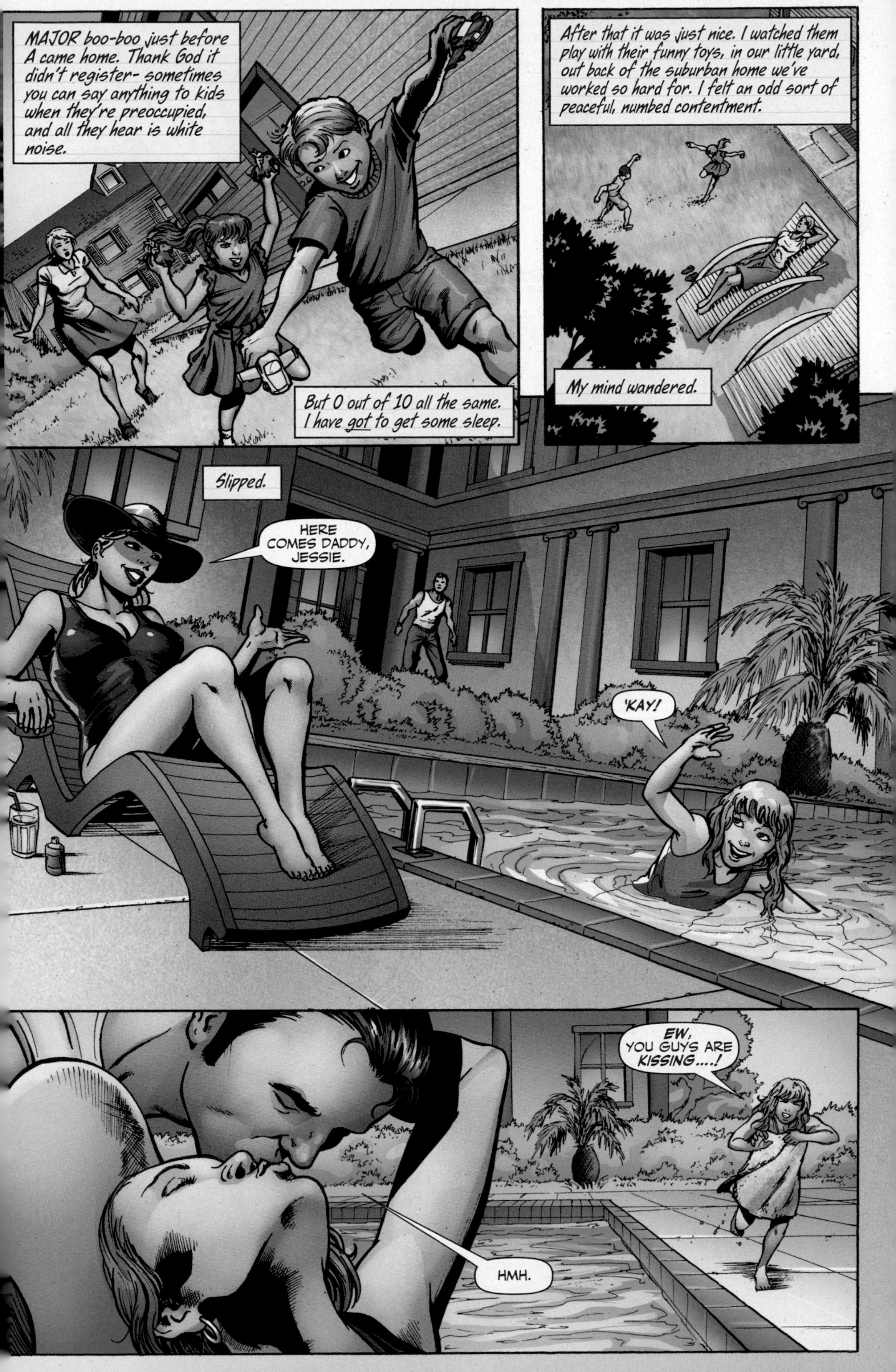
MAJOR boo-boo just before A came home. Thank God it didn't register- sometimes you can say anything to kids when they're preoccupied, and all they hear is white noise.
But 0 out of 10 all the same. I have got to get some sleep.
After that it was just nice. I watched them play with their funny toys, in our little yard, out back of the suburban home we've worked so hard for. I felt an odd sort of peaceful, numbed contentment.
My mind wandered.
Slipped.
HERE COMES DADDY, JESSIE.
'KAY!
EW, YOU GUYS ARE KISSING....!
HMH.

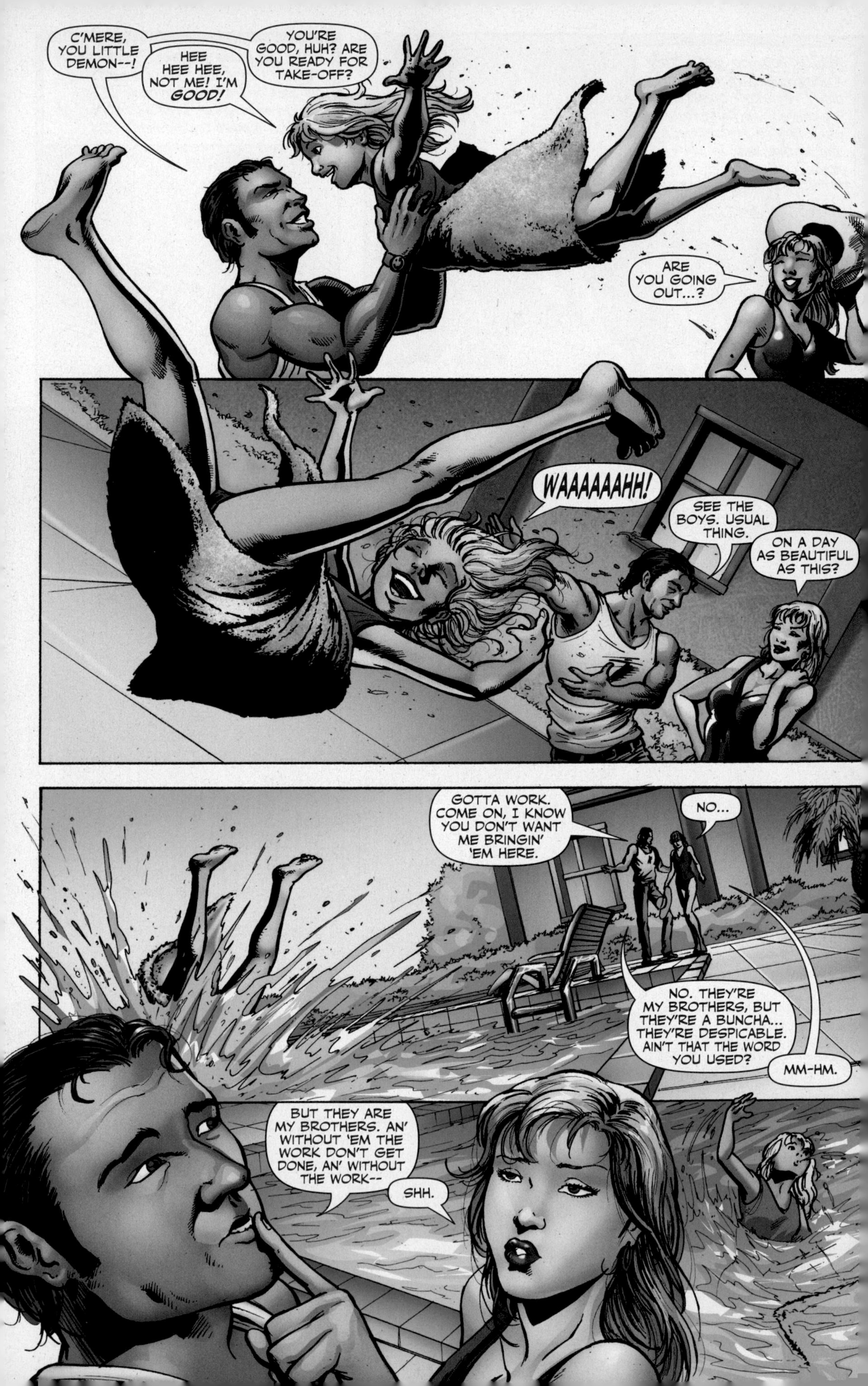
C'MERE, YOU LITTLE DEMON--!
HEE HEE HEE, NOT ME! I'M GOOD!
YOU'RE GOOD, HUH? ARE YOU READY FOR TAKE-OFF?
ARE YOU GOING OUT...?
WAAAAAAHH!
SEE THE BOYS. USUAL THING.
ON A DAY AS BEAUTIFUL AS THIS?
GOTTA WORK. COME ON, I KNOW YOU DON'T WANT ME BRINGIN' 'EM HERE.
NO...
NO. THEY'RE MY BROTHERS, BUT THEY'RE A BUNCHA... THEY'RE DESPICABLE. AIN'T THAT THE WORD YOU USED?
MM-HM.
BUT THEY ARE MY BROTHERS. AN' WITHOUT 'EM THE WORK DON'T GET DONE, AN' WITHOUT THE WORK--
SHH.

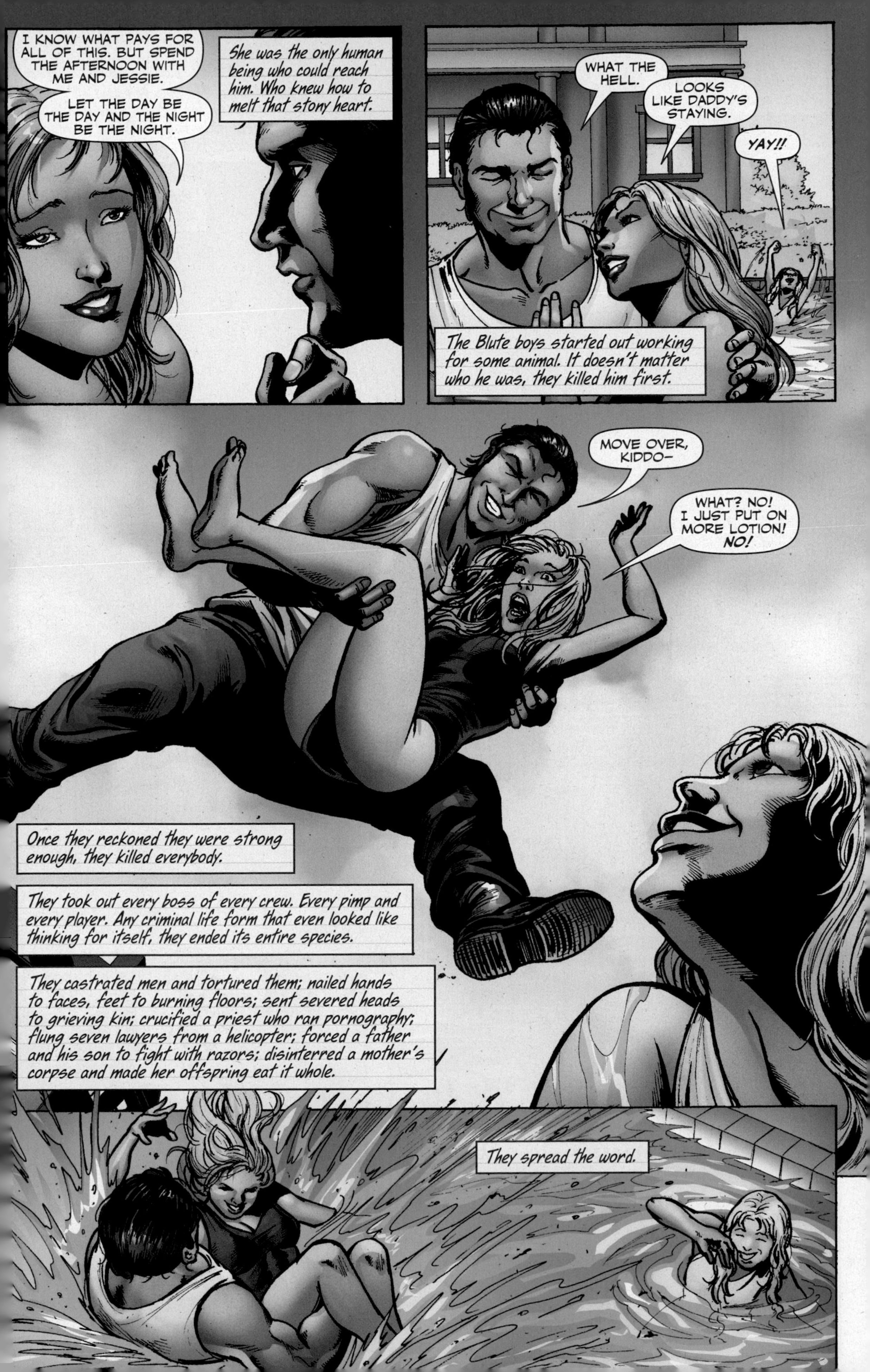
I KNOW WHAT PAYS FOR ALL OF THIS. BUT SPEND THE AFTERNOON WITH ME AND JESSIE.
LET THE DAY BE THE DAY AND THE NIGHT BE THE NIGHT.
She was the only human being who could reach him. Who knew how to melt that stony heart.
WHAT THE HELL.
LOOKS LIKE DADDY'S STAYING.
YAY!!
The Blute boys started out working for some animal. It doesn't matter who he was, they killed him first.
MOVE OVER, KIDDO–
WHAT? NO! I JUST PUT ON MORE LOTION! NO!
Once they reckoned they were strong enough, they killed everybody.
They took out every boss of every crew. Every pimp and every player. Any criminal life form that even looked like thinking for itself, they ended its entire species.
They castrated men and tortured them; nailed hands to faces, feet to burning floors; sent severed heads to grieving kin; crucified a priest who ran pornography; flung seven lawyers from a helicopter; forced a father and his son to fight with razors; disinterred a mother's corpse and made her offspring eat it whole.
They spread the word.

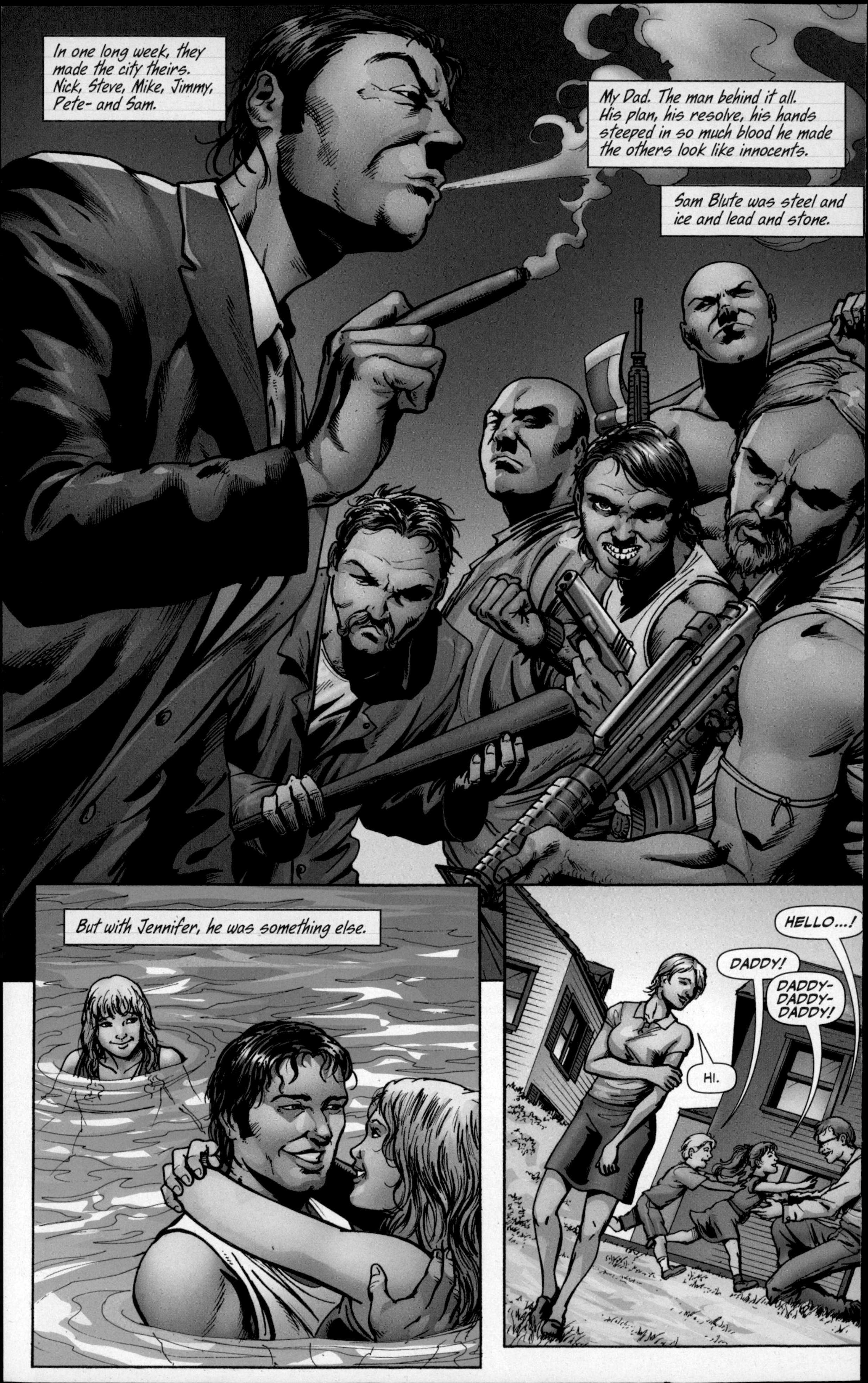
In one long week, they made the city theirs. Nick, Steve, Mike, Jimmy, Pete- and Sam.
My Dad. The man behind it all. His plan, his resolve, his hands steeped in so much blood he made the others look like innocents.
Sam Blute was steel and ice and lead and stone.
But with Jennifer, he was something else.
HELLO...!
DADDY!
DADDY-DADDY-DADDY!
HI.

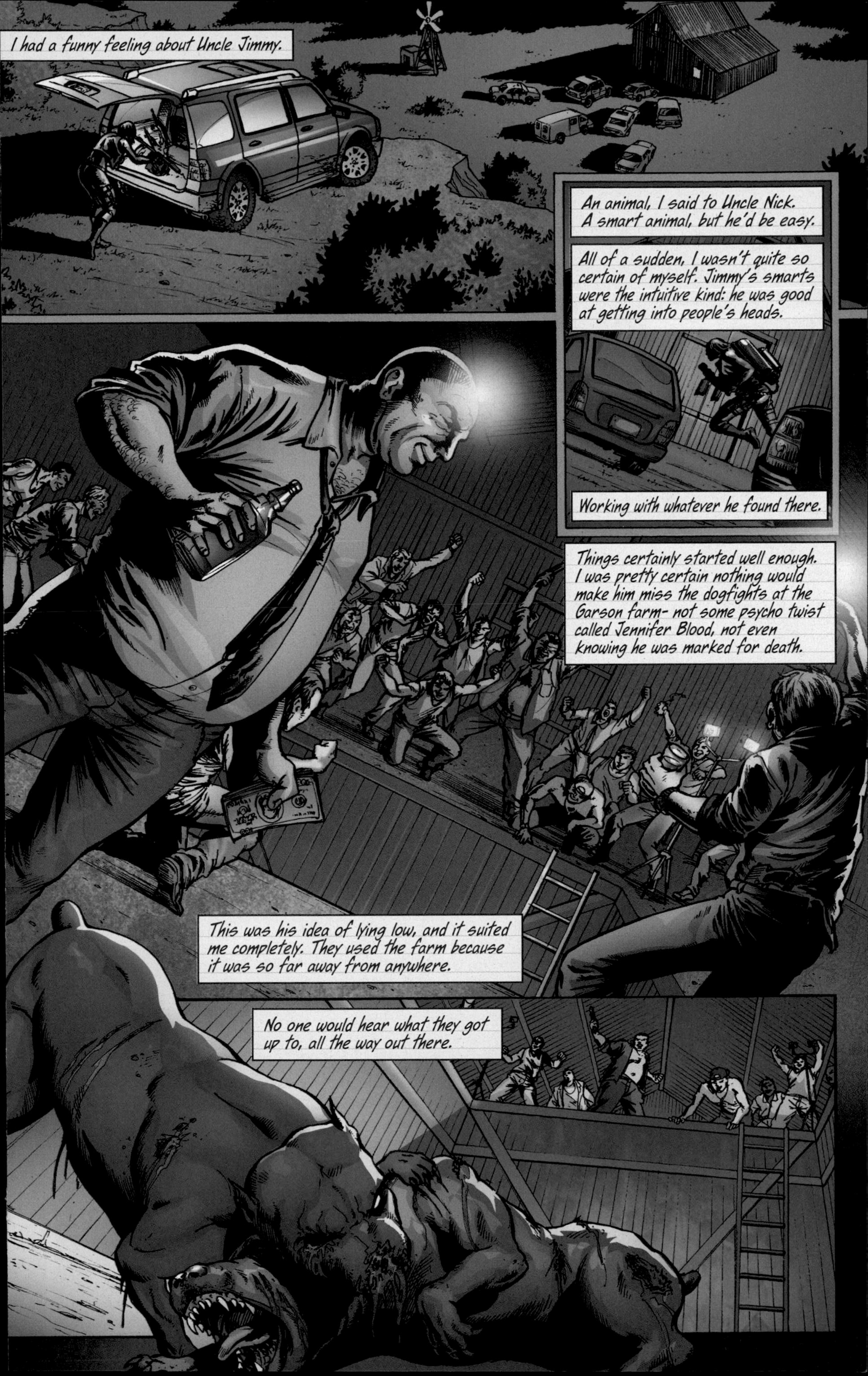

I had a funny feeling about Uncle Jimmy.
An animal, I said to Uncle Nick. A smart animal, but he'd be easy.
All of a sudden, I wasn't quite so certain of myself. Jimmy's smarts were the intuitive kind: he was good at getting into people's heads.
Working with whatever he found there.
Things certainly started well enough. I was pretty certain nothing would make him miss the dogfights at the Garson farm- not some psycho twist called Jennifer Blood, not even knowing he was marked for death.
This was his idea of lying low, and it suited me completely. They used the farm because it was so far away from anywhere.
No one would hear what they got up to, all the way out there.

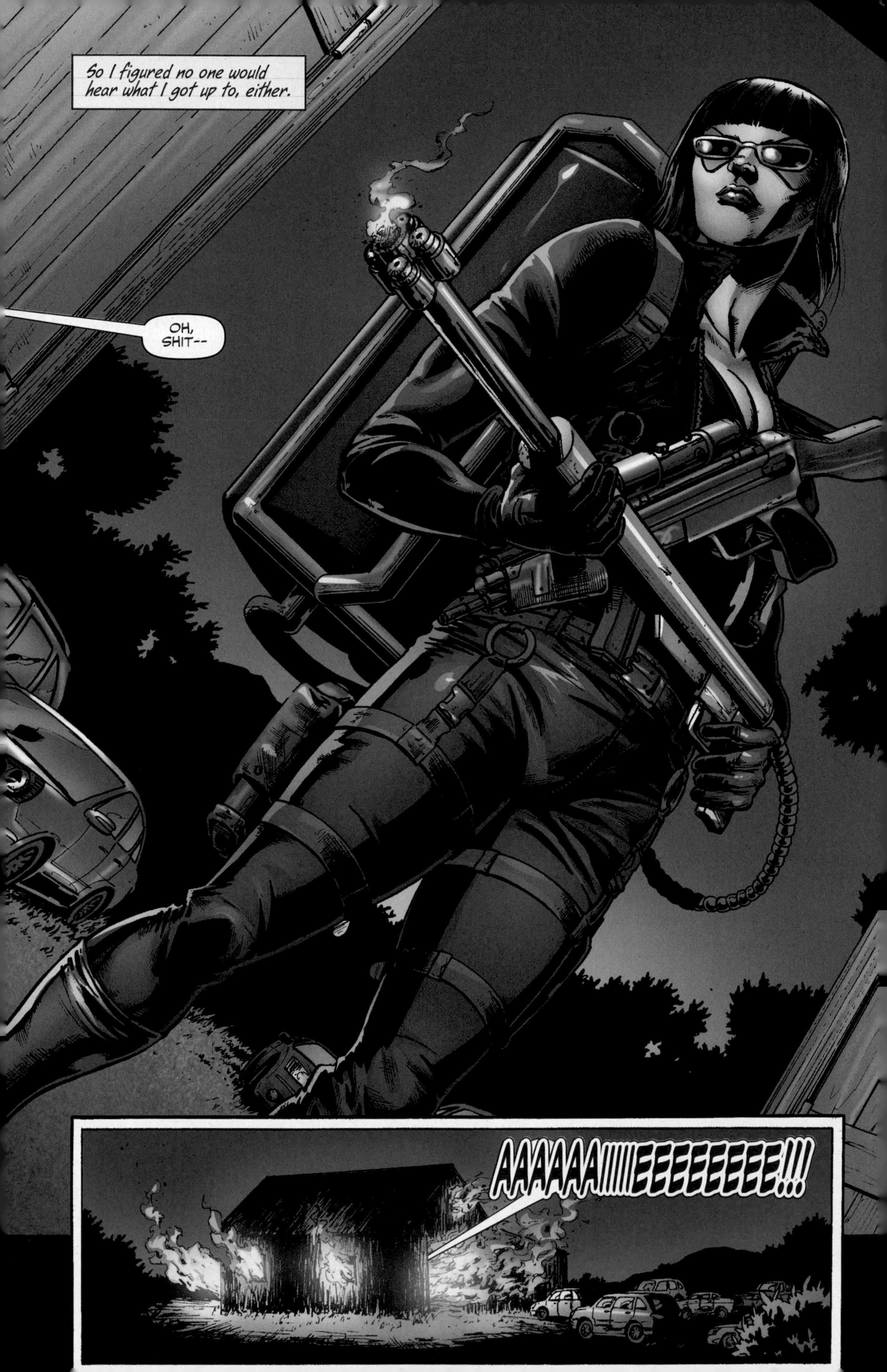
So I figured no one would hear what I got up to, either.
OH, SHIT--
AAAAAAIIIIIIEEEEEEEEE!!!

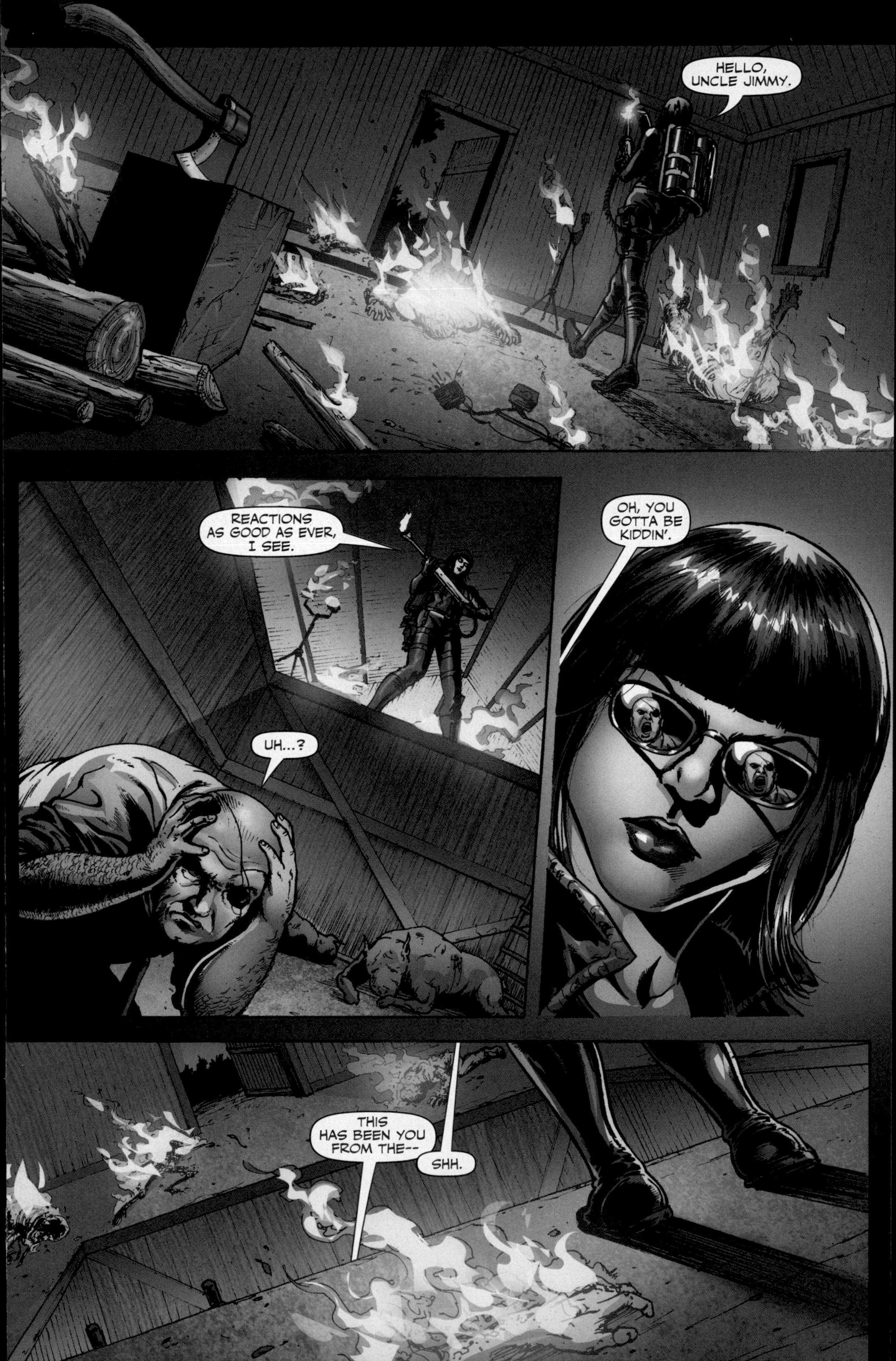
HELLO, UNCLE JIMMY.
REACTIONS AS GOOD AS EVER, I SEE.
UH...?
OH, YOU GOTTA BE KIDDIN'.
THIS HAS BEEN YOU FROM THE--
SHH.

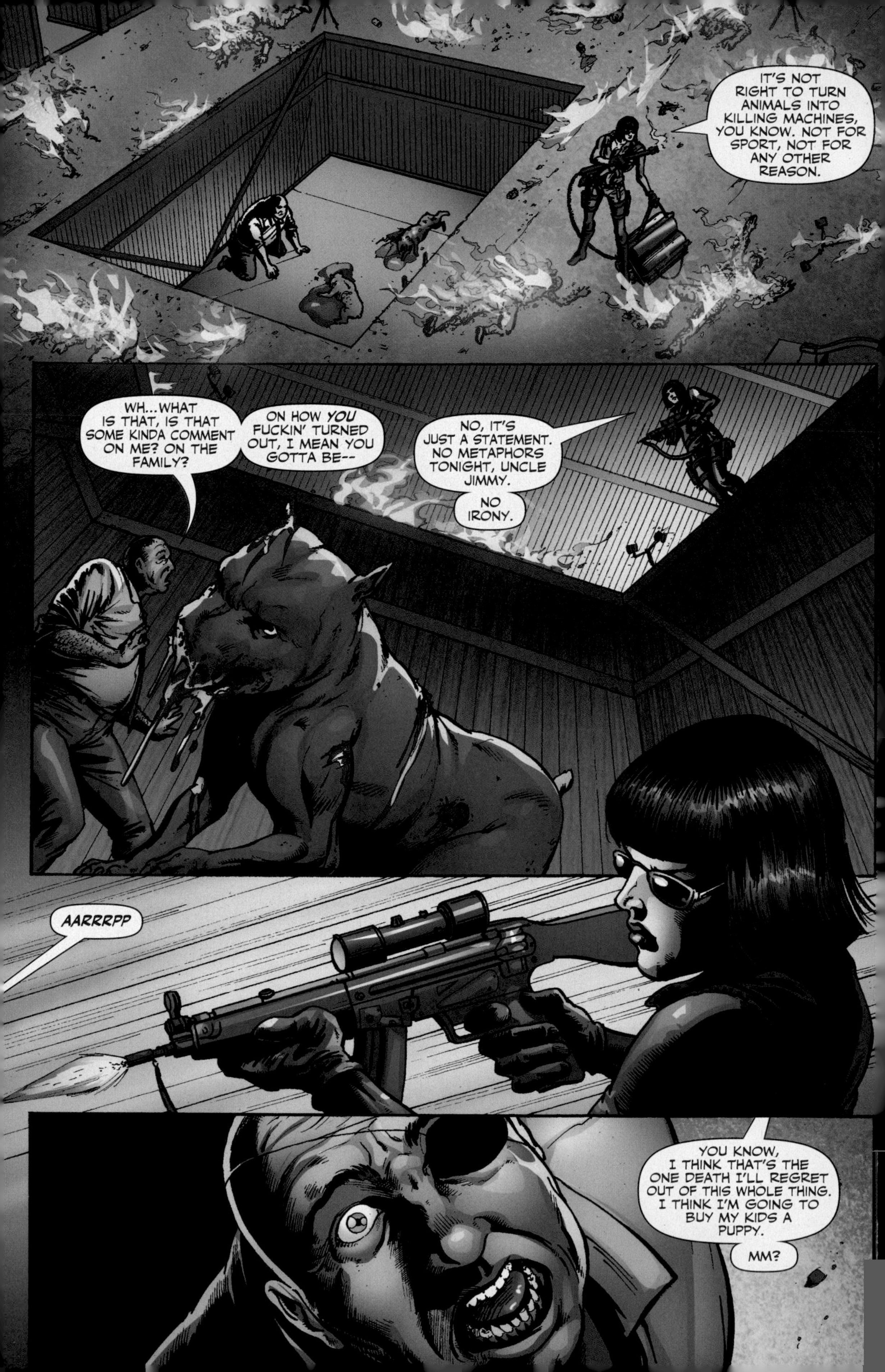

IT'S NOT RIGHT TO TURN ANIMALS INTO KILLING MACHINES, YOU KNOW. NOT FOR SPORT, NOT FOR ANY OTHER REASON.
WH...WHAT IS THAT, IS THAT SOME KINDA COMMENT ON ME? ON THE FAMILY?
ON HOW *YOU* FUCKIN' TURNED OUT, I MEAN YOU GOTTA BE--
NO, IT'S JUST A STATEMENT. NO METAPHORS TONIGHT, UNCLE JIMMY.
NO IRONY.
AARRRPP
YOU KNOW, I THINK THAT'S THE ONE DEATH I'LL REGRET OUT OF THIS WHOLE THING. I THINK I'M GOING TO BUY MY KIDS A PUPPY.
MM?

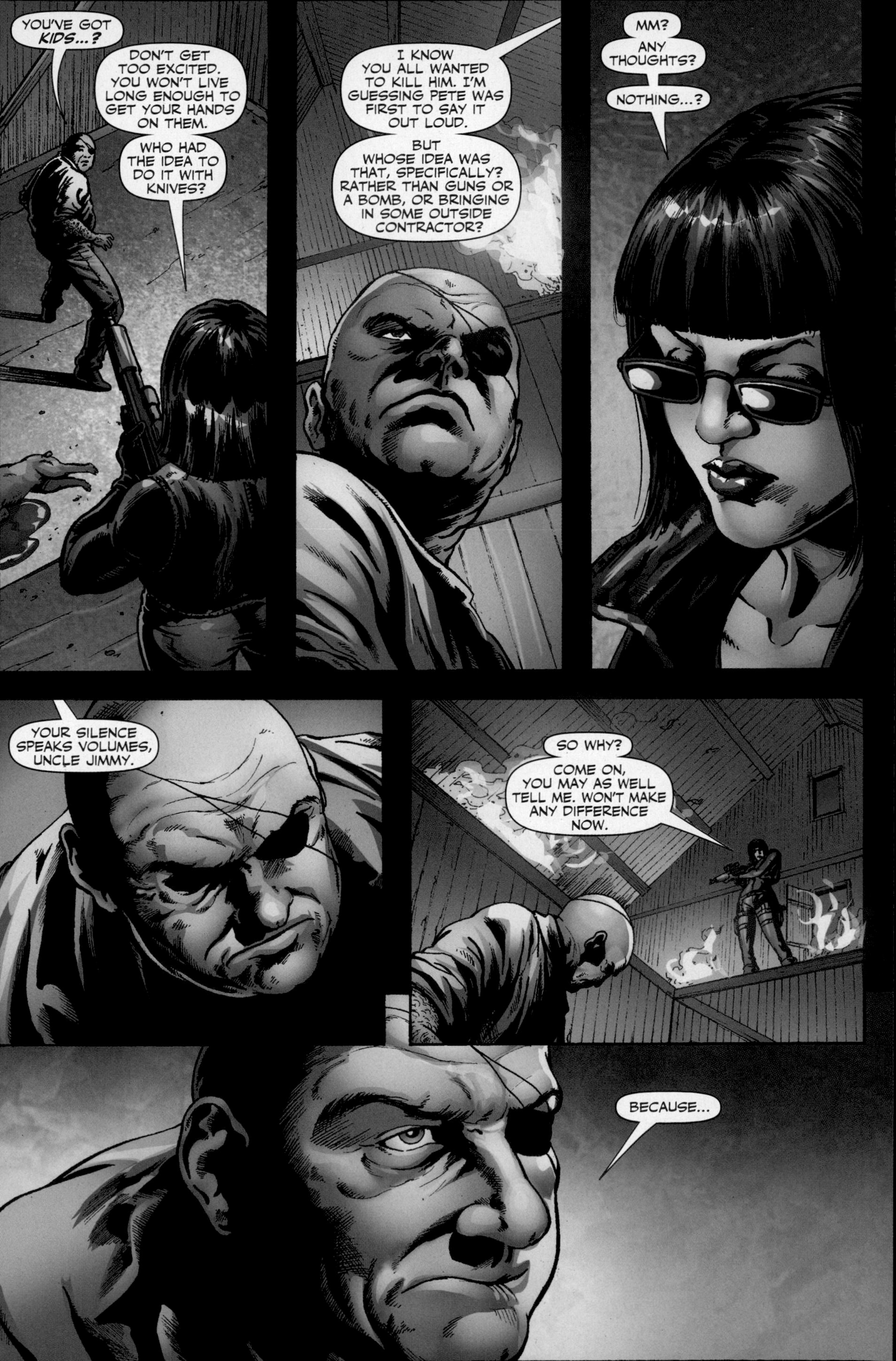
YOU'VE GOT *KIDS*...?
DON'T GET TOO EXCITED. YOU WON'T LIVE LONG ENOUGH TO GET YOUR HANDS ON THEM.
WHO HAD THE IDEA TO DO IT WITH KNIVES?
I KNOW YOU ALL WANTED TO KILL HIM. I'M GUESSING PETE WAS FIRST TO SAY IT OUT LOUD.
BUT WHOSE IDEA WAS THAT, SPECIFICALLY? RATHER THAN GUNS OR A BOMB, OR BRINGING IN SOME OUTSIDE CONTRACTOR?
MM? ANY THOUGHTS?
NOTHING...?
YOUR SILENCE SPEAKS VOLUMES, UNCLE JIMMY.
SO WHY?
COME ON, YOU MAY AS WELL TELL ME. WON'T MAKE ANY DIFFERENCE NOW.
BECAUSE...

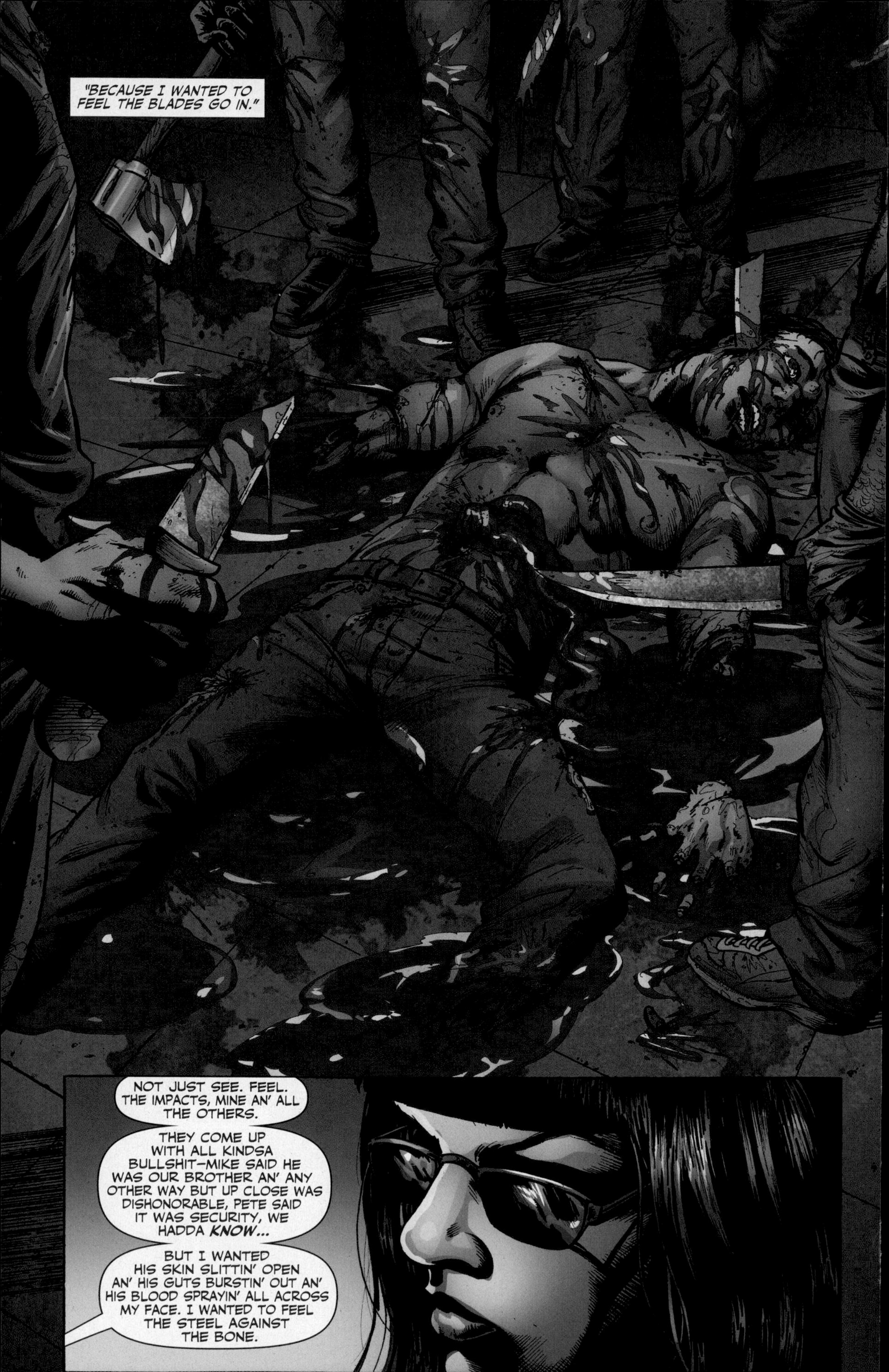
"BECAUSE I WANTED TO FEEL THE BLADES GO IN."
NOT JUST SEE. FEEL. THE IMPACTS, MINE AN' ALL THE OTHERS.
THEY COME UP WITH ALL KINDSA BULLSHIT—MIKE SAID HE WAS OUR BROTHER AN' ANY OTHER WAY BUT UP CLOSE WAS DISHONORABLE, PETE SAID IT WAS SECURITY, WE HADDA KNOW...
BUT I WANTED HIS SKIN SLITTIN' OPEN AN' HIS GUTS BURSTIN' OUT AN' HIS BLOOD SPRAYIN' ALL ACROSS MY FACE. I WANTED TO FEEL THE STEEL AGAINST THE BONE.

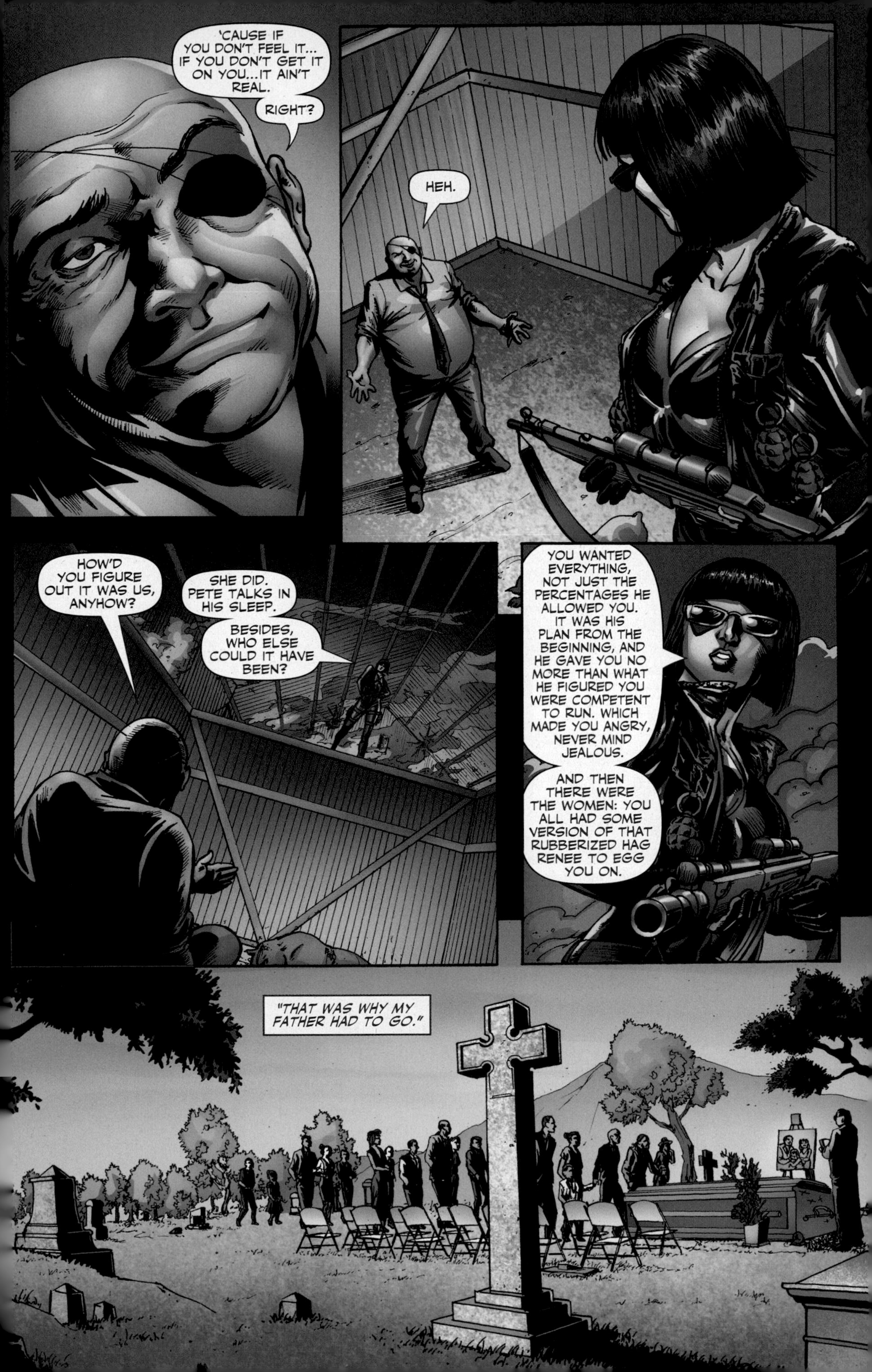
'CAUSE IF YOU DON'T FEEL IT... IF YOU DON'T GET IT ON YOU...IT AIN'T REAL.
RIGHT?
HEH.
HOW'D YOU FIGURE OUT IT WAS US, ANYHOW?
SHE DID. PETE TALKS IN HIS SLEEP.
BESIDES, WHO ELSE COULD IT HAVE BEEN?
YOU WANTED EVERYTHING, NOT JUST THE PERCENTAGES HE ALLOWED YOU. IT WAS HIS PLAN FROM THE BEGINNING, AND HE GAVE YOU NO MORE THAN WHAT HE FIGURED YOU WERE COMPETENT TO RUN. WHICH MADE YOU ANGRY, NEVER MIND JEALOUS.
AND THEN THERE WERE THE WOMEN: YOU ALL HAD SOME VERSION OF THAT RUBBERIZED HAG RENEE TO EGG YOU ON.
"THAT WAS WHY MY FATHER HAD TO GO."

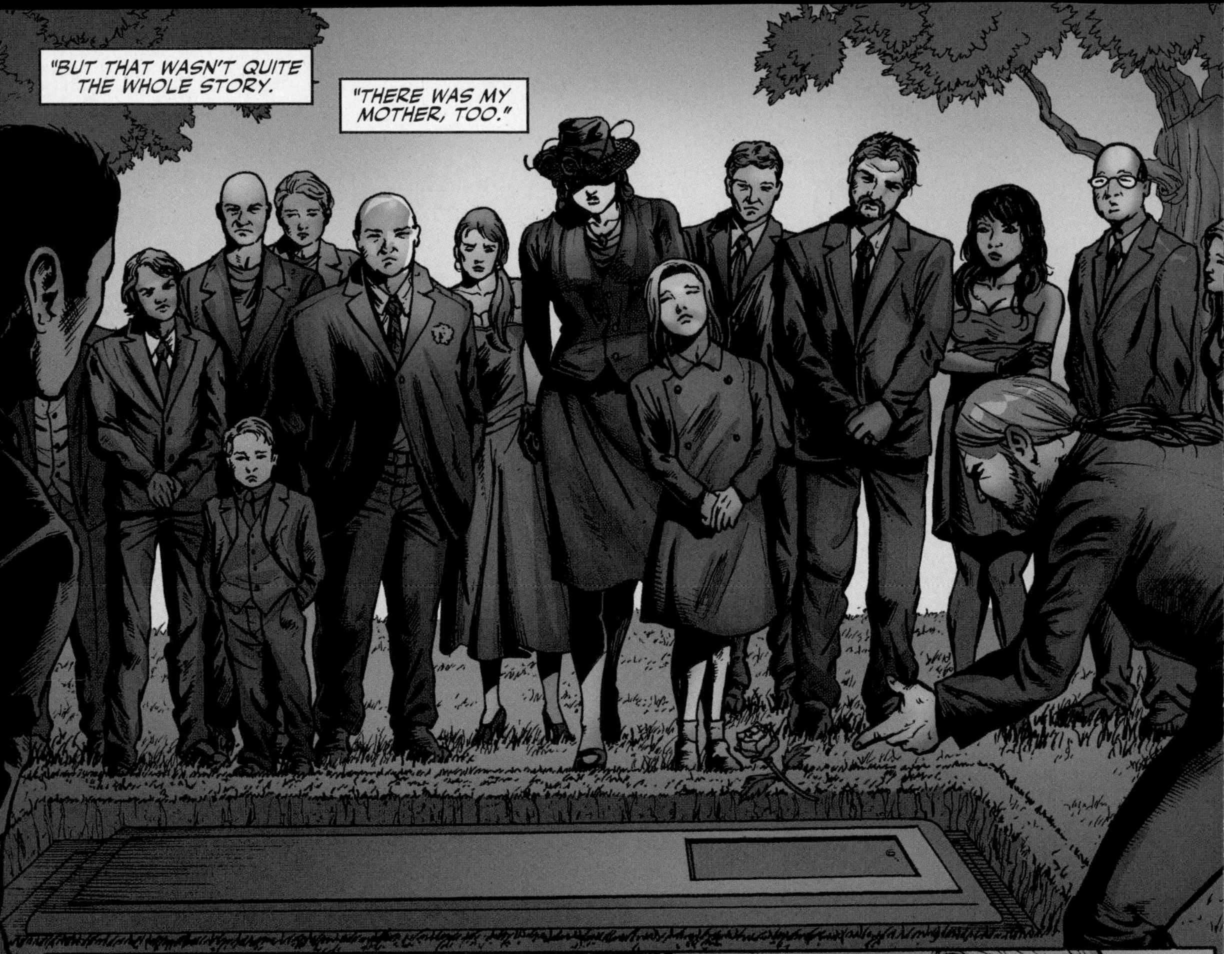
"BUT THAT WASN'T QUITE THE WHOLE STORY.
"THERE WAS MY MOTHER, TOO."

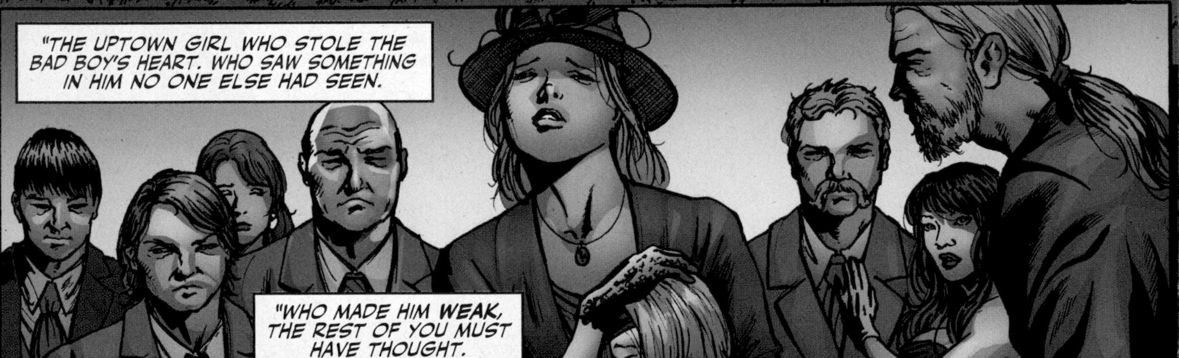
"THE UPTOWN GIRL WHO STOLE THE BAD BOY'S HEART. WHO SAW SOMETHING IN HIM NO ONE ELSE HAD SEEN.
"WHO MADE HIM WEAK, THE REST OF YOU MUST HAVE THOUGHT.
"PETE PROBABLY LOATHED HER MORE THAN ALL OF YOU PUT TOGETHER..."

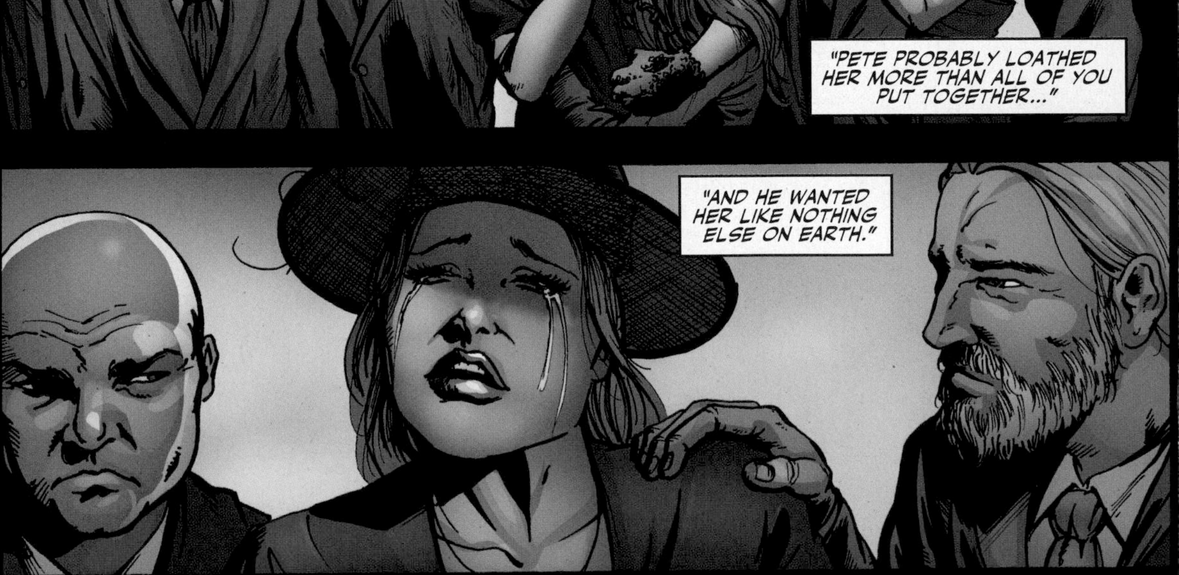
"AND HE WANTED HER LIKE NOTHING ELSE ON EARTH."

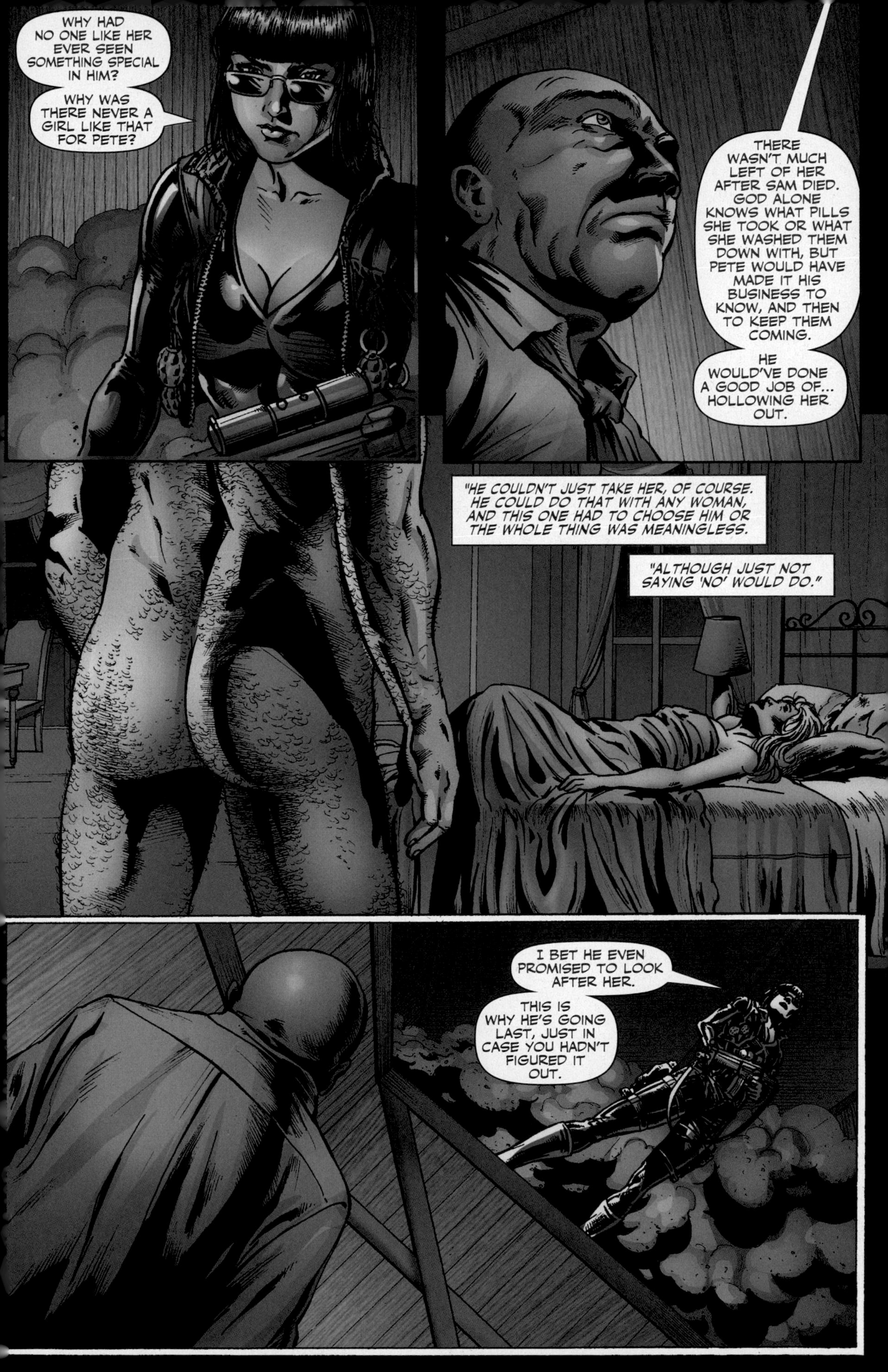
WHY HAD NO ONE LIKE HER EVER SEEN SOMETHING SPECIAL IN HIM?
WHY WAS THERE NEVER A GIRL LIKE THAT FOR PETE?
THERE WASN'T MUCH LEFT OF HER AFTER SAM DIED. GOD ALONE KNOWS WHAT PILLS SHE TOOK OR WHAT SHE WASHED THEM DOWN WITH, BUT PETE WOULD HAVE MADE IT HIS BUSINESS TO KNOW, AND THEN TO KEEP THEM COMING.
HE WOULD'VE DONE A GOOD JOB OF... HOLLOWING HER OUT.
"HE COULDN'T JUST TAKE HER, OF COURSE. HE COULD DO THAT WITH ANY WOMAN, AND THIS ONE HAD TO CHOOSE HIM OR THE WHOLE THING WAS MEANINGLESS.
"ALTHOUGH JUST NOT SAYING 'NO' WOULD DO."
I BET HE EVEN PROMISED TO LOOK AFTER HER.
THIS IS WHY HE'S GOING LAST, JUST IN CASE YOU HADN'T FIGURED IT OUT.

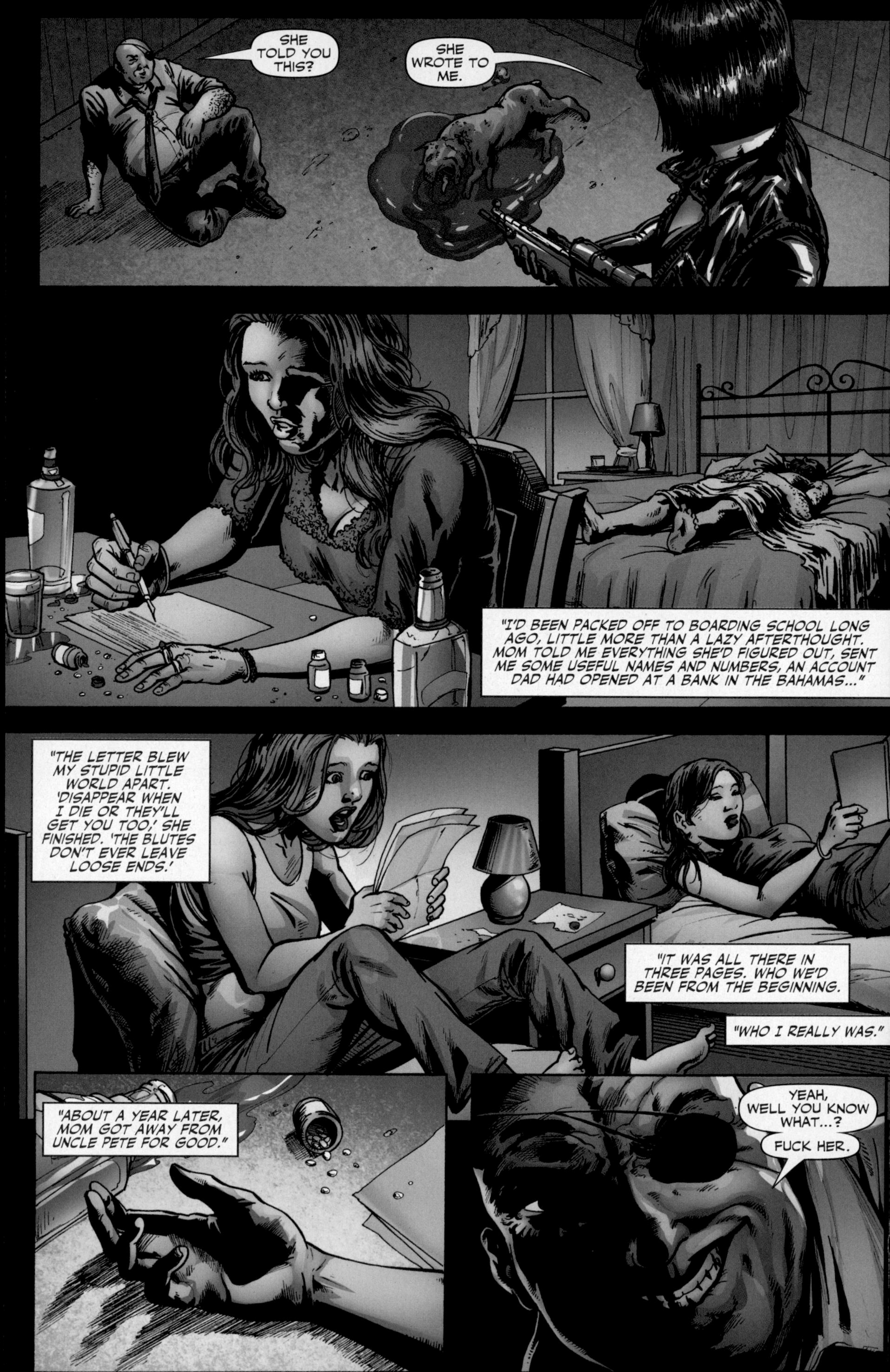
SHE TOLD YOU THIS?
SHE WROTE TO ME.
"I'D BEEN PACKED OFF TO BOARDING SCHOOL LONG AGO, LITTLE MORE THAN A LAZY AFTERTHOUGHT. MOM TOLD ME EVERYTHING SHE'D FIGURED OUT, SENT ME SOME USEFUL NAMES AND NUMBERS, AN ACCOUNT DAD HAD OPENED AT A BANK IN THE BAHAMAS..."
"THE LETTER BLEW MY STUPID LITTLE WORLD APART. 'DISAPPEAR WHEN I DIE OR THEY'LL GET YOU TOO,' SHE FINISHED. 'THE BLUTES DON'T EVER LEAVE LOOSE ENDS.'
"IT WAS ALL THERE IN THREE PAGES. WHO WE'D BEEN FROM THE BEGINNING.
"WHO I REALLY WAS."
"ABOUT A YEAR LATER, MOM GOT AWAY FROM UNCLE PETE FOR GOOD."
YEAH, WELL YOU KNOW WHAT...?
FUCK HER.

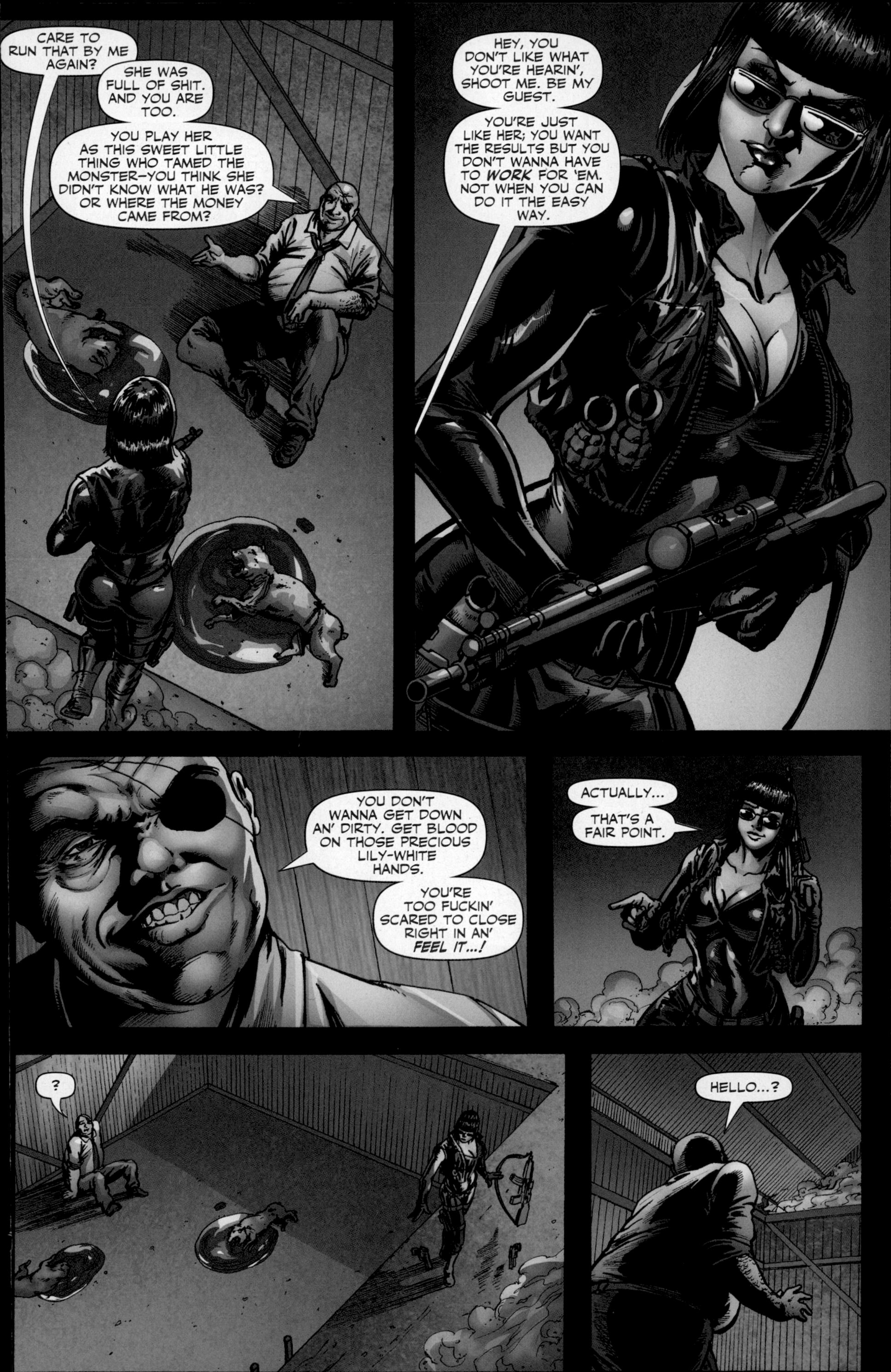
CARE TO RUN THAT BY ME AGAIN?
SHE WAS FULL OF SHIT. AND YOU ARE TOO.
YOU PLAY HER AS THIS SWEET LITTLE THING WHO TAMED THE MONSTER–YOU THINK SHE DIDN'T KNOW WHAT HE WAS? OR WHERE THE MONEY CAME FROM?
HEY, YOU DON'T LIKE WHAT YOU'RE HEARIN', SHOOT ME. BE MY GUEST.
YOU'RE JUST LIKE HER; YOU WANT THE RESULTS BUT YOU DON'T WANNA HAVE TO *WORK* FOR 'EM. NOT WHEN YOU CAN DO IT THE EASY WAY.
YOU DON'T WANNA GET DOWN AN' DIRTY. GET BLOOD ON THOSE PRECIOUS LILY-WHITE HANDS.
YOU'RE TOO FUCKIN' SCARED TO CLOSE RIGHT IN AN' *FEEL IT...!*
ACTUALLY...
THAT'S A FAIR POINT.
?
HELLO...?

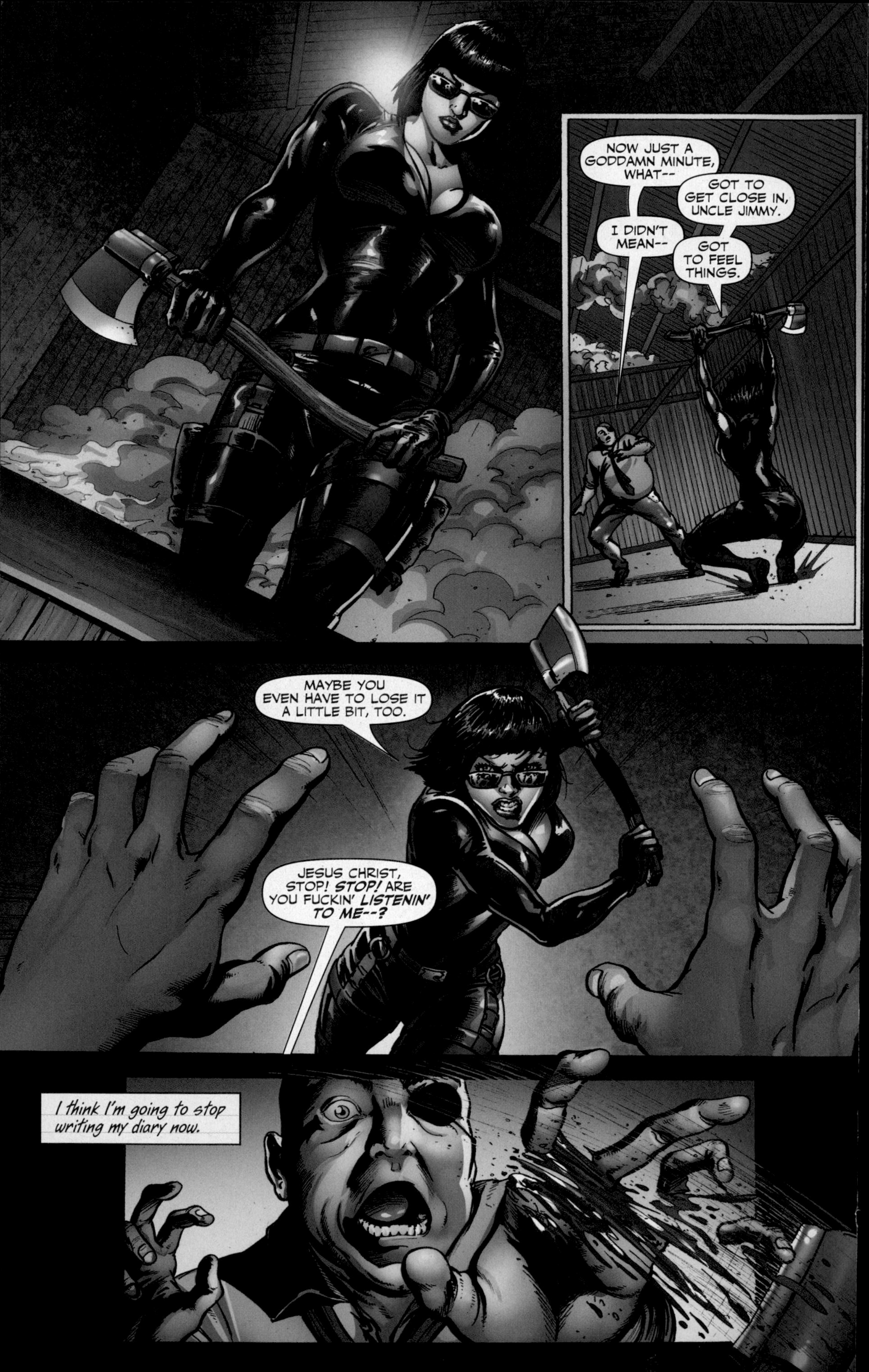

NOW JUST A GODDAMN MINUTE, WHAT--
GOT TO GET CLOSE IN, UNCLE JIMMY.
I DIDN'T MEAN--
GOT TO FEEL THINGS.
MAYBE YOU EVEN HAVE TO LOSE IT A LITTLE BIT, TOO.
JESUS CHRIST, STOP! *STOP!* ARE YOU FUCKIN' *LISTENIN'* TO ME--?
I think I'm going to stop writing my diary now.

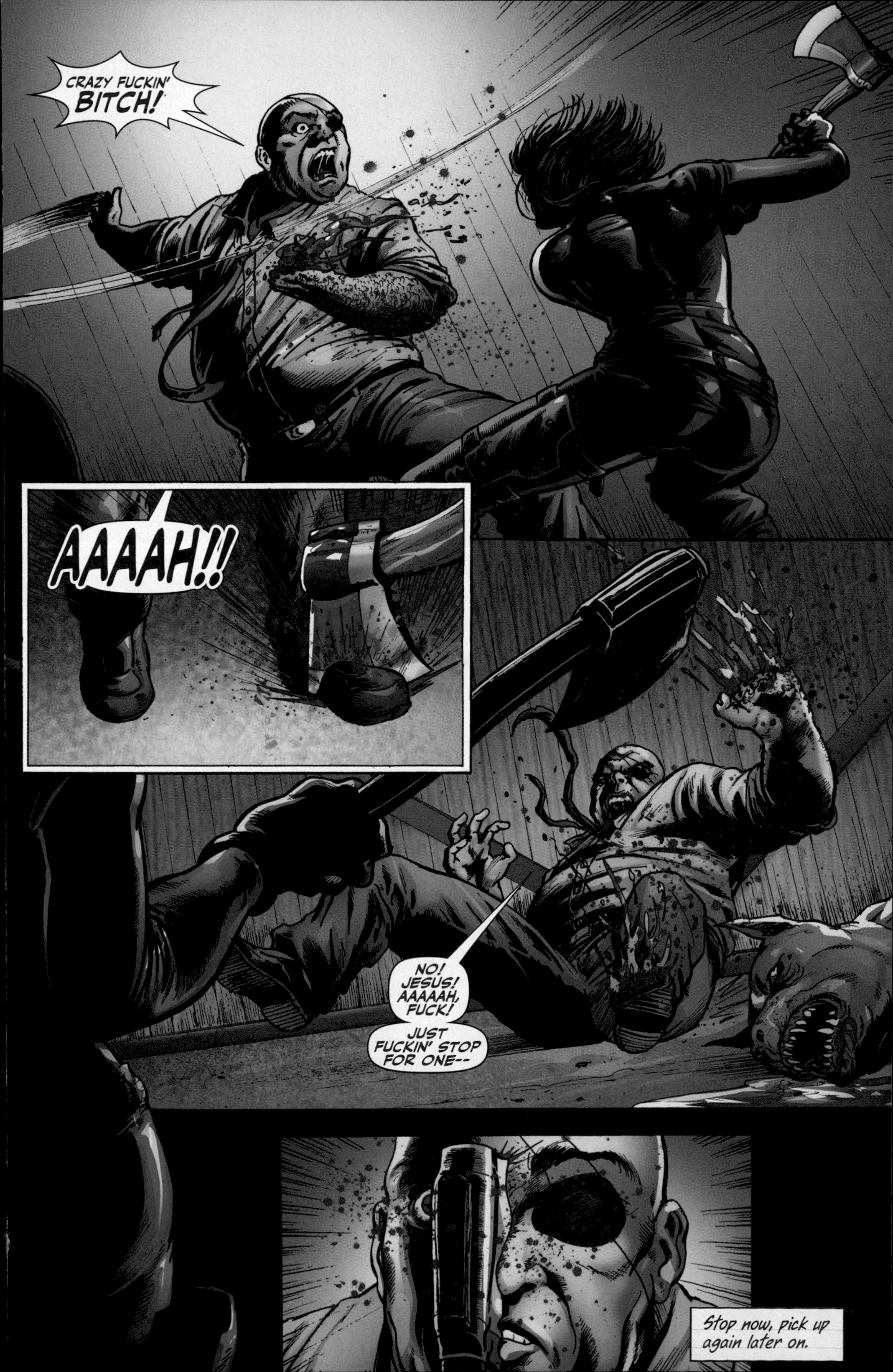
CRAZY FUCKIN' BITCH!
AAAAH!!
NO! JESUS! AAAAAH, FUCK!
JUST FUCKIN' STOP FOR ONE--
Stop now, pick up again later on.

HAWNNNNNK

I'm just so tired.

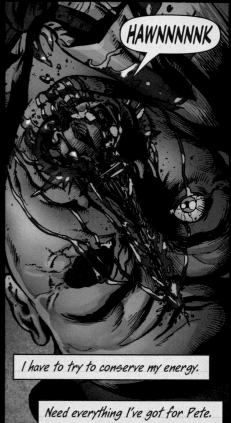

HAWNNNNNK

I have to try to conserve my energy.

Need everything I've got for Pete.

Not to mention the kids' breakfasts. A's lunch. Shopping. Laundry.

The rest.

So when I write this again, all being well, I'll be recording the violent death of the last and oldest Blute brother.

Although that should maybe be if I write this.

Come to think of it—

That could be a pretty big if.

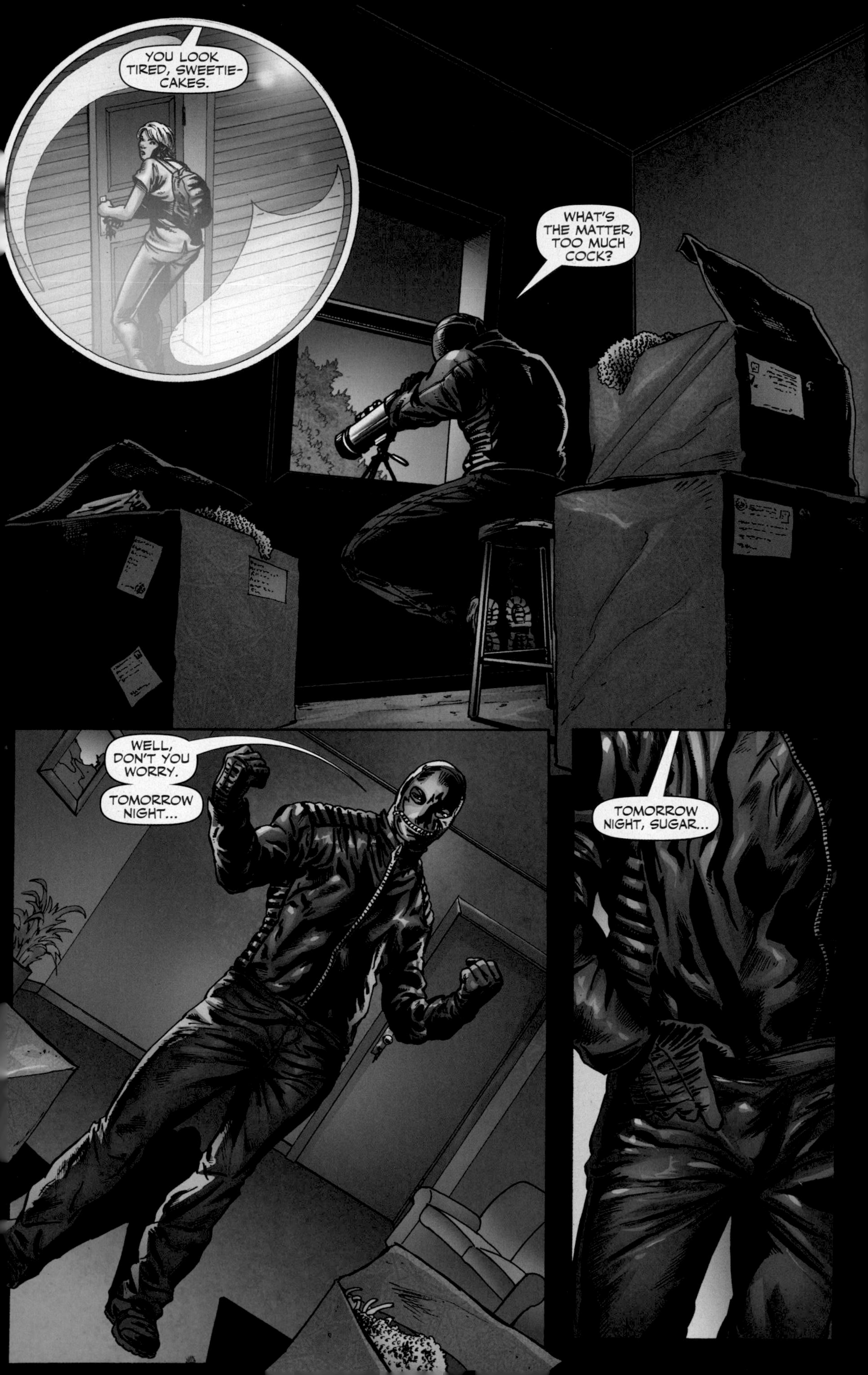
YOU LOOK TIRED, SWEETIE-CAKES.
WHAT'S THE MATTER, TOO MUCH COCK?
WELL, DON'T YOU WORRY.
TOMORROW NIGHT...
TOMORROW NIGHT, SUGAR...

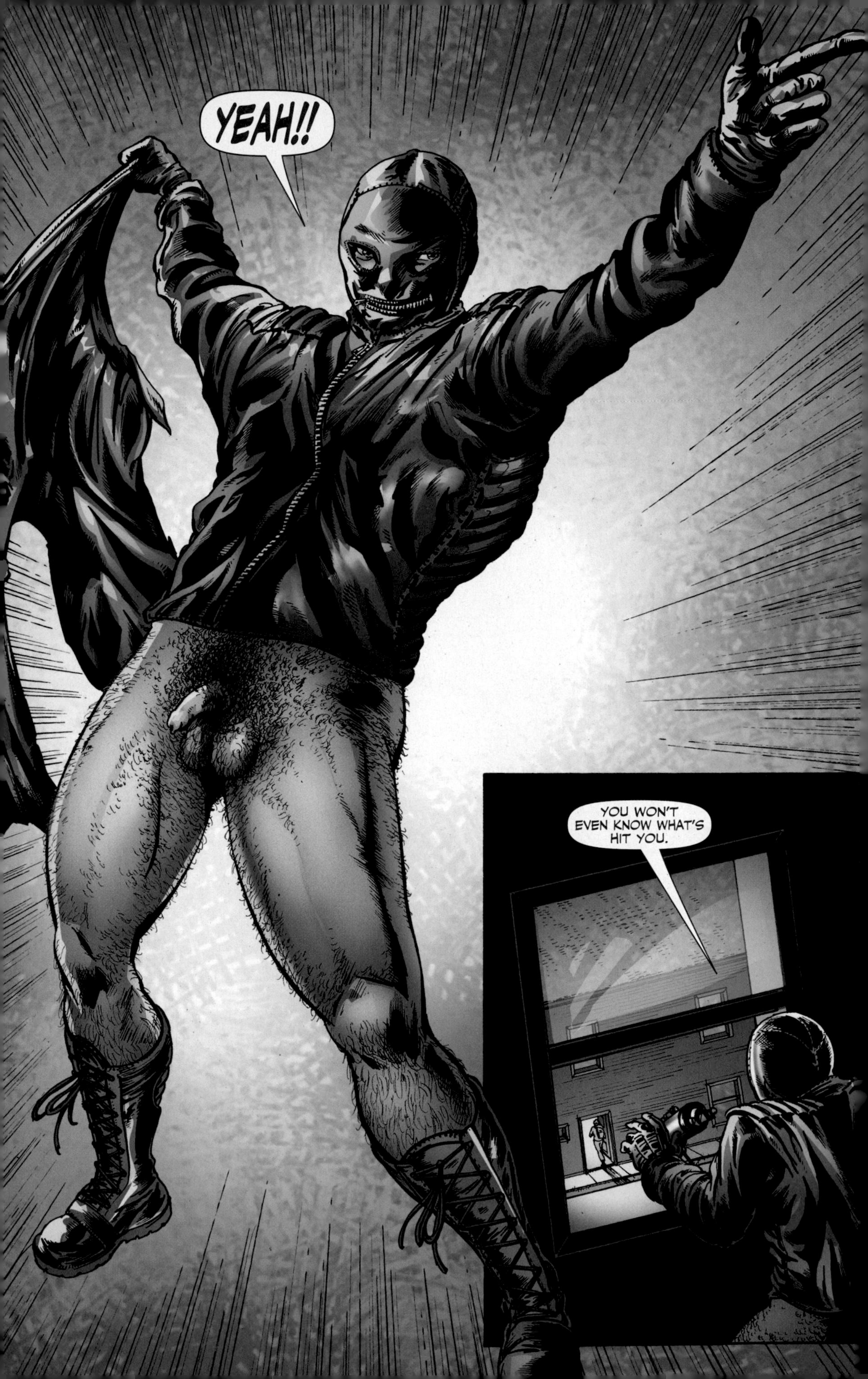
YEAH!!
YOU WON'T EVEN KNOW WHAT'S HIT YOU.

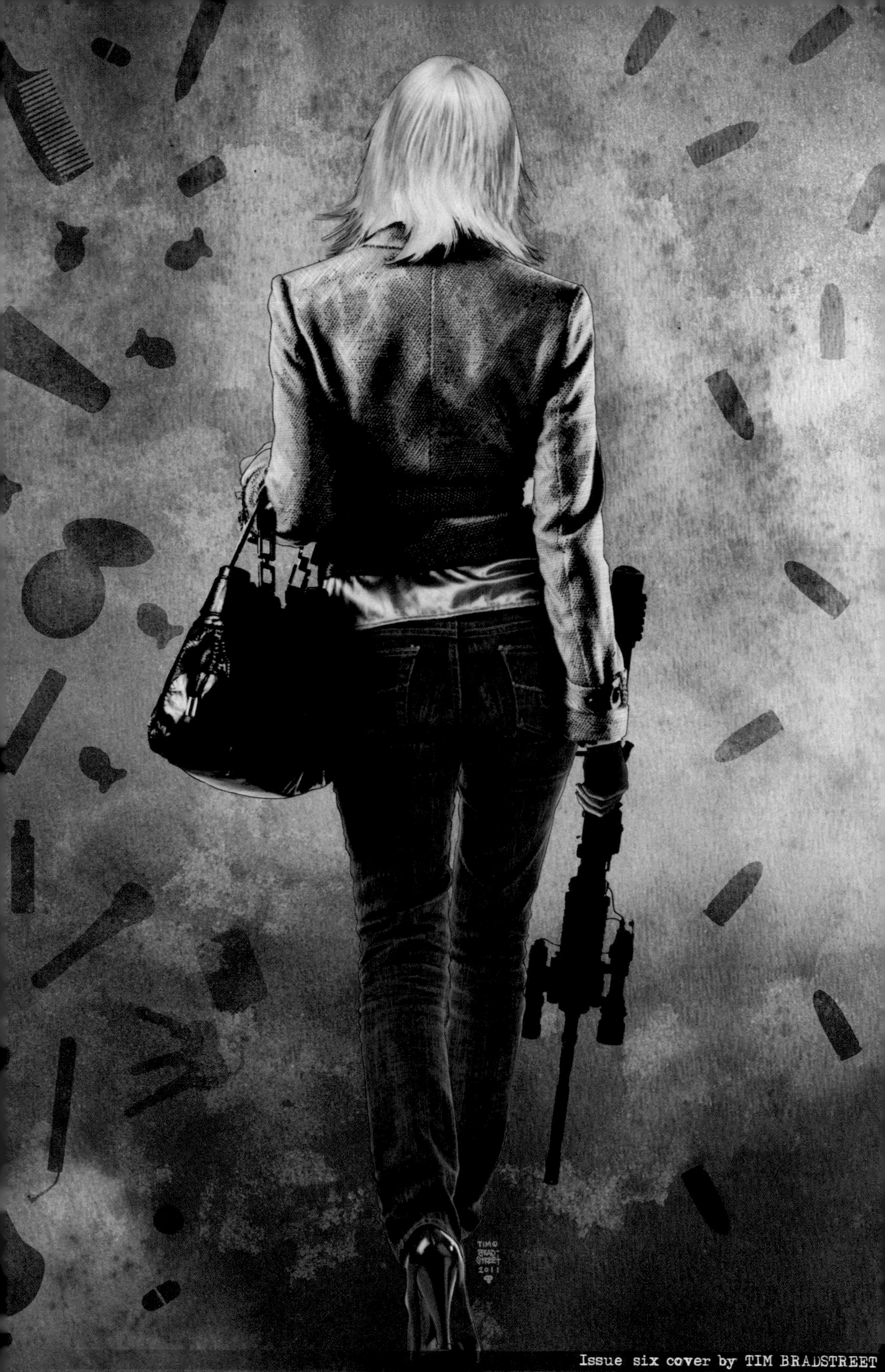
TIM
BRAD-
STREET
2011

Issue six cover by TIM BRADSTREET

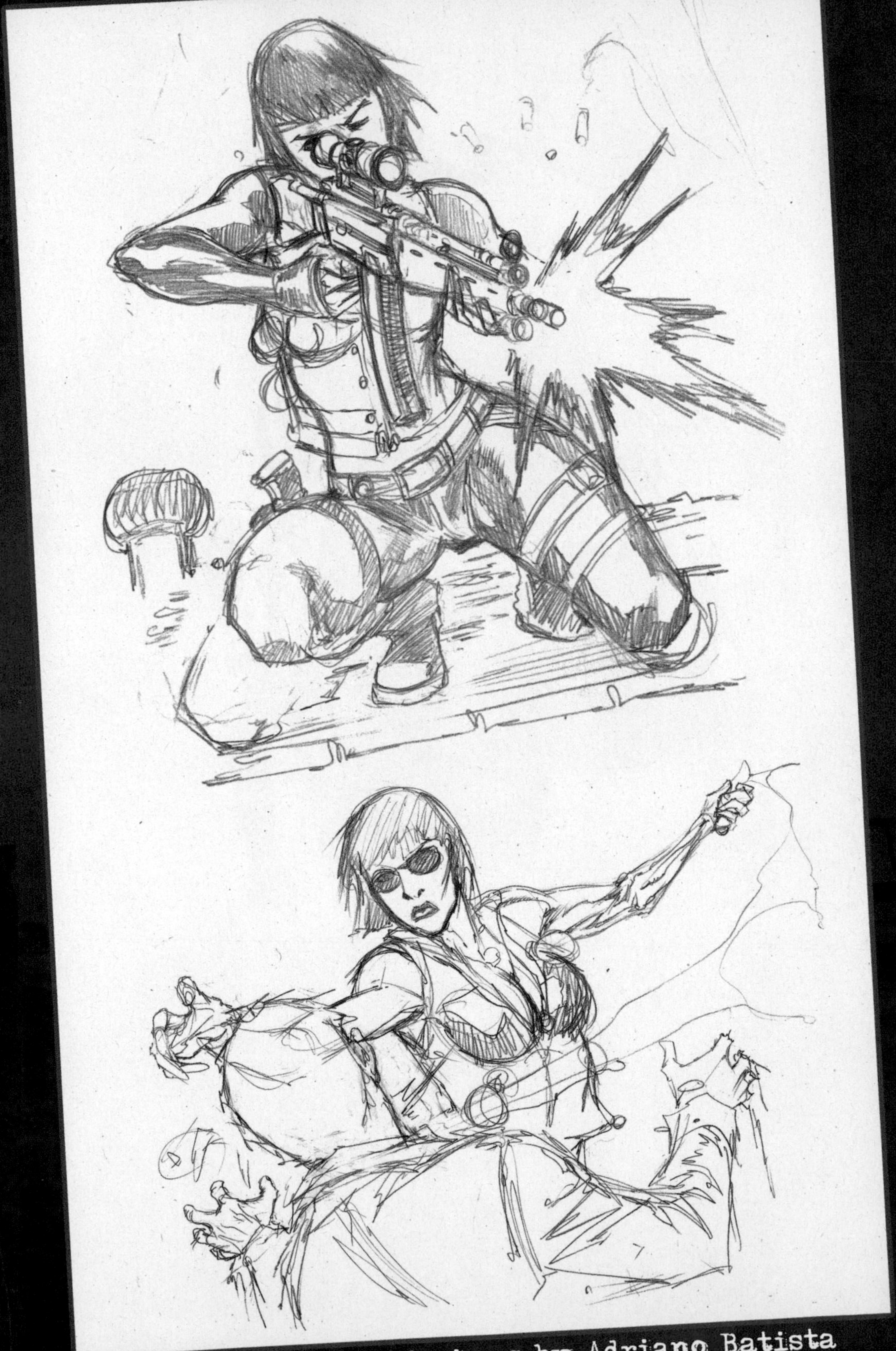

Character sketch/designs by Adriano Batista

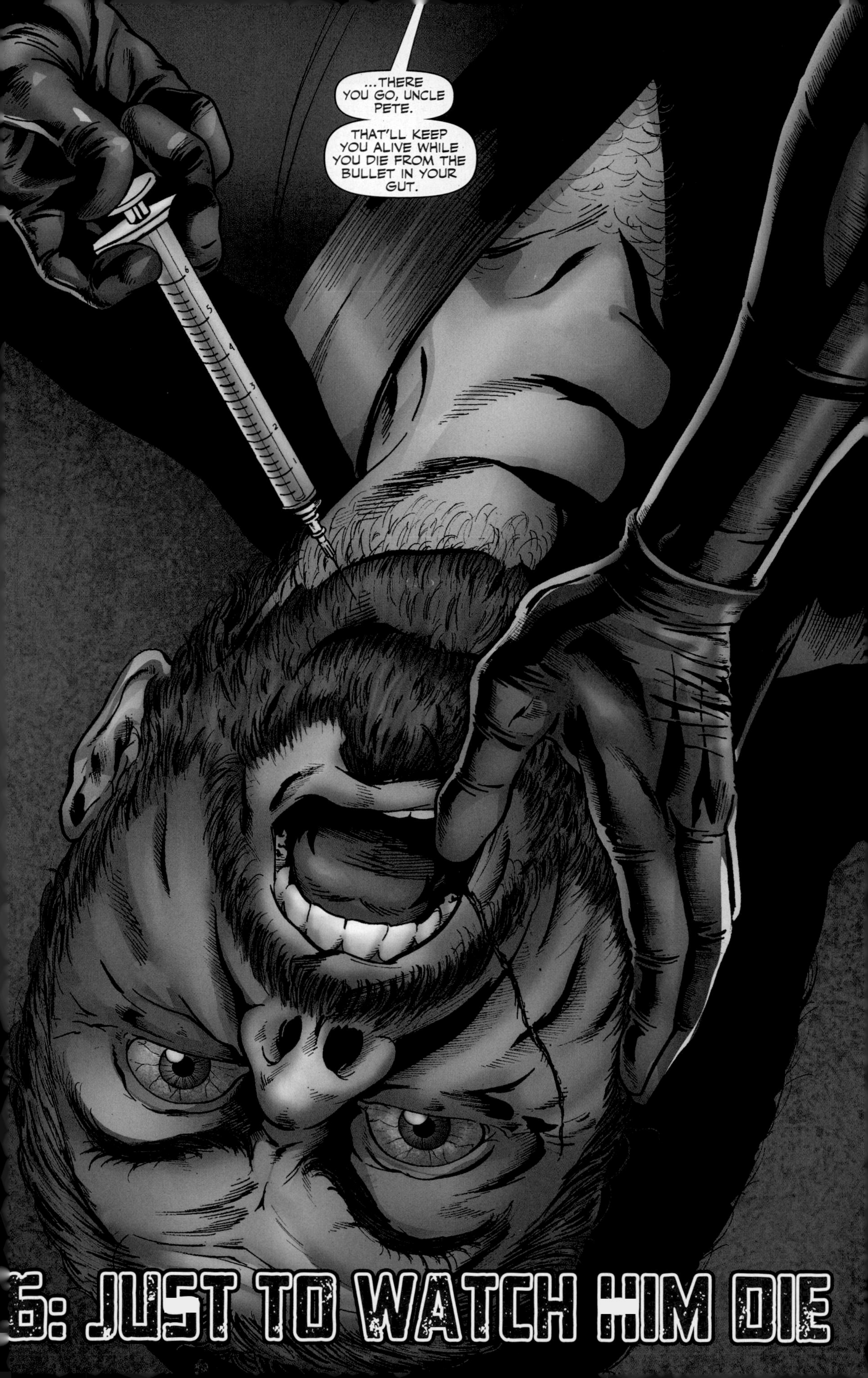
...THERE YOU GO, UNCLE PETE.
THAT'LL KEEP YOU ALIVE WHILE YOU DIE FROM THE BULLET IN YOUR GUT.
6: JUST TO WATCH HIM DIE

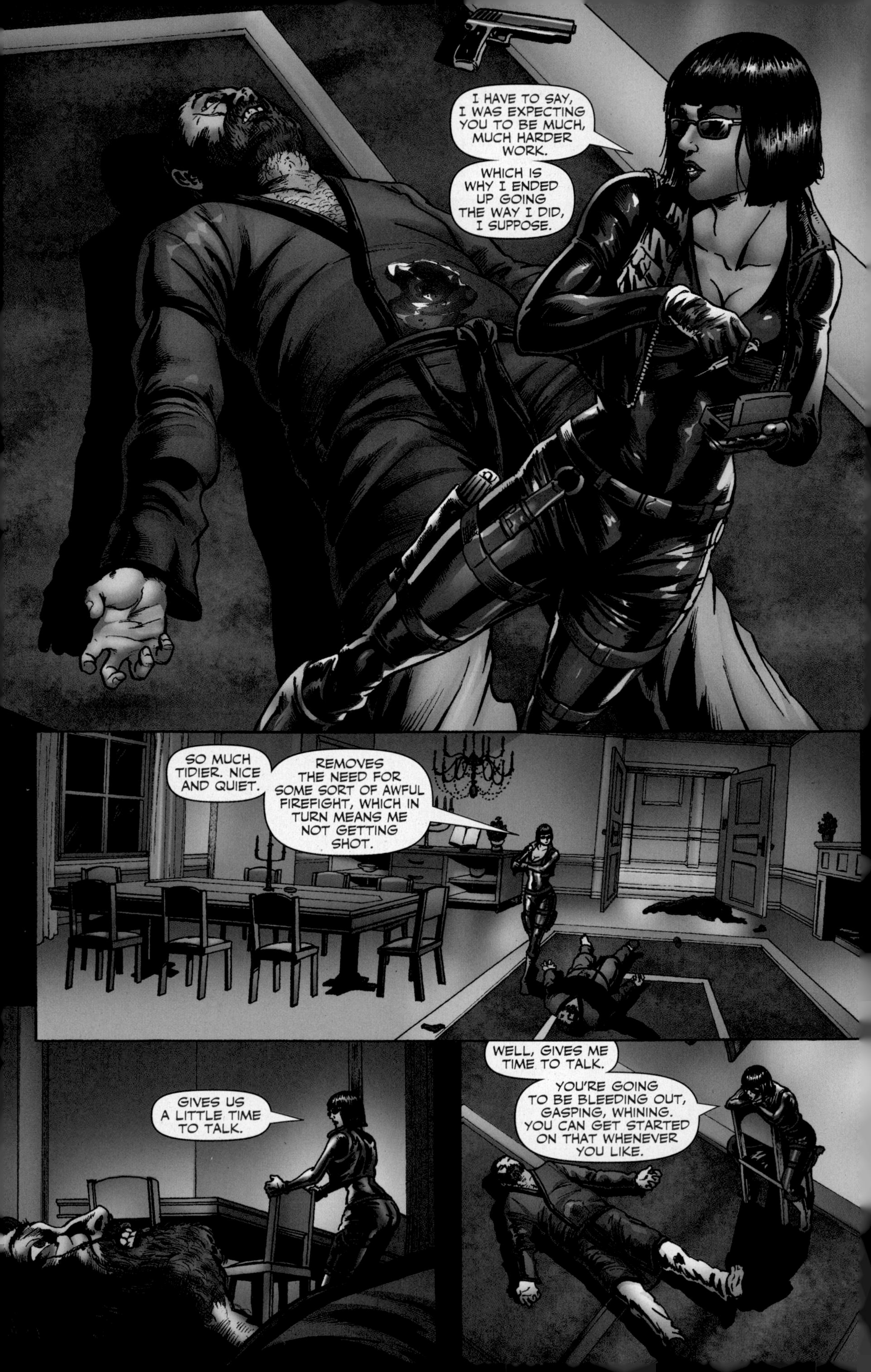
I HAVE TO SAY, I WAS EXPECTING YOU TO BE MUCH, MUCH HARDER WORK.
WHICH IS WHY I ENDED UP GOING THE WAY I DID, I SUPPOSE.
SO MUCH TIDIER. NICE AND QUIET.
REMOVES THE NEED FOR SOME SORT OF AWFUL FIREFIGHT, WHICH IN TURN MEANS ME NOT GETTING SHOT.
GIVES US A LITTLE TIME TO TALK.
WELL, GIVES ME TIME TO TALK.
YOU'RE GOING TO BE BLEEDING OUT, GASPING, WHINING. YOU CAN GET STARTED ON THAT WHENEVER YOU LIKE.

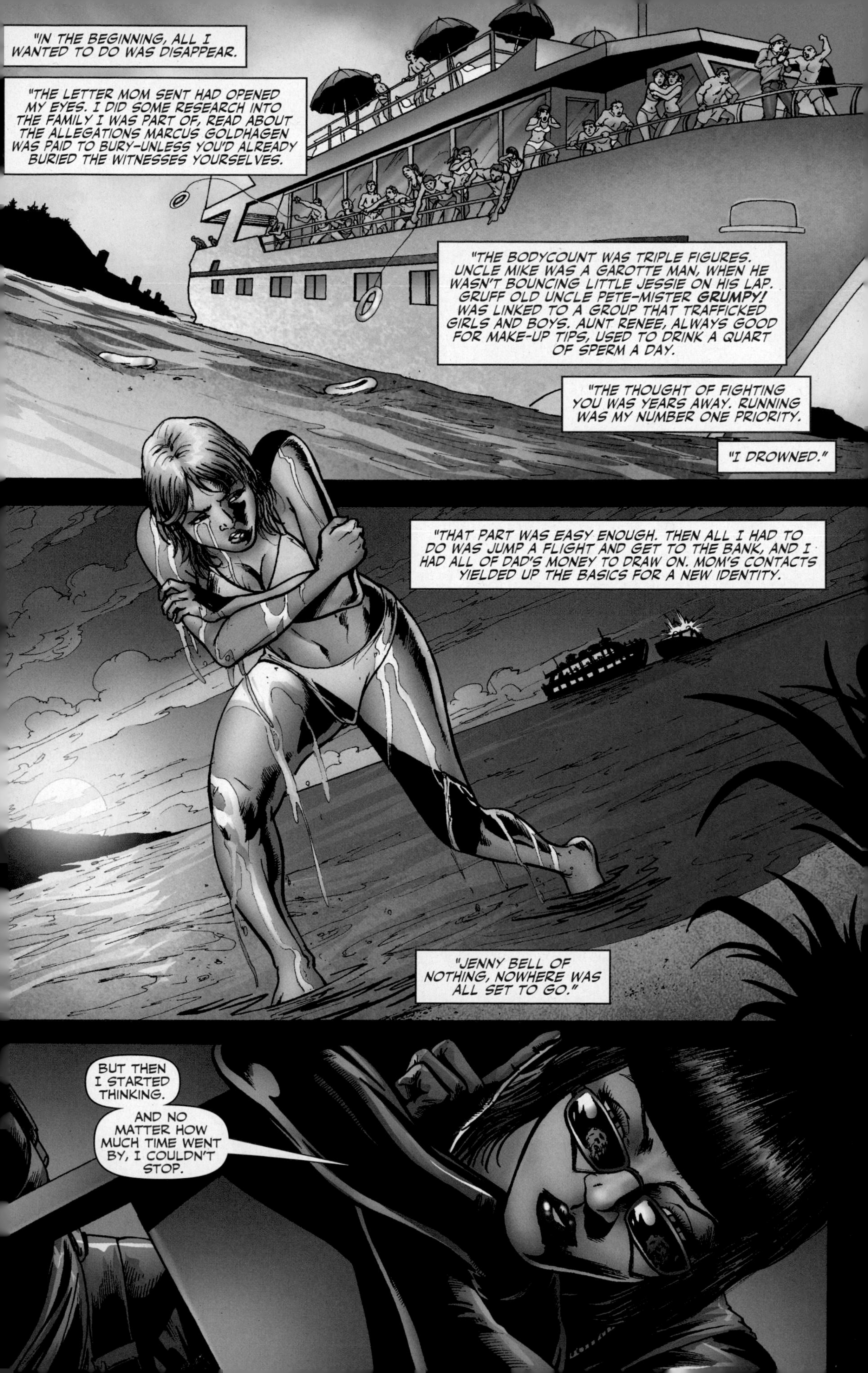
"IN THE BEGINNING, ALL I WANTED TO DO WAS DISAPPEAR.
"THE LETTER MOM SENT HAD OPENED MY EYES. I DID SOME RESEARCH INTO THE FAMILY I WAS PART OF, READ ABOUT THE ALLEGATIONS MARCUS GOLDHAGEN WAS PAID TO BURY–UNLESS YOU'D ALREADY BURIED THE WITNESSES YOURSELVES.
"THE BODYCOUNT WAS TRIPLE FIGURES. UNCLE MIKE WAS A GAROTTE MAN, WHEN HE WASN'T BOUNCING LITTLE JESSIE ON HIS LAP. GRUFF OLD UNCLE PETE–MISTER **GRUMPY!** WAS LINKED TO A GROUP THAT TRAFFICKED GIRLS AND BOYS. AUNT RENEE, ALWAYS GOOD FOR MAKE-UP TIPS, USED TO DRINK A QUART OF SPERM A DAY.
"THE THOUGHT OF FIGHTING YOU WAS YEARS AWAY. RUNNING WAS MY NUMBER ONE PRIORITY.
"I DROWNED."
"THAT PART WAS EASY ENOUGH. THEN ALL I HAD TO DO WAS JUMP A FLIGHT AND GET TO THE BANK, AND I HAD ALL OF DAD'S MONEY TO DRAW ON. MOM'S CONTACTS YIELDED UP THE BASICS FOR A NEW IDENTITY.
"JENNY BELL OF NOTHING, NOWHERE WAS ALL SET TO GO."
BUT THEN I STARTED THINKING.
AND NO MATTER HOW MUCH TIME WENT BY, I COULDN'T STOP.

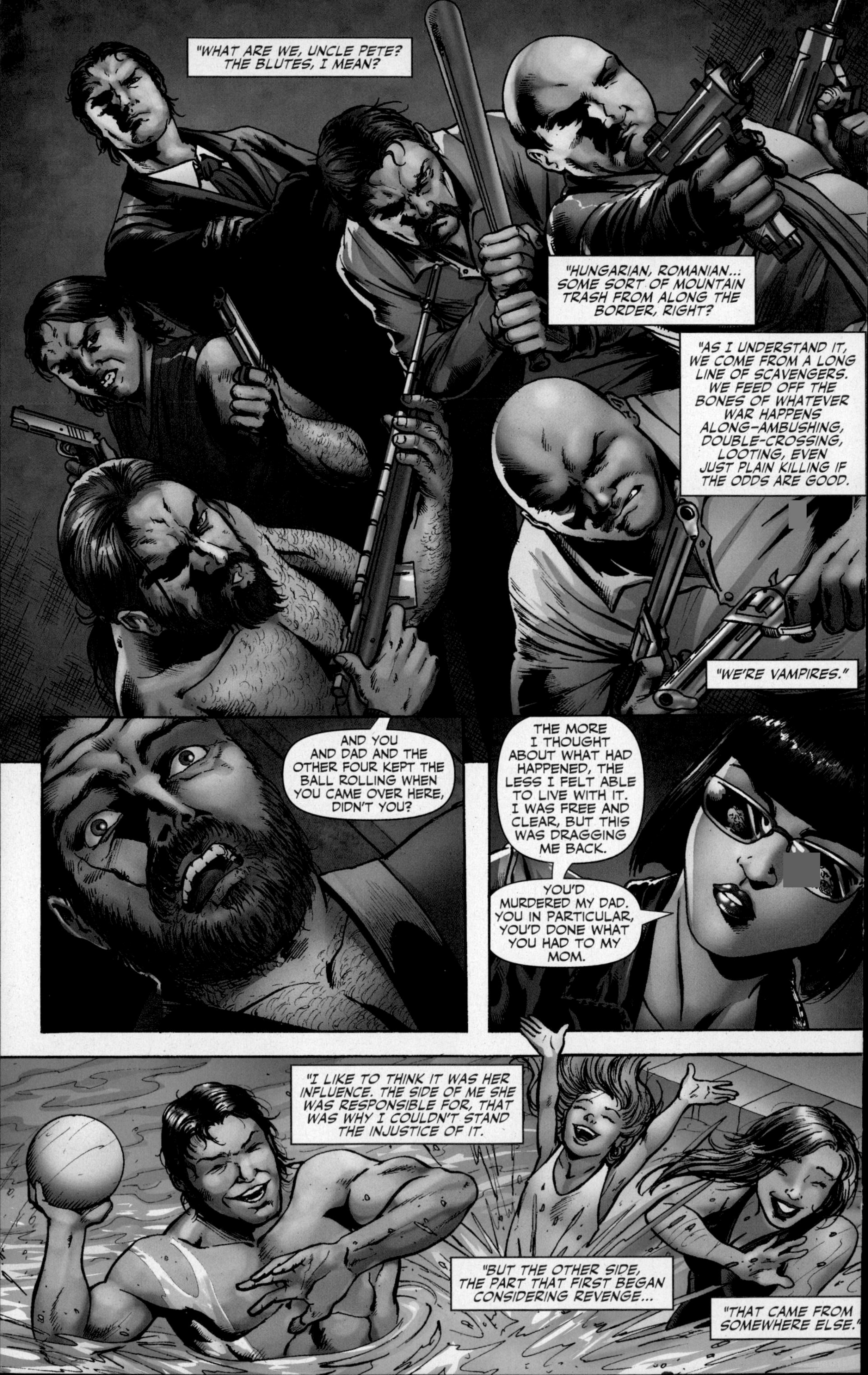
"WHAT ARE WE, UNCLE PETE? THE BLUTES, I MEAN?
"HUNGARIAN, ROMANIAN... SOME SORT OF MOUNTAIN TRASH FROM ALONG THE BORDER, RIGHT?
"AS I UNDERSTAND IT, WE COME FROM A LONG LINE OF SCAVENGERS. WE FEED OFF THE BONES OF WHATEVER WAR HAPPENS ALONG--AMBUSHING, DOUBLE-CROSSING, LOOTING, EVEN JUST PLAIN KILLING IF THE ODDS ARE GOOD.
"WE'RE VAMPIRES."
AND YOU AND DAD AND THE OTHER FOUR KEPT THE BALL ROLLING WHEN YOU CAME OVER HERE, DIDN'T YOU?
THE MORE I THOUGHT ABOUT WHAT HAD HAPPENED, THE LESS I FELT ABLE TO LIVE WITH IT. I WAS FREE AND CLEAR, BUT THIS WAS DRAGGING ME BACK.
YOU'D MURDERED MY DAD. YOU IN PARTICULAR, YOU'D DONE WHAT YOU HAD TO MY MOM.
"I LIKE TO THINK IT WAS HER INFLUENCE. THE SIDE OF ME SHE WAS RESPONSIBLE FOR, THAT WAS WHY I COULDN'T STAND THE INJUSTICE OF IT.
"BUT THE OTHER SIDE, THE PART THAT FIRST BEGAN CONSIDERING REVENGE...
"THAT CAME FROM SOMEWHERE ELSE."

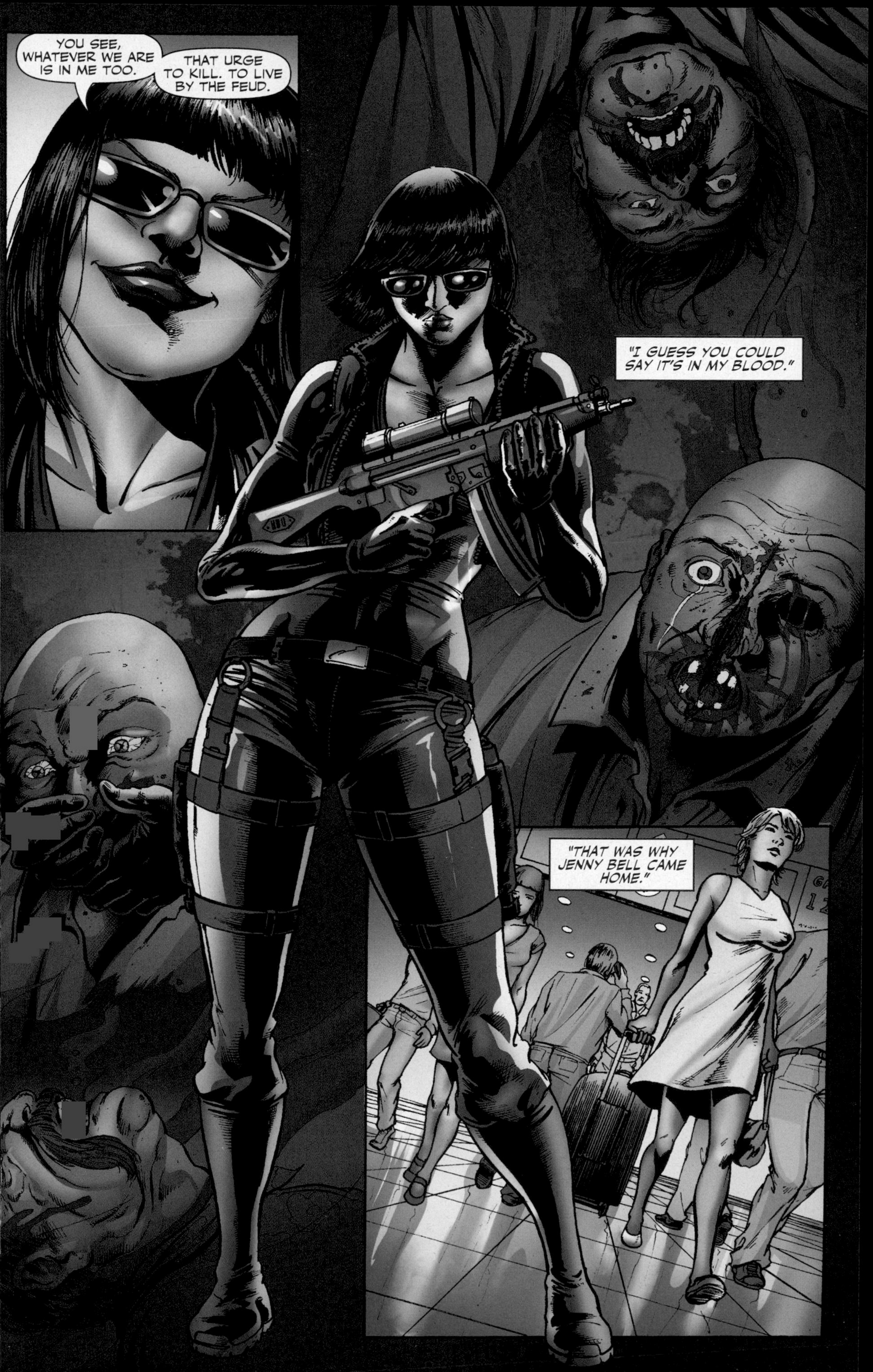
YOU SEE, WHATEVER WE ARE IS IN ME TOO.
THAT URGE TO KILL. TO LIVE BY THE FEUD.
"I GUESS YOU COULD SAY IT'S IN MY BLOOD."
"THAT WAS WHY JENNY BELL CAME HOME."

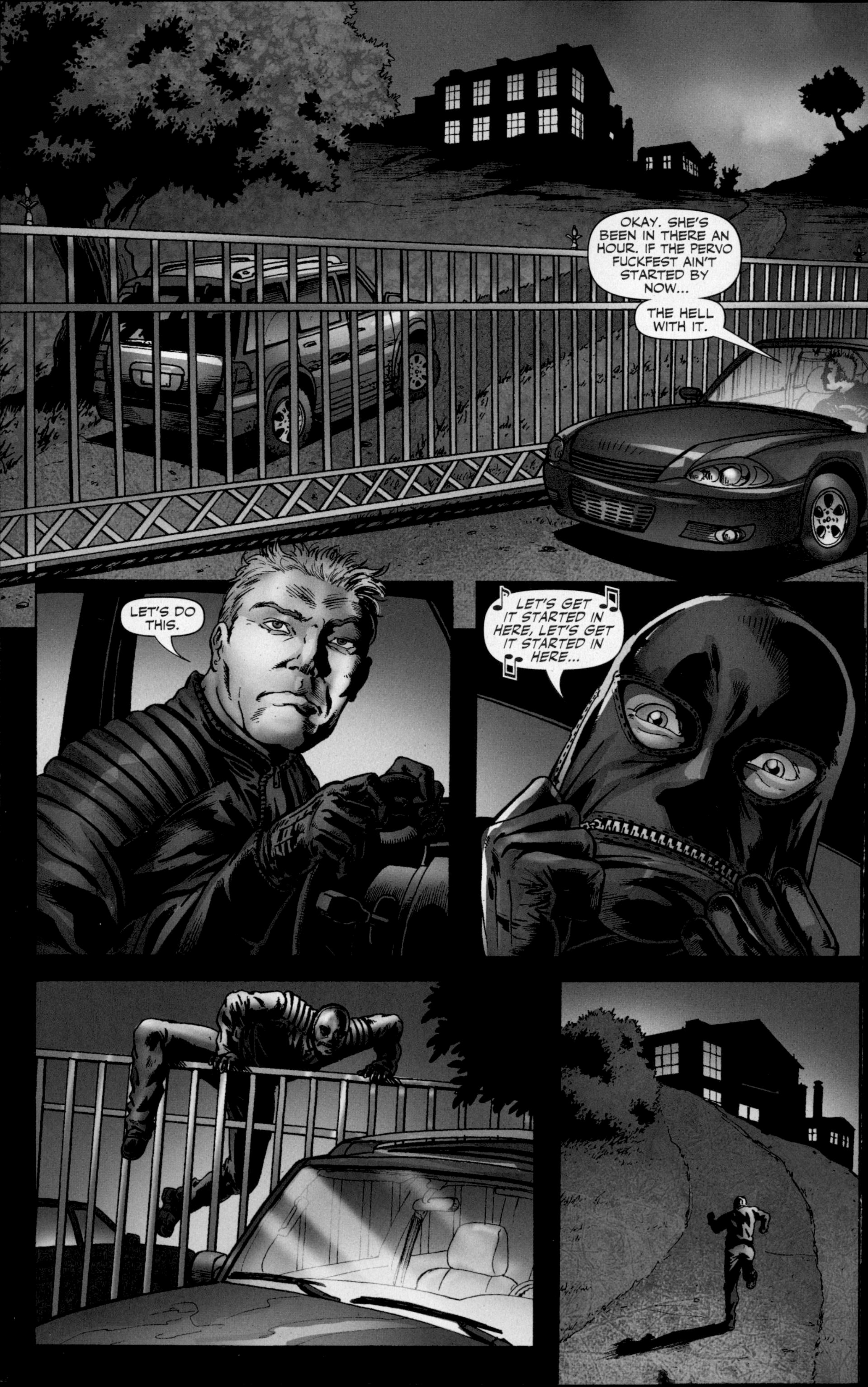
OKAY. SHE'S BEEN IN THERE AN HOUR. IF THE PERVO FUCKFEST AIN'T STARTED BY NOW...
THE HELL WITH IT.
LET'S DO THIS.
LET'S GET IT STARTED IN HERE, LET'S GET IT STARTED IN HERE...

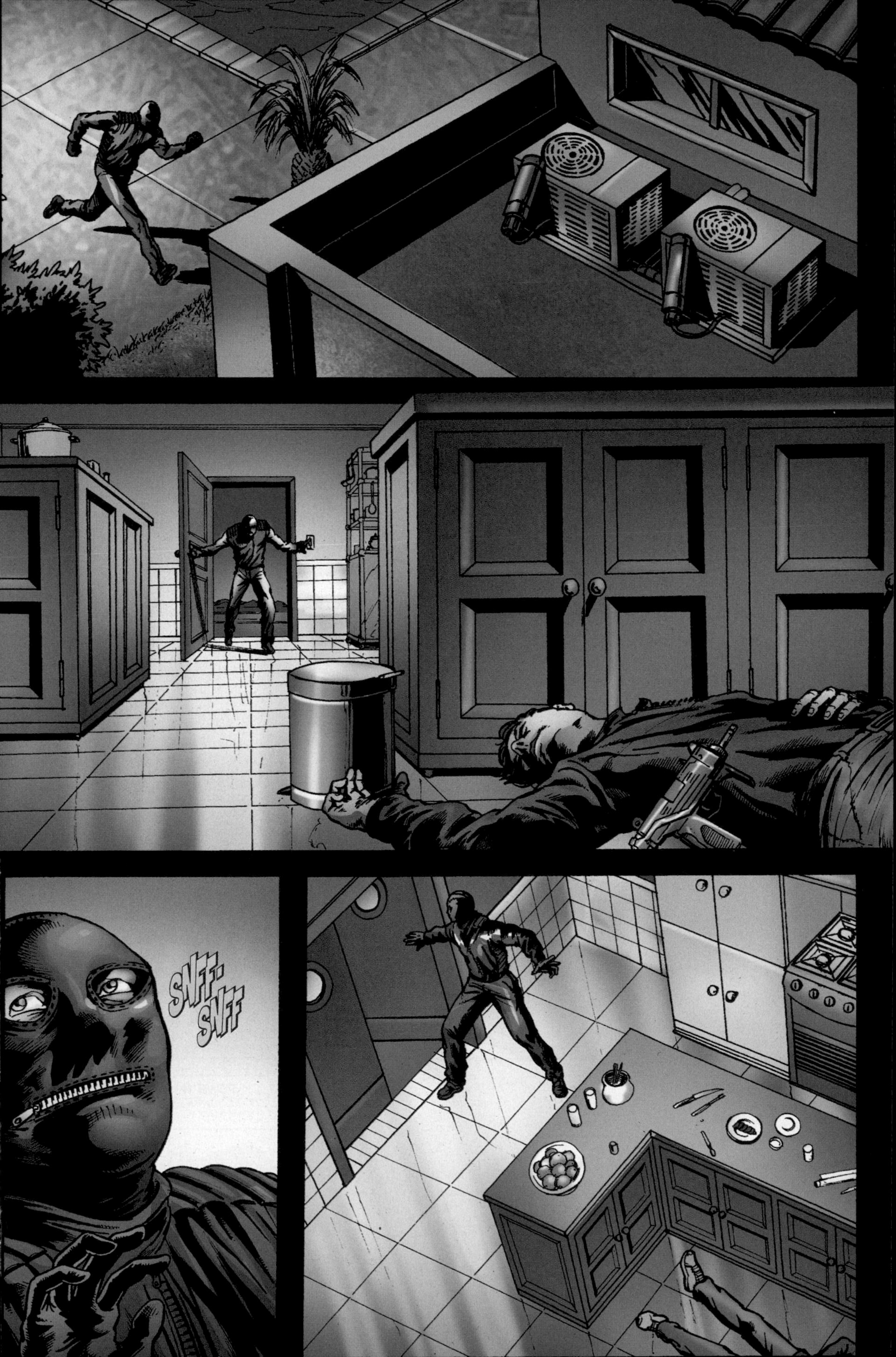
SNFF-
SNFF

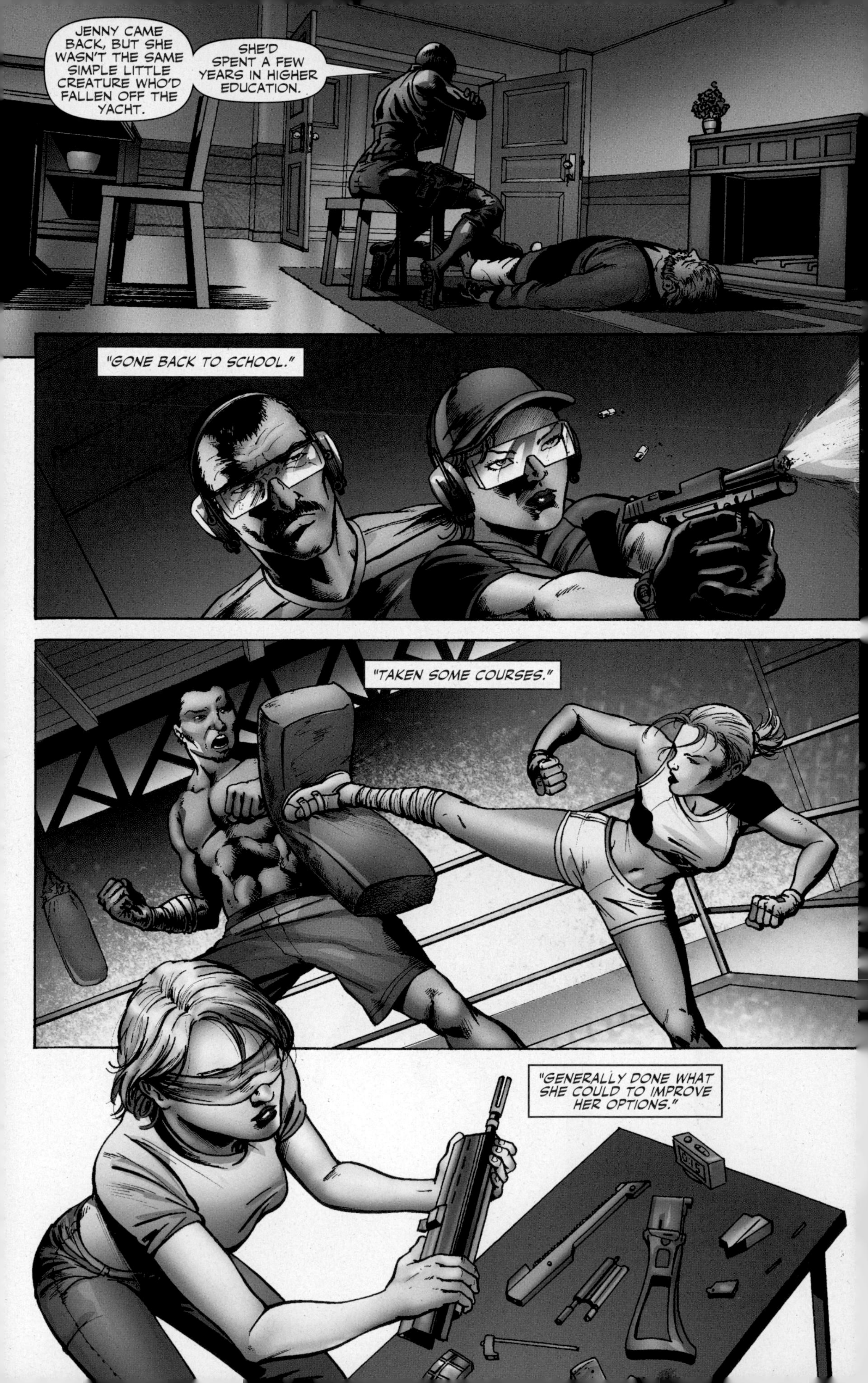
JENNY CAME BACK, BUT SHE WASN'T THE SAME SIMPLE LITTLE CREATURE WHO'D FALLEN OFF THE YACHT.
SHE'D SPENT A FEW YEARS IN HIGHER EDUCATION.
"GONE BACK TO SCHOOL."
"TAKEN SOME COURSES."
"GENERALLY DONE WHAT SHE COULD TO IMPROVE HER OPTIONS."

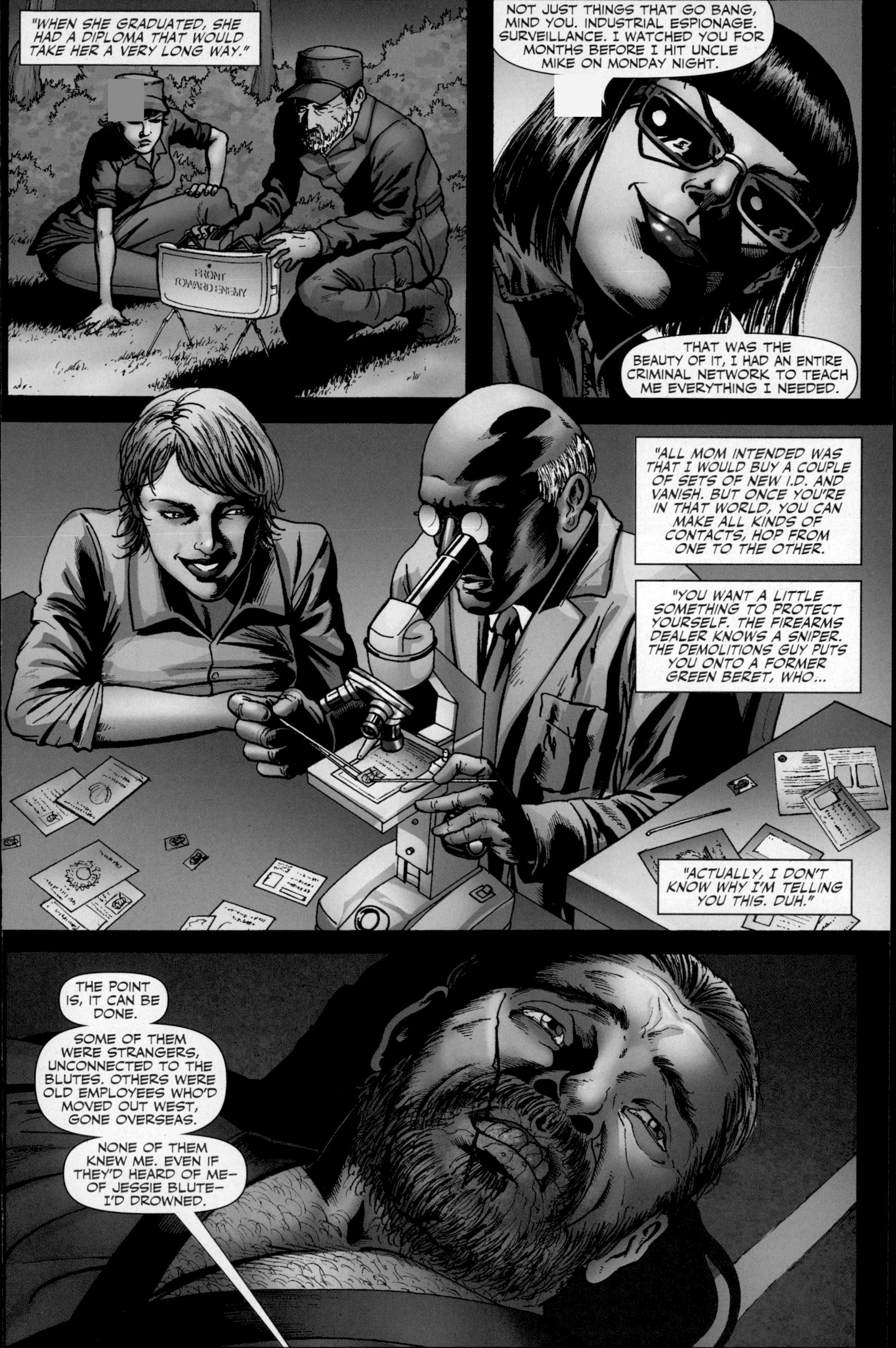
"WHEN SHE GRADUATED, SHE HAD A DIPLOMA THAT WOULD TAKE HER A VERY LONG WAY."
FRONT TOWARD ENEMY
NOT JUST THINGS THAT GO BANG, MIND YOU. INDUSTRIAL ESPIONAGE. SURVEILLANCE. I WATCHED YOU FOR MONTHS BEFORE I HIT UNCLE MIKE ON MONDAY NIGHT.
THAT WAS THE BEAUTY OF IT, I HAD AN ENTIRE CRIMINAL NETWORK TO TEACH ME EVERYTHING I NEEDED.
"ALL MOM INTENDED WAS THAT I WOULD BUY A COUPLE OF SETS OF NEW I.D. AND VANISH. BUT ONCE YOU'RE IN THAT WORLD, YOU CAN MAKE ALL KINDS OF CONTACTS, HOP FROM ONE TO THE OTHER.
"YOU WANT A LITTLE SOMETHING TO PROTECT YOURSELF. THE FIREARMS DEALER KNOWS A SNIPER. THE DEMOLITIONS GUY PUTS YOU ONTO A FORMER GREEN BERET, WHO...
"ACTUALLY, I DON'T KNOW WHY I'M TELLING YOU THIS. DUH."
THE POINT IS, IT CAN BE DONE.
SOME OF THEM WERE STRANGERS, UNCONNECTED TO THE BLUTES. OTHERS WERE OLD EMPLOYEES WHO'D MOVED OUT WEST, GONE OVERSEAS.
NONE OF THEM KNEW ME. EVEN IF THEY'D HEARD OF ME– OF JESSIE BLUTE– I'D DROWNED.

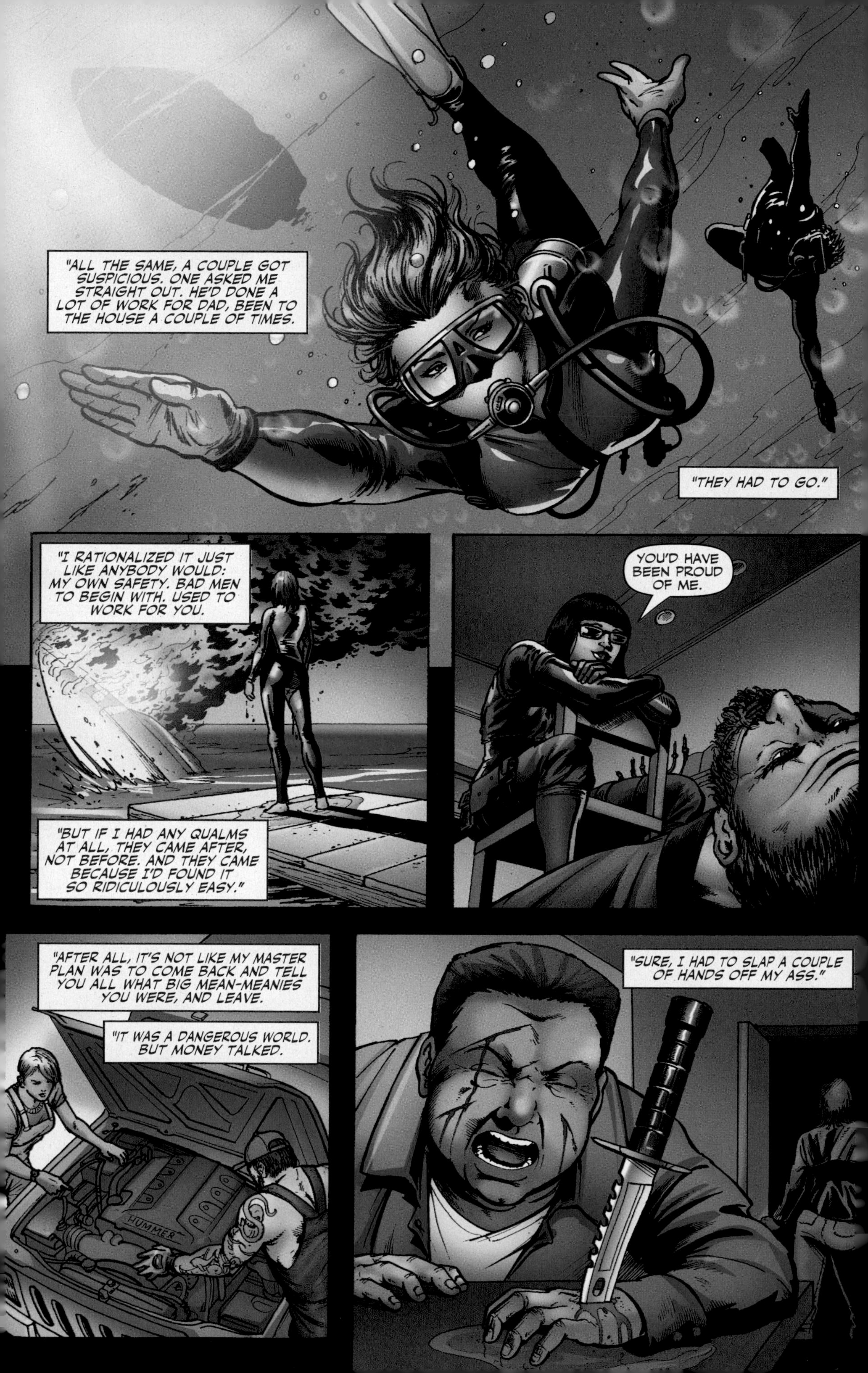
"ALL THE SAME, A COUPLE GOT SUSPICIOUS. ONE ASKED ME STRAIGHT OUT. HE'D DONE A LOT OF WORK FOR DAD, BEEN TO THE HOUSE A COUPLE OF TIMES.
"THEY HAD TO GO."
"I RATIONALIZED IT JUST LIKE ANYBODY WOULD: MY OWN SAFETY. BAD MEN TO BEGIN WITH. USED TO WORK FOR YOU.
"BUT IF I HAD ANY QUALMS AT ALL, THEY CAME AFTER, NOT BEFORE. AND THEY CAME BECAUSE I'D FOUND IT SO RIDICULOUSLY EASY."
YOU'D HAVE BEEN PROUD OF ME.
"AFTER ALL, IT'S NOT LIKE MY MASTER PLAN WAS TO COME BACK AND TELL YOU ALL WHAT BIG MEAN-MEANIES YOU WERE, AND LEAVE.
"IT WAS A DANGEROUS WORLD. BUT MONEY TALKED.
HUMMER
"SURE, I HAD TO SLAP A COUPLE OF HANDS OFF MY ASS."

I LEARNED EVERYTHING I POSSIBLY COULD. MY BRAIN WAS FULL TO BURSTING, WITH EVERYTHING FROM SETTING TIMERS TO LOSING TAILS.

IT WAS WHEN I WAS IN QUEENS, LEARNING THE ANCIENT ART OF BROKEN BOTTLE COMBAT FROM A MAN CALLED O'FEE, THAT I REALIZED I WAS JUST PREVARICATING.

I WAS READY.

IT WAS TIME TO COME AND KILL THE FIVE OF YOU.

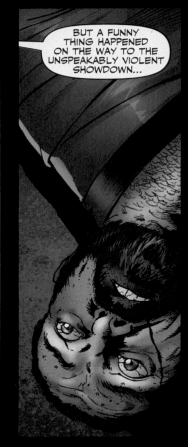

BUT A FUNNY THING HAPPENED ON THE WAY TO THE UNSPEAKABLY VIOLENT SHOWDOWN...

DID YOU HEAR THAT?

WAIT THERE A SECOND.

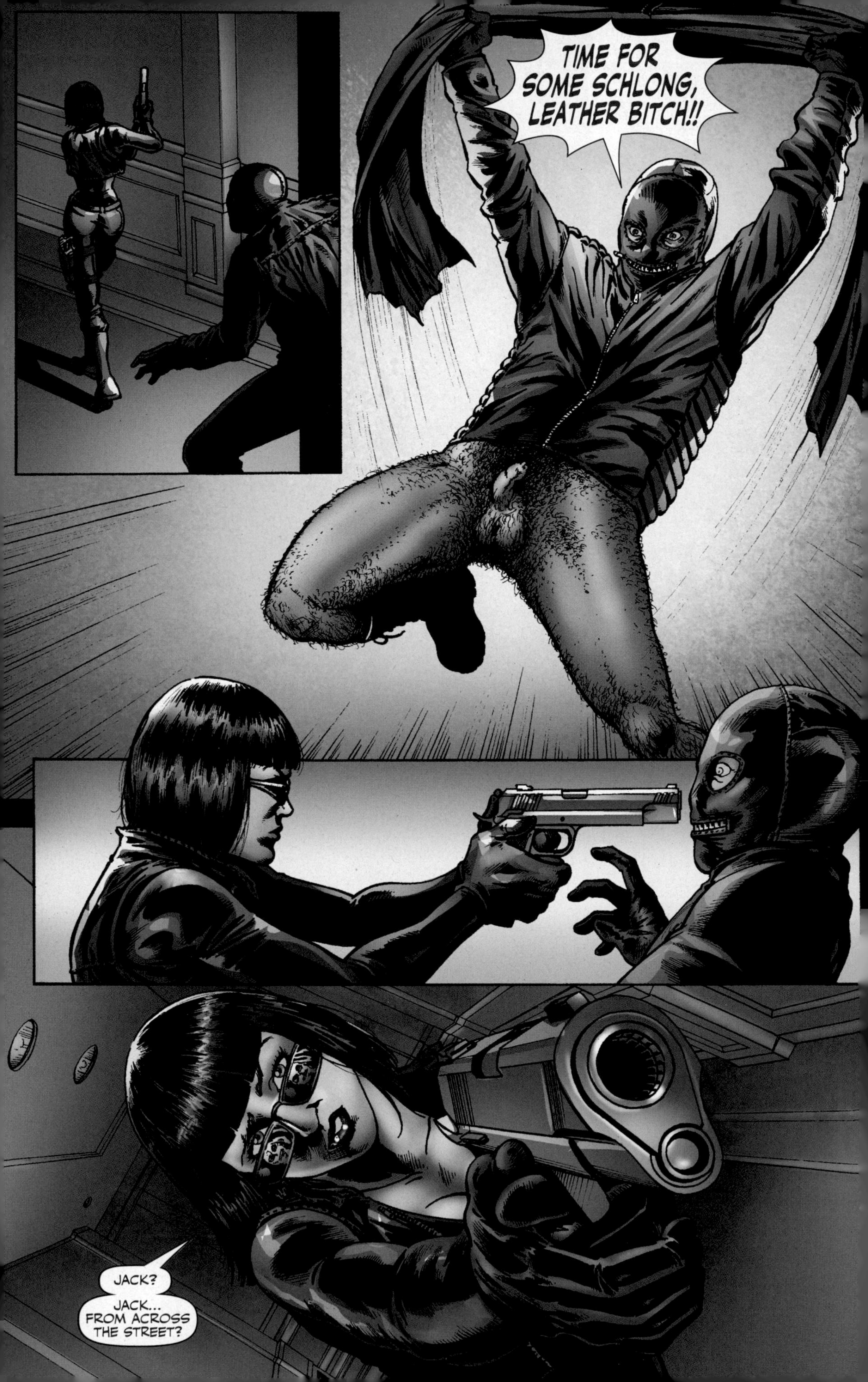
TIME FOR SOME SCHLONG, LEATHER BITCH!!
JACK?
JACK... FROM ACROSS THE STREET?

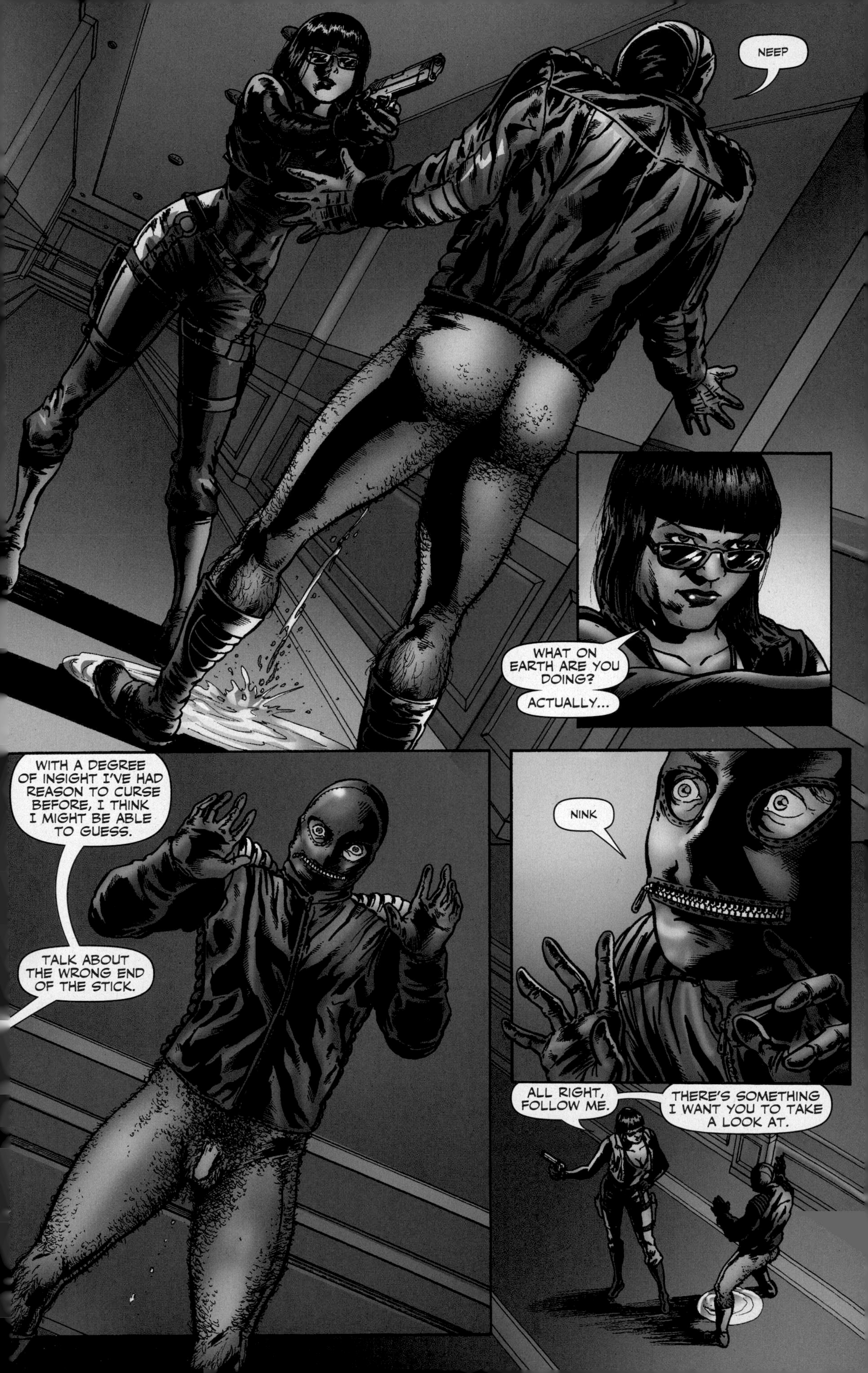
NEEP
WHAT ON EARTH ARE YOU DOING?
ACTUALLY...
WITH A DEGREE OF INSIGHT I'VE HAD REASON TO CURSE BEFORE, I THINK I MIGHT BE ABLE TO GUESS.
TALK ABOUT THE WRONG END OF THE STICK.
NINK
ALL RIGHT, FOLLOW ME.
THERE'S SOMETHING I WANT YOU TO TAKE A LOOK AT.

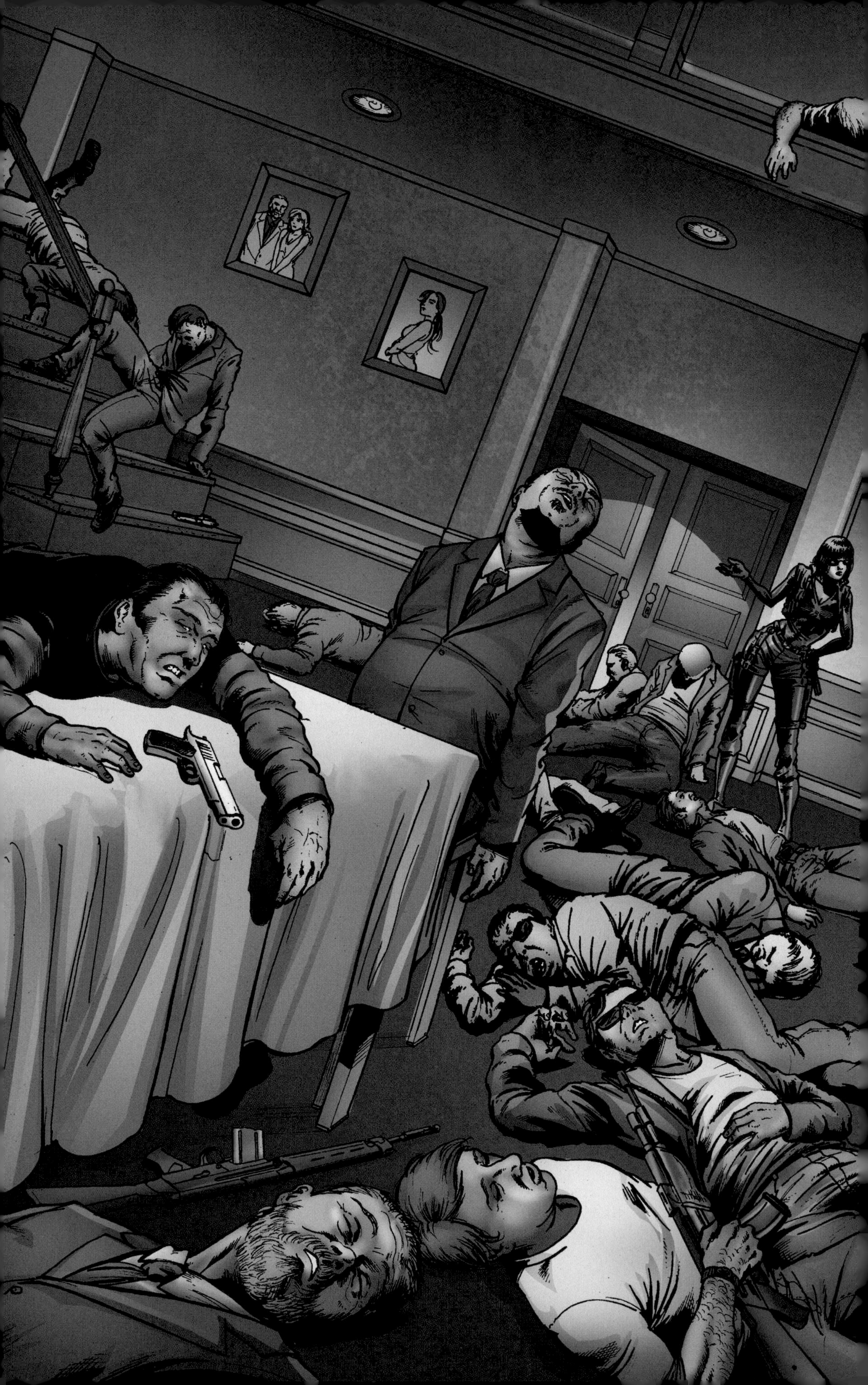

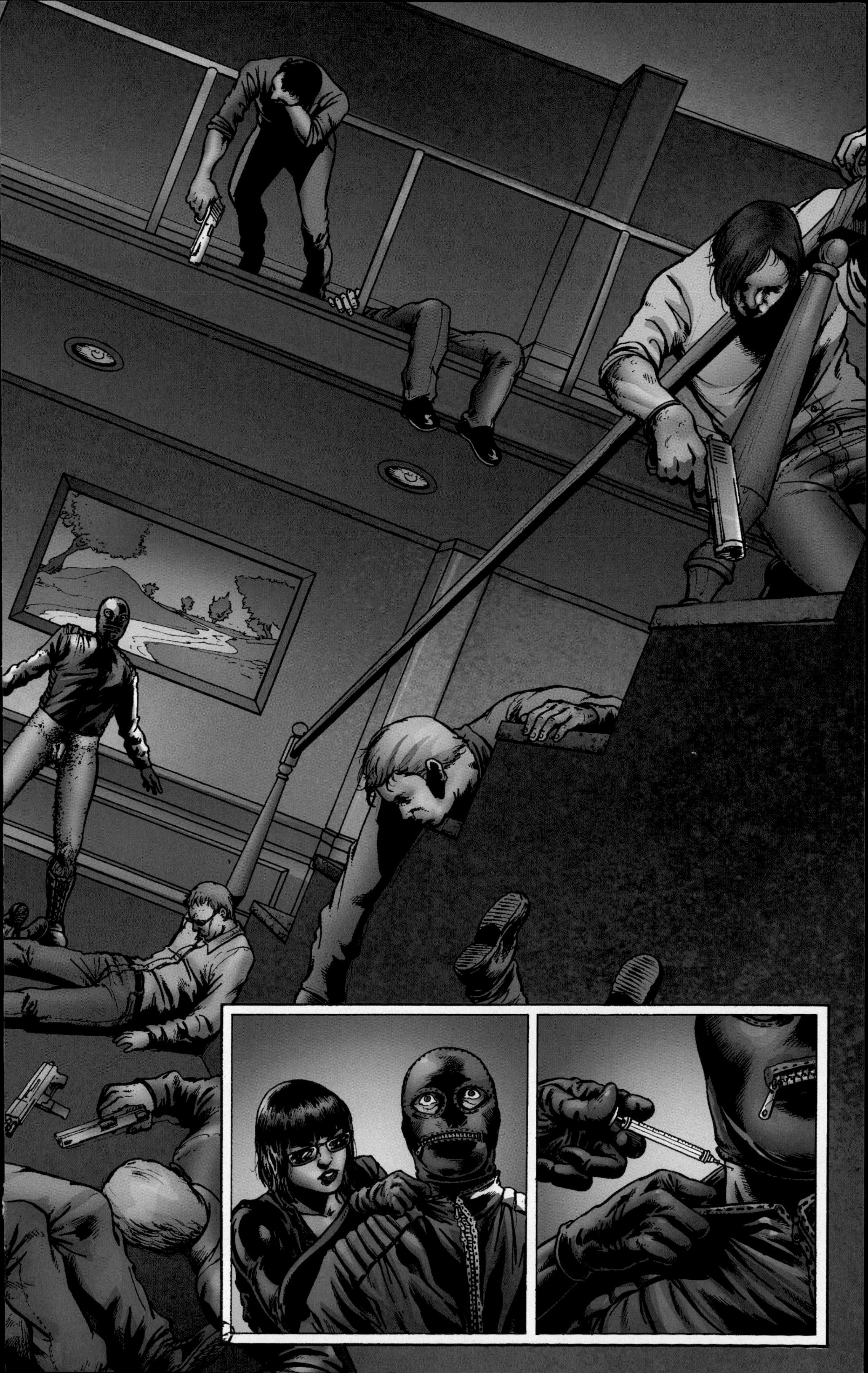

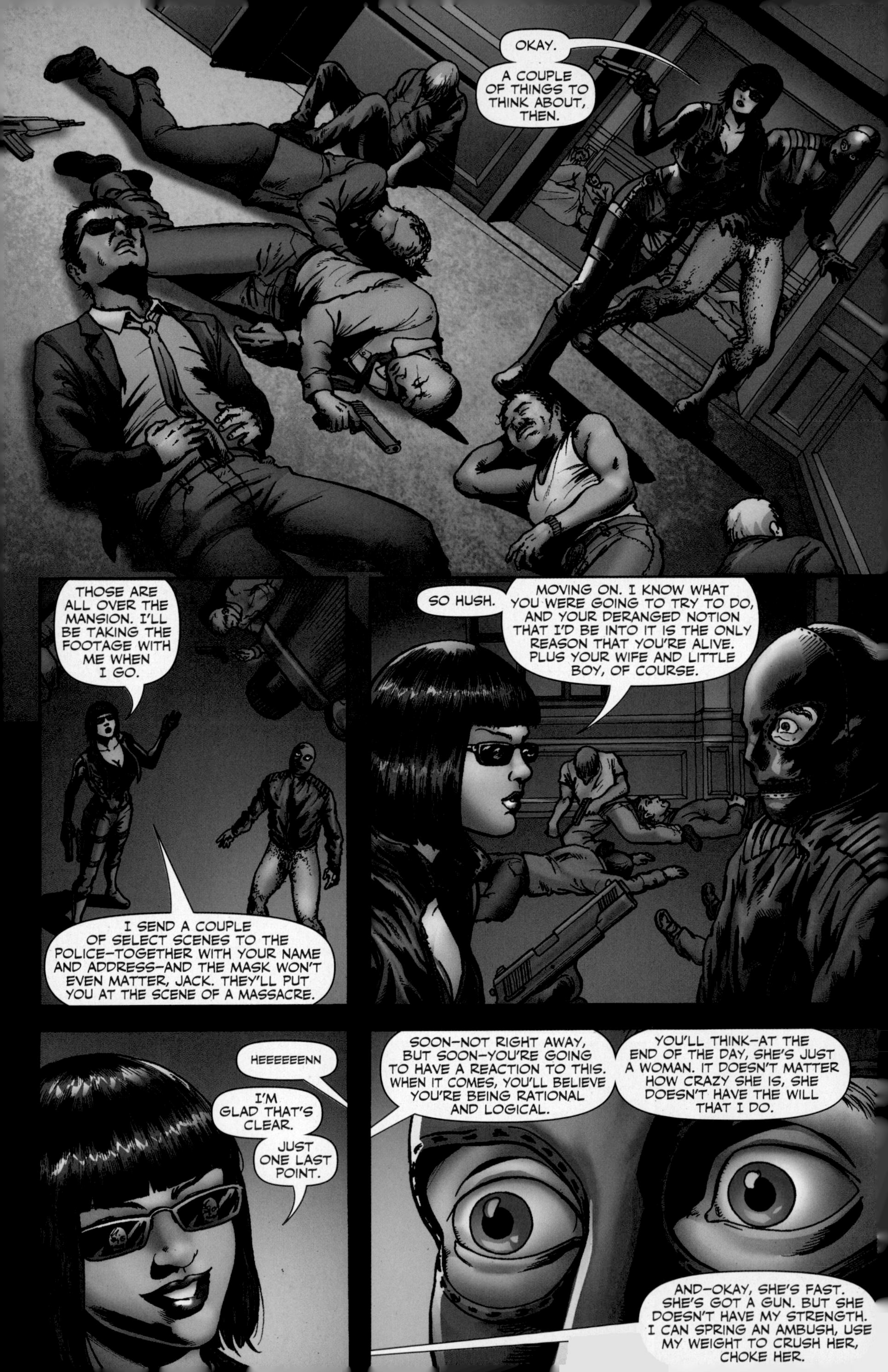
OKAY.
A COUPLE OF THINGS TO THINK ABOUT, THEN.
THOSE ARE ALL OVER THE MANSION. I'LL BE TAKING THE FOOTAGE WITH ME WHEN I GO.
I SEND A COUPLE OF SELECT SCENES TO THE POLICE—TOGETHER WITH YOUR NAME AND ADDRESS—AND THE MASK WON'T EVEN MATTER, JACK. THEY'LL PUT YOU AT THE SCENE OF A MASSACRE.
SO HUSH.
MOVING ON. I KNOW WHAT YOU WERE GOING TO TRY TO DO, AND YOUR DERANGED NOTION THAT I'D BE INTO IT IS THE ONLY REASON THAT YOU'RE ALIVE. PLUS YOUR WIFE AND LITTLE BOY, OF COURSE.
HEEEEEENN
I'M GLAD THAT'S CLEAR.
JUST ONE LAST POINT.
SOON—NOT RIGHT AWAY, BUT SOON—YOU'RE GOING TO HAVE A REACTION TO THIS. WHEN IT COMES, YOU'LL BELIEVE YOU'RE BEING RATIONAL AND LOGICAL.
YOU'LL THINK—AT THE END OF THE DAY, SHE'S JUST A WOMAN. IT DOESN'T MATTER HOW CRAZY SHE IS, SHE DOESN'T HAVE THE WILL THAT I DO.
AND—OKAY, SHE'S FAST. SHE'S GOT A GUN. BUT SHE DOESN'T HAVE MY STRENGTH. I CAN SPRING AN AMBUSH, USE MY WEIGHT TO CRUSH HER, CHOKE HER.

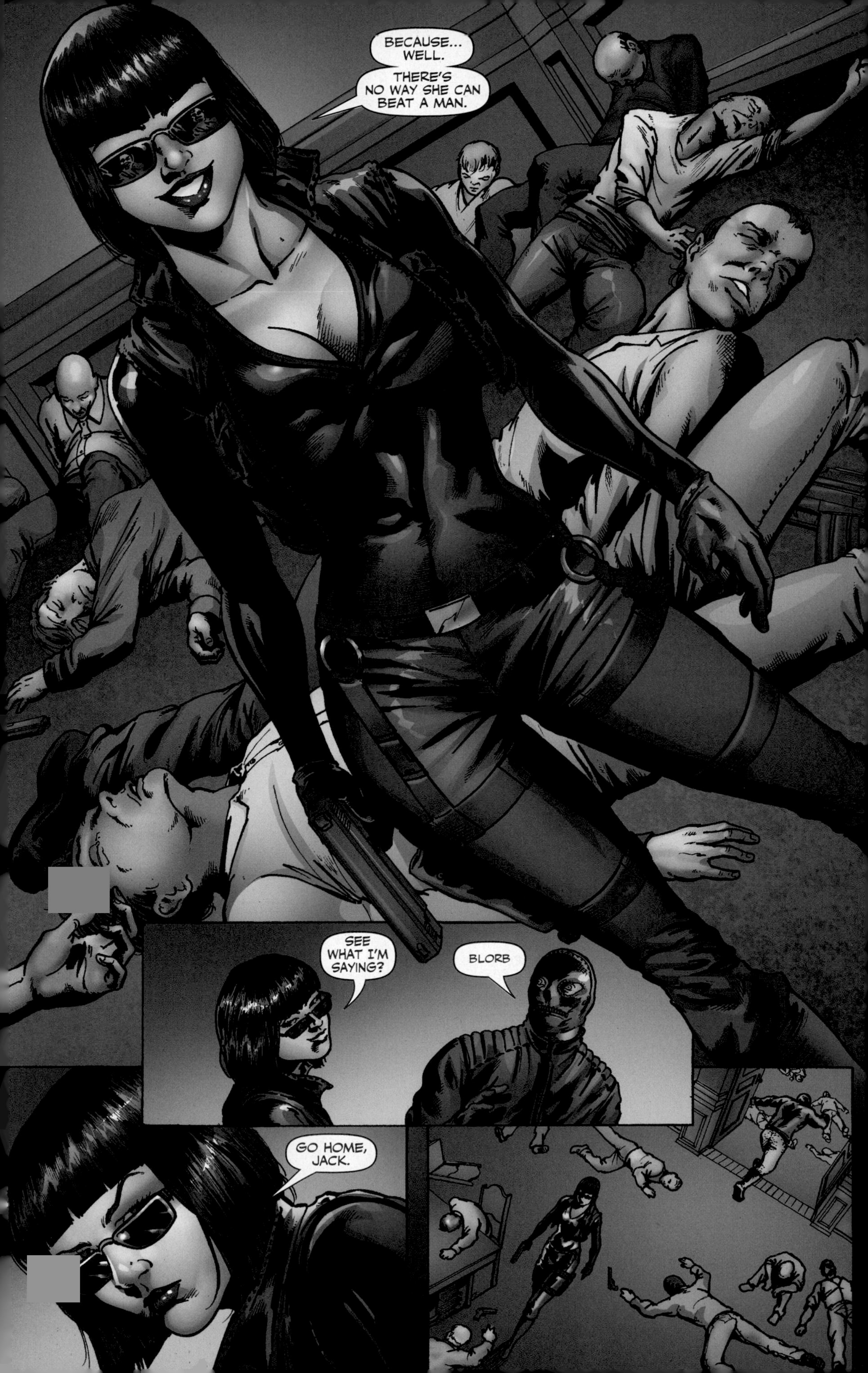
BECAUSE... WELL.
THERE'S NO WAY SHE CAN BEAT A MAN.
SEE WHAT I'M SAYING?
BLORB
GO HOME, JACK.

WHERE WERE WE?

I GOT A LITTLE SLOPPY TONIGHT AND LET SOMEONE TAIL ME, UNCLE PETE. KNEW I WASN'T GETTING ENOUGH SLEEP.

BUT I'M AFRAID THAT'S AS CARELESS AS I'M LIKELY TO GET.

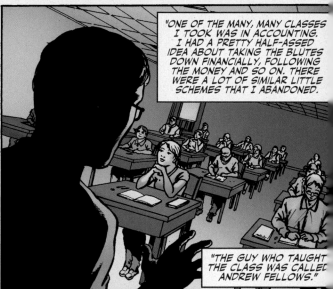

"ONE OF THE MANY, MANY CLASSES I TOOK WAS IN ACCOUNTING. I HAD A PRETTY HALF-ASSED IDEA ABOUT TAKING THE BLUTES DOWN FINANCIALLY, FOLLOWING THE MONEY AND SO ON. THERE WERE A LOT OF SIMILAR LITTLE SCHEMES THAT I ABANDONED.

"THE GUY WHO TAUGHT THE CLASS WAS CALLED ANDREW FELLOWS."

"HE WAS SWEET. GOOD-NATURED.

"HE MADE STUPID LITTLE JOKES THAT WEREN'T REMOTELY FUNNY. WENT SLIGHTLY RED IF HE MADE EYE CONTACT WITH A PRETTY GIRL. KEPT FORGETTING THINGS."

"I WOULD STARE AT HIM THROUGH THE WHOLE CLASS, TRYING TO FIGURE OUT WHAT IT WAS ABOUT HIM—

"UNTIL ONE DAY I REALIZED."

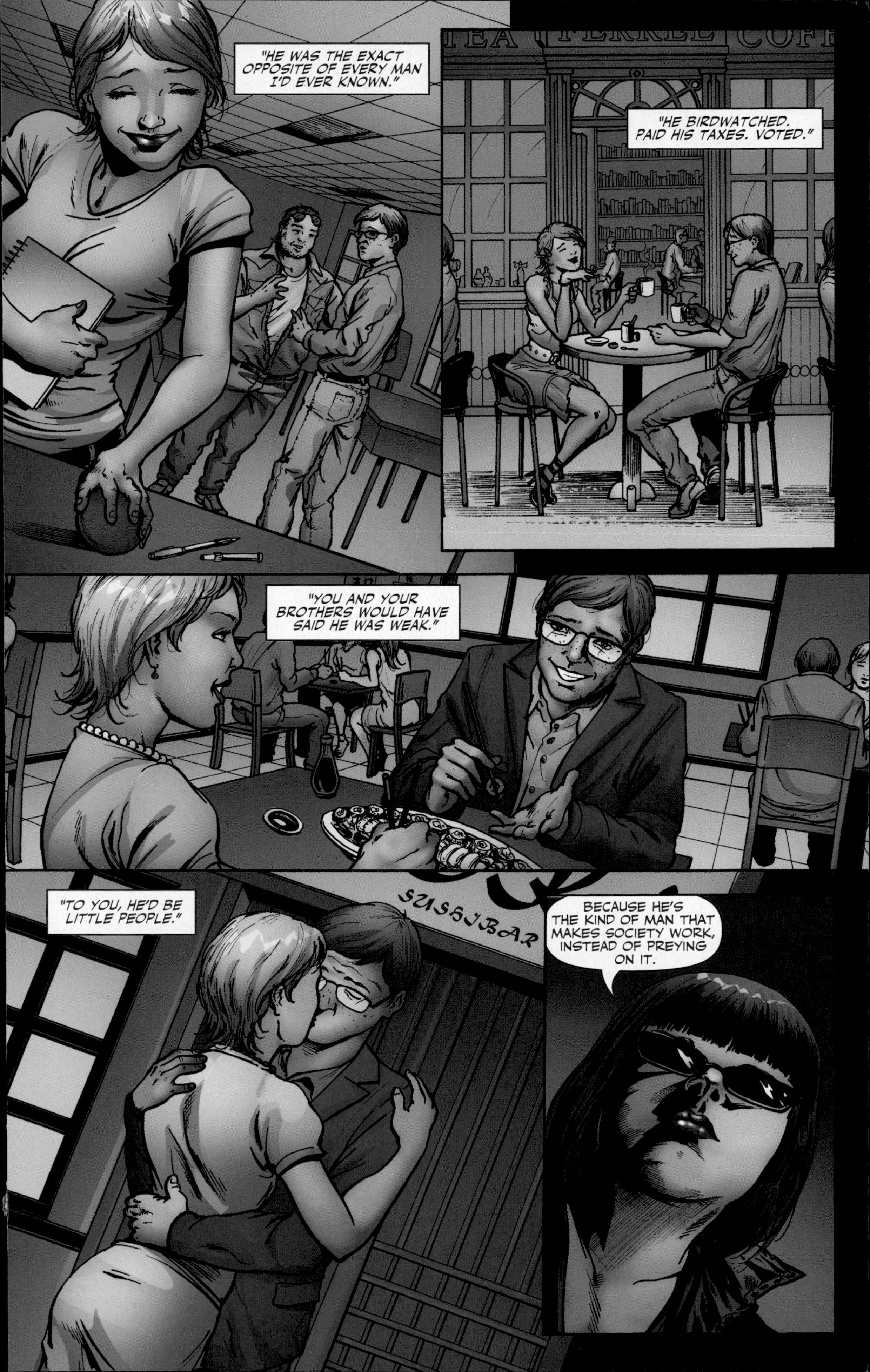

"HE WAS THE EXACT OPPOSITE OF EVERY MAN I'D EVER KNOWN."
"HE BIRDWATCHED. PAID HIS TAXES. VOTED."
"YOU AND YOUR BROTHERS WOULD HAVE SAID HE WAS WEAK."
"TO YOU, HE'D BE LITTLE PEOPLE."
SUSHIBAR
BECAUSE HE'S THE KIND OF MAN THAT MAKES SOCIETY WORK, INSTEAD OF PREYING ON IT.

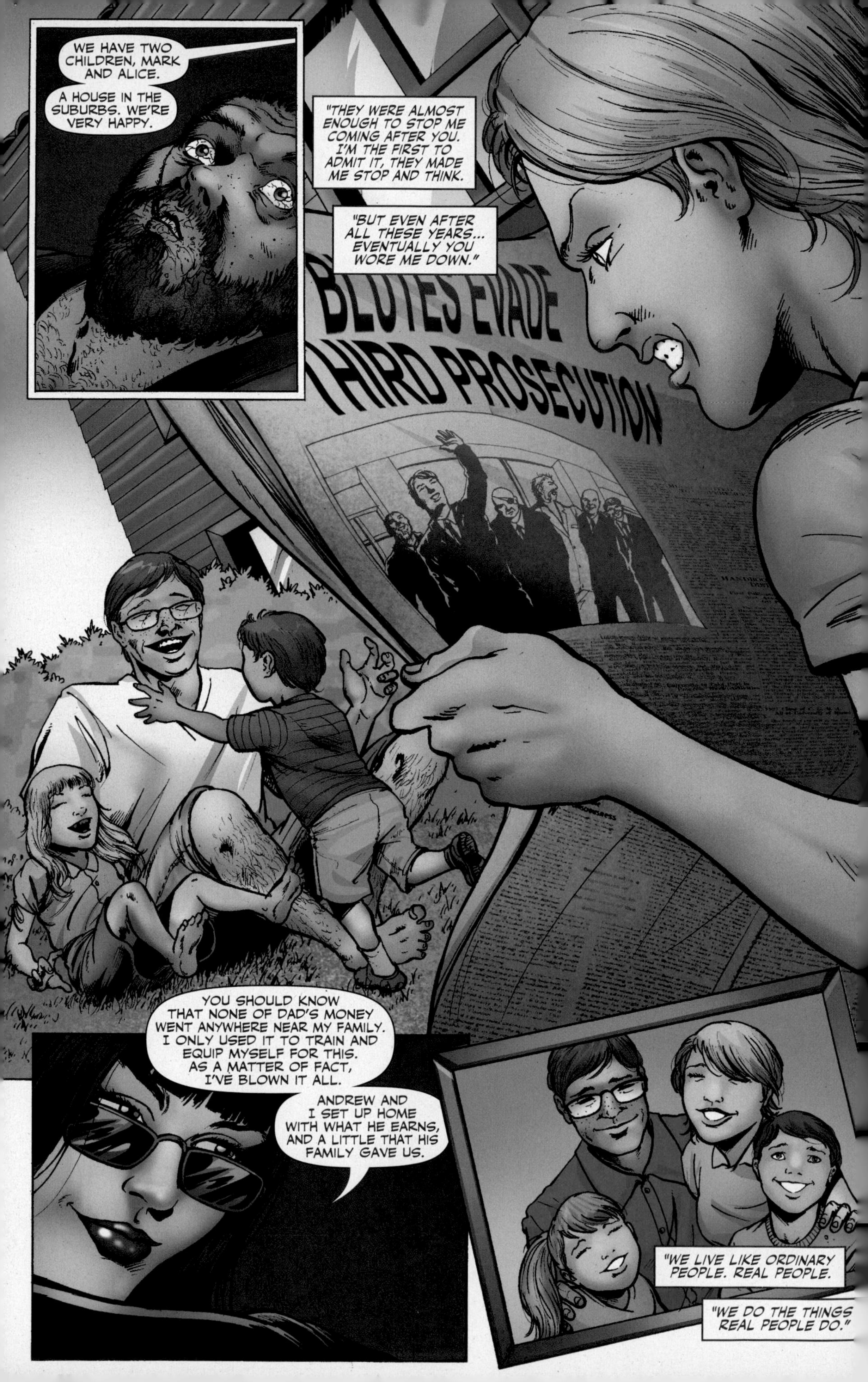
WE HAVE TWO CHILDREN, MARK AND ALICE.
A HOUSE IN THE SUBURBS. WE'RE VERY HAPPY.
"THEY WERE ALMOST ENOUGH TO STOP ME COMING AFTER YOU. I'M THE FIRST TO ADMIT IT, THEY MADE ME STOP AND THINK.
"BUT EVEN AFTER ALL THESE YEARS... EVENTUALLY YOU WORE ME DOWN."
BLUTES EVADE THIRD PROSECUTION
YOU SHOULD KNOW THAT NONE OF DAD'S MONEY WENT ANYWHERE NEAR MY FAMILY. I ONLY USED IT TO TRAIN AND EQUIP MYSELF FOR THIS. AS A MATTER OF FACT, I'VE BLOWN IT ALL.
ANDREW AND I SET UP HOME WITH WHAT HE EARNS, AND A LITTLE THAT HIS FAMILY GAVE US.
"WE LIVE LIKE ORDINARY PEOPLE. REAL PEOPLE.
"WE DO THE THINGS REAL PEOPLE DO."

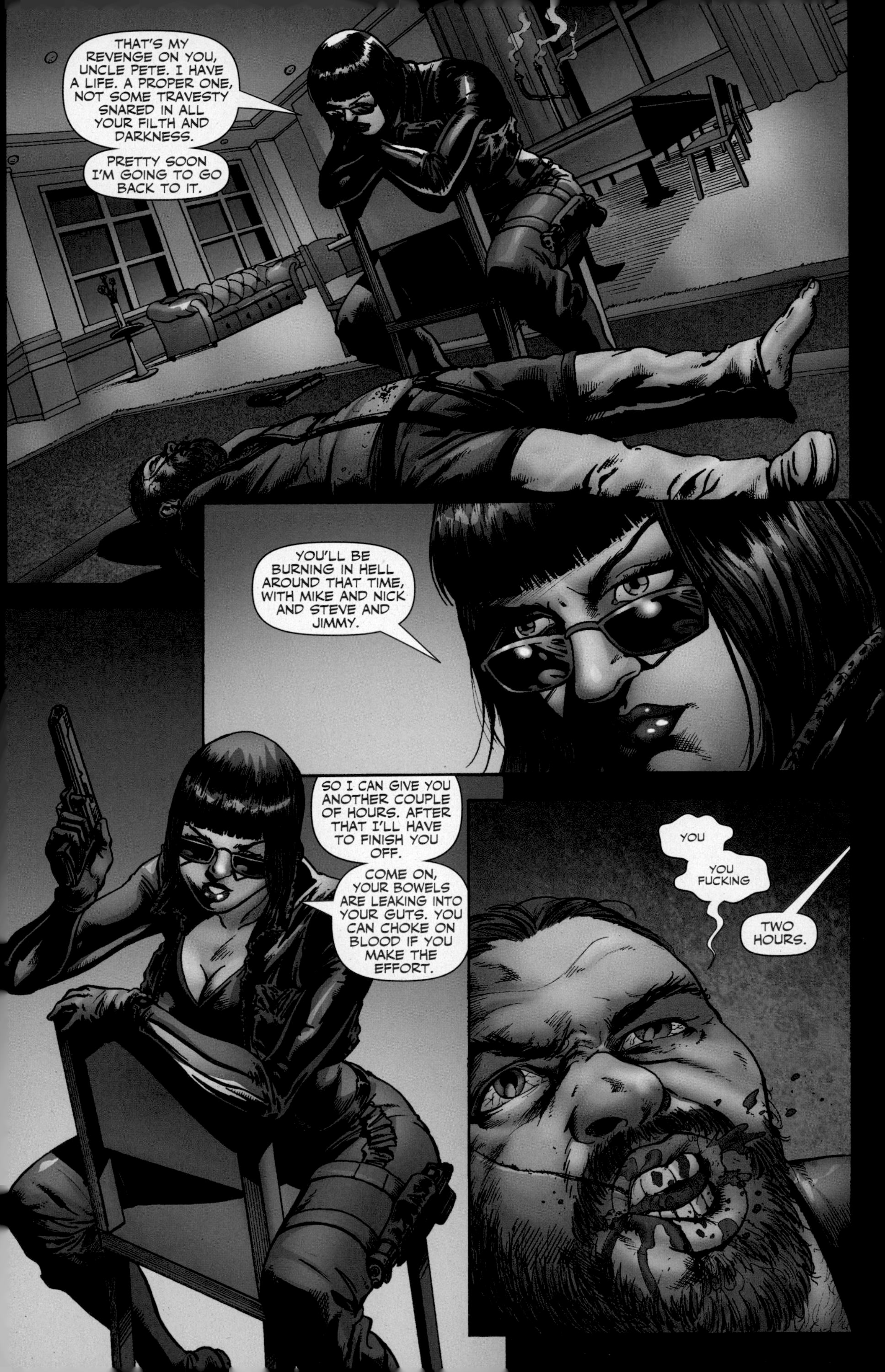
THAT'S MY REVENGE ON YOU, UNCLE PETE. I HAVE A LIFE. A PROPER ONE, NOT SOME TRAVESTY SNARED IN ALL YOUR FILTH AND DARKNESS.
PRETTY SOON I'M GOING TO GO BACK TO IT.
YOU'LL BE BURNING IN HELL AROUND THAT TIME, WITH MIKE AND NICK AND STEVE AND JIMMY.
SO I CAN GIVE YOU ANOTHER COUPLE OF HOURS. AFTER THAT I'LL HAVE TO FINISH YOU OFF.
COME ON, YOUR BOWELS ARE LEAKING INTO YOUR GUTS. YOU CAN CHOKE ON BLOOD IF YOU MAKE THE EFFORT.
YOU
YOU FUCKING
TWO HOURS.

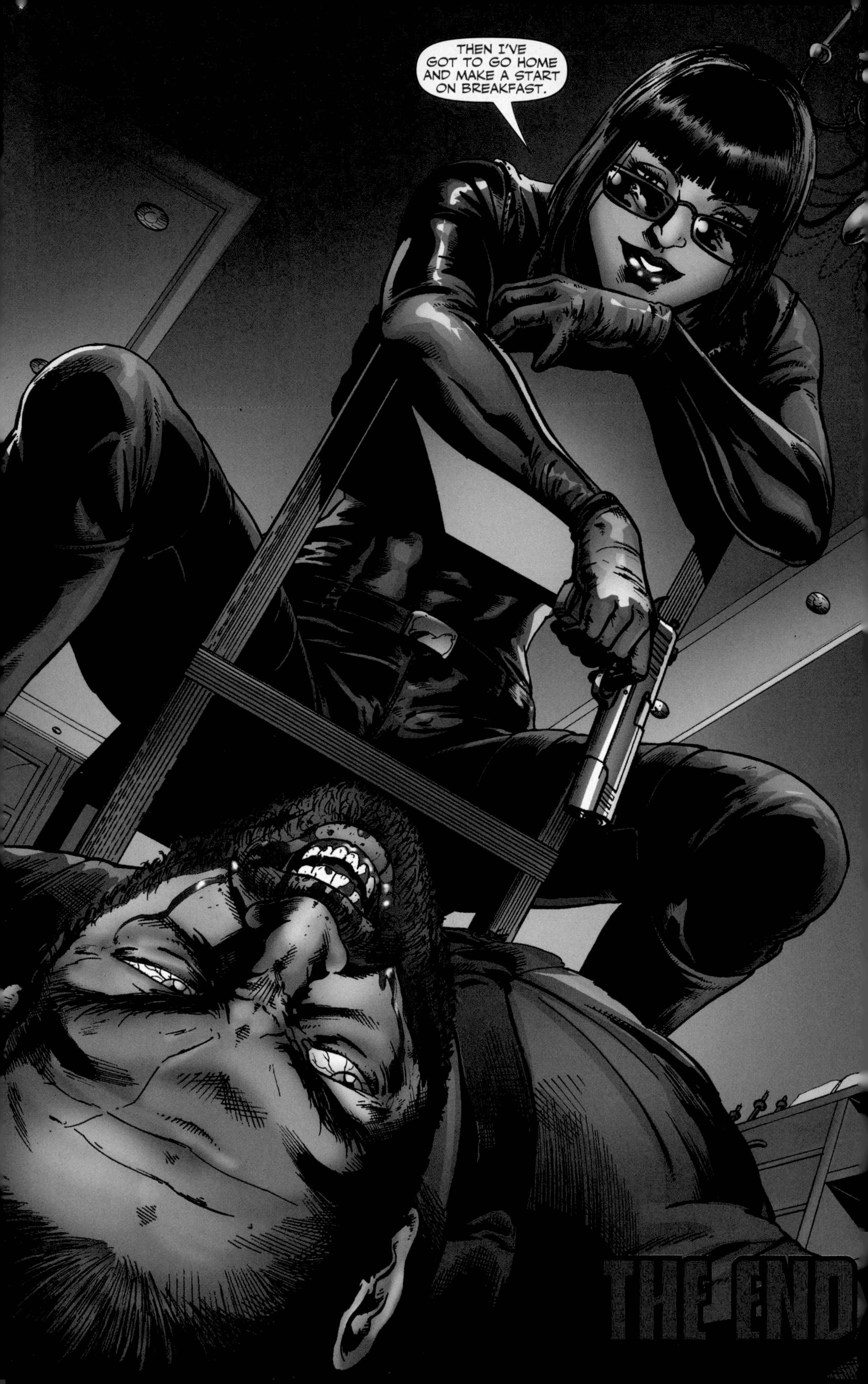
THEN I'VE GOT TO GO HOME AND MAKE A START ON BREAKFAST.
THE END

Garth Ennis Lightens up for Jennifer Blood – By Robert Greenberger

(Originally published in Jennifer Blood #1)

After crisscrossing the fields of battle and examining the underbelly of heroism, Garth Ennis has decided he was due for some fun. Of course, Garth's idea of fun involves guns, violence, and beautiful women. Coming in February is Jennifer Blood, a new miniseries that takes a fresh look at vigilantism.

"I wanted to have a bit of a laugh again. It's been a while," Ennis admits during a conversation. "Everything I've been doing recently has been getting darker and darker. *Crossed* and *Battlefields* speak for themselves; *The Boys* slides further into the shadows all the time - most notably with next summer's *Butcher* mini; even *Wormwood* gets bleaker and bleaker, and that was meant to be a comedy. So stepping back and having a laugh, maybe in the vein of *Hitman* and so on, suddenly seemed quite attractive."

Jenny is a housewife with a husband and children, but she finds herself putting the kids to bed, donning a costume of sorts and walks the streets to hand out the kind of justice cops cannot. But what could cause a woman to enter a dangerous, deadly lifestyle antithetical to her normal life?

"What would prompt anyone? The desire for revenge," Ennis explains. "Sheer anger that evil men arrogantly expect to escape retribution for their crimes. The overwhelming conviction that the target cannot be allowed to continue breathing."

In a fresh twist, the series will be told in the form of diary entries. Finding the voice of a suburban woman with a family is very different from the characters Ennis has made his reputation on. He agrees this was a bit of a stretch. "And not so much, because I know a few [housewives]. Watching your friends become parents is always interesting; you see them solve problems and reward good behavior in ways that can quite surprise you, given that you've known them since your early twenties. That gives me all sorts of material to draw on."

Ennis was born in the United Kingdom but relocated to the United States years ago and has given him a bit of an outsiders' view on the American Way. "My wife and I occasionally visit some friends of ours upstate, in a pleasantly affluent part of Westchester. When we meet their friends from the neighborhood, I'm always struck at how oddly and yet naturally people seem to segregate themselves- the men stand here and talk about this, the women stand there and talk about that. Occasionally someone snarls at a kid. There are clearer divisions and groups than I was used to in the UK. Our own friends, the couple we're visiting, are actually Brits as well, so I get to see the slight contrast between them and the locals," Ennis said. "All of which made for quite a good scene in *Jennifer Blood*, although as usual I had to ruin everything with the carnage and the nudity."

One insight is that women in a family tend to be stressed because there's never enough time between household chores and the kids' own obligations, not to mention trying to maintain a relationship with a spouse. Now imagine finding the time to go out and deliver street justice to vermin. "Well, a woman's work is never done," Ennis admits. "Jen reckons she only has to last one week- one massive effort and then she can go back to her family, job done. We'll see how that works out for her as the story progresses."

It's bound to be a bloody week so one wonders how a housewife washes it out of her work clothes. "I imagine you have to get to it before it dries and hardens. But feel free to perform an experiment or two," Ennis, who clearly has not had this problem, suggested.

"I haven't discovered too many lines she won't cross yet. She's decided that these guys have to go, and when you see what they've been up to I imagine you'll agree. As far as she's concerned they're the ones who crossed the line, and now anything goes."

Sure, many people can find the time for a special project and then get back to normal, but given that her exploits will be public events, there comes the danger that both private and public lives might clash. When asked, Ennis chuckles and replies, "Read on. You've got to wonder how long she can keep going, although she is rather good at compartmentalizing."

Since he wanted to have some fun, he confirms that the heavy moral and ethical issues that imbue his work with dramatic depth will also be taking a holiday. Instead, Jenny will be patrolling the streets on her own. Her secret will remain hers to keep. Well, not necessarily for the entire series. He teases, "A couple may find out, far too late to do them any good."

Of course, someone committing vigilante acts can't do it in a vacuum. Sooner or later, the police and/or the media will figure out there's someone at work. But Jenny has a head start, according to Ennis. "They're a long, long way in her rear-view. As far as the cops are concerned, the unofficial Punisher rules apply: someone's killing bad guys? Oh dear. How sad."

Coming along for the ride is artist Adriano Batista, a Dynamite veteran who has previously drawn women to reckon with including *Jungle Girl* and *Red Sonja*. The covers are from painter Tim Bradstreet, who has previously worked with Ennis and provided designs for Jenny. "And he did a sterling job indeed, really nailed what I was going for."

Jennifer Blood is something like a palette cleanser for Ennis. After a lengthy career exploring various genres in graphic storytelling, he admits that there's more to write about. "I'd certainly like to do more war stories," he adds. "And a bit more kitchen sink drama, like *Hellblazer* without the hocus-pocus or *Punisher* without the guns."

Since his break-in during the late 1980s, Ennis has watched the comics field change dramatically. When he arrived, imprints like DC Entertainment's Vertigo were just coming into their own. Now with Disney owning Marvel Comics and new management at DC, Ennis sees the pendulum swinging once more. "From what I can tell, we're moving away from notions like creators' rights and diversity - which people have been taking for granted for the best part of twenty years - and back towards work for hire and superheroes. The decline of Vertigo and demise of WildStorm at DC is a case in point; you can easily imagine execs at Warner going, 'Did you say creator-owned? Is that why we can't just automatically get these things into production? And who authorized this, exactly...?'

"Most new talent now seems to get automatically stuck on superhero books. And said talent seems happy enough to be there."

Another dramatic change was 2010's arrival of the iPad which seemed to be the game changer people awaited for digital comics to come into their own. Ennis happily calls himself a luddite when it comes to the technological end of comics and isn't sure how that will change matters. Instead, he happily sits at home writing his stories. Once Jennifer Blood concludes, he will be returning his attention to his other Dynamite series.

"*The Boys* still has a way to go - the monthly finishes at #72, which is nearly two years away, and there's the *Butcher* mini too. But coming up there's a new *Crossed* monthly that I've written the first three-parter for; hopefully there'll be more *Battlefields*; and there's a war series in similar format to *Battlefields* coming from Avatar. And there's one more *Wormwood* series to go, too."

But first, there's *Jennifer Blood,* a series the likes of which he has not written in far too long.

•   •   •

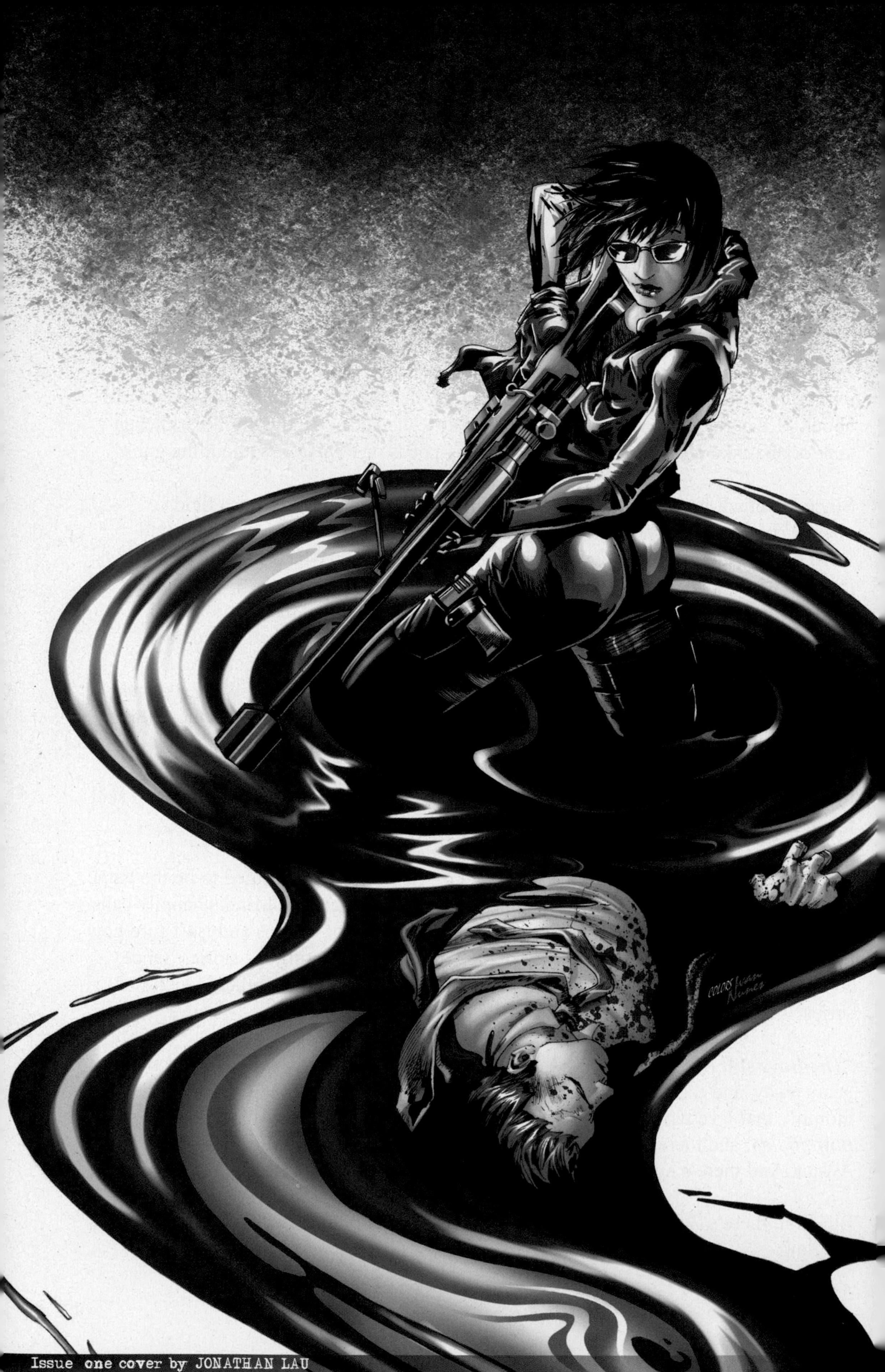

Issue one cover by JONATHAN LAU

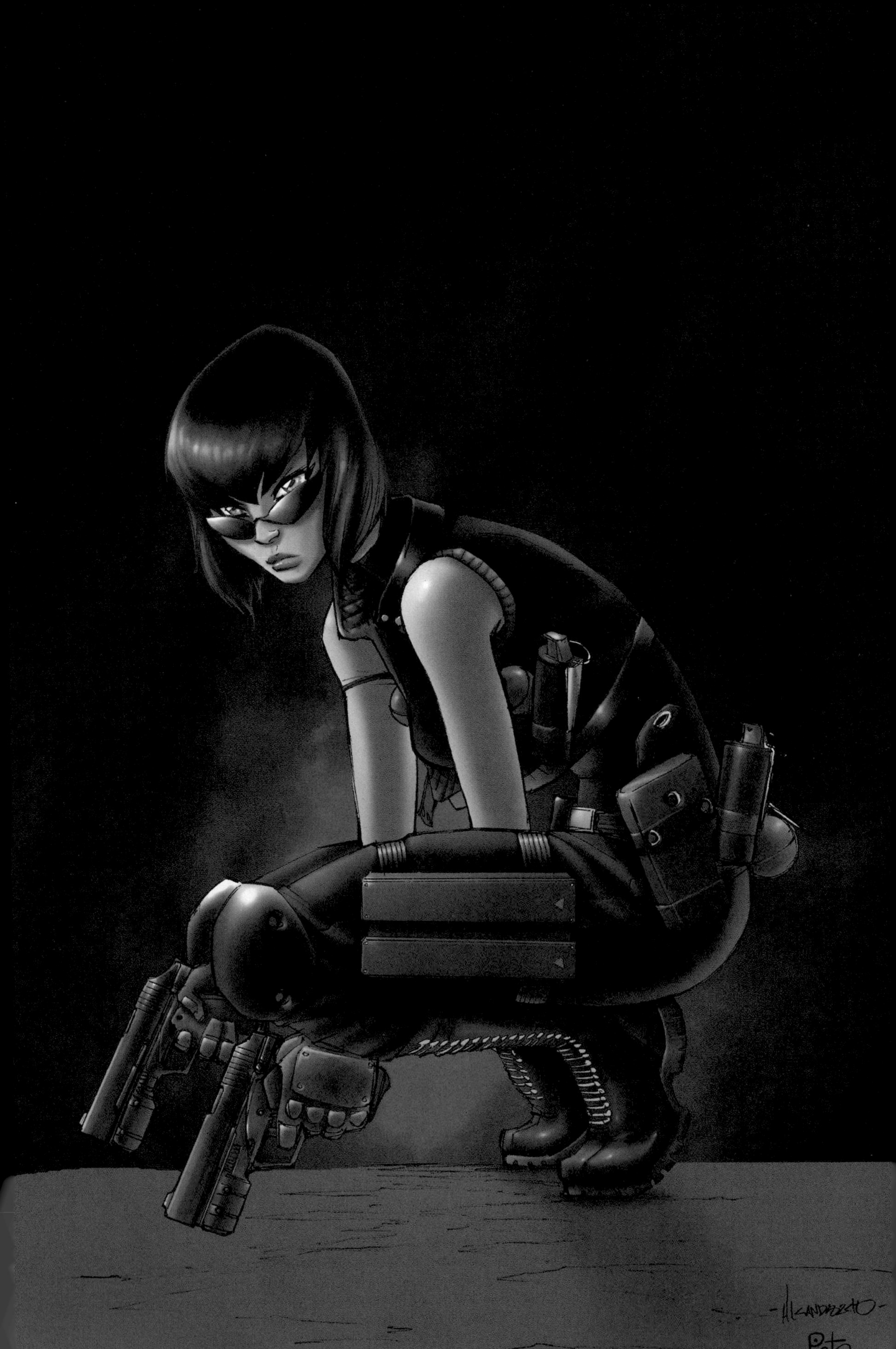

Issue one cover by ALE GARZA

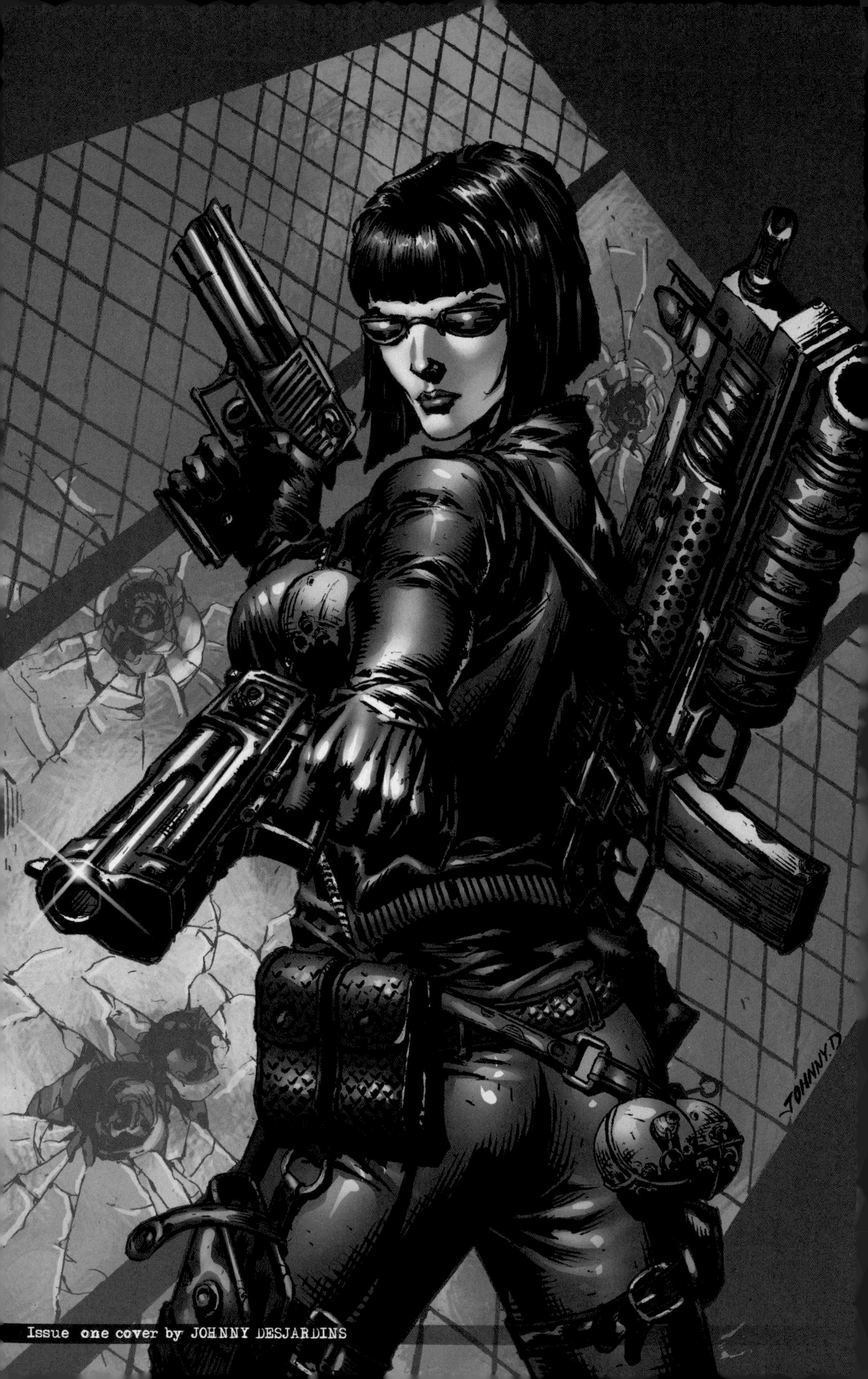
JOHNNY.D

Issue one cover by JOHNNY DESJARDINS

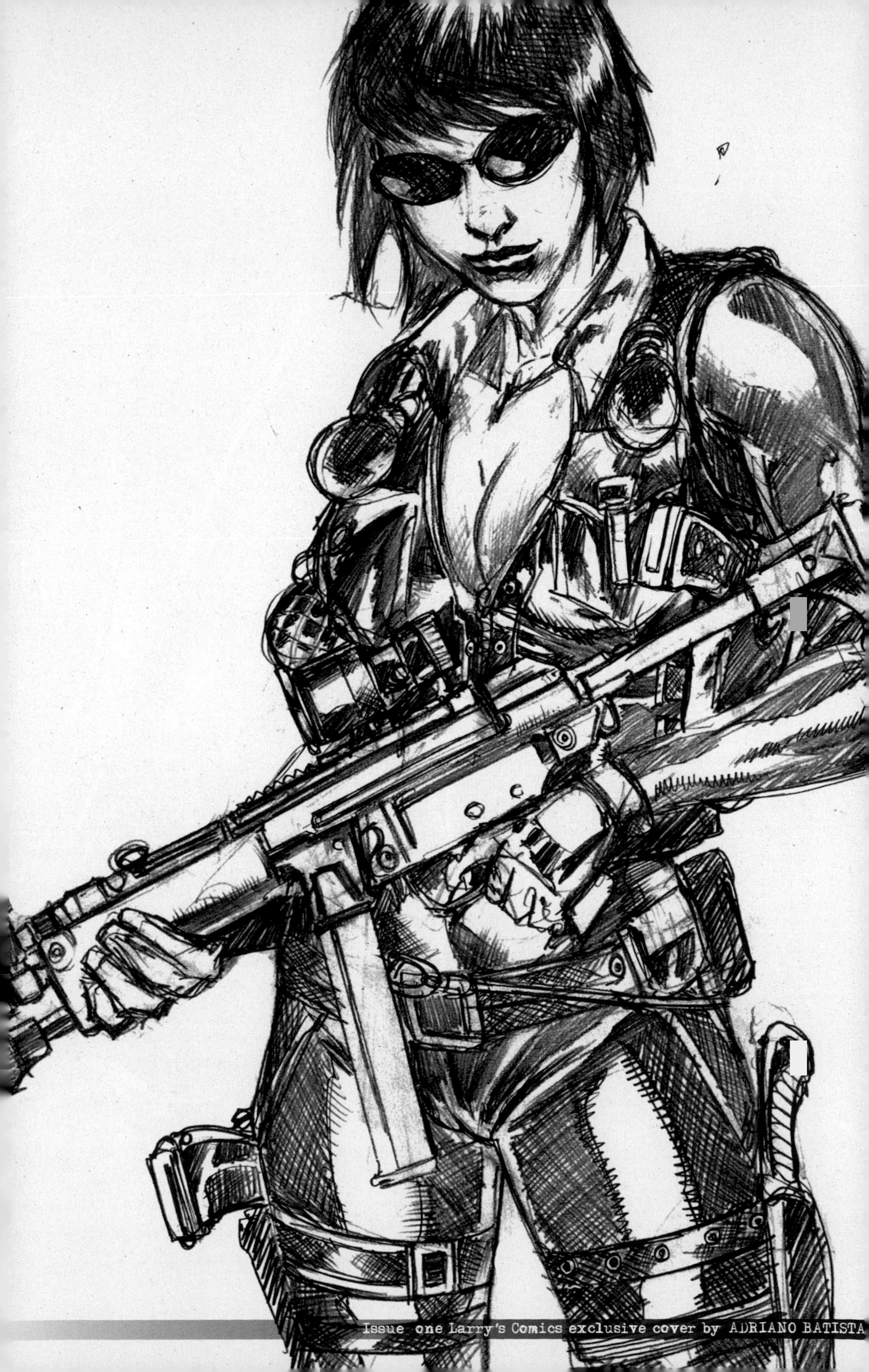

Issue one Larry's Comics exclusive cover by ADRIANO BATISTA

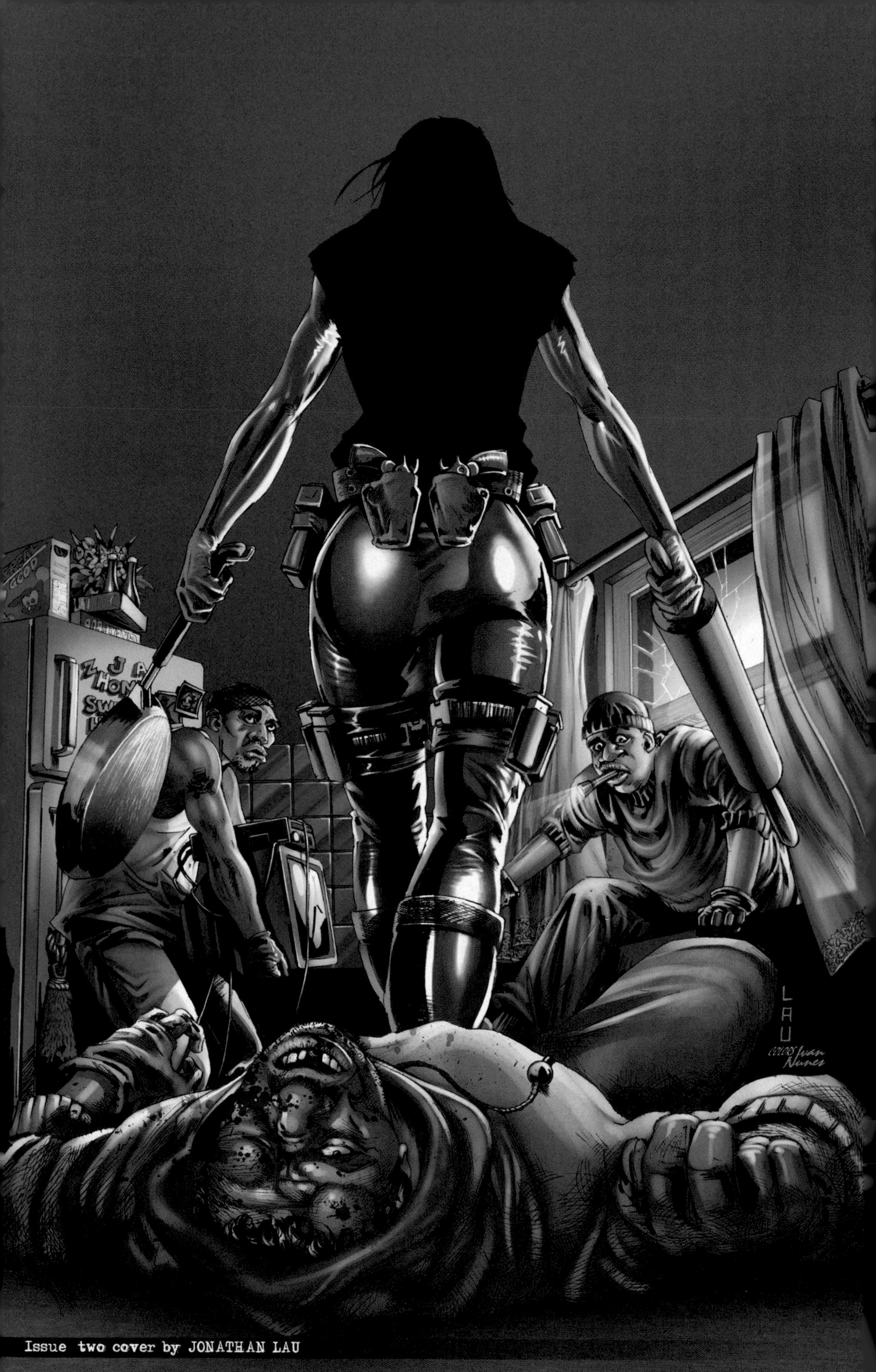
LAU
COLORS Ivan Nunes
Issue two cover by JONATHAN LAU

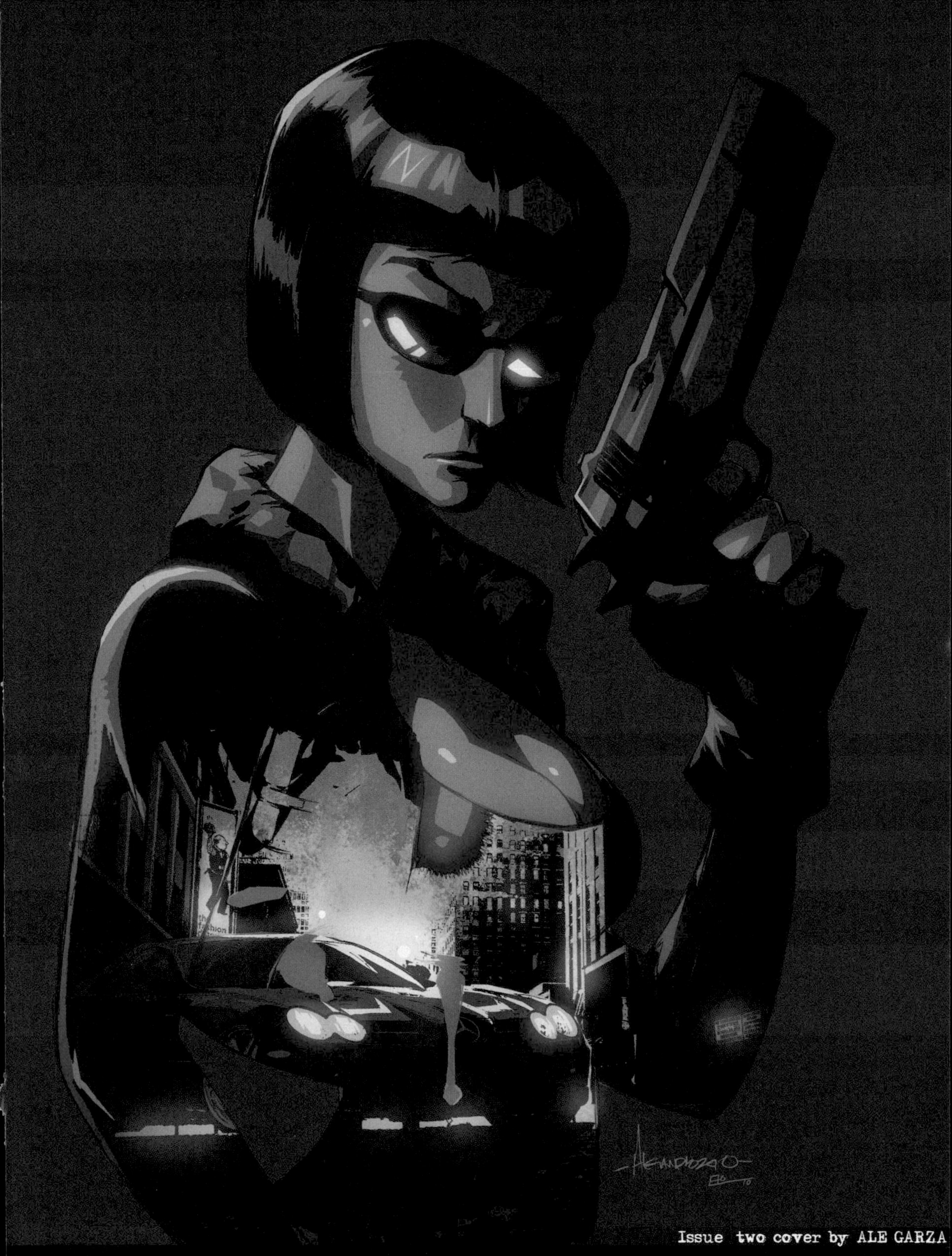

Issue two cover by ALE GARZA

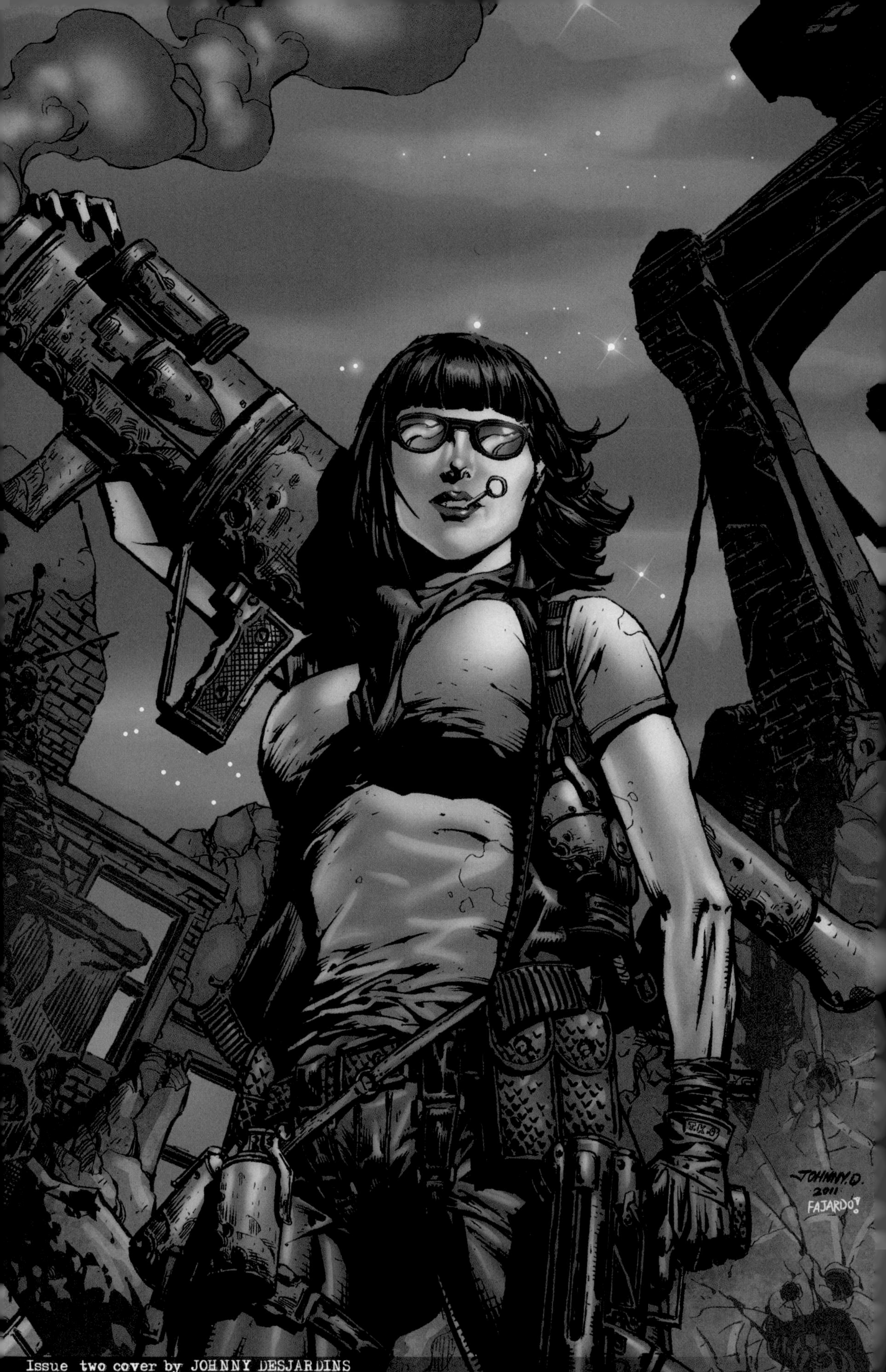
JOHNNY.D. 2011
FAJARDO!

Issue two cover by JOHNNY DESJARDINS

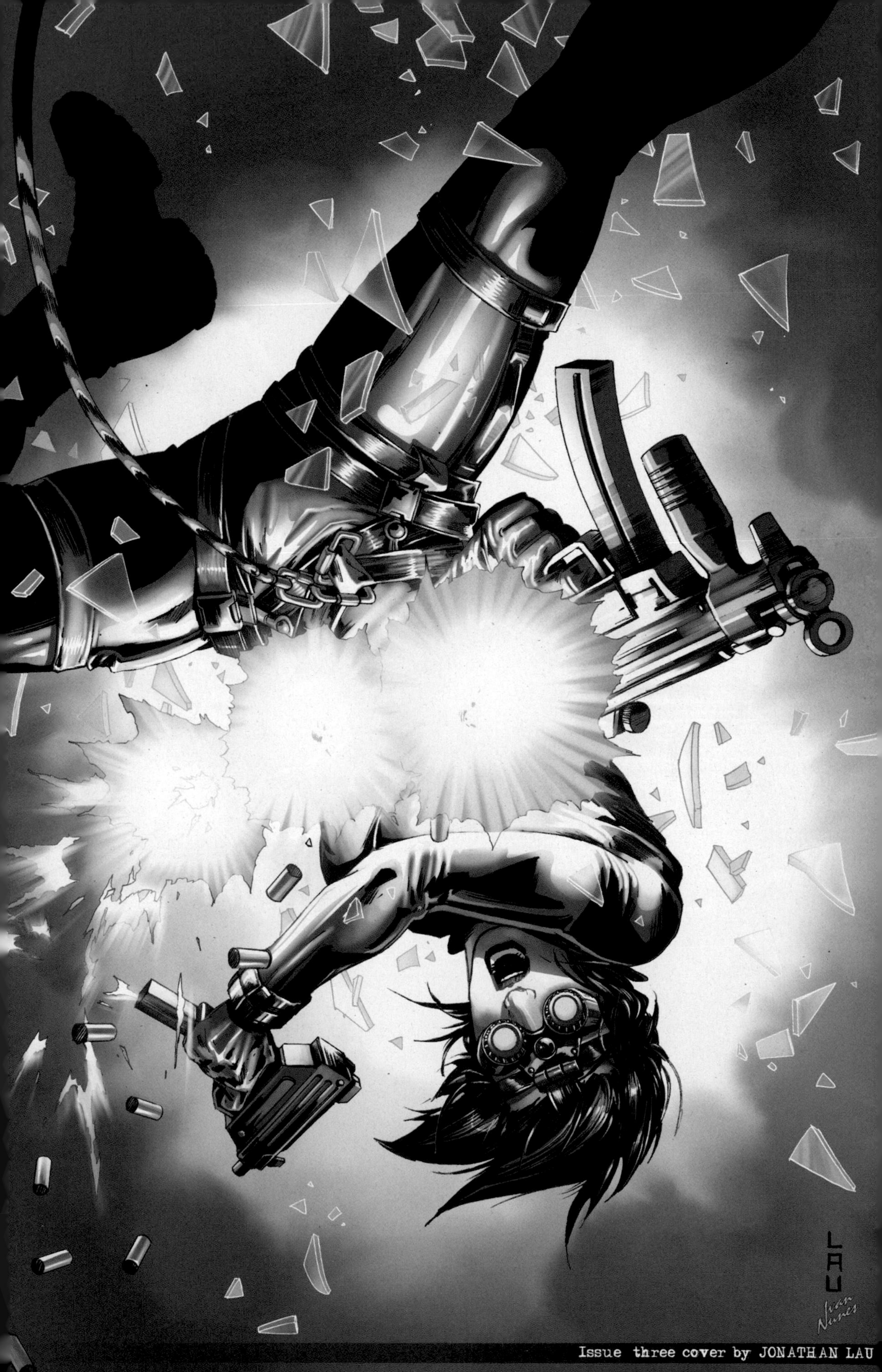
LAU
Ivan Nunes

Issue three cover by JONATHAN LAU

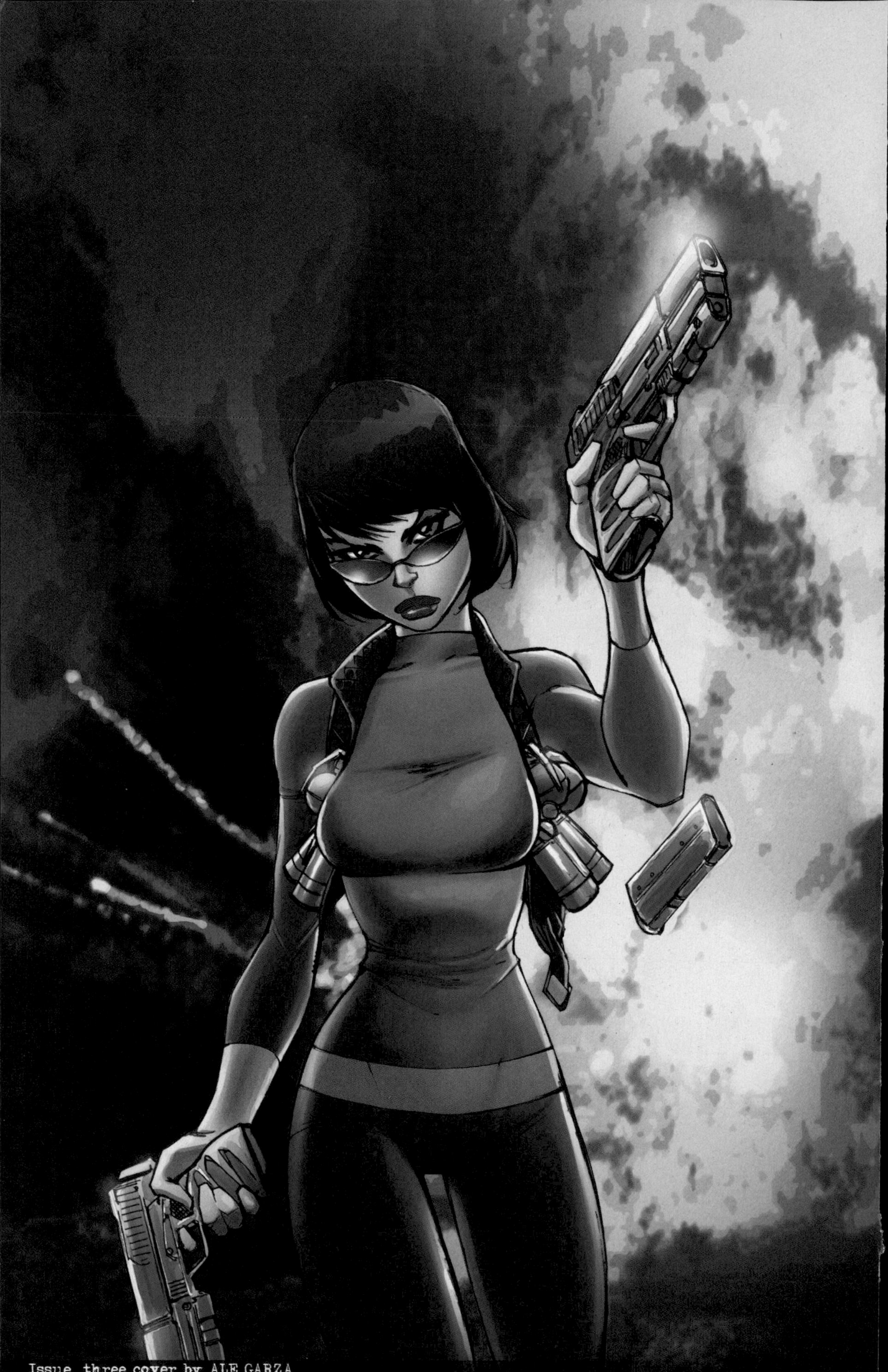

Issue three cover by ALE GARZA

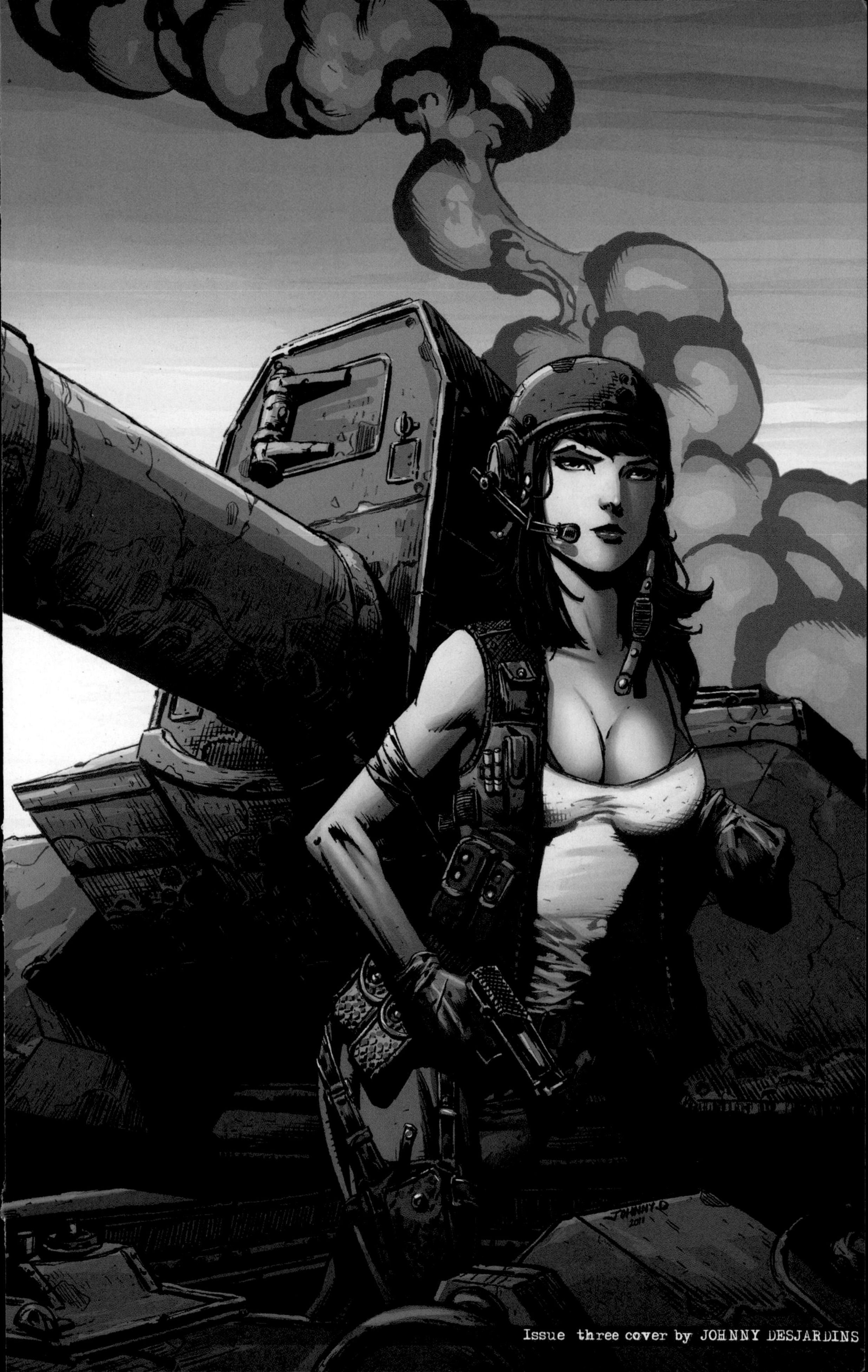
JOHNNY D
2011

Issue three cover by JOHNNY DESJARDINS

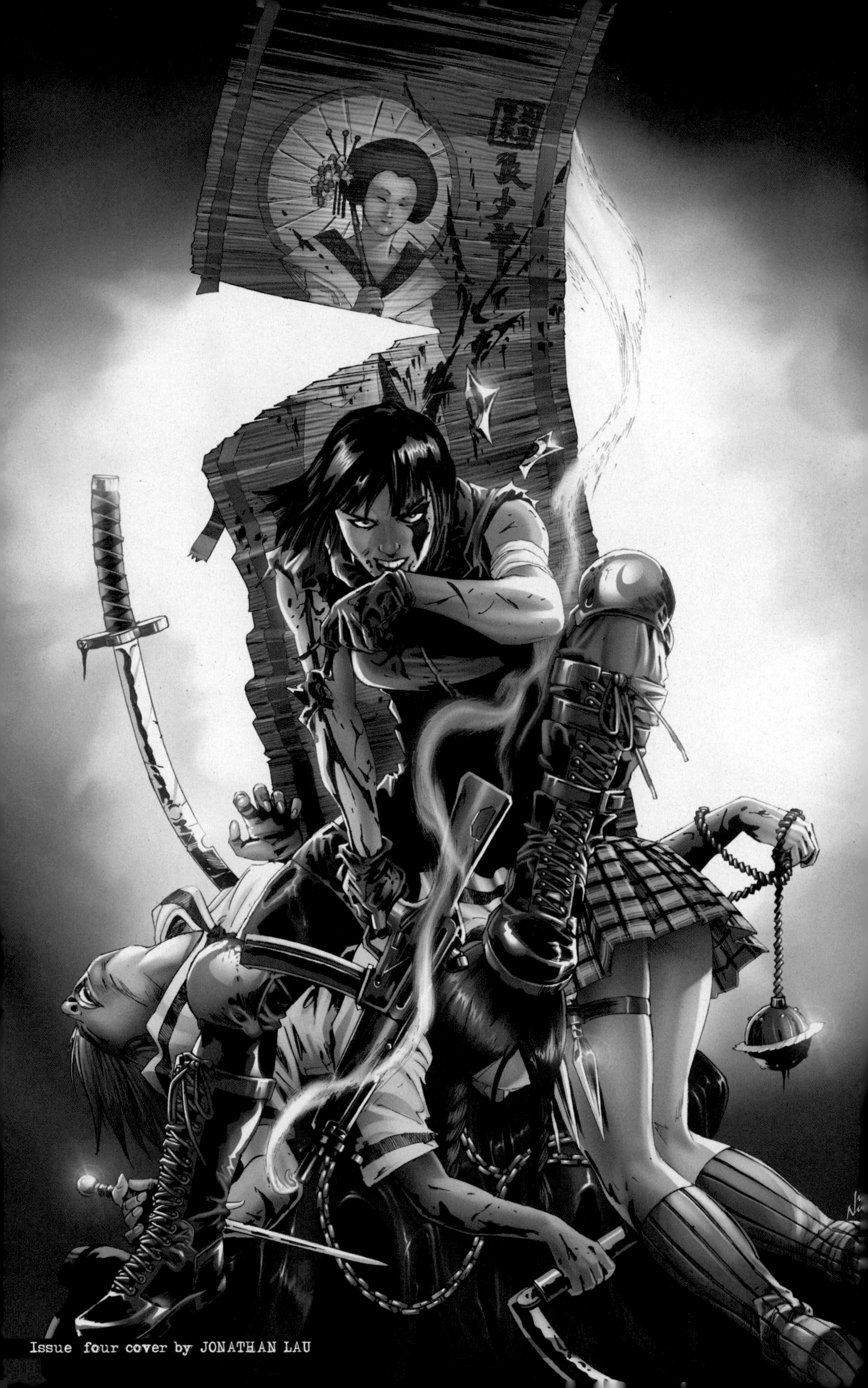

Issue four cover by JONATHAN LAU

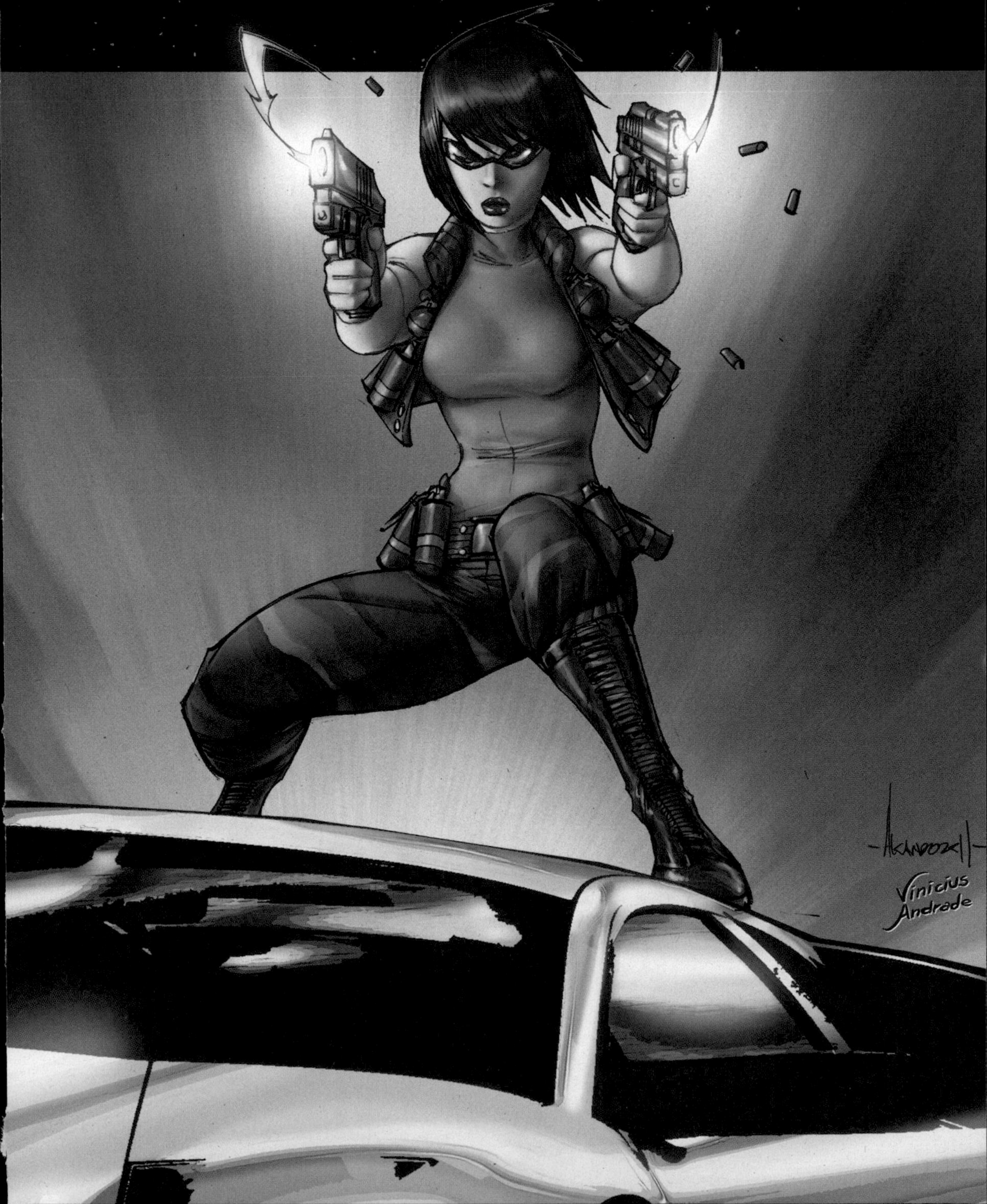
Vinicius
Andrade

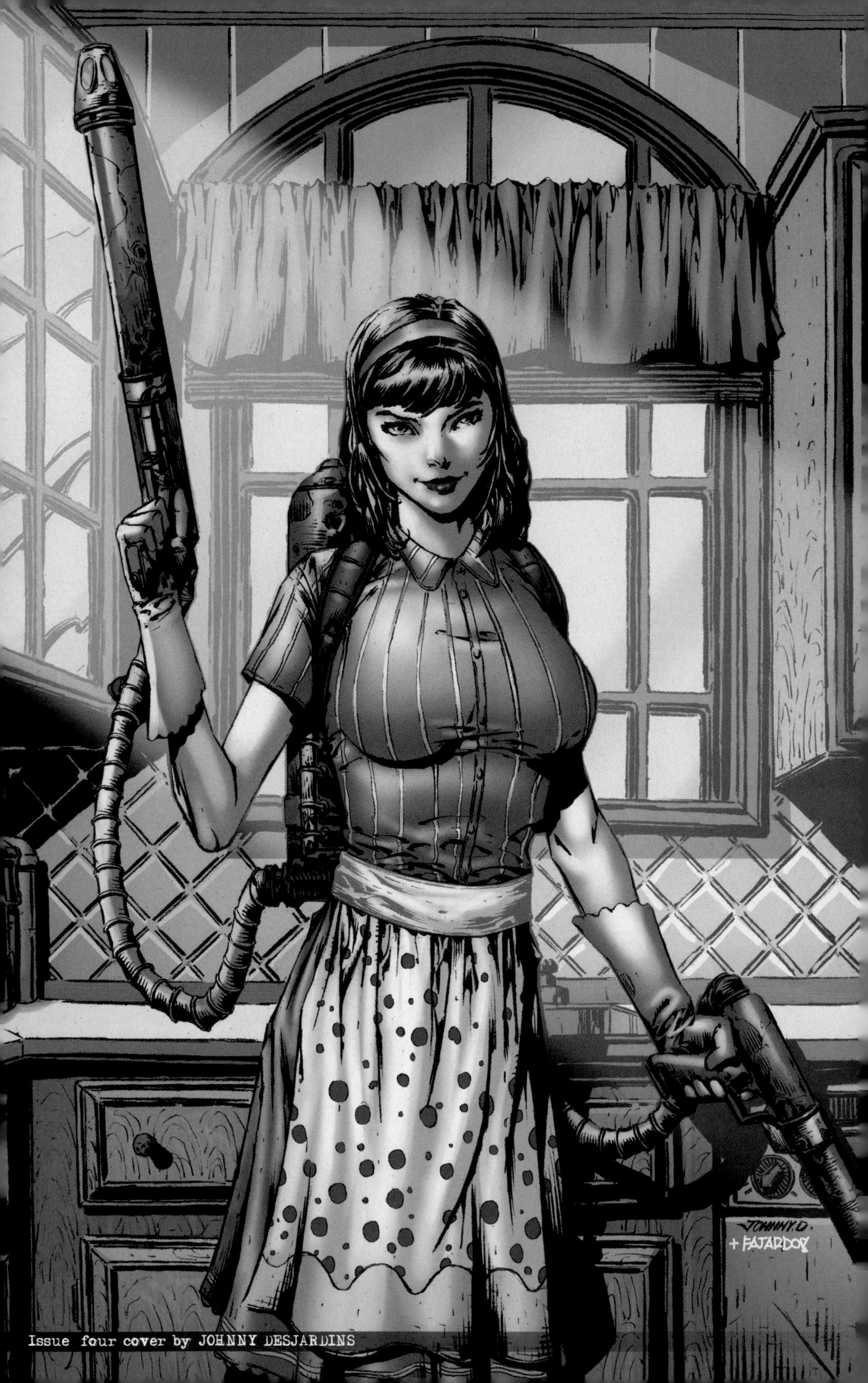
JOHNNY.D.
+ FAJARDO
Issue four cover by JOHNNY DESJARDINS

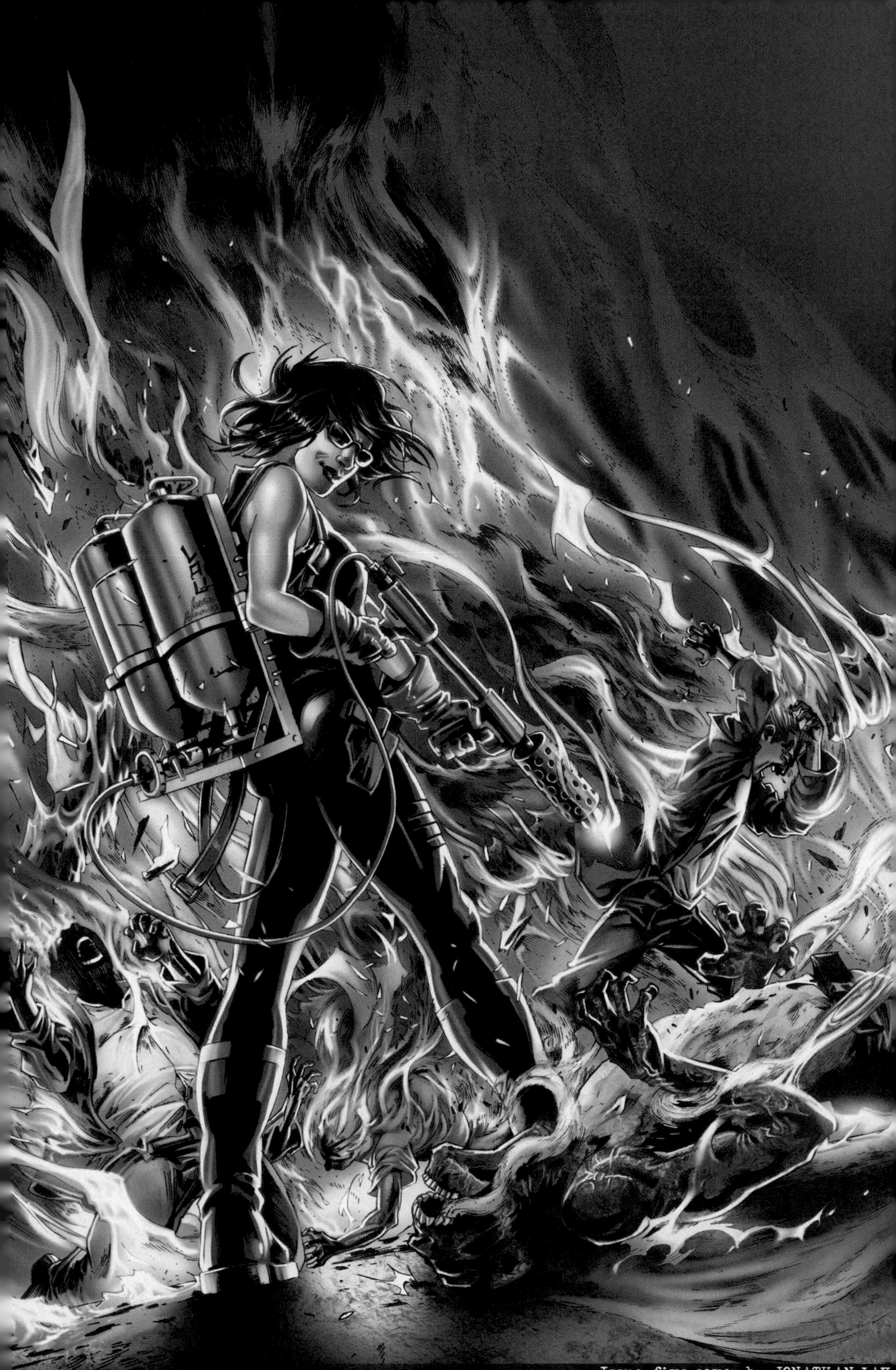

Issue five cover by JONATHAN LAU

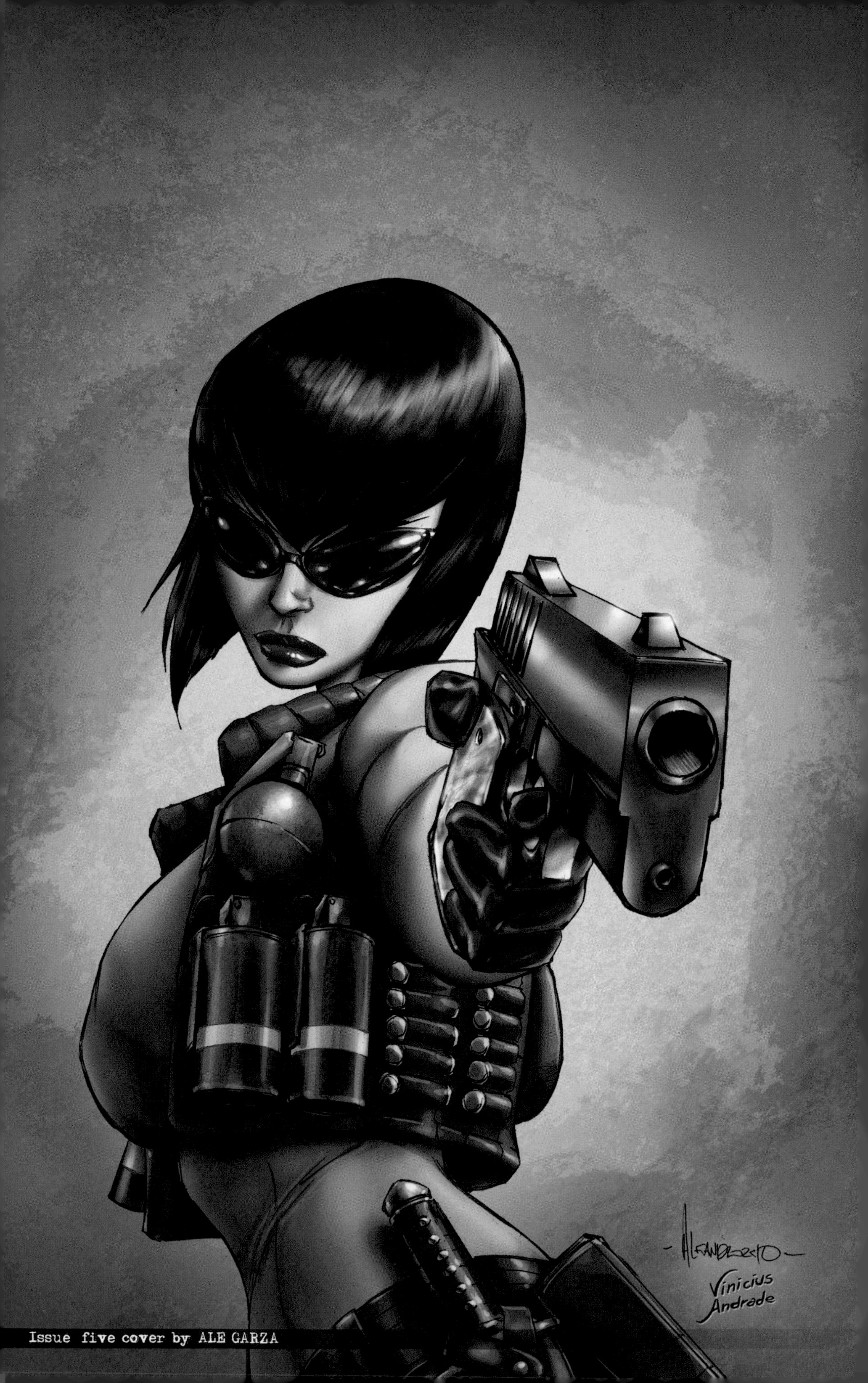
Vinicius
Andrade

Issue five cover by ALE GARZA

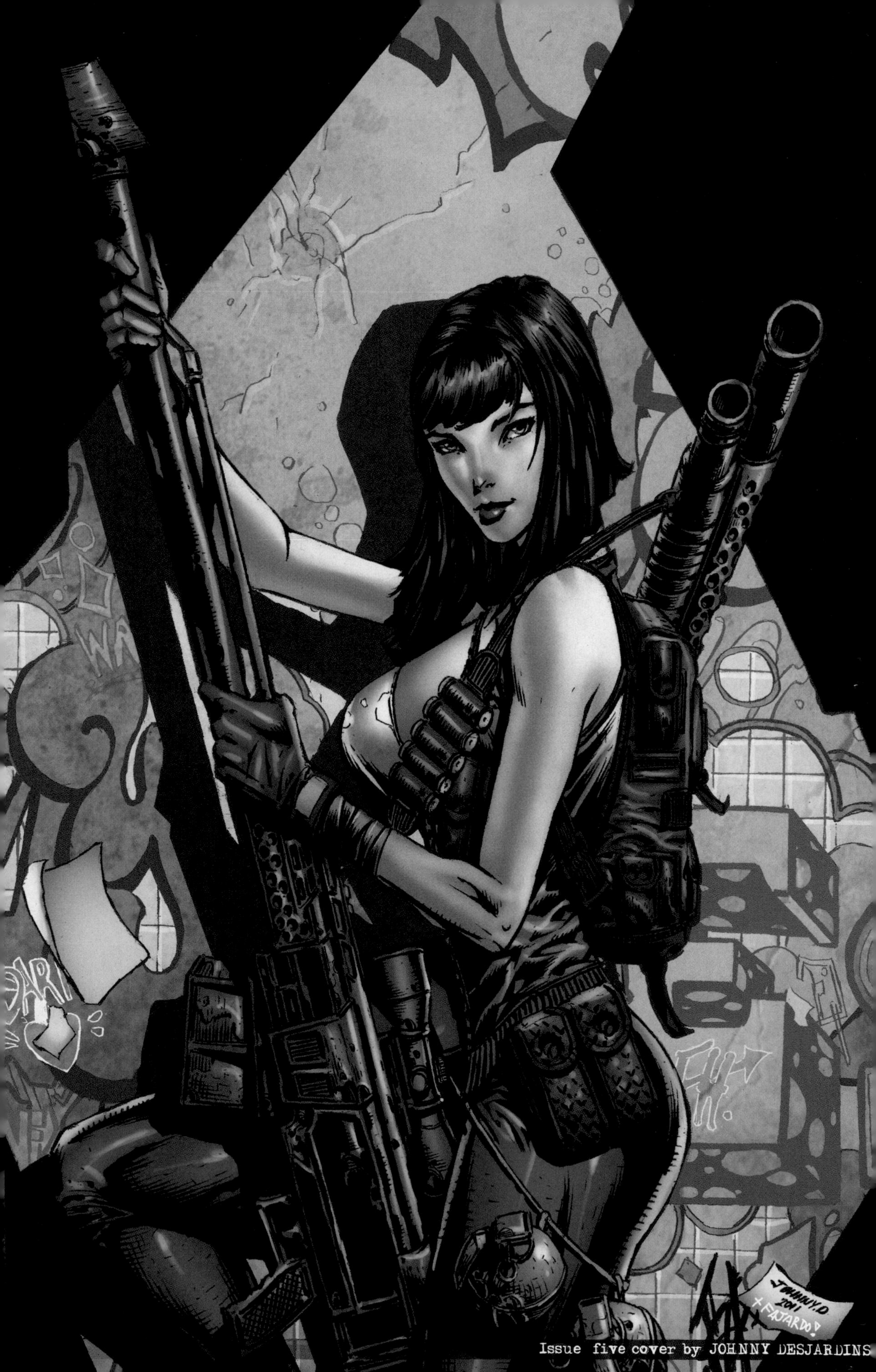
JOHNNY.D
2011
+ FAJARDO!

Issue five cover by JOHNNY DESJARDINS

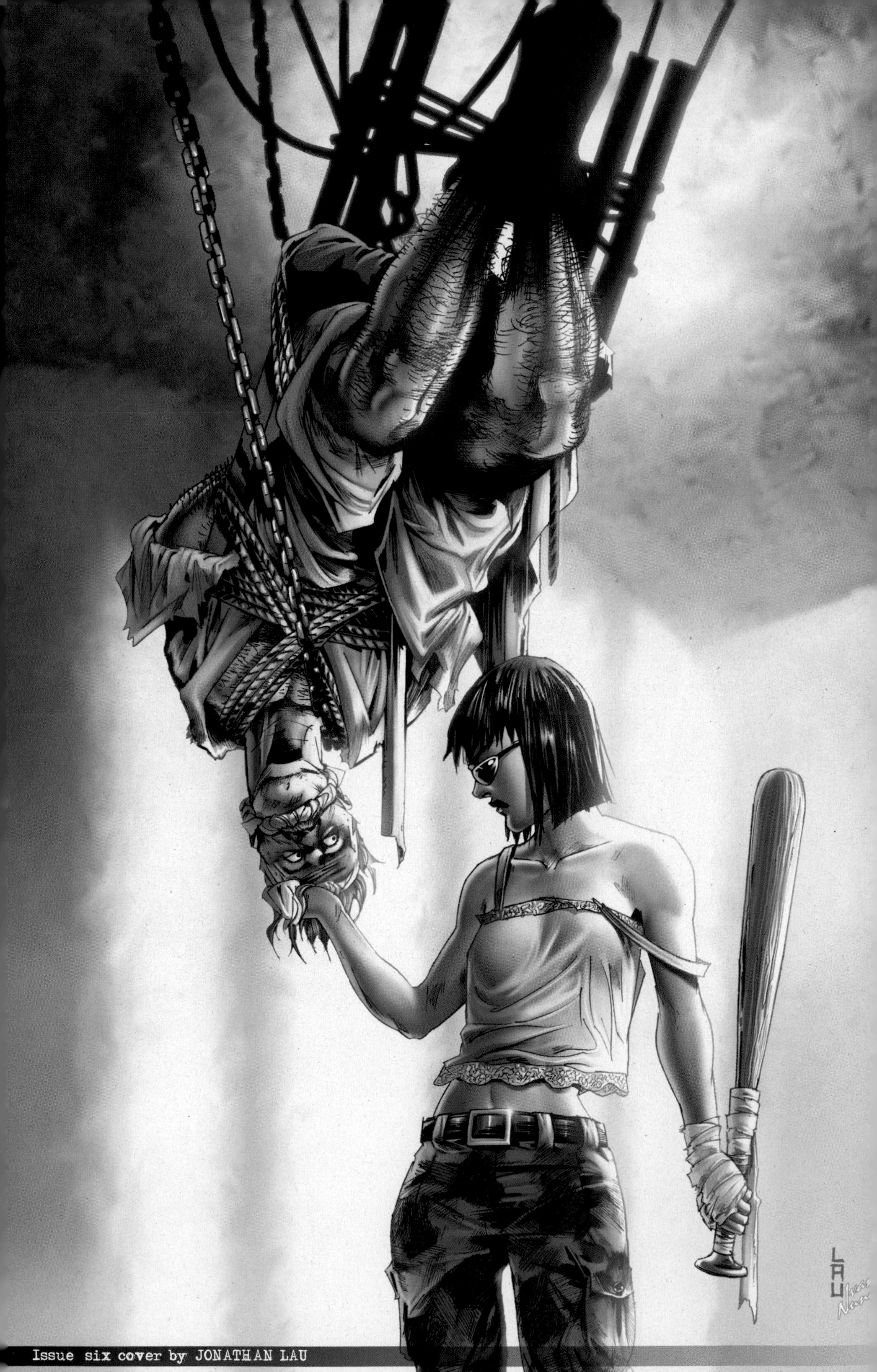
LAU

Issue six cover by JONATHAN LAU

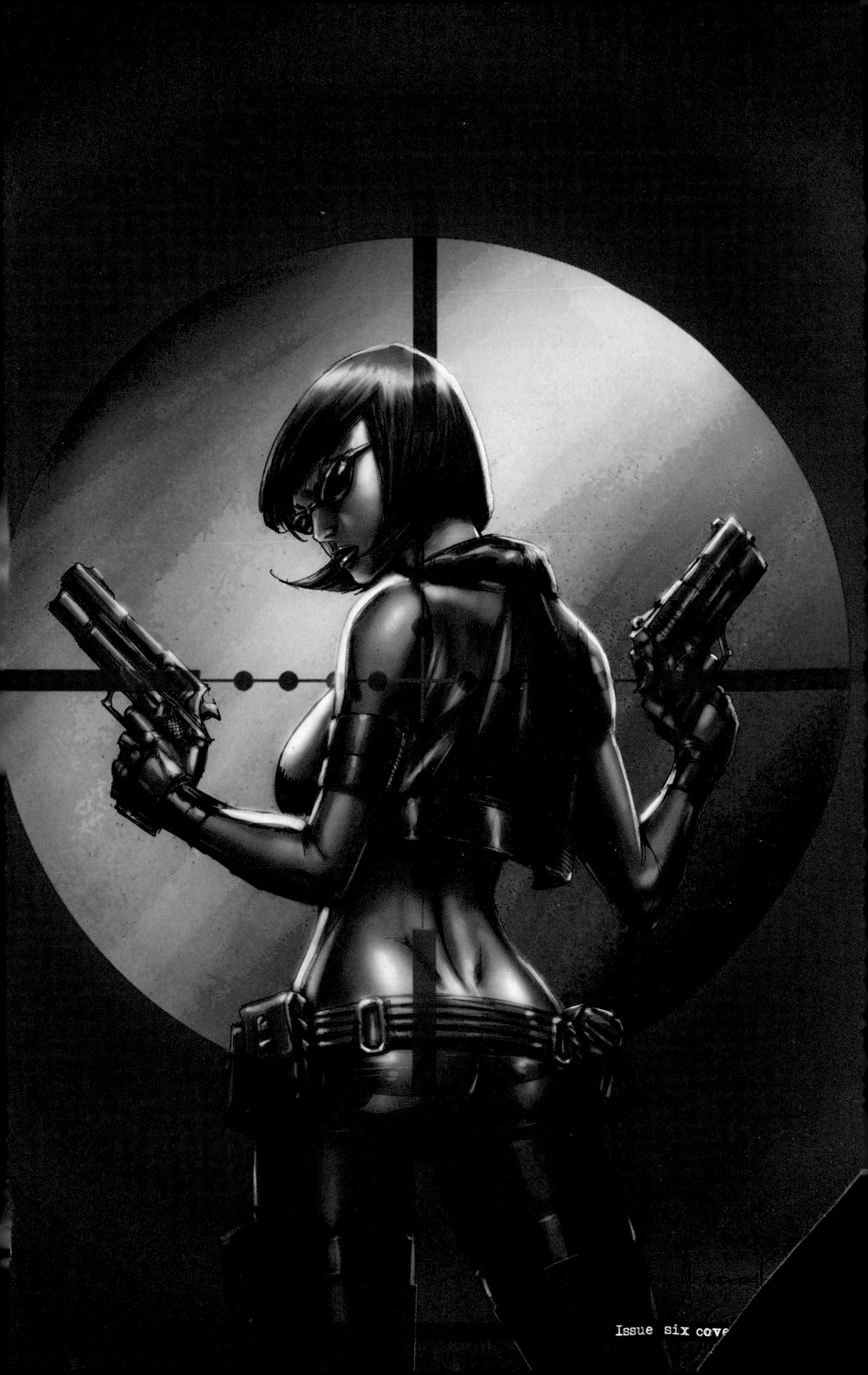

Issue six cove

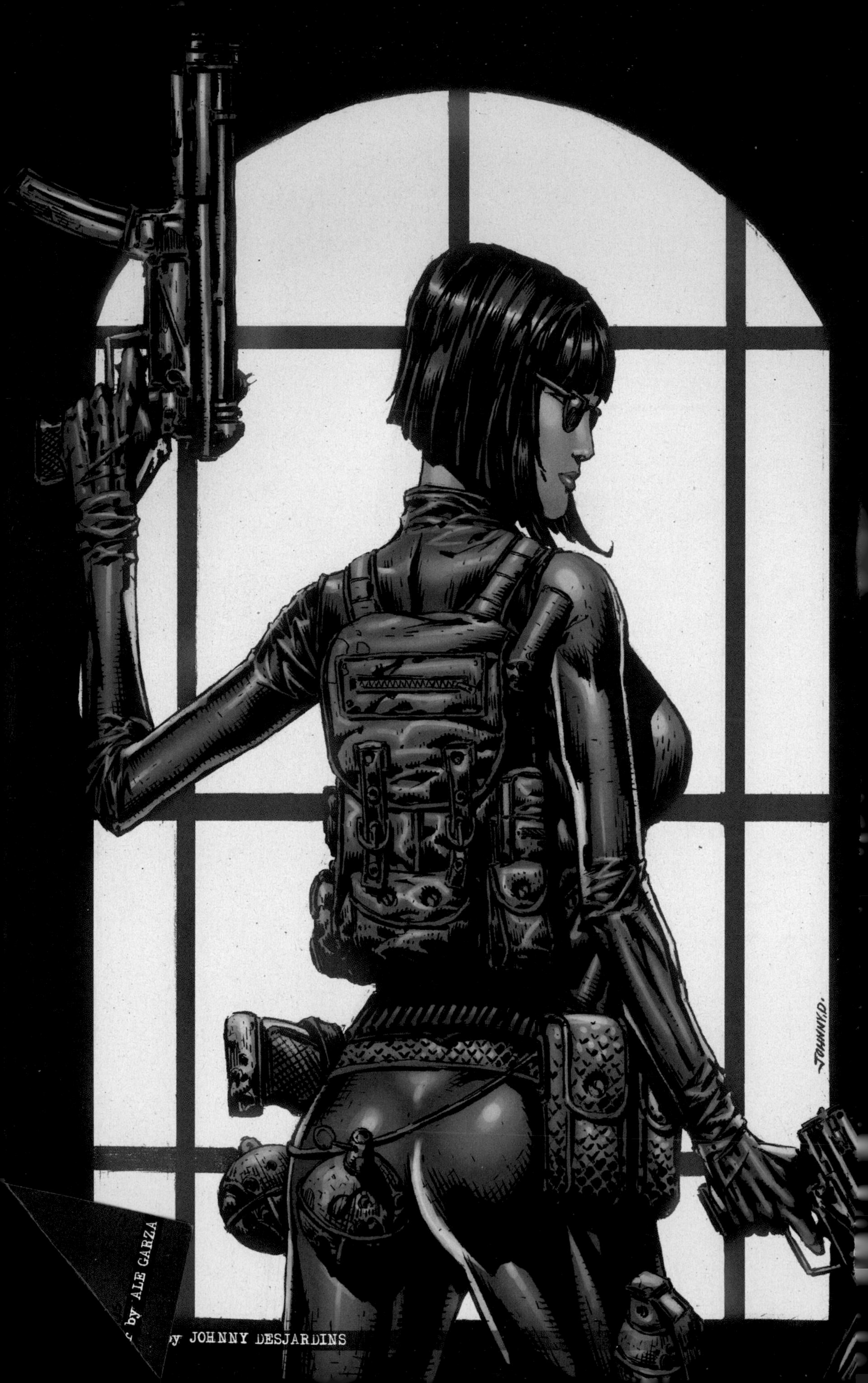
by ALE GARZA
y JOHNNY DESJARDINS
JOHNNY.D.